1996

Modernism and Mass Politics

JOYCE, WOOLF, ELIOT, YEATS

MICHAEL TRATNER

Modernism and Mass Politics

JOYCE, WOOLF, ELIOT, YEATS

STANFORD UNIVERSITY PRESS

STANFORD, CALIFORNIA

Stanford University Press
Stanford, California
© 1995 by the Board of Trustees of the
Leland Stanford Junior University
Printed in the United States of America

CIP data appear at the end of the book

Stanford University Press publications are
distributed exclusively by Stanford University
Press within the United States, Canada, Mexico,
and Central America; they are distributed
exclusively by Cambridge University Press
throughout the rest of the world.

Acknowledgments

I was fortunate to begin this project at the University of California, Berkeley as a dissertation under the direction of John Bishop and Catherine Gallagher: their ideas and critical methods underlie nearly everything I have written. I have since had the pleasure of working with Regenia Gagnier, Robert Polhemus, and Lucio Ruotolo at Stanford; they have given me the most useful support by disagreeing with each other in their detailed responses to drafts, leading me to make productive and fundamental revisions. I am indebted to many other colleagues and friends who generously criticized chapters and gave me useful advice: Carol Christ, George Dekker, Albert Gelpi, Martin Evans, R. Brandon Kershner, and Ronald Rebholz. Finally, I could never have done this work without the encouragement and patience of Leda Sportolari, Jeffrey Tratner, and Cara Tratner.

M.T.

Contents

Contents

Modernism and Mass Politics

JOYCE, WOOLF, ELIOT, YEATS

Introduction

In the first two decades of the twentieth century, a new phenomenon swept across politics: the masses. Groups that had struggled as marginal parts of the political system—particularly workers and women—suddenly exploded into vast and seemingly unstoppable movements. In England, the Labour and suffrage movements became militant before World War I, suspended actions during the war, and then achieved what seemed a remarkable success in the Reform Bill of 1918, which tripled the number of voters in national elections. In 1917, the Russian Revolution generated intense fears and hopes by providing an image of what the millions of new voters might do. At the same time, the fact that most workers' and women's parties throughout Europe had supported national war efforts revealed that mass movements that seemed to have the potential of overthrowing the system could, under the right influences, be turned into powerful supports for that same system. Politicians became intensely interested in understanding how to speak to and influence the masses. A whole subgenre of sociological-political treatises purporting to analyze the mass mind emerged all over Europe, particularly in England, where books on the subject by William McDougall, Georges Sorel, Graham Wallas, Wilfred Trotter, and Sigmund Freud were published around the time of World War I.[1]

All these texts drew heavily on the theories put forth in *The Crowd*, written in 1895 by a French writer, Gustave Le Bon, and translated into English in 1897. Le Bon developed the idea that when a crowd forms, a whole new kind of mentality that "is perpetually hovering on the borderland of un-

consciousness" replaces the conscious personalities of those in the crowd.[2]
This idea has become quite familiar under the rubric of "mob psychology,"
but in his book Le Bon did not simply condemn crowd psychology as dan-
gerously distorted thinking. Instead, he declared that to understand any
group—any political party, any religion, any nation, any mass movement—
one must understand this unusual mentality. He described in considerable
detail how crowds think.

His description should seem uncanny to literary critics, because it
sounds as if he were describing modernist literary techniques:

> A crowd thinks in images, and the image itself immediately calls up a series
> of other images, having no logical connection with the first. We can easily
> conceive this state by thinking of the fantastic succession of ideas to which
> we are sometimes led by calling up in our minds any fact. Our reason shows
> us the incoherence there is in these images, but a crowd is almost blind to
> this truth, and confuses with the real event what the deforming action of
> the imagination has superimposed thereon. A crowd scarcely distinguishes
> between the subjective and the objective.[3]

Remarkably, Le Bon presents the two basic formal features of modernist
literature—the image and the stream of consciousness—as essential traits
of the crowd mind. He also implies that the crowd has little respect for
conventions of realism, merging the subjective and the objective, the conscious and the unconscious. Georges Sorel, in a book translated by T. E.
Hulme that was influential in modernist circles, added to Le Bon's theory
the tenet that "myths" hold together the chaotic flow in the crowd mind.[4]

Examining in detail the surprising similarities between modernist literature and contemporary theories of the crowd, as the following chapters
will do, upsets many critical commonplaces concerning the character of literary modernism. I will show that many modernist literary forms emerged
out of efforts to write in the idiom of the crowd mind. Modernism was not,
then, a rejection of mass culture, but rather an effort to produce a mass
culture, perhaps for the first time, to produce a culture distinctive to the
twentieth century, which Le Bon called "The Era of the Crowd."[5] The contest between modernist and realist literary forms was thus not a contest
between literature for a coterie and literature for the masses, but rather a
contest between different ways of speaking to and from the mass mind, a
contest based on different conceptions of how the masses think.[6]

Much of what modernist writers said they were doing fits such a view.
T. S. Eliot wrote that he sought the mysteries of modernism—and later
Catholicism—because the intellectuals such as Irving Babbitt who had influenced him as a young man at Harvard had "nothing to offer the mob"
and thus "left a space not only for the mob, but (what is more important)
for the mob part of the mind in themselves."[7] Eliot's equation of the mob
and the mob part of the mind inside intellectuals, inside the cultured elite,

is a key to understanding how theories of the mass mind such as Le Bon's intersected with modernism. Le Bon argued that the crowd mind resides, hidden, in every person's unconscious; a similar vision underlay Eliot's aesthetic theory in "Tradition and the Individual Talent." Eliot said that a poet must undergo a process of "continual extinction of personality" to become aware that "the mind of Europe—the mind of his own country—is . . . much more important than his own private mind."[8] Yeats similarly declared that a writer must use "symbols that have numberless meanings" beyond what the writer knows in order to escape the "barrenness and shallowness of a too conscious arrangement."[9] In *A Room of One's Own*, Woolf describes the role of the mass mind in the development of literary works: "masterpieces are not single and solitary births; they are the outcome of many years of thinking in common, of thinking by the body of the people, so that the experience of the mass is behind the single voice."[10] The later novels of Woolf and Joyce are structured around moments when single voices disappear and we can glimpse the experience of the mass, for example, the dinner parties in *The Waves*, during which the people lose their own identities and finally feel, as Bernard puts it: "there is no division between me and them. As I talked I felt, 'I am you.' This difference we make so much of, this identity we so feverishly cherish, was overcome."[11] *Finnegans Wake* portrays the extremely crowded mind that appears when a single person's conscious personality is extinguished. Many of the experimental features of modernist texts may be understood as efforts by authors to disrupt their own conscious personalities (and the conscious personalities of their readers) in order to reveal and perhaps alter the socially structured mentality hidden inside each person's unconscious.

Writers as diverse as Georg Lukács and Maurice Beebe have held that the modernist era marked a retreat from Victorian concern with social issues into introspection, solipsism, or aesthetic detachment.[12] In what follows, I will argue precisely the opposite: that modernism was an effort to escape the limitations of nineteenth-century individualist conventions and write about distinctively "collectivist" phenomena. To define the transition from the Victorians to the modernists in this way brings literary history into line with political histories such as those written by A. V. Dicey, Samuel Beer, Charles Maier, and Theodore Lowi, who have characterized the transformations of English, European, and American politics that occurred in the early twentieth century as the shift from individualism (or liberalism) to collectivism.[13] Collectivist political theories, theories of the mass mind, and modernist literature all were intertwined as part of a general change in discourse, based on the "modern" premise that individuals cannot control their own lives or even understand their own experiences, that vast collective entities such as classes, genders, and nationalities shape the individual mind and can, at times, even act independently of any individual.

That modernism contributed to or is a product of the undermining of the individual (and hence was part of the demise of individualism)—has been argued by literary critics of nearly all schools.[14] The critique of the individual, though, has rarely been taken as leading to any alternative to individualism, but rather to psychological or philosophical changes in the individual. Edmund Wilson, for example, described the poets who developed early forms of modernism as people who rejected the bourgeois, individualist world but were "incapable" of believing in any alternative; they became thus "peculiarly maladjusted persons."[15] Post-structuralist theorists have developed a complex methodology of dismantling the individual and include modernism as one version of what results from doing so—but the deconstruction of the individual seems to leave individuals engaged in an endless process of subversion of the self without turning the self into anything else, such as part of a mass.[16] Deconstruction functions as well to dismantle collectivist systems based on mass structures: it serves politically as a critical tool, not as a way to construct alternatives. A few critics have seen modernism as seeking a communal alternative. In 1934, V. F. Calverton argued that Eliot was an "inverted Marxian" who shared the Marxist critique of "nineteenth-century individualism" but proposed a Catholic rather than a Communist community as the replacement.[17] Recent critics have begun developing a formal analysis of modernism in terms of communal structures. Rachel Blau DuPlessis argues that Woolf's later novels are structured around "a collective *Bildung* and a communal affect";[18] Allen McLaurin has similarly characterized Woolf's works as presenting a "wave of consciousness."[19] John Paul Riquelme has described the streams of consciousness in Joyce's works as "tributaries that merge" to create a river of "cultural consciousness."[20] And Michael André Bernstein has used Pound's own words to describe *The Cantos* as the "tale of the tribe," the voice of the culture, not of any distinct individual.[21]

This criticism has demonstrated modernism's antipathy to individualism and its affinity to communal structures, but it has largely overlooked the political theories and practices that embodied the communal alternatives to individualism. The dismantling of the individual during the modernist era was not merely an intellectual, aesthetic, or psychological revelation, but a central feature of political debates, a topic of election speeches, a basis of policy, and a commonplace of newspaper and magazine articles. If we place modernism in the context of such mainstream political debates, we can see surprising relationships between literary innovations and real parties and policies.[22] To seek to understand how the aesthetic value of a literary work may be connected to the political uses of the aesthetic is, needless to say, not to declare a methodological prejudice against purely aesthetic analyses: rather, it is to begin to understand how the aesthetic functions as a social and political category and practice, and how social and political concerns enter into aesthetics.

According to most literary histories until very recently, politics impinged on British modernism only in the 1930's, when the Depression, Fascism, and impending war pressed too hard to allow the leisure of modernist experimentation. As the most recent *Norton Anthology* puts it, "Auden and his contemporaries looked out at an England of industrial stagnation and mass unemployment, seeing not the metaphorical Waste Land of Eliot but a more literal Waste Land of poverty and 'depressed areas.' . . . [Auden] preferred to confront modern problems directly rather than filter them, as Eliot did, through symbolic situations." Eliot at least is credited with symbolically recognizing modern social problems. Virginia Woolf is presented as the quintessential aesthete, a writer whose "world was from the beginning the cultured world of the middle-class and upper-middle class London intelligentsia," a person who "entertained . . . literary and artistic friends at evening gatherings where the conversation sparkled."[23] Before the 1970's, the *Norton* ignored her essays completely and summarized her career by saying "She was comfortably off, she had leisure to cultivate her sensibility, she wrote because she wanted to."[24] In recent editions, this sentence has been cut and a paragraph added that begins: "Woolf was increasingly concerned with the position of women, especially professional women."[25]

In the change in the *Norton*'s presentation of Woolf, we can see that the view of modernists as leisure-class aesthetes is slowly being revised. But it is actually surprising that such a view ever held sway. Woolf, for example, was declared during her life "the most brilliant pamphleteer in England" for *Three Guineas*, a work of biting social criticism that expresses concerns about considerably more than the position of professional women: it equates and attacks empire, property, and patriarchy.[26] Woolf actively sought to change the social system: holding weekly meetings at her house of a working-class women's organization, the Women's Cooperative Association; publishing articles in the *Daily Worker* in which she declared, for example, that "the artist is the first of the workers to suffer"; and working as secretary of the Rodmell Labour Party.[27] Given Woolf's activism, it seems plausible to consider her literary works in the context of the debates about socialism, imperialism, and suffrage—the debates that relied on and influenced theories of the mass mind. The essays and letters of Eliot, Joyce, and Yeats reveal similar interest and involvement in these debates.

In viewing modernist works from within such political contexts, I do not wish to supplant other interpretations: I am not claiming that all modernist works were written with political goals in mind. I hope only to complicate our understanding of these works, to show political corollaries to the personal, psychological, aesthetic, or philosophical issues that previous critics have explored in such depth. I do not limit myself to works that overtly thematize political issues; in fact, I seek in particular to show political dimensions of poems and novels that appear to be about private life.

Certain features of the political issues of the early twentieth century lead me to this methodology. For one thing, the question of whether or not anyone could escape politics—whether a private sphere exists at all—was at the center of the controversy between individualists and collectivists. I will try to show that eventually Joyce, Woolf, Eliot, and Yeats all concluded that there is no private realm, not in the house and not in the mind. This does not mean that they did not feel strong desires to escape politics, to live private lives, to think private thoughts; they all expressed such desires. But the new developments in politics and the new disciplines of psychology, anthropology, and sociology convinced these modernists that vast social forces permeate and shape private relationships, private thoughts, and even the desire for privacy. To understand why they embraced such a view, it makes sense to look at the most private, least political moments in their works—moments when they seem to be trying to resist the masses—to see if we can find within such moments subtle doubts about the value of privacy or hints that they felt they could not escape impersonal social forces. At times, especially in analyses of early works, I will focus on small moments that contradict what seems the overall "meaning" of the work. Such elements reveal what eventually led the writers to reject their youthful beliefs. I will often focus on an image or a phrase in a seemingly apolitical literary work that reappears in a political essay by the same author. Such repetitions do not imply a political thought was in the mind of the author when the literary work was written, but they do allow us to draw connections between the ways these authors thought about politics and the ways they thought about their personal relationships and their writing.

This book is about a change in discourse, in verbal forms, but I do not see discourses as residing entirely within language or within the mind, with a change in discourse therefore preceding or causing changes in political practices. Rather, I regard texts as forms of symbolic action that interact with other types of social and political action. Emerging together in the early twentieth century were modernist literary forms, collectivist political theories, new intellectual disciplines such as sociology and anthropology, mass movements such as socialism, feminism, and Fascism, and new collective or corporate structures of mass society such as unions, welfare systems, corporations, and modern political parties. The lines of influence went in all directions. It is also important to my argument to conceive of discourses as available to be used by all camps in political or social debates.[28] In particular, to describe the new discourse as "collectivist" does not imply that it is particularly supportive of either left-wing or right-wing movements: I use the term as Samuel Beer does when he says that the twentieth century is a "collectivist age" and that both the Conservative and the Labour Parties in Britain are collectivist.[29]

The basic conceptions of the masses and of collectivist politics did not simply emerge from nowhere in the twentieth century; they dated back at least to the feudal period. Many writers of the early twentieth century invoked this long history by treating the move from individualism to collectivism as in some ways a return to the Middle Ages. Edmund Wilson was correct to characterize modernists as seeking a "castle," but this was not, as he argued, merely an effort to escape modern mass society.[30] Rather, in the early twentieth century it was a common and apparently quite believable political tenet that some elements of the Middle Ages, such as the social structure of castles, were about to return. Conservatives such as Harold Macmillan could talk about resurrecting the "organic" hierarchy of the Middle Ages, while the Labour Party could label their program "Guild Socialism."[31] John Ruskin's admiration for Gothic cathedrals and the supposedly wonderful social order they symbolized served to inspire both the left and the right in their opposition to liberal capitalism. The two sides differed on what it would mean to return to building cathedrals or castles: the Right argued that it meant returning to a society structured around a glorious aristocracy or even a monarchy, with an accompanying restoration of the power of religion; the Left argued that it meant turning to the collective ownership of all property that was embodied in a cathedral.

Collectivism—a politics based on large groups or masses rather than on individuals—was thus not only a new political philosophy, but also the revival of elements of a very old one. Even so, most histories of the shift from individualism to collectivism have focused on the nineteenth century as "the individualist past," and there is good reason for this narrow focus: when social commentators have looked back from the twentieth century, the nineteenth has appeared both the peak and the end of individualism. In the nineteenth century, the debate between individualism and collectivism emerged in its modern form, as can be seen in the fact that the words *individualism* and *collectivism* both first appeared in the English language during this century, along with the related words *liberalism*, *socialism*, and *communism*.[32]

Collectivism and *individualism* appeared at roughly the same time because the two terms can be defined only in terms of each other—and largely as contrary ways of conceiving of the relationship of the individual and the mass. The first definition of *individualism* in English, in Alexis de Tocqueville's *Democracy in America* (1835), presents the concept as a "feeling, which disposes each member of the community to sever himself from the mass of his fellow-creatures, and to draw apart with his family and friends."[33] De Tocqueville set out the basic issue in the debate between individualism and collectivism: the question of whether or not there should be a division between a private sphere (a world of family and friends) and public life. Individualists believe that there are and should be spaces in which persons can escape the illusions and pressures of society, and hence seek to divide the social order up into public and private areas, keeping the public as small as possible. Collectivists believe that the social order requires the interrelationship of all parts, and so seek to reduce the disconnected or private sectors as much as possible. Each philosophy gains its power from showing the evils of the other: individualists portray the loss of identity and the dictatorial powers that result when private spaces disappear, and, as they conceive of it, people become masses or herds; collectivists portray the alienation and oppression that result when people withdraw into private disconnection from the rest of society, particularly by becoming self-centered entrepreneurs. The two remain, in effect, dependent on each other: if either seemed to triumph completely, the terms of political debate would change.

During the nineteenth century, the private realm seemed to steadily shrink as both government and mass movements seemed to permeate everything, pressing into what used to be the private sphere of the individual. By the end of the century, an anxiety arose that it might no longer be possible to "draw apart" from the masses. Social commentators began theorizing that the individual might need a social medium, not a free space, to even exist. As T. H. Green postulated around the turn of the century, "social life is to personality what language is to thought."[34] After World War I, Wilfred Trotter produced a more ominous version of that epigram: "the only medium in which man's mind can function satisfactorily is the herd."[35] In collectivist theories, a person who retreats from social life, from the herd, does not become independent, as individualists claim, but rather suffers distortions of personality and of mental functioning. As F. H. Bradley, the subject of Eliot's doctoral dissertation, put it, "the mere individual is a delusion of theory; and the attempt to realize it in practice is the starvation and mutilation of human nature, with total sterility or the production of monstrosities."[36]

The conception of a necessary "medium" often merged with the conception of the "unconscious." T. S. Eliot described what he considered the fundamental medium for thought, "culture," as an "unconscious background."[37] When the historian George Dangerfield tried to explain how mass movements caused the "Strange Death of Liberal England," he ended up saying that "the unconscious desires" of vast social groups controlled the politicians and even the leaders of those movements, who were little more than "puppets."[38]

The existence of an unconscious background that shapes individual thought and action does not imply so much the destruction of the self as its multiplication: a single act becomes the composite result of several types of mentality operating simultaneously. Such a vision of the complex sources of actions and ideas makes the task of describing a person's life difficult. Virginia Woolf described the problem in explaining how hard it was to write her memoirs: "Consider what immense forces society brings to play upon each of us, how that society changes from decade to decade; and also from class to class; well, if we cannot analyze these invisible presences, we know very little of the subject of the memoir and . . . how futile life-writing becomes. I see myself as a fish in a stream; deflected; held in place; but cannot describe the stream."[39] A literature developed to reveal the influence of "invisible presences" would not, then, show them to us, but would attempt to make us aware of much more than we can see. An individual portrayed or implied by such literature—a character or an author—is only a phenomenon whose movements, like those of a fish, are there to reveal the action of "the stream," the social medium. Modernism had the peculiar task of trying to engage with that invisible stream, to reveal and alter it—in other words, to speak the language of the mass unconscious—and to do so was tantamount to breaking free of the Western metaphysics of individuals and distinct objects.

Feminist theorists have described what I am calling the idiom of the unconscious mass mind as the socially repressed feminine, and have called efforts to express it *"écriture feminine."* Luce Irigaray has said that "to an extent, the unconscious is historically censored femaleness."[40] Alice Jardine has described the disruptions of modern literature as "the putting into discourse of 'woman.' "[41] Julia Kristeva says that speaking subjects are conceived of as occupying a "phallic position" as "masters of their speech"; the experimentation of modernism is, she argues, a challenge to "everything considered phallic." Writers such as Joyce and Woolf were seeking "refuge in the valorization of a silent underwater body."[42] To identify the buried form of mentality emerging in the early twentieth century as the feminine is an important development in criticism and in our understanding of history. It also makes sense to interpret attitudes toward the masses as ultimately deriving from reactions to the feminine because, as Andreas Huyssen argues, "political, psychological, and aesthetic discourse around the turn of the century consistently and obsessively genders mass culture and the masses as feminine."[43] Klaus Theweleit demonstrates in his massive work, *Male Fantasies*, that the strongest imagery expressing fear of the masses in Fascist literature derived from unconscious fear of the feminine.[44] Marianne DeKoven, building on Theweleit's and Huyssen's work, has explored the ways that the gender of modernist writers had much to do with how they reacted to the prospect of social revolution: the rise of the masses became the threat or promise of the feminine or the maternal.

I wish to fill in the other half of the equation of the masses and the feminine—to show how the varied political constructions of "the masses" (e.g., as "workers," "folk," or "natives") shaped varied conceptions of the feminine and the maternal. It makes as much sense to speak of the masses emerging and of mass mind and its own type of writing as it does to speak of *"écriture feminine."* I am not claiming that the mass mind is fundamental and that the feminine mind is not: the mass, the feminine, the proletariat, the racial other, the primitive, the unconscious, and the id all have functioned as metaphors of each other.[45] I also do not wish to suggest that there is some one underlying otherness that merely appears at times to be the masses and at other times the feminine. Rather, I am interested in the tensions that emerge when these various others are equated with each other. When, for example, the feminine is equated with the masses who wait underneath the English upper classes, the desire of an upper-class woman to liberate herself from the limitations of gender roles can become fraught with fears of descending to the "bottom of the sea" of humanity, as I will show (in Chapter 3) happens in Woolf's first novel, *The Voyage Out*. Or when the id, the mob of sexual impulses, is equated with the immigrants pouring into the United States, a midwestern male such as T. S. Eliot may feel that he has to leave the country to integrate his own body (as I discuss in Chapter 4).

By focusing on the varied ways that the unconscious and the mass mind were interpreted in the early twentieth century, we can resolve one of the problems that has plagued efforts to explain the "politics of modernism": why it is that modernists held such diametrically opposed views and yet wrote in such similar ways. Critics have shown the relationship between the politics and the literary works of individual modernists, but have always encountered difficulty using the overall category of modernism in political analyses.[46] Eliot, Yeats, and Pound can be dealt with together because they at least are all conservatives: they suggest modernism is a movement to maintain traditions and shore up the authority of an elite.[47] Similarly, Joyce and Woolf occasionally end up together in political analyses of modernist innovation as a tactic for undermining phallogocentric authority.[48] Critics analyzing one or the other of these political camps usually have to explicitly exclude the other. For example, Michael North, in a book on the conservative modernist poets, says in his introduction that "it is not possible to argue that the politics of Yeats, Eliot and Pound are typical of a movement that also includes Joyce and Woolf."[49] Cairns Craig argues that modernist poets, but not novelists, were connected to a distinctly conservative, even Fascist, politics.[50] Since in my account of the later works of modernists (but not their earlier works) I set novelists against poets, I might seem to support such a view. However, I do not believe that modernist novels and poems should be separated at all in political analyses. I argue that Joyce's first novel was tending toward Fascism, and Wyndham Lewis shows that there can be Fascist modernist novels. Conversely, Yeats was strongly influenced by William Morris, going so far as to attend socialist meetings, and William Carlos Williams was a modernist poet whose politics seem closer to Joyce's and Woolf's than to Pound's. So if modernist poetic forms have had any relationship to politics, it must be such that these forms have served quite opposed political ends.

By seeing modernism as part of the reconceptualizing of social issues in terms of masses rather than individuals, we can make sense of how modernism could be used both to shore up and to undermine all authority and how a writer such as Joyce could be influenced simultaneously by the proto-Fascist Gabriele D'Annunzio and the anarcho-socialist Arturo Labriola. We might say that the advent of collectivism rotated the axis of political debate, so that the ends of the spectrum changed simultaneously and in closely related ways. Or we can follow Russell Berman's analysis and focus on the common political element in left-wing and right-wing modernism, as in left-wing and right-wing collectivism, namely, opposition to nineteenth-century liberalism.[51] All the modernists I am focusing on opposed capitalism and individualism: all sought to release a part of the social order and of the psyche that capitalism has hidden or repressed.

Fredric Jameson and Perry Anderson have developed political interpretations of the way that modernism seems to point to something hidden, something beyond comprehension. Jameson has interpreted the modernist trope of pointing to something beyond consciousness as a reflection of the imperialist economic system, which rendered vast parts of the economic structure (colonial territories) invisible.[52] Anderson similarly sees modernist ambiguity as deriving from the "imaginative proximity" of a whole range of social revolutions, whose outcomes seemed, during the modernist era, "profoundly ambiguous."[53] In Jameson's and Anderson's theories, modernism developed from the need to write about matters that were in fact beyond anyone's consciousness. I propose a slightly different interpretation of the relationship of modernism, politics, and the unknowable: in the early twentieth century, the trope of speaking about and appealing to what is beyond consciousness was a commonplace of political debates and functioned to promote diverse ends. Politicians justified their positions by referring to the invisible medium lying around or beneath the conscious individual mind, and they did so generally not because of doubts about their own understanding, but rather because by doing so they could claim to represent the masses in a way that capitalism had failed to do. The hidden substance surrounding capitalism was, most often, presented as the unconscious mass mind.

Political debates then took the form of opposed theories of what was buried underneath capitalism—what the masses would be if released from current forms of oppression. Conservatives described the masses as "the people" or "the folk" and argued that mass riots expressed dissatisfaction with industrialization and the destruction of culture. Capitalism, in its focus on economic man, on private life, and on a rationality supposed to transcend culture, had broken up the social body, producing, in Eliot's words, "bodies of men and women—of all classes—detached from tradition, alienated from religion, and susceptible to mass suggestion; in other words, a mob."[54] The opposite of the mob was a people, a group held together by traditions that could never be created out of rational planning because traditions are, Eliot says, "of the blood, so to speak, rather than of the brain."[55] Listening to the blood rather than the brain would restore what Harold Macmillan called the "organic conception of society which was the distinct contribution of medieval thought" and the cure for laissez-faire individualism.[56] Conservatives drew heavily on biological metaphors, arguing that they were opposed to the materialism of both capitalism and socialism: the masses were not rebelling for property, they claimed, but for a restoration of the lost social body. Especially important in conservative theory was restoring the "natural" head for the social body, the aristocracy, something the masses were supposed to deeply desire. As Disraeli put it, "I believe the wider the popular suffrage, the more powerful would be the natural aristocracy."[57] The "natural aristocrats," recognized and elected by the masses and feeling blood ties to them, would take care of the working class in a way that self-centered, materialist capitalists had not. As Harold Macmillan put it, "Toryism has always been a form of paternalistic socialism."[58]

Socialists argued in contrast that the masses were not the "folk" but "the proletariat" and did not wish any sort of aristocracy, but rather sought a classless society based on alterations in the system of property. Socialists also disagreed with conservatives in describing what was wrong with capitalist individualism: it had not fragmented society into atomized individuals at all. Individualism was in fact an illusion that served to coalesce society into two vast groups in strict hierarchical arrangement. Individualism accomplished this by restricting the definition of "free individuals" to males who live in private houses and have good educations. The solution to capitalist oppression, then, was to stop valuing the so-called free individual and to empower directly those others, those who do not have the right property, the right gender, or the right education. Some Labour theorists dreamed of a society with no distinctions among groups, an international brotherhood and sisterhood of workers. The willingness of workers' parties to go to war in 1914 undermined such a dream, and socialists turned instead to pluralist theories based on the idea that solidarity requires smaller units than an international class. G. D. H. Cole and Harold Laski developed what was called "Guild Socialism" based on the tenet that the differences in the mentalities of people in different groups meant that there could be no unified government for all. Instead, Guild Socialists advocated providing separate forms of government for every separate social organization, particularly unions and consumer groups, but the theory extended easily to religions, gender groups, and even nationalities (such as ex-colonies). Cole's and Laski's theories implied not only the breakup of government, but the breakup of the individual voter: a person was not conceived of as an individual at all, but as a collection of separate parts of groups that were not even all present at the same time. As a result, Cole argued, "a human being, as an individual, is fundamentally incapable of being represented."[59] Cole suggested that government represent all the parts of a person separately: "a person requires as many forms of representation as he has distinct organisable interests or points of view."[60] The nation and the individual would move in many directions at once. Cole's comments could describe the novels of Joyce and Woolf as well as they describe pluralist governmental systems: the multiplicity of "forms of representation," of styles and points of view in these literary works, serve to break up the unities of personality—of characters and of narrators—that had structured the traditional nineteenth-century novel. Like the British pluralists, Joyce and Woolf sought through this breakup of forms of representation to reduce domination, to release varied forms of consciousness that had been suppressed by liberal capitalism.

The debate between conservative national unity and socialist international multiplicity turned a debate about class relations into a debate about cultures. This was a crucial transformation that I want to trace in some detail because of the importance of culture (particularly in the form of myth) as a structural element in modernist texts. Conservatives argued that the culture that held England together had almost disappeared—both high culture and folk culture had been consumed by middle-class materialism. As Anthony Ludovici put it in 1921, "The common culture had been replaced by a congeries of pseudo-cultures, all in active conflict."[61] This conservative argument slid into a belief that the middle class was not even really part of the culture: the money men were internationalists, and reestablishing the "organic" relation of upper and lower classes would involve expelling these money men as "aliens." Yeats's play *The Countess Cathleen* traces a version of this theory: in it, demons disguise themselves as world-traveling merchants who take advantage of Irish poverty to buy the souls of the poor, destroying Irish culture, until the Countess gives away her soul to get enough money to save the poor, whereupon the merchants are expelled, the Countess ascends to heaven anyway, and the poor at the end are on their knees worshipping the image of the Countess. Yeats implies that the workers' taste for money and indeed the workers' movements originated in middle-class corruption of the minds of the poor from their natural deference for the aristocracy. Restoring culture would thus restore the two "real" classes and eliminate the middle—and would transform the nation into a religious entity, not a monetary one. The equation of the money-lending middle class and mysterious "foreign" demons translates class issues into national ones: Yeats can blame the English for bringing bourgeois thought into Ireland. Such arguments were also available to the English through the identification of the Jews as the international financiers who created the anticulture of money and liberalism. As George Lane-Fox Pitt-Rivers put it in 1920, the loss of culture in England was due to "free commercial exploitation by all and sundry middlemen, usurers, Jews; and the translation of all values into money-values, by which alone can be realised that ideal of personal equality, dead-levelness and compulsory mediocrity in which she glories under the name of Liberalism and Democracy."[62]

In Yeats's play, the only way to escape money values and reestablish the aristocracy is to reestablish "supernatural" beliefs: the Countess Cathleen has to be transformed from a human to a heavenly body. This was a basic

conservative tenet—that the nation would be unified not by human leadership but by restoration of the superhuman or mythic underpinnings of
the social order. The importance of myth to theories of the mass mind
derived from Georges Sorel, who sought to turn Le Bon's theories into a
methodology for producing mass movements. Sorel theorized that at certain times the chaotic images passing through the crowd mind coalesced
into a "myth"—an illogical, unanalyzable complex that could overcome
all rational argument.[63] Sorel's most famous text, *Reflections on Violence*,
proposed a myth of a general strike in conjunction with acts of unexpected
violence, in effect a theory and practice of pure rupture, as the only way
out of the powerful hold of capitalist rationality. The book presented the
general strike as a method of reaching socialism, but Sorel at various times
also supported nationalism and monarchy as possible ways to escape capitalism. Sorel had a direct influence on the four modernists I examine here,
and as I will show, myth and violence functioned together in their literary
works very much as Sorel postulated they function in society.

Conservatives such as Eliot and Yeats found in traditional myths support for the view that there is an inherent need for cultural or national
leadership, for kings and aristocracy, and they developed historical narratives that implied that the present was moving through a period of restoration of such ancient forms. The masses were rising up to overthrow
current leadership in order to clear the way for the restoration of older
forms of leadership: the present was a stage in the cycle of history, a period
of violently laying waste to the land, of clearing out overgrown social forms
to allow old roots to flourish again. The rebellion of workers and women
would transform into the restored greatness of the nation, the culture.

World War I lent great support to such a theory: calls to national unity
seemed to resonate in the blood and overwhelm socialist and feminist agendas. Joyce and Woolf viewed the triumph of nationalism over socialism and
feminism with horror. But Guild Socialism, the pluralist Labour theory of
the twenties that I described earlier, provided an answer on which Joyce
and Woolf could draw: socialism should not try to destroy national ties, but
should accept that every person is a product of multiple group alliances. A
group could go to war only when the alliances that cross its borders could
be suppressed. The answer to war was then not simply replacing one group
unity with another, but rather building up the voices of suppressed groups
and reducing but not eliminating the voices of the dominant groups, so that
multiplicity and not unity became the norm.

Therefore, Joyce and Woolf countered conservative emphasis on national and aristocratic traditions by drawing on alternative traditions, the
traditions of oppressed groups: Jews, women, homosexuals, the working
classes, all the members of Woolf's "Outsiders' Society."[64] These authors
were not claiming that such outsiders are universal persons free of any
specific culture; indeed, the specificity of the traditions of these oppressed

groups was essential to their providing an alternative to the dominant traditions. The key traditions they searched for were ones that allowed a group to have a cultural identity without requiring them to dominate all other cultures—a quality Joyce saw in Jews and Woolf saw in the "daughters of gentlemen."

The crux of the argument between conservatives and socialist pluralists ultimately came down to this question: could a culture continue to exist without a repressive system of hierarchy or dominance? Conservatives argued it could not and hence believed that if workers and women were to gain power, they would simply take over the system of dominance and suppress the upper-class males. Woolf and Joyce did not accept this conclusion: they did not valorize oppressed groups in order to turn everyone into Jews or daughters of gentlemen. So they also created in their novels versions of the high culture and national traditions conservatives valorized, but versions that did not imply a system of domination. Instead of creating as a model a glorious aristocrat such as the Countess Cathleen who expels all international merchants (English or Jewish), Joyce equated the traditional noble hero-king with a Jewish salesman, producing Bloom/Ulysses, a hero who does not need to kill the seducers of his people because he does not need to preserve a fraudulent image of national purity. Woolf directly portrayed the overthrow of the mythic hero-king in *The Waves*, showing Eliot's grail knight Percival falling into a sea of humanity. Joyce's and Woolf's later works are full of images of the tides overthrowing and breaking up the leader's body and the social body. And yet their books are also full of moments of communal unity: they sought to show that the joys of solidarity are accessible without recourse to either violence or authoritarian leadership.

To bring out the sociopolitical underpinnings of modernism, I have organized the book around a common development in literary form in the works of four writers and a parallel development in politics. World War I serves to mark a division within these parallel developments: before the war, many modernists and most politicians in government feared being drowned by the masses; after the war, they feared being left out of the mass movements transforming society. I focus on Joyce, Woolf, Eliot, and Yeats because they all underwent this transition: by following their development, we can see the connection between modernist experimentation and attitudes toward the masses. That the four changed similarly suggests that the changes they went through were not simply results of personal growth. But I am not claiming that what happened was a movement that identically transformed the thoughts of every person. Writers such as H. G. Wells embraced socialism and yet continued writing in premodernist literary forms: for such writers, socialism was envisioned in terms of individual liberation and so was in effect a continuation of liberal goals via new methods. Many English writers who are classified as modernists never accepted collectivism and never moved to the late, fragmented mode of modernism. E. M. Forster, Joseph Conrad, and D. H. Lawrence continued after the war to portray individuals who seek to escape the masses: their novels are concerned with ways that individuality can coexist with the "dark forces" surrounding everyone. As Michael Levenson and Vincent Pecora have argued in quite different ways, even Henry James can be placed in this category of writers who struggled to preserve some kind of individuality in a postliberal era.[65] Wyndham Lewis actively supported Fascism but was only briefly a collectivist, never fully embracing the concept that the masses are the heart of the social order. He ended his life advocating a very strange form of liberalism, one that allowed him to support Hitler, as Fredric Jameson has shown.[66] I will show in Chapter 5 how Fascism could appeal to those who wished to preserve the strong individual from mass influence. William Faulkner and Djuna Barnes, whose writing careers began after World War I, did not have significant early modernist phases. One writer I have left out who would fit in this book is Ezra Pound; I refer to his works frequently, but do not give him equal space because his later, collectivist works were entwined with economic theories that I believe go beyond interwar collectivism. Pound's focus on interest rates anticipated a social transformation that started in the 1930's and was not completed until the 1960's: the normalization of being in debt as a part of everyday life and of government policy.

I begin with two chapters that provide an overview of the whole development of collectivism and modernism: first, a chapter on political, aesthetic, and psychological theories of the mass mind that explicates those theories in terms of the concerns and practices of literary modernism; second, a chapter on political and literary works that present the mass unconscious erupting as an event that equally disrupts historical chronology and fictional narrative: *To the Lighthouse, Ulysses,* and *The Strange Death of Liberal England.* In these three works, the unconscious is identified with the working class and women, and the emergence onto the public stage of these previously invisible social groups is coded within the works themselves as entwined with, if not the cause of, the disruption of narrative form.

After these chapters of theory and history, I provide three chapters on prewar modernism and politics, focusing particularly on the way that the masses were presented as causing the dissolution of the individual. These early works were caught in the tension between individualism and collectivism: dissolution appears tantalizing, inevitable, and horrible. I include in this part of the book only chapters on Woolf, Eliot, and Joyce; I found that to define the transition in Yeats's writing required me to discuss his early and late works together. During and after the war, the image of individuals dissolving into a mass changed valence: it became a hopeful sign. Such dissolution did not seem to lead to chaos, but to certain mass structures that somehow could combine the loss of individual personality and the provision of an even better-defined self: to surrender to certain social bodies seems to increase the individual's sense of his or her own power and even morality. As Samuel Beer defines the basis of collectivist politics, "the individual finds in the group a sphere of moral fulfillment and a basis for political action."[67] New collective structures appeared—unions, corporations, modern political parties, and mass movements—and old institutions such as the church, the military, and the nation gained new formulations. Interwar modernism, which seems to me the fully developed form of modernism, was an effort to join in the production of new social structures that operated differently than previous ones did. Instead of seeking to construct individuals who freely join together because they share certain principles, these new social structures relied on and operated through the social medium, through the unconscious mass mind.

In the last four chapters, I explore four different but overlapping ways of building a new, collectivist social order—ways of drawing on the unconscious, collective mind as the basis of social order and literary form. Yeats developed a Sorelian theory of violence as releasing and at the same time mutating the mass; translated into a poetic and an educational philosophy, it became a methodology of radical and violent self-alteration, including change of gender. Eliot developed a method of dissolving or fragmenting the self to allow something suprahuman to take over and hold the fragments together: the intellectual sinks into the mass in an effort to fill his own consciousness with the culture buried in the "mob part of the mind in himself." Joyce conceived of society and texts as formed by multiple institutions that share authority and authorship, a version of pluralism uncannily close to Italian syndicalism and British pluralism. And finally, Woolf postulated the possibility of enlisting historical forces to change and perhaps escape ideology, the unconscious images that cause everyone to conceive of themselves as individuals. Violence, culture, institutions, and ideology: each of the four modernists I examine sketched a method by which social order is created and may possibly be changed through the action of the mass mind. These methods intertwine, so when one is foregrounded in a chapter, elements of the other three appear in the background.

I end the book with thoughts on the failure of all these projects, the failure of the masses to overthrow capitalism. Modernism's central period was quite short, lasting only from the end of World War I to the beginning of the Spanish Civil War, a period when modern mass society and collectivist politics seemed full of promise. This period did not produce a literature of despair or retreat, though it may seem that way to us, because we no longer have much faith in any vision of a collective reform of society. Though modernism was, as Woolf put it, a literature full of the sound of things breaking, it was not merely destructive. The sense of wholesale destruction in modernism derived from the sense of being engaged in subversive activities, and in the early twentieth century, both the left-wing and the right-wing modernists saw themselves as subversive, both sides saw themselves as undermining hegemonic capitalism in order to empower marginal groups who had been suppressed almost out of existence, and both sides saw themselves as breaking up the individual that had been at the center of literature and politics. Modernism essentially invented all the tropes that have become so familiar in recent political readings of texts. We critics tend to forget what was transparent during this period: these tropes have had political power precisely because they are available to opposite positions. What appears as the undoing of discourse—modernism—was rather a new form of discourse, a new medium in which to continue some very old political debates.

PART I

Contexts

CHAPTER I

Mass Minds and Modernist Forms

Political, Aesthetic, and Psychological Theories

Two French political theorists set the terms for most analyses of the mass mind in the early twentieth century: Gustave Le Bon, in *The Crowd* (1895), and Georges Sorel, who extended Le Bon's ideas into a method for inciting mass movements in *Reflections on Violence* (1906). Sorel's theory became the basis of syndicalism, which powerfully influenced such diverse movements as the International Workers of the World in the United States and the Fascists in Italy. (Mussolini began his career as a syndicalist.)

Much of the power of Le Bon's and Sorel's theories came from their usefulness to both the Left and the Right. Le Bon's influence on twentieth-century politics was somewhat paradoxical, since he declared in 1896 that the coming "Era of the Crowd" marked the end of all civilization. Previously in history, he claimed, the crowd had gained power only in brief "barbarian phases" between periods of "elevated . . . culture." The crowd always had slipped back into passivity when a new "intellectual aristocracy" arose. But in the twentieth century, Le Bon feared, there would be no new aristocracy because the masses were not only destroying leadership, they were taking it over: "The destinies of nations are elaborated at present in the heart of the masses, and no longer in the councils of princes" (p. xv). What Le Bon did not predict was that politicians and social analysts would study "the heart of the masses" and would use his analysis of the unusual mentality found there as the basis of new kinds of political appeals. And modernist writers were as attracted as any contemporary intellectuals by those appeals, the sociopolitical analyses that lay behind them, and the techniques of representation and address those analyses made possible.

At first, such appeals seemed to involve abandoning reason and culture, placing a "heart of darkness" at the center of the social order. But
gradually, new political philosophies gained power that inverted Le Bon's
evaluation of the rise of the crowd: arguing that rationality is not the basis
of civilization but only of the capitalist system, a system that had destroyed
culture, such theorists concluded that empowering the masses was a way
of restoring civilization.

We might expect such arguments to have come largely from the Left.
Le Bon himself equated the rising power of the masses and the remarkable
rise of socialist or communist politics:

> Today the claims of the masses are becoming more and more sharply de-
> fined, and amount to nothing less than a determination to utterly destroy
> society as it now exists, with a view to making it hark back to that primitive
> communism which was the normal condition of all human groups before
> the dawn of civilisation. Limitations of the hours of labour, the nationali-
> sation of mines, railways, factories and the soil, the equal distribution of all
> products, the elimination of the upper classes for the benefit of the popular
> classes, etc., such are these claims. (p. xvi)

But Le Bon went on to suggest that leaders could draw on the nature of the
crowd to counter this communist trend: Crowds are "powerless . . . to hold
any opinions other than those which are imposed upon them, and it is not
with rules based on theories of pure equity that they are to be led, but by
seeking what produces an impression on them and what seduces them. . . .
In practice the most unjust may be the best for the masses" (p. xx). In other
words, there was nothing inherent in the crowd's fascination with communism: rather, communism was simply what was being "imposed" on the
workers in 1895, and they could be seduced to some other philosophy that
would restore civilization.

Le Bon had little hope of using the crowd mind to develop civilization because, he argued, "civilizations as yet have only been created and
directed by a small intellectual aristocracy, never by crowds. . . . A civilization involves fixed rules, discipline, a passing from the instinctive to the
rational state, forethought for the future, an elevated degree of culture—all
of them conditions that crowds, left to themselves, have invariably shown
themselves incapable of realising" (p. xviii). The crowd at best would clear
the ground for a new civilization, but if such a new order were to arise, according to Le Bon, it would owe nothing to the crowd mind, but would be
merely a new aristocracy imposing itself. The conservatives who followed
Le Bon, however, developed a different idea of the relation between the aristocracy that builds culture and the masses. The new conservatives, such
as Georges Sorel, Charles Maurras, and Giovanni Gentile—social theorists
that Yeats and Eliot followed—argued that the aristocracy is the part of
society best able to express and make conscious what is in the crowd mind.

Such conservatives argued for a culture based on instinct and irrationality, a culture growing out of the crowd, and hence a culture opposed to the old middle-class leaders. Le Bon noted some of this already going on in the 1880's: for example, he commented that many middle-class leaders, in response to the rise of the crowd, were turning to Catholicism, but he argued that it was a futile effort because "the masses repudiate to-day the gods which [the middle class] repudiated yesterday and helped to destroy. There is no power, Divine or human, that can oblige a stream to flow back to its source" (p. xvii). Eliot clearly disagreed, hoping for a Catholic revival. And Eliot could draw on Le Bon for support in this belief: though Le Bon believed that entirely new gods must emerge to restore civilization, he also said that the crowd always responded most powerfully to the oldest traditions, to the "soul of the race" (p. 67). Le Bon's contradictions made his theory useful to both the Left and the Right.

How to Think Like a Crowd

The key to Le Bon's influence did not lie in his predictions of which beliefs the crowd would continue to hold, but in his analysis of how the crowd functions. This analysis begins with his description of the moment of transformation of a collection of people into a crowd: "The sentiments and ideas of all the persons in the gathering take one and the same direction, and their conscious personality vanishes. A collective mind is formed, doubtless transitory, but presenting very clearly defined characteristics. The gathering has thus become what, in the absence of a better expression, I will call an organised crowd, or . . . a psychological crowd. It forms a single being" (p. 2). Such a transformation does not always occur with gatherings of people, but only under certain conditions. A few may become a crowd in the midst of hundreds who do not join together, or "an entire nation, though there may be no visible agglomeration, may become a crowd under the action of certain influences" (p. 3). Le Bon argued that the collective mind that emerges is not at all composed of the sum of the minds of the individuals who participate in it—"exactly as the cells which constitute a living body form by their reunion a new being which displays characteristics very different from those possessed by each of the cells singly" (p. 6). A single individual can be transformed in many different ways by different crowds, and hence Le Bon concluded that the kind of consistent character that had been glorified by literature is largely a fraud: "It is only in novels that individuals are found to traverse their whole life with an unvarying character. It is only the apparent uniformity of the environment that creates the apparent uniformity of character. . . . Among the most savage members of the French Convention were to be found inoffensive citizens who, under ordinary circumstances, would have been peaceful notaries" (pp. 4–5).

Le Bon's call for a literature that would show how character changes as environment changes is closely related to the attitudes that led to modernism. One of the basic differences between Victorian and modernist literature is a change in the relationship between environment or setting and character. In Victorian novels, the setting remains fairly constant while the characters move across it and eventually develop personalities that in some sense fit the environment. In *The Way of the World*, Franco Moretti describes the nineteenth-century *Bildungsroman* in such terms: the "individual's formation and socialization . . . is conceivable only if . . . social norms, for their part, enjoy a substantial stability." Moretti goes on to say that the nineteenth-century novel cannot really portray social and political change because the novel "revolves around individual destinies, while politics moves to collective rhythms." Moretti ends with the comment that the *Bildungsroman* disappeared when "in ideology after ideology, the individual figured simply as part of the whole"—in other words, when the movement of the collective appeared to be more fundamental than the movement of the individual.[1]

But the *Bildungsroman* did not disappear; it just changed form: writers developed methods of building novels around "collective rhythms" rather than around "individual destinies." Most of Woolf's major novels are *Bildungsromanen* in which the social setting changes, and those changes form the basic structure of the book. As Rachel Blau DuPlessis has argued, Woolf's later works are based on "a collective *Bildung* and communal affect" and so "suggest the structures of social change in the structures of narrative."[2] The individual is presented precisely as a "part of the whole" and as such changes along with the setting. The most striking example is *Orlando*, where a young person grows through four hundred years of English history, changing personality and even sex with each shift of period. Instead of suggesting that Orlando's inherent character is developed or hindered by these social influences, Woolf simply shows him/her having different traits in different eras—and all these traits end up layered on top of each other at the end. The book creates no sense of finality; it simply reaches the present, after which one expects that the next social shift will simply produce another layer of character to add to Orlando.

In modernist novels, setting is no longer a constant background against which individual character is defined but the main agent moving the "plot" along and determining what characters think and do. When we are following a character, we often lose track of the supposedly major issues of his life as his thoughts and actions get taken over by the concerns of the groups or the places he wanders through. How this differs from Victorian novels can be made clear by contrasting a dinner scene in Dickens and one in Joyce or Woolf. If people go to dinner in Dickens, we may read about the food they eat and the random conversation, but we are waiting for the clues to the destiny of the hero that are scattered throughout the scene. We are willing to enjoy the dinner, but expect the tale to pick up speed again as clues to the plot proliferate. In *Ulysses* and *To The Lighthouse*, in contrast, when people gather to eat, they talk and think about food, the house they are in, or each other, and major issues in individuals' lives fade into the background. A group of people coming together in these novels ends up defining the topics of conversation and even the thoughts that occur in the minds of the people in that group; each person is transformed. Woolf provides a metaphor for this process in *The Years*: she says that when two people join in conversation, weights underneath the skin of each of them shift to new positions, so that the two people do not even look the same as they did before they started talking. They have different bodies, different faces, different minds in the conversation than they would have had in other ones.[3] The mind is not an internal substance that can be molded to conform to a stable set of moral or intellectual principles; it is rather a space through which pass numerous streams of contradictory words, images, and feelings, most of which never even become conscious.

In *Ulysses*, changes of social setting are marked by changes of style so complete that we often lose track of which characters we are following. Most of the styles used in the text are, as Karen Lawrence has described them, "anonymous, collective discourse," so that sentences seem to derive from institutions that shape characters and author alike rather than from any individual mind.[4] In *The Waves*, Woolf shows six people all changing their thoughts together, not as they wander about the city, but as they age. Woolf emphasizes that setting is what is causing these changes, and not individual actions, by presenting before each chapter a setting that slowly changes throughout the book, tracing the cycle of a day, the sun rising and sinking. These "interludes" reveal the collective rhythm of the life of the group, and indeed of all of England, which rises to a moment of group glory in the triumphant group enterprise of imperialism and then falls with the sinking of the imperial sun.

Eliot and Yeats, in their later poems, also reverse the relationship of background and figure: instead of creating social worlds to define what the poet escapes in moments of lyrical reverie, they make us focus on the setting and suggest that the setting is the only agent in the poem. Yeats's poems often directly proclaim that the images in his brain are products of the surrounding social order and of the past, not of his own "genius." He is constantly trying to decide whether his images have truly emerged from a deep social tide, from the "blood" of the people, or from mere passing "winds" blowing about. In Eliot's poem "The Hollow Men," similarly, the images the writer uses do not emerge from his head (which is hollow), but from the surroundings. These later Yeats and Eliot poems are all epics that, in Pound's phrase, "contain history," poems structured around the collective rhythms of vast and shifting social landscapes. They present characters as minor, fleeting images that blend into the background. The poets present themselves not as individuals, but as parts of eras, of currents of history, of traditions.

Part of the reason that modernism involved such a change in the form of literature was that, according to contemporary theories of crowd psychology, the new mind that a person acquires by joining a crowd is not simply "another" personality: it is a different kind of mentality. Le Bon described the crowd mind in terms that are quite close to Freud's view of the id—pure desires running rampant and constantly shifting due to external stimulation:

> Isolated, he may be a cultivated individual; in a crowd, he is a barbarian— that is, he is a creature acting by instinct. He possesses the spontaneity, the violence, the ferocity, and also the enthusiasm and heroism of primitive beings, whom he further tends to resemble by the facility with which he allows himself to be impressed by words and images . . . and to be induced to commit acts contrary to his most obvious interests and his best-known habits. An individual in a crowd is a grain of sand amid other grains of sand, which the wind stirs up at will. (pp. 12–13)

Le Bon was clearly ambivalent about the crowd: it is violent, ferocious, primitive, but also spontaneous, heroic, and enthusiastic. The crowd becomes the ideal mobilizer of revolution, the vehicle of social change. As Le Bon notes, "It is crowds that have furnished the torrents of blood requisite for the triumph of every belief" (p. 18). Collectivists on the Left and the Right (anarcho-syndicalists, Fascists) drew on the power of the crowd and glorified violence, myths, and irrational images for their ability to produce enthusiasm and spontaneity and overcome the dull bourgeois life, effects that pacifists like Joyce and Woolf sought as well.

Modernist literary techniques, like the techniques of modern political rhetoric and its parent, advertising, developed at least in part in order to speak to and from this crowd mind, to extinguish "conscious personality" in audience and writer alike and appeal instead to the mass unconscious supposed to take its place. It is often presented as a prima facie commonplace of modernist criticism that stream of consciousness and Imagism are aesthetic devices that mark a rejection of social concerns and identify "high-brow" literature as the extreme opposite of "mass" literature. The obscurity and contradictoriness of modernism are said to prove that such literature cannot have been seeking to influence the masses. Mass art supposedly consists of clear, simple stories and straightforward images. Yet the forms taken by advertising and political campaigning in recent years contradict this view. Advertising has shown that the mass mind is influenced by utterly bizarre images and words. Politicians have borrowed such tactics, moving more and more toward the Imagist poetry of "sound bites" as modern media have become more and more mass media. Modernist lit-

erature itself contradicts the critical commonplace as well. If we extract "sound bites" from modernist works, we can find moments quite as propagandistic, pandering, randomly violent, titillating, and banal as anything in any ad. Modernist works are full of short passages that would be at home in horror movies, pornography, or late-night TV, just as advertising juxtaposes images from Shakespeare, Wagner, Marx, the Bible, and T. S. Eliot as freely as did Eliot himself.

Many modernists believed that they were gaining contact with the mass mind by using their strange forms; they also believed that if they wrote in clear, easily comprehensible, realistic forms, they would be disconnected from the masses, thus merely serving the nineteenth-century capitalist system. Yeats expressed this idea very strongly throughout his career; he even developed two different kinds of obscurity—Romantic and modernist—in opposition to what he perceived as capitalist realism. His early position can be seen in his essay "What Is Popular Poetry?"

> what we call 'popular poetry' never came from the people at all. . . . There is only one kind of good poetry, for the poetry of the coteries, which presupposes the written tradition, does not differ in kind from the true poetry of the people, which presupposes the unwritten tradition. Both are alike strange and obscure, and unreal to all who have not understanding, and both, instead of that manifest logic, that clear rhetoric of the 'popular poetry,' glimmer with thoughts and images.[5]

Yeats says that the manifest logic and clear rhetoric of what passes for "popular poetry" was created by "the counting-house" as part of its creation of a "new class." Before "the counting-house" had "set this art and this class between the hut and the castle, and between the hut and the cloister, the art of the people was . . . closely mingled with the art of the coteries."[6] Yeats's early poetry used Romantic strangeness to break out of the middle-class "clear rhetoric" and once again unite the masses and the coteries.

Later, Yeats defined the defects of clear and realistic forms of literature in somewhat different terms. In "Fighting the Waves," in 1934, he describes realism as part of the industrialism that brutalizes people into mechanical objects. Modernism, in all its obscurity, is part of the movement to escape this alienation:

> When Stendahl described a masterpiece as a 'mirror dawdling down a lane,' he expressed the mechanical philosophy of the French eighteenth century. Gradually literature conformed to his ideal . . . till, by the end of the nineteenth century . . . characters . . . had been brutalized into the likeness of mechanical objects. But Europe is changing its philosophy. . . . Certain typical books—*Ulysses*, Virginia Woolf's *The Waves*, Mr. Ezra Pound's *Draft of XXX Cantos*—suggest a philosophy like that of the *Samkara* school of ancient India, mental and physical objects alike material, a deluge of ex-

perience breaking over and within us, melting limits whether of line or tine; man no hard bright mirror dawdling by the dry sticks of a hedge, but a swimmer, or rather the waves themselves. In this literature . . . man in himself is nothing.[7]

The unrealistic modernist literature of flow, of tides, of waves, is thus part of a social movement to end the domination of mechanical, middle-class capitalism. Man in himself—the conscious personality of the individual— becomes nothing, extinguished in the greater social waves. In contrast, the popular realism of writers such as H. G. Wells, Yeats says, is "the opium of the suburbs."[8]

The moves away from realism in the later works of all the authors I am studying here, similarly, were efforts to escape "the suburbs," to break out of the clean, clear shapes of private life. Modernist efforts to eliminate "man in himself" were efforts to write of the underlying social medium. Both novelists and poets moved in their more radical works toward producing streams of images that were overtly identified as the flow of images of a crowd or, perhaps, a culture. *The Waste Land* is a stream of images in the consciousness of "the land," perhaps England, perhaps Europe, perhaps all of Western civilization. *Ulysses* repeatedly shows individuals being engulfed by flows of images that cross all the minds in a given social institution.

Most stream-of-consciousness novels entwine a whole collection of individual streams and trace the group movement that is not controlled by any one person. (Think of *As I Lay Dying* or *To the Lighthouse*.) The streams entwine different people together in a portrayal of a social unit, a crowd. The process of creating a united social body involves not merely finding some common history, but becoming part of intertwined streams of conscious and unconscious thought. Early in Yeats's life, he thought that all he needed was to find the central image of Irish history to accomplish this goal; later, he found that the mind of the nation is "multiform." When he describes this multiform mind, he sounds very much as if he is describing a modernist multiple stream-of-consciousness novel:

Is there a nationwide multiform reverie, every mind passing through a stream of suggestion, and all streams acting and reacting upon one another no matter how distant the minds, how dumb the lips? A man walked, as it were, casting a shadow, and yet one could never say which was man and which was shadow, or how many the shadows he cast. Was not a nation, as distinguished from a crowd of chance comers, bound together by this interchange among streams or shadows; that Unity of Image, which I sought in national literature, being but an originating symbol? . . . How could I judge any scheme of education or of social reform, when I could not measure what the different classes and occupations contributed to that invisible commerce of reverie and of sleep: and what is luxury and what necessity when a fragment of gold braid, or a flower in the wallpaper, may be an originating impulse to revolution or to philosophy?[9]

Yeats summarized his anxiety in a phrase that could characterize all of modernism: "Was modern civilization a conspiracy of the subconscious?"[10]

Woolf's novels frequently focus on tiny fragments, such as a flower in the wallpaper, and suggest that such elements have great power. When Mrs. Dalloway asks if her roses are as important as her husband's political causes, she is not just being self-centered; it is a legitimate question of the sort that tormented both Yeats and Woolf in their efforts to discover the springs of social revolution. Yeats's description of the complexity of the "invisible commerce" that passes between "different classes and occupations" is quite similar to Woolf's description of the "invisible presences . . . immense forces that society brings to bear upon us," forces that cross classes and even decades of history.[11] Like Yeats, she believed that she needed to examine vast nets of unconscious influence that crisscross society if she was to make sense of her world.

Yeats went so far as to investigate supernatural phenomena. These investigations are considered by most readers as absurd and irrelevant to any real political effects his poetry may have. However, Le Bon gives strong credence to a belief in a certain kind of magic and supernaturalism. He says that the images that move crowds

> do not always lie ready to hand, but it is possible to evoke them by the judicious employment of words and formulas. Handled with art, they possess in sober truth the mysterious power formerly attributed to them by the adepts of magic. They cause the birth in the minds of crowds of the most formidable tempests, which in turn they are capable of stilling. . . . Reason and arguments are incapable of combatting certain words and formulas. . . . By many they are considered as natural forces, as supernatural powers. (pp. 95–96)

Le Bon's comments suggest that Yeats's investigations of supernatural phenomena ought not to be seen as disconnected from his politics. Yeats writes at one point that when he passes an Irish cottage, he has stepped outside of Europe into the realm of the supernatural, the realm of the "most violent force in history."[12]

These writers believed that in the twentieth century, political battles were not going to be waged by logical arguments read by individuals in private rooms: the battles were going to be waged between competing streams of images in the crowd mind. Logic has little to do with such streams: "These imagelike ideas are not connected by any logical bond of analogy or succession, and may take each other's place like the slides of a magic-lantern which the operator withdraws from the groove in which they were placed one above the other. This explains how it is that the most contradictory ideas may be seen to be simultaneously current in crowds" (p. 47). Many of the most distinctive modernist effects seem to be described here: the juxtaposing, overlapping, and rapid shifting of disparate images, the overlay of one image on top of another, the rapid shifting of images. Con-

versely, it is not an accident that the most famous Imagist poem, "In a
Station of the Metro," is about a crowd:

> The apparition of these faces in the crowd
> Petals on a wet, black bough.[13]

From the title to the end of this poem, we pass from the mechanical, realistic world of subway stations, through the faces of individuals, into the
collective world of a single organic unit, a bough. This transformation also
involves moving from dry to wet and from light to dark—dissolving the
visible world into the dark unconscious wave that carries everyone along.

Pound's poem sets up an opposition between the almost weightless
individual faces, flitting apparitions or petals, and the deep solidity of the
social branch that holds them together. The poem could be referring to all
the short Imagist poems themselves, which exist each as a small petal in a
large book and are held together only by the dark spine that is not visible
in any single poem. The passage beyond realism is the passage into the
unconscious basis of social unity. The realistic world is merely an ephemeral surface, flickering over something deeper. Le Bon similarly sees it as
useful to divide the ideas that inspire the images in the crowd mind into
two categories:

> In one we shall place accidental and passing ideas created by the influences
> of the moment; infatuation for an individual or a doctrine, for instance. In
> the other will be classed the fundamental ideas, to which the environment,
> the laws of heredity, and public opinion give a very great stability; such
> ideas are the religious beliefs of the past and the social and democratic ideas
> of to-day.
>
> These fundamental ideas resemble the volume of the water of a stream
> slowly pursuing its course; the transitory ideas are like the small waves,
> for ever changing, which agitate the surface, and are more visible than the
> progress of the stream itself although without real importance.
>
> At the present day the great fundamental ideas which were the mainstay
> of our fathers are tottering more and more. They have lost all solidity, and
> at the same time the institutions resting upon them are severely shaken.
> Every day there are formed a great many of those transitory minor ideas
> of which I have just been speaking; but very few of them to all appear-
> ance seem endowed with vitality and destined to acquire a preponderating
> influence. (pp. 46–47)

Le Bon's vision here is very similar to Pound's, Eliot's, and Yeats's: they
all defined the goal of social change and of their art as the producing of a
deep wave—a restored cultural center, a wet, black bough—that will hold
together the chaotic small waves agitating society now. If the bough is in
place, the leaves can randomly wave about all they want; if it is not, the
leaves will blow apart in chaos. Modernist writers all recognized that it

is very difficult to gain access to the invisible depths where deep waves are generated. In their poems, they constantly show their uncertainty—at times confidently presenting images of a new, deep order emerging, and at other times describing the impossibility of finding anything but dry, sterile words. The voice of thunder that brings water to the dry waste land, the beast that replaces the chaotic circling tides with a slow but unified motion of a giant social body, are presented as images of a new, unified social order—and both disappear in endings that express the doubts of the poets about their power to penetrate the current agitation of chaotic small waves.

Eliot and Yeats also shared Le Bon's belief that heredity and environment are the sources of the deep waves. Yeats went so far as to advocate eugenics as a way of altering the stream of images. Eliot also suggested racial and environmental criteria for producing the culture he would like, as I discuss in some detail in Chapter 4. Le Bon implied strongly that one needs some kind of hereditary unity to have a deep wave at all. He writes that people in the modern world often seem to have multiple and contradictory personalities because they are exposed to so many different influences and cultures. But "these contradictions are more apparent than real, for it is only hereditary ideas that have sufficient influence over the isolated individual to become the motives of conduct. It is only when, as the result of the intermingling of different races, a man is placed between different hereditary tendencies that his acts from one moment to another may be really entirely contradictory" (p. 48). Le Bon concludes that the "inferior characteristics of crowds are less accentuated in proportion as the spirit of the race is strong. . . . It is by the acquisition of a solidly constituted collective spirit that the race frees itself to a greater and greater extent from the unreflecting power of crowds" (p. 161).

Eliot's and Yeats's ideas of cultural unity are well known; what Le Bon provides is a way of linking those ideas to the wildly fragmented and contradictory flows of images that we find in their poems. Instead of trying to write out clearly the fundamental ideas that underlie deep waves (which would leave their writing in the conscious, surface mind), these poets were trying to operate in the medium of the unconscious crowd mind itself. Le Bon says that "ideas," especially "somewhat lofty philosophic or scientific ideas," must "undergo the most thoroughgoing transformations to become popular" (p. 48). This is a very unusual kind of popularizing, not via simple books that make complex ideas clear to the poorly educated, but via images that operate on the unconscious. The books that we would consider popularizing versions of great ideas engage only the conscious mind or the shallowest waves. Joyce, Woolf, Eliot, and Yeats were not seeking to do that at all: they did not wish to speak comprehensibly to average men because doing so was irrelevant to the job of creating deep waves.

Le Bon's distinction between deep and surface waves thus suggests an answer to the problem of how obscure poems and novels, to be read only by a few, might be written with the intent of influencing the masses and even popularizing lofty ideas. The surface of these works engages only the intellectuals, but the depths supposedly touch on the waves carrying the whole society along. Moreover, the whole problem with the threatening anarchy of the early twentieth century was not truly a problem with the masses because most theorists regarded them as carrying the tide of the future. It was the intellectuals who were thought to be weak and out of touch with these tides. As Yeats put it, the way to "deepen the political passion of the nation" is to make "current among the educated classes" the stories and images found among the "uneducated classes."[14]

The novels of Joyce and Woolf are similarly directed at the cultured few, trying to bring them to join with the masses—but in a subtly different way. Joyce and Woolf were seeking to bring high culture to serve socialist mass movements, and in particular were seeking to break with the whole idea of leadership, of ruling classes or individuals. Furthermore, Joyce and Woolf wanted to bring about the kind of hereditary mixture that Le Bon says produces contradictory personalities: Joyce and Woolf advocated such contradictoriness as a way out of the oppression that results from one race trying to hold itself separate and pure from others. We might even say that Joyce and Woolf inverted Le Bon's description of deep and shallow waves: the deep waves, in their view, are multiple and contradictory, and the appearance of a unified wave is a surface illusion produced by oppressive politics. Civilization can be made to appear orderly and disciplined by suppressing into the depths the waves that pass through the minds of, say, women, lower classes, and marginalized ethnic groups.

Le Bon joined in the debate between contrasting versions of an ideal collectivist state when he analyzed the factors that shape the deep waves that are fundamental to the shape of civilization. He describes two as essential: race and traditions. He says, "crowds are the most obstinate maintainers of traditional ideas," reaching the remarkable conclusion that the crowd is the most conservative part of society. We can see why conservatives embraced his theory even though he had at other points in his book equated the crowd with socialism. He also says that "political and social institutions" and "education" are very weak influences, almost negligible: "they are effects, not causes. Nations are not capable of choosing what appear to them the best institutions" (p. 66). Hence the emphasis in so much early-twentieth-century politics on ignoring overt political institutions and education, the cornerstones of liberal politics.

Collectivism was a politics that took place outside the political arena. This explains much of what appears to be the antipolitical attitude of modernists. Samuel Beer and Charles Maier both argue that the new mass politics involved a shift in the center of power to extraparliamentary institutions.[15] As Joyce wrote his brother Stanislaus in 1906 about the Italian syndicalists: "Their weapons are unions and strikes. They decline to interfere in politics or religion or legal questions" because "public powers" always end up supporting "the middle-class government."[16] In *Ulysses*, as I will show, Joyce developed a form of literary syndicalism: he attempted to change Ireland by acting on the collective consciousnesses, the "mental unions," we might say, that underlie institutions throughout the social order. He did not seek, however, to replace the government leaders or alter the religions or laws from within. Rather, so strongly did he believe in the need to alter those institutions that he could not work from within them: he thought they remained too completely tied to middle-class capitalism.

In order to make use of traditions and the "soul of the race" to move the crowd to join into unions, mass movements, or cultural wholes, the basic tools are the "magical power of words and formulas" and "the social illusion [that] reigns to-day upon all the heaped-up ruins of the past, and to it belongs the future" (p. 105). The most important illusions are those of legendary, marvelous events, especially those involving heroes. Le Bon therefore concludes that

> works of history must be considered as works of pure imagination. They are fanciful accounts of ill-observed facts, accompanied by explanations. . . . To write such books is the most absolute waste of time. Had not the past left us its literary, artistic, and monumental works, we should know absolutely nothing in reality in regard to bygone times. . . . Our interest is to know what our great men were as they are presented by popular legend. It is legendary heroes, and not for a moment real heroes, who have impressed the minds of crowds. (p. 31)

The importance of legends and heroes derives from Le Bon's belief in the "instinctive need of all beings forming a crowd to obey a leader" (p. 112). Le Bon concluded that all crowds, even those forming socialist movements, are essentially religious, with a deep need for gods and priests.

It is easy to see how Yeats, Eliot, and other conservatives found such analyses congenial: Le Bon seemed to argue that the crowd will maintain religion, leadership, and a belief in great men. Joyce, Woolf, and the socialists who sought to free the masses from religion and ruling classes struggled against Le Bon's conclusion that crowds inevitably view their leaders as gods. The debate between Left and Right was finally in many ways a debate about whether or not crowds require images of superhuman leaders to hold them together.

Myths and Violence

Debates about the masses' desire for leaders did not focus as much on images as on another literary form: myth. The importance of myth in early-twentieth-century theory of the mass mind derived from Georges Sorel, who modified Le Bon in ways that were influential on both the Left and the

Right. Sorel sought to understand how to turn a crowd into a movement, and he decided that the essential trick was to find a "group of images" that functioned as a "myth":

> men who are participating in a great social movement always picture their coming action as a battle in which their cause is certain to triumph. These constructions, knowledge of which is so important for historians, I pro- pose to call myths; the syndicalist "general strike" and Marx's catastrophic revolution are such myths . . . [as are] those which were constructed by primitive Christianity, by the Reformation, by the Revolution and by the followers of Mazzini. . . . We should not attempt to analyse such groups of images in the way that we analyse a thing into its elements, but . . . they must be taken as a whole, as historical forces. (pp. 48–49)

Sorel's "myths" in this description are not what we usually think of as myths: he is speaking about what could be called histories of the future— theories of the social forces and currents moving the world that predict that a certain movement is going to triumph. During the early twentieth cen- tury, theories of history that described the present as on the cusp of some major change proliferated and were highly influential on the modernists. Yeats's cycles and Eliot's theory of the dissociation of sensibility dating from the seventeenth century are overt historical presentations; Woolf's later novels repeatedly trace history up to the present. Sorel suggested that the central point in any theory of the currents of history passing through the present is how such a theory motivates groups of people to act now.

Sorel dismissed the traditional forms of history and literature, saying the business of the true historian "is to *understand what is least indi- vidual* in the course of events; the questions which interest the chroniclers and excite novelists are those which he most willingly leaves on one side" (p. 70). We can begin to see why Sorel's theories would imply a change in the nineteenth-century novel and in Romantic poetry. For one thing, Sorel's project was opposed to individualist theories of psychology: "I want to find out how the feelings by which the masses are moved form them- selves into groups; all the discussion of the moralists about the motives for the actions of prominent men, and all psychological analyses of character, are, then, quite secondary in importance and even altogether negligible" (p. 68). Sorel objected to character for an unusual reason: because it is in his view a restriction on individual freedom. Character is formed of habits that keep people doing the same thing over and over again. So Sorel looked for moments when people "break the bonds of habit which enclose us"— and he concluded that the key to breaking habits is bringing people to be swept up in the enthusiasm of a mass movement (p. 55). Sorel was similarly opposed to liberal individualism because he viewed it as restricting people to thinking about their small, private lives. Sorel could thus regard the loss of conscious personality and individual psychology that occurs when people join the crowd as a liberation of the self, an improvement of the individual. By defining the crowd mind as the superior and deeper mind and the conscious personality as a dull complex of habits, Sorel inverted Le Bon's evaluations.

Sorel also separated what he was interested in from politics. He said that socialists became discouraged when it seemed "trades union organization was . . . becoming a kind of politics, a means of getting on" (p. 82). Sorel labeled as "politics," as means of getting on, such things as elections, governmental policies, and redistribution of income. Sorel, then, was as apolitical as he was anti-economic, even though he was seeking to cause a socialist (and hence an economic) revolution. Sorel sought to break free of all concerns about "getting on," all thoughts about goods, economic interests, or status. He asks, "Is there an economic epic capable of stimulating the enthusiasm of the workers?" (p. 276). He notes that "economic progress goes far beyond the individual life . . . but does it give glory?" (p. 276). Sorel disliked politics and economics precisely because they do not inspire enthusiasm, and such inspiration was his entire goal. Indeed, the myth that Sorel believed would bring about a socialist revolution was the myth of the general strike, a myth of stopping the economic system, a myth of an anti-economics, a refusal to care about goods entirely, no matter how distributed.

Sorel argued that the general strike could develop as a myth as a result of one particular tactic: violence. Violence and the general strike are quite similar as methods: they both are in essence disruptions that cause an intense need for something to happen with no sense of what that something will be. For Sorel, the moment of complete disruption, the general strike, is the best state of all, and an end in itself. The myth of the general strike "gives to socialism such high moral value and such great sincerity" because this myth has the "character of infinity" in its complete undefinability and its complete resistance to "argument" (p. 53). Modernists themselves have at times seemed also to valorize complete disruption. In a very Sorelian line, Yeats writes in "Under Ben Bulben" that "war completes the partial mind"—in the instant of action one becomes whole. Stephen Dedalus's desire to eliminate all space and time in a stroke of a Wagnerian sword named *Nothung* is an image of this general strike: Stephen strikes out at the whole world, seeking to free himself from space and time. And critics have valorized modernism for its embrace of these disruptions. Colin MacCabe sees *Ulysses* as enacting the "revolution of the word."[17] Lucio Ruotolo has argued that "interrupted moments" in Woolf's works provide access to a world beyond ordinary reality—and has suggested that Woolf was an anarchist.[18] Frank Kermode provides a subtly different vision of the importance of complete disruption in modernism: he sees modernists as dreaming of "apocalypse" and hence leading to totalitarianism (particularly Fascism).[19]

As part of my methodology of considering literary texts as participating in political debates, I regard modernist visions of ultimate revolutions of consciousness or of society—anarchistic, mystical, or apocalyptic
moves beyond everyday reality—as ways of advocating or rejecting particular social changes. Modernist works themselves suggest that apocalyptic
imagery may function as a transitional device. In many modernist works,
the apocalyptic images appear in the middle, and show the world passing
through complete or nearly complete annihilation. Both *To the Lighthouse*
and Dangerfield's history use the apocalyptic imagery of a general strike to
indicate such a moment of transition, a moment of political change. Similarly, *The Waste Land* passes through "death by water" to present an image
of something beyond the sea change produced by social tides swamping the
old capitalist system.

We can even apply this methodological principle to Sorel himself, treating his "theory of myth" as a political tactic, a narrative that functions to
bring about a particular historical change. Sorel does much to make his
theory of myth ahistorical: his use of many previous historical myths and
the revolutions they produced imply that he is examining some eternally
repeatable phenomenon, not something particular to his era. But as his
own theory says, histories such as his own always serve simply to create a
sense of inevitability about some future change. His history of myths adds
a feeling of inevitability to the particular myth he is promoting: the general
strike takes its place in the sequence of successful revolutionary myths
that he presents.

There is an even stronger way in which Sorel's entire theory and history
of myths served one particular political goal of his era, that of breaking the
rule of middle-class capitalism. He presents all earlier revolutions as pre-
cursors of the break with capitalist individualism. In each of these earlier
revolutions, Sorel claims, myths disrupted the desire to "get on" and also
disrupted "rational argument." Rational argument and the desire to get on
may have always operated to keep people from joining revolutionary movements, and so may have always been the obstacle that myths overcome,
but these two things are practically defining features of middle-class capitalism, according to Sorel. So Sorel can define the goal of his whole theory
(including his accounts of ancient history) as helping "to ruin the prestige of
middle-class culture" (p. 62). Sorel's history shows the decline of the Western world from the "mythic" life of the Greeks, especially the Spartans,
into bourgeois individualism.

In his account of this decline, "myth" changes from referring to any
collection of images that creates a sense of inevitability to referring to the
collection of stories that have been labeled "myths," particularly the Greek
ones. Sorel claims that in every revolution, the participants have felt they
participated in *"truly Homeric conflicts,"* so Homeric epics provide the

model for all other myths (p. 268). He blurs these two different senses of myth so that he can then say that the emergence of *any* myth will transform the people of any country into essentially Greek heroes and heroines.

These two different senses of "myth"—as the history of the future and as elements taken from ancient tales that will revive ancient values lost in capitalist society—appear in modernist works extensively. Yeats's *Vision* is a theory of history that produces a sense of the inevitability of certain changes about to occur, but Yeats supplements this extremely abstract history with powerful images drawn from what we would more easily recognize as mythic sources (particularly Greek and Irish tales) to add another kind of power to his history. The "scientific" history and the images together were supposed to produce a mass movement, and frequently Yeats describes his goal in terms that sound very much as if he were seeking a general strike—a complete disruption of current production (especially cultural production)—in order to allow a radical change in the social order that is inevitable. Eliot says that myths, as Joyce used them in *Ulysses*, function as "a way of controlling, of ordering, of giving a shape and a significance to the immense panorama of futility and anarchy which is contemporary history."[20] Eliot thus blurs together the use of ancient texts and the provision of direction for current mass movements—"shaping anarchy."

Eliot also treated Joyce as seeking to restore the kind of hierarchical order characteristic of Greek society. Joyce was strongly influenced by syndicalism and by Sorel's formulations, but I will show later that the novel's relation to history and to social change has been seriously misrepresented by Eliot. Eliot's essay is an effort to take a work that was written to serve left-wing anarcho-syndicalism and turn it to the right-wing corporatism of Eliot himself. Such an effort to transform works was not at all unusual in the early twentieth century—politicians switched sides constantly, and they frequently reinterpreted their own works written while aligned on one side as arguments for the other side. Eliot treated Sorel's text in precisely the same way, praising *Reflections on Violence* as one of the five central texts in the movement for a return to a royalist Europe.[21] That Sorel's book was written with clearly socialist goals did not disturb Eliot in the least, possibly because Sorel himself slid back and forth between right-wing and left-wing movements.

To understand the relationship of Sorel's theories to modernism, then, it is important to examine how they served opposed political movements. The two completely opposed directions syndicalism took are epitomized by pluralism and nationalism: the earliest syndicalists, at least in Italy, were, as the historian A. James Gregor puts it, "radically antistate, antinationalist, anticlerical, and antimilitant," and this form of syndicalism evolved into the nonviolent British pluralism of figures such as Harold Laski.[22] Another branch of syndicalism developed into a powerful part of nationalist (and racialist) movements in Italy (Benito Mussolini) and in Ireland (James Connolly), and in these movements syndicalism became synonymous with violence.

One way to understand the opposed developments is to see them as deriving from two opposed interpretations of a single clause in *Reflections on Violence*. Sorel says that syndicalism is based on "corporate exclusiveness, which resembles the local or racial spirit" (p. 80). The pluralists emphasized the importance of the word "local," while the nationalists emphasized "racial": the pluralists argued that only in very small groups can there be the feeling of corporate unity, while the nationalists believed that size isn't the issue, but rather "common blood"—and hence that racial and national groups are not only possible, but preferable to small units.

Socialist syndicalists moved toward nationalism in Italy and Ireland because they became convinced that the nation embodied the myth that most unified people.[23] Part of this conviction was due to their belief that their countries were too poorly developed to have a coherent proletariat that could respond to the image of the general strike. Socialists thus adopted nationalist and developmental goals—building up the industrial base of the country—as a step toward the socialist revolution. Le Bon's analysis of the crowd also supported switching from a class to a national or racial basis: he argued that the crowd is best formed by drawing on "the soul of the race."

In Sorel's works, there are also strong hints that he was particularly interested in a *French* general strike, not an international one. For example, he describes as the ideal revolutionary the "soldier of Napoleon . . . [who] felt that the epic in which he was taking part would be eternal, that he would live in the glory of France." Sorel then asks, "do there exist among the workmen forces capable of producing enthusiasm equivalent to those?" (p. 276). Sorel often seems to equate the "glory of France" with the results of the socialist revolution he advocates. Similarly, the Italian syndicalists who formed the core of Fascism (Roberto Michels, Paolo Orano, etc.) merged together the restoration of Italy as a glorious empire and the ending of the economic troubles of Italian workers.

The particular form of nationalist syndicalism that evolved in Europe required one more element: the theory of elites. This is a central feature of the particular visions of ideal cultures in Eliot and Yeats and a central element opposed by Joyce and Woolf. Arguments for elites derived from many sources, but for modernists Sorel provided two justifications for an elite that were especially important: an elite is necessary to produce the myths to which the masses will respond, and images of an elite, of an aristocracy, are always part of the mythic imagery that motivates the masses. Italian philosophers and social psychologists developed these two halves of the theory of elites and were highly influential on the modernists I am discussing. Vilfredo Pareto and Gaetano de Mosca argued that myths are always the product of an elite. Roberto Michels states the second point in its strongest form: "among the masses there is a profound impulse to venerate those who are their superiors. In their primitive idealism, they have a need for a secular 'divinity.' . . . This need is accompanied by a genuine cult for the leaders, who are regarded as heroes."[24]

As such theories suggest, syndicalism became intertwined with aristocratic and right-wing movements in many countries. In France, Charles Maurras developed a theory of "socialist monarchy" that relied on the monarch to provide the intense veneration that would hold together the nation and replace the capitalist leadership that was, in his view, destroying the underlying cultural unity. The solidarity of socialism, he argued, is in its essence identical to the unity provided by a king. Eliot, in his 1916 lectures on French literature and on Sorel, developed similar ideas, arguing that socialism and royalism were actually relatively similar alternatives to capitalism in that both led to "centralization in government."[25] Yeats put together the necessity of violence and of an elite in the thoroughly Sorelian poems praising the Irish syndicalist James Connolly written in reaction to the events in Ireland from 1916 until independence. His later poems anxiously consider the impossibility of restoring the Irish aristocracy and the consequent necessity of some further violence (Fascism or war) to develop some new form of leadership.

Though Sorel himself followed the nationalist trajectory of syndicalism, there is another part of the analysis in Sorel's *Reflections on Violence* that radically opposes the forms that syndicalist nationalism became. This part of syndicalist theory served as inspiration for the anti-elitism, anti-Fascism, and antimilitarism of Joyce and Woolf. Sorel argued that his myths do not produce the kind of enthusiasm that leads people to obey leaders. In fact, Sorel saw myths as serving the "transformation of the men of to-day into the free producers of to-morrow working in manufactories where there are no masters" (p. 264). These workers without masters, he claimed, would be similar to the peasants fighting for Napoleon; their labors would be "collections of heroic exploits accomplished by individuals under the influence of an extraordinary enthusiasm" (p. 267). The syndicalist revolution, in turn, would then be

> an immense uprising which yet may be called individualistic; each working with the greatest possible zeal, each acting on his own account, and not troubling himself much to subordinate his conduct to a great and scientifically combined plan. This character of the proletarian general strike has often been pointed out, and it has the effect of frightening the greedy politicians, who understand perfectly well that a Revolution conducted in this way would do away with their chances of seizing the Government. (p. 269)

We must distinguish this kind of "individualistic" life from liberal individualism: this is the individual as so completely a part of the group that he is devoted entirely as an individual to group goals. Sorel argued intriguingly that the individual who feels an epic enthusiasm does not lose himself, does not submit to domination by others, but becomes freer: "It might at first be supposed that it would be sufficient to say that, at such moments, we are dominated by an overwhelming emotion; but everybody now recognises that movement is the essence of emotional life, and it is, then, in terms of movement that we must speak of creative consciousness" (p. 55). Sorel's replacing of the phrase "dominated by an overwhelming emotion" with the term "creative consciousness" marks his denial of the common image of collectivism as an authoritarian system. Sorel defined the ideal revolutionary movement as one that eliminates authority, freeing each person from domination and to "creative consciousness." In a mass movement, every person becomes an artist.[26]

British pluralists drew a different conclusion than nationalists did from Sorel's argument that syndicates needed the "corporate exclusiveness that resembled local or racial spirit." Sorel overtly denied that mass movements turn people into "passive instruments who do not need to think." Such passivity is a *"morality of the weak"* promoted by those who would turn revolutionary syndicalism into the bourgeois fraud of "State Socialism" (p. 264). Sorel argued that his myths would eliminate large government and the division of society into rulers and followers. Labour theorists also spoke frequently about empowering the masses directly and eliminating any "ruling elite": in effect, they were against leadership. The organization of the British Labour Party thus reflected the theory of anarcho-syndicalism. The party conference dictated policy, and elected officials were delegates of this conference, not leaders of the party. The party had a strongly unified ideology, but that was not inherent in the structure: indeed, the party was set up to allow trade unions autonomy and to disperse control among multiple party bodies. Harold Laski wrote an influential book called *The Foundations of Sovereignty* in which he argued that there should be no sovereign power at all, no central leadership of the state. He and G. D. H. Cole developed pluralist theories that suggested government be divided into separate bodies for every social organization. These writers emphasized that the corporate unity of feeling could exist only in small groups. It is to maintain the enthusiasm and dissolution of self in the social body, they believed, that government should be broken up and leaders eliminated.

Woolf's "Outsiders' Society" was very much an image of revolutionary syndicalism in this sense of people sharing an enthusiasm without leadership. Woolf of course knew Laski and Cole well through Leonard Woolf and her own involvement with the Labour Party. Joyce reached much the same ideas through his fascination with early syndicalism in Italy and through his rejection of later syndicalism, with its nationalism and epic militarism.

Much of the debate in modernism thus consisted of efforts to separate the contradictory parts of Sorel's theory: Joyce and Woolf tried to show that one can have enthusiasm, the joys of group unity, and even myths, without elites, without "common blood," and without violence. Eliot and Yeats tried to show that one needs elites and blood ties to have the enthusiasm of group unity, and Yeats defended the necessity of violence.

Critics have frequently criticized Yeats for his advocacy of violence; in contrast, Joyce and Woolf are often praised for their seeming pacifism.[27] I want to question such distinctions, because Sorel's claim that violence is essential to liberation, to the release of what lies buried in the unconscious, haunts and undermines Joyce's and Woolf's supposedly nonviolent works. In their novels, though violence is condemned, it still serves a necessary function. In both *To the Lighthouse* and *Ulysses*, the authors use overt acts of violence connected in odd, indirect ways to war in order to bring about a transition from one dominant form of consciousness to another: a soldier knocks out Stephen Dedalus; Mrs. Ramsay dies in the midst of World War I—and these acts seem necessary to allow Leopold Bloom and Lily Briscoe to take charge and become in some sense images of the authors' new, modernist selves.

Throughout Woolf's novels, uncanny acts of violence liberate characters from oppressive relationships. Because they feel mistreated, her characters' minds are full of murderous wishes: these wishes are never carried out, but other violent acts occur that seem to accidentally and indirectly accomplish the same purpose. In the beginning of *To the Lighthouse*, nearly everyone is full of violent anger at Mr. Ramsay, yet it is Mrs. Ramsay who dies suddenly and whose death seems to alleviate much of the oppressiveness of the Ramsay household. In *The Voyage Out*, Rachel's father and Mr. Dalloway seem to abuse her and cause her to have monstrous dreams of cutting men's heads off, yet she is the one who dies, and her death just before her marriage has been taken by critics as a symbolic act of escaping abusive male sexuality in general (see Chapter 3). In *The Waves*, the six characters are full of angry desires to destroy each other, yet it is the seventh who never speaks, the leader, Percival, who dies and seems to release them from their competitiveness. Woolf created novels about the need for violent release from oppression, but did not allow anyone's anger to be directly expressed in action. She disconnected her characters from the mechanisms that bring about the violent liberations that fulfill their dreams. Her novels embody a problem that runs throughout her essays: she analyzes brilliantly the violence of the social system but refuses to countenance aggressive reactions to it. In *A Room of One's Own*, Woolf shows the violence surrounding the women's movement as a male reaction; she ignores or minimizes the violence performed by the movement itself. We have to be careful if we want to valorize Woolf's nonviolence: is she condemning methods of liberation of which she takes advantage?

Joyce also creates in his novels worlds of such oppression that characters dream of violent responses; he even shows them at times becoming violent, but such violent acts are presented as futile, generally a result of drunkenness, and always misdirected: Stephen, dreaming of using a Wagnerian sword to free himself from everything, slashes a prostitute's lamp shade with a stick; the poor man in "Counterparts," in anger at his boss's unfairness, hits his own son; the citizen, fulminating against the British, throws a tin at the Jew, Bloom; in *Finnegans Wake*, such absurd violence becomes a repeated motif, particularly in the tale of a military figure being shot in the bottom while relieving himself.

Joyce's works also include numerous allusions to historical violent acts that have only an indirect relationship to the everyday lives being presented, e.g., lengthy discussions of murders and allusions to the violence of figures such as "skin-the-cat" in *Ulysses* and accounts of Napoleonic battles in *Finnegans Wake*. The role of these allusions is similar to the role of allusions to World War I in *To the Lighthouse* and *The Waste Land*: they create a sense that violent forces are at work somewhere else, in a hazy but quite real political world that we cannot help but feel has a close relationship to the unconscious, violent impulses revealed inside everyone.

Joyce and Woolf thus recognized the power of violence to express and satisfy the unconscious desires for liberation created by social oppression, but they struggled to find some other method of change. While my sympathies lie with Joyce and Woolf in their projects to break up what seems an inherent connection linking radical change, violence, and militarism, I cannot dismiss Yeats's position that violence must be advocated at certain times, particularly in the effort to escape colonial rule. Modernism has a particularly strong relationship to postcolonial writers, who have never had any trouble seeing the sociopolitical underpinnings of this art form. Edward Said says that Yeats has been accepted as a great national poet of the postcolonial world; Yeats's advocacy of violence has been a source of that acceptance.[28] At the same time, Feroza Jussawalla and Reed Way Dasenbrock claim that "Joyce remains a central figure for many of the postcolonial writers in English."[29] We might, then, consider how postcolonial theories illuminate the debates within modernism. Frantz Fanon has argued that only a violent national movement can bring about the demise of a colonial government, a version of Yeats's position.[30] If Fanon is correct, the political agendas in Joyce's and Woolf's works may not only be unrealistic, they may even serve to support certain oppressive systems that Yeats's visions would help overthrow. By advocating "outsiders' societies" with no treasurers, no leadership, and no unity, and by refusing to be part of movements that are arranged hierarchically and act militantly, Joyce's and Woolf's works may in effect support oppressive regimes by undermining the only possible oppositional movement.

On the other hand, theorists of the subaltern such as Partha Chatterjee have argued that nationalist liberation movements, in their insistence on unity, too often end up recreating hierarchical and oppressive states after colonial rule has ended. Chatterjee advocates instead a form of social organization that sounds modernist, composed of what he calls "fragments."[31] Such a theory helps us see the political value of the fragmentary pluralism practiced by writers such as Joyce and Woolf, particularly as an antidote to the cultural homogeneity advocated by Eliot and Yeats.

Psychological Theories

During the modernist era, psychologists developed competing theories of the unconscious that played significant roles in the debates growing out of Sorel's work. Though Freud should be labeled a classical liberal in the scheme I have been employing, in which both socialism and conservatism stand at odds with liberalism, his own theories of the unconscious mostly supported the new conservatives because he argued that groups are held together by images of great male leaders, which merge with the unconscious mental formation that in English is called the super-ego. In a book on mass psychology (*Massenpsychologie und Ich-Analyse*, mistranslated as *Group Psychology and Analysis of the Ego*), Freud declared that a group such as an army, church, or nation is unified by an "I-ideal," or what Freud later called the "super-I," an image of the perfect self that everyone in the group admires and tries to emulate, and by whom everyone feels criticized and judged. The individual becomes a docile group member because joining the group allows the individual to identify with the super-I and thereby become a greater person. The ego, accepting the limitations of society and reality, recognizes that it cannot satisfy all desires. But by identifying with a leader or an image of a leader who functions as an ideal, "a man, when he cannot be satisfied with his ego itself, may nevertheless be able to find satisfaction in the ego-ideal." Joining such a group allows a return to primal feelings of unlimitedness and allows an "exaltation or intensification of emotion," especially feelings of love, or, as Freud puts it, libidinal ties. Humans, then, form mass movements not because of a natural need to be in herds, a kind of docility and unwillingness to stand alone, as Wilfred Trotter had argued, but because of a need to identify with and love a "primal father." Freud says he must "correct Trotter's pronouncement that man is a herd animal and assert that he is rather a horde animal, an individual creature in a horde led by a chief."[32]

Freud's theory of the super-ego was not so much a source of the modern politics of the leader as a part of the developing collectivist notions emerging all over Europe. He mirrored the attitudes of Le Bon and Sorel in declaring that the old ties that held social groups together, based on the religious worship of a "father god," were weakening: he celebrated this, arguing that the "weakening of religious feelings and the libidinal ties which depend on them" have reduced the "intolerance" in the world, or at least made it "less violent and cruel as in former centuries." But Freud warned that "if another group tie takes the place of the religious one—and the socialistic tie seems to be succeeding in doing so—there will be the same intolerance toward outsiders as in the age of the Wars of Religion."[33] Freud saw the socialist parties as following out his theories. Theodor Adorno says that Freud got it wrong, that Freud's essay actually serves much better to describe the power of Fascism;[34] but in the 1930's, theories of crowd and group psychology moved with strange ease from one end of the political spectrum to the other. Indeed, the reason that Freud's theories seem similar to Fascist practices is that Fascist propaganda was developed by people who originally sought to develop a syndicalist, socialist psychology—Roberto Michels and Paolo Orano. But even the fairly moderate Conservative Party in England believed in the natural deference of the masses and so sought to appeal to the masses by glorifying leaders and producing images of mythic national figures that formed a tradition in which to place current leaders.

The Labour Party in England and the anarcho-syndicalists who opposed the Fascists found support for their rejection of leadership in other theories of psychology. Harold Laski defended a pluralist political system as a way of adapting government to fit British theories of social psychology. Unified, sovereign governments with single leaders were based, he claimed, on outdated psychological theories that presumed individuals (both citizens and leaders) are unified wholes. Social psychologists had instead shown that "personality is a complex thing and the institutions—religious, industrial, political—in which it clothes itself are as a consequence manifold. The pluralistic state is an endeavor to express in terms of structure the facts we thus encounter."[35]

Laski was following up a peculiarly British vision of social psychology, one that modified Freudian theory. As the historian Greta Jones notes, Freud's belief in one central instinct, sexuality, that could transform itself into every human motive, struck the British as "anarchistic" because it would deny the basis for the multiplicity of institutions in society.[36] Laski's vision of the complexity of personality derived from the dominant psychology text in England in the early twentieth century, William McDougall's *Social Psychology*, which was organized around a long list of different instincts and purported to show how various social institutions were connected to these various instincts.[37] The debate between conservative focus on leadership and Laski's attack on sovereignty was then in part a mirror of the debate between Freud's theory of the necessity of a single object for the single dominant instinct in humans and McDougall's theory of multiple objects that appeal to multiple instincts.

Joyce and Woolf were influenced by the McDougall side of this debate about human psychology. The multiple-instinct schools of psychology appear in Woolf's writing about "contrary instincts" bred into women by society, about "severances and oppositions in the mind," about two sexes in the brain.[38] In the chart Joyce prepared to explain *Ulysses*, Joyce also developed a model of personality similar to the multiple-instinct schools. He presents the mind as influenced quite separately by different organs of the body and connects the influence of these organs to the influence of different social institutions. The alimentary system is connected to restaurants, the lungs to newspapers. We may read these connections as merely metaphorical, but Joyce was certainly presenting a person's mind as functioning differently at different times of the day and in different locations. He was showing, as was Woolf, that people's bodies are filled and shaped by social institutions in ways they cannot control, ways that also shape their consciousnesses. As Bloom says, "Never know whose thoughts you're chewing."[39]

Joyce referred directly to a psychologist Morton Prince, who carried the theory of multiple instincts further than McDougall, to a belief that every person has multiple personalities. Joyce indicated his affinity for Prince's psychology by basing Issy in *Finnegans Wake* on Prince's 1908 description of Christine Beauchamp, a woman with multiple personalities. Prince described the individual in terms similar to Le Bon's, as formed of multiple "systems" so that character is constantly changing: "this switching out and switching in, suppression and repression and resuscitation of enduring systems result in the ephemeral normal alterations of character in everyday life." He suggested we think of a person "as if he were a magic lantern with many colored slides passing in sequence before his eyes, and through which he looked; and as the world would be colored by those slides, so he felt and thought about it."[40] Prince argued, as did Le Bon, that this view of character ought to change literature. In an essay in 1924 entitled "The Problem of Personality: How Many Selves Have We?" Prince wrote out what could be a program for the novels of Joyce and Woolf:

> nearly all writers of fiction and even biographers have failed to recognize—what in these modern days the most advanced criminologists and penologists have recognized—that man is a many-sided creature. . . . No one is wholly good or wholly bad; or wholly hard, or wholly sentimental. . . . In the realm of fiction the dramatist is forced by the conventional canons of his art, if not by lack of wisdom, and for the purposes of dramatic effect, to depict but one side of the personalities of his characters. Consequently there is probably not a character of the drama, excepting Dr. Jekyll and Mr. Hyde, of which the whole personality has been portrayed. Iago, devil that he was, probably at home with his children, if he had a home and children, might have been the picture of an angel father. Melancholy Jacques, if he had had a couple of cocktails before dinner, might have forgotten his pessimism and shown *in vino veritas*, another side of his personality and entertained his company as a hilarious jester. Even Hamlet, though a good subject for a psychopathic hospital, if he had returned to his University at Wittenberg would have probably forgotten for one night, at least, all about his philosophies of life and his lamented father and exhibited himself in that other joyous, rollicking mood. . . . The world still awaits the great dramatist who will draw, if it be possible, a complete picture of a human personality, true to nature and under the confining canons of art.[41]

Joyce read Prince, but clearly Prince did not read Joyce, for *Ulysses* does just what Prince wanted—portrays all the sides of its main characters. Stephen is a Hamlet who does relax into jolly humor in the newspaper office, and into general pleasant talk in Bloom's living room; Bloom is a coward who hides from Blazes Boylan and then becomes a hero standing alone against the anti-Semitism of his friends and neighbors.

The break-up of character in *Ulysses*, as in other novels by Joyce and Woolf, was designed to reduce domination, to free the varieties of individual consciousness within society. In both psychological theories and modernist texts, domination has been figured often in relation to the sexuality of father figures. Prince developed his theory of multiple personalities partly out of a case in which an adult male tutor became frightening to a young woman; this is the case that Joyce refers to in *Finnegans Wake*. In Prince's case history and in Joyce's novel, there is a sense that the great power of father figures leads them to be implicated in sadistic or incestuous relations to their followers/family. Freud similarly commented on the "sadistic/masochistic" character of the relationship of masses and leaders who become "I-ideals." Woolf also equated Fascism and the sexual jealousies that cause fathers to mistreat their daughters.[42] Believing that people are inherently multiple, Joyce and Woolf presented all efforts to produce a single, all-encompassing relationship or identity—in a family, a social group, or a nation—as versions of dominating sexuality. They advocated instead multiple, partial, incomplete sexual relations and group identities.

In contrast, Eliot and Yeats frequently used images of restored passion and complete surrender to represent restored cultural wholeness. Incomplete and partial sexuality is, in their views, the result of alienation. They advocated a unified flood of emotion in the entire nation—the restored power of blood—while Joyce and Woolf feared such unified emotions. Joyce and Woolf were not seeking individual isolation, but rather the syndicalist local unities, local passions—a turbulent mix of passions that keeps any from dominating.

Both sides thus argued that they sought to release the passions of group involvement that capitalism had suppressed. Using Freudian terms, we can specify the difference in an intriguing way: both sides wanted to release the power of the id from the control of the "realist" ego. Both believed that domination by the ego is the result of capitalism, which empowers the calculating, rational part of the mind, the part that seeks the means of "getting on." Thus, all four of the modernists I am examining disagreed with Freud, who based his therapeutic practice on expanding the ego. His famous edict, "where id was, there ego shall be," could be interpreted as a method of maintaining a liberal order in the age of the masses, which is why, Adorno to the contrary, I have put him in that category. The ego, that is, rational, middle-class science, claims to be able to go where the id is buried, to speak for it, and to harness its power. In contrast to Freud, for conservatives such as Eliot and Yeats, the way to make use of the power of the id was by providing a real super-ego figure, a male leader: in a crowd with a powerful leader, everyone is released into passionate love of the leader, a return to the primal affections. Joyce and Woolf represented a third, socialist, possibility, that letting go of all super-ego figures and of rational, private selfhood are both necessary to experience the pleasure of communal unity, the pleasure of being part of the mass. In short, the modernism of both the Left and the Right sought to replace the politics of the ego with a politics of the id, to replace rational discourse based on the reality principle with unconscious discourse based on the pleasure principle. Modernism was an effort to write from and to the id, the mass unconscious.

CHAPTER 2

The Unconscious
Enters History

Working-Class Women in 'To the Lighthouse,' 'Ulysses,' and 'The Strange Death of Liberal England'

T he rise of mass movements and new theories implying that the individual is moved about by vast collective entities reshaped the way people conceived of the plots of their own lives. Aneurin Bevan commented, for example, that for young people at the turn of the century, the "texture of our lives shaped the question" of how to succeed "into a class and not an individual form. . . . We were products of an industrial civilization and our psychology corresponded to that fact. . . . The streams of individual initiative therefore flowed along collective channels already formed for us by our environment. Society presented itself to us as an area of conflicting social forces and not as a plexus of individual striving."[1]

Similarly, when Virginia Woolf, in her memoirs, described the process of writing *To the Lighthouse* as in effect a psychoanalytic treatment for her obsession with her mother's death, she found that she could not regard her mother as an individual with whom she had had a relationship. Instead, she found she had to think of her mother as "one of the invisible presences who after all play so important a part in every life. This influence, by which I mean the consciousness of other groups impinging on ourselves; public opinion; what other people say and think; all those magnets which attract us this way to be like that, or repel us the other and make us different from that; has never been analysed in any of those Lives which I so much enjoy reading." It was then that she declared she saw herself as "a fish in a stream; deflected; held in place; but cannot describe the stream."[2]

Social forces become visible beneath an overlay of a "familiar," or, we might say, a "familial" way of thinking. Woolf was struggling to stop viewing her life in terms of individual characters and families and private affairs, to turn instead to thinking about vast collective entities such as classes, genders, and cultures. *To the Lighthouse* was a product of such a struggle.

Woolf's sense that to understand her family and herself she needed to consider vast public issues may have been a reaction to her father's fame as a biographer. Leslie Stephen was the principal author for the Macmillan English Men of Letters series that, as Stefan Collini notes, played an important role in constructing a notion of English culture at the turn of the century.[3] Stephen used his biographies to promote what he repeatedly called "manly" qualities, which were not merely properties of individuals: he wrote of manly institutions, methods of intellectual research, styles of argument, and courses of political action.[4] In writing an autobiographical novel focusing on women, Woolf could not then view her family as a locus of private relationships because her father had devoted his life to using the gender structures internal to that family as the framework for constructing images of Englishness that permeated the national scene.

T. S. Eliot also recognized a historical shift from an individual to a social perspective that occurred during his life. In the introduction to *Nightwood*, he wrote:

> In the Puritan morality that I remember, it was tacitly assumed that if one was thrifty, enterprising, intelligent, practical and prudent in not violating social conventions, one ought to have a happy and "successful" life. Failure was due to some weakness or perversity in the individual; but the decent man need have no nightmares. It is now rather more common to assume that all individual misery is the fault of "society" and is remediable by alterations from without.[5]

Eliot went on to argue for an even greater move away from individual responsibility—to the heavenly, to Catholicism. Even so, Eliot clearly placed his advocacy of Catholicism in the context of the general move to a collectivist consciousness occurring throughout Europe and America.

All these early-twentieth-century writers concluded that it was important to see the most personal and disturbing parts of one's own psyche—including even obsessions and nightmares—as entwined with vast collective structures and immense social forces. One has to pass beyond the visible world that creates the illusions that individuals are self-contained entities and have private psychologies and look instead at patterns that are only dimly perceptible from the study of decades of history.

The most visible forces altering the social order during this period were the mass movements of workers, women, and colonials. The theories of mass mind suggested that these movements operated through invisible or unconscious elements in every person's psyche. The unconscious might then be conceived of as, at least in part, lower-class, female, and racially

other. The change to the twentieth century was accompanied by the erup-
tion of this multiply marginalized unconscious into visibility, swamping
the conscious, controlled mind of the individual. Most famously, *Heart
of Darkness* equates the descent into the unconscious and a journey into
Africa. As Albert Guerard writes, Marlow and Kurz travel on a " 'night journey' into that unconscious mind which, some of the anthropologists and
psychologists tell us, is the same as the primitive and prehistoric mind."[6]

Figures in the Dark

To the Lighthouse and *Ulysses* both contain chapters that trace de-
scents into the night side of life, into the unconscious: "Time Passes" and
"Circe."[7] Critics have little noted the striking fact that in both novels, these
night worlds are presented as realms ruled by working-class women of
"minor" ethnicity: Mrs. McNab, the Scot, and Bella Cohen, the Jew. The appearance of these women represents a change in the structure of the social
unconscious, the emergence into visibility of hidden realms of the social
orders in which these authors grew up. These women also represent parts of
the authors themselves and of literature, elements that had been repressed
because they were classified as lower-class, female, or culturally suspect.
In many ways, these chapters are set up by the rest of the novel to appear to
reveal what has been kept invisible or unconscious: in "Circe," Bloom visualizes his wife's adultery and his father's suicide, events he has struggled to
keep out of his consciousness elsewhere. In "Time Passes," the war seems
to have no relation at all to the preceding chapter, yet it emerges from a distinctly developed undercurrent in the first part of the novel: the violence
and destruction that fills the unconscious fantasies of nearly everyone in
the Ramsay household. James wants to knife his father; Nancy imagines
a holocaust inflicted on sea creatures; Jasper shoots birds with a toy gun,
exploding Lily's thoughts. In this way, Woolf connects World War I with the
repressions and tensions within European families, a view she developed
at length in *Three Guineas*. And she employs the small central chapter
to represent what is buried under Mrs. Ramsay's consciousness: when she
lets go of her personality for a moment in the first chapter, she finds herself
descending into a "wedge of darkness," where she is free of limitations and
imagines herself in India. The center of the novel is that wedge of darkness, a realm where the personalities of the Ramsays disappear and acts
impossible in everyday life occur.

The dark chapters in these two novels also contain their most radical
breaks with narrative structure, disrupting the well-developed novelistic
convention of making narration appear to be the product of some person's
consciousness. Woolf switches to an impersonal style and Joyce to the form
of drama, with no overt narrator. Both novels code the breakdown of the
narratorial form as a historical event: the rupture in the flow of conscious-

nesses is at the same time a rupture in the flow of history. "Time Passes" represents the transition between Victorian and modern (or modernist) worlds. The flow of time changes, so that ten years pass in the space it took a few minutes to pass in the first chapter. As Alex Zwerdling comments, the novel's "discontinuous structure is largely determined by her wish to highlight historical and ideological shifts."[8]

In *Ulysses*, to see that Joyce was coding the move into the unconscious as a vast social change we have to look carefully at the way he sets up the move into Nighttown. In the chapter preceding "Circe," Joyce traces a sequence of prose styles that are identifiable as great authors' styles: these prose styles represent distinct forms of consciousness—ideal, well-developed individual minds. Joyce's chart labels the technique of this chapter "embryonic development," so we would expect a steady form of growth or progress leading up to the present. Yet he makes the breaks between styles abrupt; he does not highlight slowly changing common features, as we might expect him to do if he were in fact treating the styles as an embryo developing. As Hugh Kenner notes, in this chapter, "Joyce is refusing the most pervasive idea of the century in which he was born, the idea of continuity."[9]

The last style in the sequence emphatically breaks any sense of a smooth development; just when the history of styles is about to reach the twentieth century, it explodes into a conglomeration of slang expressions from all over the world. This break could represent "birth," but it is very strange that the embryonic development of great authors would give birth to a chaotic mix of lowly expressions. This final conglomeration also could be seen as simply a way of representing the drunkenness of the characters whose discussion has been reported in all the different styles, but that does not explain why Joyce ended the sequence of great stylists with an image of loss of control over language. This break represents something that is being revealed in the twentieth century as shaping the writing of the greatest authors, something that is no longer under the conscious control of authors: a mass mind that brings in influences from every class and from all over the world. By having this nonindividual mentality emerge from within the conscious mind by a process of losing control (intoxication), Joyce also suggests that all the previous well-formed images of consciousness have been created in part by exclusion: great authors have had to distort and repress parts of themselves to maintain the illusion of self-control. In the twentieth century, historical change has made such self-control and self-containment no longer possible, so that for Joyce or Woolf to retell their own lives requires bringing in voices, styles, and invisible presences that seem distant, strange, and discontinuous.

In the commonwealth slangs that erupt, class and national otherness are the new elements shaping writing. The scene also points to another hidden influence haunting the styles of great authors: women. In "Oxen," a group of men are talking in a maternity hospital, so that there is a strong sense of women just beyond the door. Joyce also oddly excludes from his sequence of styles the already canonized women writers, such as Jane Austen and George Eliot, even though the books he consulted to construct this chapter included them.[10] Sandra Gilbert and Susan Gubar have argued that "Oxen" was part of the general early-twentieth-century effort to establish a "new patrilinguistic epoch" so that Joyce could place himself in the great tradition of male authors.[11] I find far more convincing the views of Bonnie Kime Scott and Karen Lawrence, who argue that the chapter serves to undermine the authority of the great tradition. Scott has shown that in the first paragraph the words, "Hoopsa boyaboy," comprise a traditional midwife's cry, suggesting that the entire parade is "born" from female words.[12] Lawrence argues that "the anonymous power of woman's body is felt within this chapter as a power to undo the male patronym."[13] The structure of the chapter highlights far too much the feeling of exclusion and the pain of those excluded (the women screaming in the next room) for it to represent the shoring up of male power.

Joyce included only male canonized authors in this chapter not because he wished the canon were revised to exclude women, but rather because he wanted to focus on male writers like himself to show that inside the male mind there have always been women's voices, as there have always been lower-class and "foreign" voices. Throughout the scene, the conversation reveals anxieties about such influences, about what happens to men when they become involved with women, about what has happened to Ireland due to English "rape." In other words, the forms of otherness that have been repressed by the traditional methods of constructing literary consciousnesses are constantly leaking into this scene. It is simply no longer possible to maintain these traditional styles any more due to social change, not simply to literary developments. The end of this scene, the product of the embryonic development of male literary styles, is the explosive "birth" that expels these men from the maternity hospital into the world of Nighttown, the world of the triply marginalized Jewish working-class woman, Bella Cohen. If Leopold Bloom represents throughout the novel the excluded and ostracized other because of his Jewishness, it is highly significant that the only place he finally has a relationship with another Jew is in Nighttown. Leopold Bloom's and Bella Cohen's interactions may seem perverse and reduced to mere fantasy, but this sexual encounter is one of the few times Bloom is not alien to the person with whom he is involved.

In both *To the Lighthouse* and *Ulysses*, a change of psychology, a change of literary form, and a change of historical era are all invoked by the emergence into the text of working-class women of marginal ethnicity. The movement from "Oxen of the Sun" into Nighttown is a breaking down of barriers that define exclusive social groups: the door that separates the men and the women in "Oxen" opens into the world of the brothel, where male

and female, upper and lower class, become confused. Woolf, too, emphasizes that the move into the darkness of "Time Passes" is a breakdown of
barriers between social groups, and she does so in a way quite similar to
Joyce's: she precedes the move into the world of night by a party, a scene
of seeming social unity that the dark world exposes as a fraud. In *To the
Lighthouse*, the dinner party brings together people of one class rather than
people of one gender, as in *Ulysses*. The people eating at the Ramsays' share
a vision of themselves as forming an isolated party on an island, making
"common cause against that fluidity out there" (p. 147); they end up feeling
"as if the walls of partition had become so thin that practically . . . it was
all one stream, and chairs, tables, maps, were hers, were theirs, it did not
matter whose" (p. 170). This seems a unity of all humanity against nature,
and a unity that breaks down the barriers created by private property. However, this partitionless unity is a fraud, because there is a distinct partition
within this house separating humans into two groups, divided by property ownership. That partition is the kitchen door, which hides not just
Mildred the cook, but Mrs. McNab, who, though unmentioned during the
dinner scene, is back there washing the dishes. In "Time Passes," the upper
class disappears and the hidden working-class women enter the rooms they
have been excluded from: Mrs. McNab and Mrs. Bast drink tea in the bedroom and the study and talk about Mildred. The dark chapter reveals that
the beautiful unity of the dinner party and of upper-class consciousness
has actually been created by those who have been excluded from it. The
alteration of the upper-class mind, allowing its unconscious to be seen, is
entwined with the rise of lower-class minds into visibility.

In an essay, "Mr. Bennett and Mrs. Brown," Woolf provides an explanation of why modernist authors would use working-class women this
way. The essay is about the origins of modernism, yet what Woolf focuses
on throughout the essay is the question of how a working-class woman,
Mrs. Brown, would be presented by various writers. Arnold Bennett is condemned because he would describe Mrs. Brown entirely in terms of her
"house," and would thereby confine her to her class and gender roles, even
if he were to include comments on the unfairness of poverty. Woolf, in
contrast, argues that there actually are or should be no limits on what
Mrs. Brown might be like: "You should insist that she is an old lady of
unlimited capacity and infinite variety; capable of appearing in any place;
wearing any dress; saying anything and doing heaven knows what . . . for she
is, of course, the spirit we live by, life itself." If such women are understood
as living limited lives, then "we," upper-class artists, and the literature "we"
write will also be limited. So altering the presentation of working-class
women was entwined with the project of freeing Woolf herself.

Woolf went much further in equating the liberations that had allowed
her to write with changes in the lives of working-class women. In the same
essay, she describes these crucial changes in the famous line, "on or about

December, 1910, human character changed." To define this change of character, Woolf starts by saying it was first noticeable in "the books of Samuel
Butler" and "the plays of Bernard Shaw," but then goes on:

> In life one can see the change, if I may use a homely illustration, in the
> character of one's cook. The Victorian cook lived like a leviathan in the
> lower depths, formidable, silent, obscure, inscrutable; the Georgian cook
> is a creature of sunshine and fresh air; in and out of the drawing-room,
> now to borrow the *Daily Herald*, now to ask advice about a hat. Do you
> ask for more solemn instance of the power of the human race to change?
> Read the *Agamemnon*, and see whether, in process of time, your sympa-
> thies are not almost entirely with Clytemnestra. Or consider the married
> life of the Carlyles and bewail the waste, the futility, for him and for her,
> of the horrible domestic tradition which made it seemly for a woman of
> genius to spend her time chasing beetles, scouring saucepans, instead of
> writing books. All human relations have shifted—those between masters
> and servants, husbands and wives, parents and children. And when human
> relations change there is at the same time a change in religion, conduct,
> politics, and literature.[14]

This passage begins and ends with a change in literature, but in the middle
it uses as its example of what has happened in real life to bring about this
change the transformation of working-class women. In her last illustration,
Woolf connects her own life with the lives of working women: the same
change in human relations releases the cook into the drawing room and
allows a woman of genius to write books instead of scouring saucepans.
Woolf here once again emphasizes the political dimension of her critique of
Arnold Bennett's style: literature that would portray Mrs. Brown in terms
of her house props up the social system that entraps all women, including
Mrs. Carlyle and Mrs. Woolf, in houses.

    The necessity of escaping the chains of domestic tradition in order to
write is a central issue in *To the Lighthouse*. This is obviously a feminist
issue, but Woolf's essay suggests that she conceived of it as a socialist issue
as well. Woolf hints at the role of socialism in her little scene in "Mr. Bennett and Mrs. Brown" by mentioning the *Daily Herald*, the Labour Party
paper: the Georgian cook and her employer (say, Virginia Woolf) would thus
seem both to be supporters of the Labour Party, unlike, we may surmise,
the Edwardian cook and employer (or Arnold Bennett). Woolf's choice of
December 1910 also alludes to a specific event in political history: that was
the date of the last election won by the Liberal Party, the last election in
which the Labour Party was only a minor third. Since there were two elections that year, the month is significant. The change in human relations
she specifies includes, then, a quite precise change in political relations, a
shift to a contest between Labour and Conservative rather than between
Liberal and Conservative Parties: after 1910, the working class left its obscurity and began to read and write and exercise its own genius in public,

in Parliament. The rise of the Labour Party was a major topic in the Woolf household while she wrote "Mr. Bennett and Mrs. Brown" in 1924 because that was the year the Labour Party (including her husband as an M.P.) had its first opportunity to organize a government.

To the Lighthouse was written a few years after her essay, and it traces the change in human character she describes. Once we begin considering issues of class and work in this novel, we can see how they form its basic framework, which is overlain by and supports the novel's focus on family life and aesthetic issues. The novel focuses mostly on changes in the relations of husbands and wives, parents and children, and artists, but it also draws attention to the changes in the relations of master and servants. Woolf reenacts the little scene of the cook emerging from obscurity when Mrs. McNab and Mrs. Bast pause in the study to drink tea, entering the roles and spaces of upper-class life. Woolf even suggests that these women were present, though invisible, in the first part of the novel by having them discuss staying up late washing dishes after parties such as the dinner party that concludes just before "Time Passes." In *To the Lighthouse*, the emergence of obscure parts of society is a necessary part of the process that would allow Lily Briscoe to paint and not to marry.

Since Lily's painting is heavily coded as modernist, the novel implies, as does "Mr. Bennett and Mrs. Brown," that the origins of modernist art have been powered by changes in human relations (say, the success of the suffrage movement and the explosive growth of the Labour Party) that overcame the inscrutability of working-class women—that allowed them to speak and write and paint, to be heard, read, and seen. Woolf joined in that process of enabling lower-class women's voices directly, writing an introduction to a collection of autobiographies written by working-class women, in addition to hosting meetings of the Women's Cooperative Association at her house every week, as we already have seen.[15]

Another intriguing connection between the essay and the novel is that in both she uses an image of emerging leviathans to represent the transitions in history. In her essay, she says the Victorian cook who lived "like a leviathan in the lower depths" now rises into fresh air. As Mrs. McNab and Mrs. Bast emerge in "Time Passes," Woolf mentions that "leviathans" are seen rising in the sea and tumbling about. These leviathans are described as "amorphous bulks . . . whose brows are pierced by no light of reason" (p. 202–3). Mrs. McNab and Mrs. Bast are similarly described as "a force working; something not highly conscious; something that leered, something that lurched" (p. 209). The description of these two women as "not highly conscious" and "lurching" is in part a reflection of Woolf's snobbery, and almost grounds enough for seeing Woolf's socialism as hypocritical, but there is also a way to see this insult as actually directed at liberal capitalism, not these women. The prime virtues of nineteenth-century liberals and novelists were "reason" and "consciousness," and for Woolf to focus on nonconscious forces at work is to identify what liberalism overlooked. When Woolf describes the women as "not highly conscious," she is talking about the force that saved the "whole house" from plunging "to the depths to lie upon the sands of oblivion" (p. 209), actually crediting the nonconscious force of the working-class masses with saving England from destruction. Woolf ends the passage with a rhythmic tribute to work: "some rusty laborious birth seemed to be taking place, as the women, stooping, rising, groaning, singing, slapped and slammed, upstairs now, now down in the cellars. Oh, they said, the work!" (p. 210), inscribing the birth of Labour itself as a visible and valued part of the English social order. Woolf's act of giving working-class women credit for saving England repeats what happened during World War I, when women's work became much more visible than it had been, and this visibility was crucial in bringing about the passage of the Reform Bill of 1918, which gave women that fundamental voice in the social order, the vote. It is not hard to see a relationship between women gaining the vote and being allowed "to paint, to write," and so it makes sense that Woolf would credit working-class women with transforming society so that she and Lily Briscoe could work as artists.

Issues of class and work frame the novel in other ways, as well. The lighthouse has generated considerable critical interest as a symbol, yet it plays a clear enough and scarcely symbolic role in this underlying framework: when the characters actually reach it, it is revealed as a small domestic community, a place where the lower classes live and work. The novel is built around the relationship between two houses, one full of rich people and one full of workers. The title, then, focuses attention on the question of whether the upper classes can find a way to travel to the lower classes.

The tripartite structure of the novel, interpreted in terms of the fairy tale Mrs. Ramsay reads to James, also mirrors the history of the emergence of the working class and women. The tale is about a poor woman who badgers her husband to ask a magical fish he has caught to improve their lives: the fish complies, moving them into a big house, and then, on further requests from the wife, making her king, emperor, and pope. Each time the man goes back to the fish the sea is progressively wilder, until it has become a raging storm. The woman finally asks to become God, and at that the fish swims away, the sea becomes calm, and the fisherman and his wife are back in their little house again. Many critics have seen this as a tale about a woman taking over male power, but it is at least as much a tale about the working class taking over the power of the upper class. Woolf structures her novel around this fairy tale: when Mrs. McNab and Mrs. Bast take over the big house, the sea rages—and it is calm again when they leave. Woolf emphasizes the connection by placing the very first "ominous sounds" of wartime explosions immediately after Mrs. McNab has been described as moving so beautifully through the Ramsay household that she "looked like a tropical fish oaring its way through sun-lanced waters" (p. 200).

Woolf is here blurring together issues of class tensions and international tensions. One fact provides considerable support for such a view: as Kate Flint has documented, Woolf was writing "Time Passes" during the General Strike of 1926; Woolf wrote letters requesting amnesty for strikers as she finished this section of the novel.[16] As she sought to convince a Conservative government of what she felt workers deserved, she would naturally turn back to World War I to remind the government of what was owed the Labour Party and women for saving the nation from the brink of destruction.

If the violence of the sea in the novel is read in terms of the social unrest caused by the rising of working-class leviathans, the opening conversations in the book prove to involve more than meteorology. The question of Mrs. Ramsay's taking her gifts to the lighthouse men during such threatening weather raises the issue of the safety and propriety of the upper class visiting the working class with patronizing gifts. Will the lighthouse men be insulted and demand more than noblesse oblige?

The question of what the working class deserves arises in the question of what to take to the lighthouse. Nancy asks the question, and the text goes on: "At any other time Lily could have suggested reasonably tea, tobacco, newspapers. But this morning everything seemed so extraordinarily queer that a question like Nancy's—What does one send to the Lighthouse?—opened doors in one's mind that went banging and swinging to and fro and made one keep asking, in a stupefied gape, What does one send? What does one do? Why is one sitting here, after all?" (p. 218). The image of doors opening in the mind parallels the opening of the physical and political barriers, such as kitchen doors and disenfranchisement, that used to separate working-class women from the upper class. Those mental doors used to keep upper-class people from thinking about what else they ought to give the working class besides tobacco and old newspapers. But after the expansion of the vote to women in 1918, and after the Labour Party had organized a government in 1924, after upper-class institutions had been expanded to include working-class women, people began to think different things. Lily is perplexed, uncertain—and this novel never says what one "does send to the Lighthouse." Woolf was equally uncertain about just what, if any, political message about class relations this novel could contain.

When Woolf began writing the novel, she had a much clearer sense of what she was doing by bringing in Mrs. McNab. The woman was not a comic figure as she is now, and she had an important role in opposition to the war. James M. Haule says that in the early manuscripts, "The charwomen . . . represent a creative, saving force that, along with nature, rescues the earth from the destruction of war. Mrs. McNab in particular begins as an ageless seer who cooperates with the 'ghostly presences' all about her."[17] Mrs. McNab thus functions as the visible embodiment of those "invisible presences" that Woolf discussed in her memoir. Woolf first planned to write "Time Passes" as Mrs. McNab's internal monologue.[18] In the early draft, then, Mrs. McNab was intended to be one of the central consciousnesses of the novel. But Woolf backed away from presenting Mrs. McNab as such an important figure; she finally turned Mrs. McNab into someone who is devoted to resurrecting the Ramsay household and cleaning a space in which Lily can paint. For reasons I will discuss below, Woolf was ambivalent about the transformation of working-class women: she may have seen their liberation as part of the change in human relations that freed her, she may have shared her *Daily Herald* with them and may have served tea to them in her sitting room, but she still relied on them to clean the house so that she could be free to write.

Woolf's essay "Mr. Bennett and Mrs. Brown" suggests a way of understanding how she could view working-class women both as emblems of artistic innovation and as fairly obtuse figures: she did not view working-class women such as Mrs. Brown or the Victorian cook as seers or poetic voices that could replace upper-class artists, but as the visible manifestation of hidden forces that could release buried voices within those artists. Mrs. McNab and Mrs. Bast help release the vision inside Lily; they do not bring any original vision of their own into the novel (though they may have in early drafts). Modernist artists drew inspiration from the others politically challenging the social order, but what the modernists eventually produced they presented as deriving entirely from the otherness within themselves.

Woolf's ambivalence about her debt to working-class women was shared by all the modernists. Working-class women often emerge in modernist works as images of alternative voices, but usually these voices are coded as buried within the artist, not as deriving from the women themselves. The way art historians have dealt with Picasso's *Demoiselles D'Avignon* provides an example of this phenomenon. This painting of five prostitutes is almost universally hailed as the founding work of modernist painting, and for decades critics have debated how much it was indebted to African art because its most radically strange figures resemble African masks. Picasso claimed that he had not seen any African masks before painting *Demoiselles*, even though he went on to acquire a large collection of such masks. Some art historians obligingly derive the non-European influence on this painting from Iberian sculpture—in other words, from within Picasso's Spanish background.[19] Even when art historians admit African influence, they declare that ultimately it is irrelevant, because all African art did was stimulate Picasso's genius. For example, H. W. Janson, in a college textbook widely used until the 1970's, declares that Picasso transcended whatever was due to African influence when he moved from *Demoiselles* to Cubism. Comparing a later Cubist portrait with *Demoiselles*, Janson writes: "the canvas has the balance and refinement of a fully mature style. . . . Of the 'barbaric' distortions in the *Demoiselles* there is now no trace; they had served their purpose. Cubism has become an abstract style within the purely Western sense."[20]

Janson's art history creates a narrative of Picasso's artistic life that is strikingly similar to what we see in *To the Lighthouse*: the move to modernism requires a dark, transitional period or chapter of barbarism and distortion, a chapter outside traditional European forms, after which there is a return to the "enlightened" world of "purely Western" culture. As one critic of postcolonial literature puts it, "at the moment of formation of the central texts of modernism . . . the encounter with the Other in the form of non-European cultures is crucial. From now on the 'discovery' of cultures essentially different from Europe . . . is a central factor in the production and reproduction of European art itself."[21]

The necessity of seeing the dark period as a time when cultural others play an important role leaves a peculiar flaw in the overall history of Western genius and technical development that usually surrounds modernism: the crucial transformation that creates our most technological era requires the visible influence of workers, women, and "alien" cultures, which at the same time are all presented as utterly devoid of technical sophistication. Janson is driven to remarkable logic to explain why African masks should be "abstract" when that term seems to identify the latest, most sophisticated and technical style of European art. He says,

> Must we then credit the primitive artist and his public with an interest in abstraction for its own sake? That hardly sounds plausible. There is, I think, a far easier explanation: the increasingly abstract quality of [African sculpture] resulted from endless repetition. . . . Any gesture or shape that is endlessly repeated tends to lose its original character—it becomes ground down, simplified, more abstract. . . . One might term what happened to them "abstraction by inbreeding." We have discussed the process at such length because it is a fundamental characteristic of Neolithic and primitive art.[22]

Instead of crediting African artists with inventing abstract art in all its complexity, Janson describes them as essentially lazy and thoughtless, cutting corners and hence creating simpler and more abstract figures. Abstraction in African art becomes a result of perversion, a defect in reproduction, that Janson terms "inbreeding." Picasso's painting of prostitutes is defective for its similar "barbaric distortion" of artistic form, for its immaturity, but Picasso, unlike the African abstract artists, moved on to a "fully mature" style.

Janson's argument is a particularly explicit restating of what is implicit in numerous modernist works and histories of modernism: though the content of the works may suggest cultural and political issues, the works are understood almost entirely in terms of technical or formal structures devoid of cultural referent other than a general parallel to the technical sophistication of the modern world. The very use of "primitive" images in modernist works becomes a marker of the sophistication and technical complexity of the artists and writers—the modern genius is so complex it can contain multiple cultures.[23] Technical innovation becomes the explanation of all change, ignoring the evidence within the works themselves of the influence of political events and cultural influences.

Marianna Torgovnick has analyzed how such a view of modernism was developed in the 1920's by critics such as Roger Fry.[24] In order to explain the importance of "primitive" arts to modernists, Fry declared that the "reestablishment of purely aesthetic criteria," "principles of structural design and harmony," removed cultural barriers: modernists could then borrow from artists of other cultures without in any way borrowing those cultures because of "the isolation of the aesthetic from all other human activities." Fry even claimed that in some cases, "a people who produced such great artists did not produce a culture in our sense of the word."[25]

Modernists claimed to borrow from outside Europe only to release what was buried within Europe—in Fry's terms, to further a "general aesthetic awakening" that could revitalize European traditions.[26] Thus, it is important in *To the Lighthouse* that we see the house almost fall apart and then be rebuilt: the English world is to be restructured, not replaced. Otherness serves to break up the stale culture, but then must be incorporated within the culture it has broken up: hence, modernism took the form of the mixture and blurring of historical and cultural forms. Early-twentieth-century writers conceived of the new arts emerging as representing a European cultural unconscious, not as something that originated elsewhere.

Breaking Up History Texts

The most popular history of England in this era, *The Strange Death of Liberal England* by George Dangerfield, presented the transformations of the social order and of artistic styles in very much these terms. Dangerfield's book provides a view of the relationship of modernism to mass politics from the other side, from a historian's view of mass movements. The book also provides an intriguing way of understanding why modernism was driven to formal innovation: as Dangerfield attempted to explain the changes in the social order brought about by mass movements, his own narrative was forced into the strange shapes characteristic of modernist novels.

Dangerfield's book actually traces three political rebellions—the Tories', the workers', and the women's. For Dangerfield, what tied them all together was that they all turned to violence and nonparliamentary action because they all felt silenced by parliamentary rule. In parliamentary rule, the speakers present themselves as individuals, and through discussion, reason is supposed to adjudicate differences between them. But these new political groups denied that there is a universal reason: they argued that the previous debates within politics were illusory, because only a very limited group was allowed to participate. As Charles Maier says about the changes occurring all over Europe at this time, "in the emerging corporatist system, new social elements had to be consulted, above all labor leaders who had earlier been outside the system. Domestic policy no longer emerged intact from the foyers of the ruling class, no longer just represented the shared premises of the era's 'best and the brightest' . . . party competition was changing from a clubby and whiggish rivalry into a professional mobilization of opinion through electoral machines."[27]

The professional mobilization of opinion that replaced parliamentary debate involved the development of a new array of techniques and academic disciplines whose goal was to analyze and influence the mass mind—demographic research, advertising, sociology. Politicians began to enter discussions backed not only by votes, but by research that purported to reveal the unconscious desires of vast social groups: the size of groups and the power of their desires became more important than the logic of the arguments put forth by the politicians. Mass movements create policy in very different ways than individuals do. The central institutions of representative democracy, Parliament and Congress, lost much of their power to extraparliamentary structures such as government commissions, party conferences, and organized interest groups. Members of Parliament became delegates from other bodies, rather than individuals creating policies themselves. Government still appeared formally to be the representative of a consensus reached by individuals voting separately, but it gained what Beer calls an "informal" structure of policy making that mirrored the group structure of the nation.[28] Maier describes Parliament as only "registering" and not "shaping" policy decisions, with a consequent "bleeding away of parliamentary authority" in the "twilight of sovereignty."[29] He is not being literary in using such vivid phrases; he is borrowing language used extensively in the early twentieth century. There was a sense of twilight, of a sun setting and a new regime of darkness emerging; there was a sense of injury and loss of containment—bleeding—that made the boundaries of the body politic hard to define; and there was a sense that society was in the future going to be ruled by hidden forces that, like earthquakes, could only be registered, not shaped.

Dangerfield summarized his entire work in just these terms: the epilogue of his book is called "The Lofty Shade." But Dangerfield chose a surprising emblem of what was going into the darkness: the poet Rupert Brooke. For Dangerfield, a change in artistic style encapsulated the changes wrought by violent mass movements. Oddly, Dangerfield devoted less space to Brooke's poetry than to the poet's appearance, his "beautiful head, the wild blond hair threaded with metallic gold, the incredibly clean features" (p. 427); when Brooke died, according to Dangerfield, an array of dark new styles, including political ones, replaced his blond beauty. Early in his history, Dangerfield described these new styles: "There was talk of wild young people in London . . . of night clubs; of negroid dances. People gazed in horror at the paintings of Gauguin and listened with delighted alarm to the barbaric measures of Stravinsky. The old order, the old bland world, was dying fast, and the Parliament Act [of 1911] was its not too premature obituary" (p. 67). The words "wild" and "barbaric" in the context of "negroid dances" and Gauguin's Tahitian scenes make this whole list resonate with the sense of "dark" cultures replacing the bland and blond English ideal represented by Rupert Brooke. We might expect these "dark" cultures to be presented as foreign invasions, but the passage implies that they emerged from within the unconscious minds of cultural leaders such as Gauguin, Stravinsky, and members of Parliament. The Parliament Bill of 1911 seems a strange addition to this list, but it took the veto away from the House of Lords and so seemed to expel the lords from Parliament and send them into the same realm of political obscurity that women and workers were struggling to escape.

One of the strangest effects of Dangerfield's narrative is to equate the actions of Tories with those of women and workers, as if these quite different groups were in fact merely three visible parts of one invisible tide sweeping across England and the whole Western world, wrecking liberalism and at the same time killing Rupert Brooke and replacing his blonde and beautiful art with the modernist forms of Gauguin and Stravinsky. Even stranger is that Dangerfield argued that only by looking at the actions of the women could the deep, underlying causes of all three movements be understood. Dangerfield began his book tracing the Tory rebellion, but then concluded he had missed something, which he called the "neurosis" underlying the actions of politicians: "though the Tory Rebellion refuses to reveal . . . the irrational nature of this phase, the historian cannot excuse himself from seeking it elsewhere. . . . The politicians refuse to be anything but politicians; there remain the women. What can hardly be seen in the activities of one sex, may possibly discover itself—however reluctantly—in those of the other" (p. 142). To understand what was operating deep inside everyone, from aristocrat to suffragette, Dangerfield used suffrage leaders—the Pankhursts—much as the modernists used working-class women—as emblems of the unconscious of everyone, particularly upper-class males.

The turn from the Tories, who refused to reveal the irrational parts of themselves, to the suffrage leaders, who, as Dangerfield described them, became the visible manifestation of the irrational, was also a turn from one kind of character to another, a change in narrative form that produced strange effects throughout Dangerfield's text. The strains produced in Dangerfield's narrative, resulting from allowing the mass mind thus to enter it, illustrate the innovations in forms of discourse brought by the new political movements.

The mass unconscious that became visible in the actions of the Pankhursts simply could not exist within the narrative forms of nineteenth-century novels and histories. Repeatedly within Dangerfield's book, especially in his accounts of the women's rebellion, he was consequently forced to reject the narrative forms he had constructed. He did not become a modernist, but baldly declared that the characters and plots he had developed for hundreds of pages were basically irrelevant to the story he had been telling. For example, when discussing the events leading up the passage of the Suffrage Bill, he spends dozens of pages revealing the characters of Sylvia Pankhurst and Lord Asquith, the prime minister; then he brings these two leaders together in a tense confrontation. Just when we expect a decisive victory of one or the other, something else takes control of everyone and moves them about like "puppets," resolving conflicts without the leaders even being aware of what has happened. The Suffrage Bill gets approved, but not because of any decisions of any of the leaders Dangerfield has so carefully described: rather, "Woman . . . had pulled the strings . . . and while, in one corner of the stage . . . militants whirled through their abandoned paces, the other corner was occupied by no less a puppet group than the Liberal Cabinet, nodding its ministerial head in dignified and helpless acquiescence" (p. 385).

In such passages, the Pankhursts become a dream of the mass unconscious:

> It is surely one of the minor ironies of history that it was the unconscious desires of all Englishwomen, who abominated militancy, which made militancy possible; and that womanhood, half waking from its long Victorian sleep, so filled with unrecognized fantasies and unremembered nightmares, should have expelled, like a sigh or a groan—the Pankhursts. . . . The Pankhursts were the slaves of a vital but timid desire for freedom; they were its puppets, its projections, and, as is sometimes the unfortunate habit of projections, they began to assume a more and more demoniac form. (p. 185)

Dangerfield therefore could claim that as dynamic a leader as Christabel Pankhurst was "used by life to express a meaning unknown to herself" (p. 199). The Pankhursts became for Dangerfield very much what working-class women were in modernist texts: emblems of a vast social change of which they were unaware, a change that only the writer could interpret. It was not only sexism that caused Dangerfield to claim that the Pankhursts had no idea what they were doing; he said much the same thing about all the political leaders in his history. He consequently created a text with a double structure: people have characters that shape their actions and thoughts, but underlying everything is another set of forces that determine results regardless of what the characters do.

Dangerfield worried about the tensions between the conscious and the unconscious narratives he was telling, and his worries emerged as a question about two different forms of representation. Overtly, he wondered what it is that democratic governments represent, but he was also asking about what he was representing by means of the strange double narrative of agency in this history:

> Is it possible that governments, even democratic government, respond not merely to the opinions but to the deepest, the most hidden feelings of the countries they govern? that those sudden decisions, which so often surprise us in history, are due less to ministerial whimsy than to some unconscious and almost unimaginable prompting of the whole people? Could it be that representative governments actually *represent*? and represent in a most subtle and mysterious way? (p. 384)

Dangerfield attempted to represent both: all his ministers are whimsical, eccentric, and willful; at the same time, all the important events in this novel are eruptions of "the unimaginable," described in the melodramatic language of Gothic fantasies and nightmares. The peculiar mixture is strikingly similar to modernist texts. *To the Lighthouse* divides up into whimsical talk (a debate about the weather) and mysterious, nightmarish imagery (the dark middle section); Yeats's later poems are about silly old men, schoolchildren, and drunken soldiers who are transformed when mysterious "shades" or "images" erupt into the scene from a collective unconscious; *The Waste Land* alternates between urbane satire and vast, impersonal horror; *Ulysses* is simultaneously a comic novel about a few insignificant people and a work that seems to bring the unimaginable into view. In these novels, as in Dangerfield's history, a mysterious mass unconscious coexists with the surface scenes of ordinary everyday life.

Dangerfield escaped modernism because he never considered how his own consciousness would be undermined if the "unimaginable prompting of the whole" actually sought to express itself through his own writing. He seems to have considered himself comfortably removed from the process he was describing and thus felt little doubt about his own ability to see and describe both whimsical characters and unimaginable wholes. There was no alteration in his personal life to be represented by the history he told. The modernist texts of Joyce and Woolf, on the other hand, present themselves as arising mostly from personal experiences. Modernism derived from the effort to press together the private and the public, and hence it undid liberalism, which depended on the separation of those two realms.

Modernists tried to reach the collective from inside themselves, not from the general overview that Dangerfield presents. Unlike Dangerfield, Woolf and Joyce never presented their narratorial voices as sure of what they were saying or as removed from the forces pressing on the characters; in their novels there is a constant sense of something invisible or unconscious beyond even the narrator's purview. Woolf and Joyce not only wanted to reveal invisible presences, they wanted to make their readers, too, have to struggle to see and to interact with the invisible, the social, hidden inside the most private parts of life.

The way Dangerfield, Joyce, and Woolf used working-class women was in one sense a form of co-optation: they are credited with shaking things up, but they are not seen as replacing "us," the writers, who can shape the meaning of their acts. Mrs. McNab, Mrs. Bast, and Bella Cohen all are returned to darkness at the end of the novels—as the Pankhursts in Dangerfield's history perform their unconscious role and then are dismissed. But there is another side to the use of working-class women in these texts: a genuine sense of having gained something from them, of having followed their lead in moving toward something new.

New Models of Authorship

Woolf and Joyce used working-class women as models on which to construct new selves. Joyce's and Woolf's works belong to the socialist tradition, even though these writers did not simply valorize working-class figures. Because Joyce and Woolf were revising their upper-middle-class selves into something modeled on the lower classes, they reversed the methods of socialist realism: instead of turning a member of the masses into a developed individual character, they turned highly developed individuals into parts of masses. Instead of reducing working-class obscurity and unconsciousness, they added realms of obscurity and unconsciousness to upper-class minds.

In both novels, the working-class women who emerge in the dark become models on which new images of authorship are constructed: by identifying with these figures, Joyce and Woolf found ways to escape nineteenth-century conventions of authorship that paralyzed them. Mrs. McNab provided a model that Lily and Woolf needed as an alternative to Mrs. Ramsay: a working woman, a woman whose teatime conversation is with other working women, a woman who rarely mentions her own family. Mrs. McNab is also a model of the artist. She sits and "unwinds her ball of memories" of Mrs. Ramsay to Mrs. Bast, and then goes about painting those memories all over the house: her cleaning is described as a "yellow beam" projecting "a lady in a grey cloak"—Mrs. Ramsay—"over the bedroom wall, up the dressing-table, across the wash-stand" (p. 205). At the end of the novel, Lily is not looking at Mrs. Ramsay, but at Mrs. McNab's re-creation of Mrs. Ramsay's spirit in the cleaned-up house. And Lily is finally able to complete her painting by imitating Mrs. McNab: Lily locates herself, like Mrs. McNab, as a worker in the company of another worker, another unmarried artist—Mr. Carmichael. In that company, Lily "unwinds her ball of memories" of Mrs. Ramsay to paint a house much as Mrs. McNab did.

The prostitutes similarly serve as an image of authorship that Stephen needs to embrace to escape the paralysis he suffers. The relation of writing to prostitution is most clearly stated in the early work *Stephen Hero*, where Lynch equates Stephen's selling his verses with prostitution. Stephen defends himself by saying that there is a part of himself that is not for sale: "I do not sell . . . the divine afflatus: I do not swear to love, honour and obey the public until my dying day."[30] In *Portrait*, Stephen says that avoiding literary prostitution involves using language according to the "literary tradition" rather than the "tradition of the marketplace." But the distinction of the two traditions is presented in the text in terms of two meanings of "detained" that get confused. Is there a literary meaning to Cardinal Newman's sentence about the Blessed Virgin being "detained in the full company of saints" that does not imply Mary was restrained, held back, in such company?[31] This question is equally a question about Stephen: can he use language so as to remain in the company of saints, preserving a literary virginity, in any way except by restraining his speech? Joyce did not think so, and showed Stephen trying to avoid being a literary prostitute by simply holding back his "divine afflatus," his inspiration, his breath, which eventually results in his being unable to speak his literature at all. To avoid marketplace usage, Stephen lapses into silence. In *Ulysses*, of course, Bloom lets his wind pass freely, so that his afflatus, his farts, make important speeches in the text. In "Circe," there is an image of a virgin losing control of her divine afflatus: the nymph who emerges from an advertisement claims to be purely ethereal, but then cracks open and releases smelly gases. Like the nymph, Stephen will have to accept that he is at least as much a part of the smelly world of advertising as of the ethereal world of art. And at end of "Oxen of the Sun," the effort to maintain the restraining walls separating the literary tradition from other traditions breaks down, letting out the afflatus of language, releasing all the foul, unliterary, prostituted marketplace languages that Joyce used so well to write *Ulysses*. By *Finnegans Wake*, Joyce was no longer holding anything back in his relationship with the public: the washerwomen there say about the great male figure, "He married his markets, cheap by foul."[32] Not only does he accept that his writing is cheap and foul, but he relies on "cheep cheep" of that "fowl," or bird, that low-class female Kate the Hen, to provide him the letters he writes with.

We do not have to turn to *Finnegans Wake* to see that Joyce credited working-class women with creating the male writer's voice. In *Portrait*, when Stephen goes to a prostitute to escape his weak, timid, paralyzed self, her cure consists of putting her tongue into his mouth, whereupon he feels a pressure on his brain like a "vague speech": she is giving him the tongue and the speech that he needs to write.[33] Stephen goes to prostitutes for the same purpose in *Ulysses*. In "Circe," Stephen says to Lynch that he is seeking in Nighttown the "gift of tongues" because it would provide a "universal language" (15.107). And in the middle of the chapter, a prostitute reads Stephen's palm and says it is a "woman's hand," to which Stephen replies that he "never could read His handwriting"—the "his" having a capital *H* (15.3679). Stephen thus gains from the prostitutes an explanation of why he has had difficulty understanding God's male handwriting: because Stephen has a woman's tongue in his mouth, writes with a woman's hand, and so can fully understand only women's handwriting.[34] He will be a paralyzed writer until he can accept his female anatomy, until he can accept that he cannot write as men have written before, that he must write at least in part as a woman. In *Ulysses*, he begins to learn this new kind of writing from prostitutes, just as Lily learns a new way to paint from Mrs. McNab.

Joyce even uses the central symbol in *To the Lighthouse*: the light by which the artist writes or paints. In *Portrait*, Stephen says that he is writing by the "lamp" of Aristotle and Aquinas, but adds, "If it does not give light enough I shall sell it and buy another."[35] In *Ulysses*, Stephen's entry into the marketplace tradition includes his paying for a lamp, a prostitute's. It may seem that I am stretching a bit here: after all, he seems to pay for the privilege of destroying that lamp, not writing by it. But according to a stage direction at the beginning of "Circe," Stephen's act of striking the lamp is an effort to liberate the light. The stage direction says that Stephen "flourishes his ashplant, shivering the lamp image, shattering light over the world" (15.99–100). The later gesture of smashing Bella's lamp is Stephen's way of spreading the prostitute's light over the world, not of destroying the lamp; note that all he destroys is the paper shade that limits the spread of the light. He is breaking the working-class women's light out of the shade of Nighttown.

At the end of *Ulysses*, Joyce sought to write by this female light, or, to switch metaphors, to speak with a woman's tongue. In effect, he was trying to give back to women what they gave him—their voices. Similarly, the end of *To the Lighthouse* is an effort to give back to the working class some of the light they have provided for Woolf to use to view the upper class. Although Woolf never identifies what is in the parcel Mr. Ramsay carries to the lighthouse, it is clearly meant as some new kind of gift, even if Woolf could not quite imagine what it might be. Just as Molly is paid for her voice, the lighthouse family is given new kinds of gifts for their light: these authors attempted to repay the debts they owed for the gifts of authorship they received from these others.

Molly's soliloquy and Lily's painting serve much the same purpose in these two novels: they are each a final vision from the outside of the group that the author has been struggling to escape. Lily paints the house, the upper-class family; Molly describes men. One feature of these final visions is crucial to the overall project of breaking out of class and gender limitations: in both cases, individuals have been reduced to parts of masses. Lily's talk about her painting in terms of "masses" of color seems to be a discussion of technical aesthetic issues, but there is an unusual political resonance to her words. Lily says that to finish her painting she has to figure out "how to connect this mass on the right hand with that on the left" (pp. 82–83). One of Lily's oddest lines becomes comprehensible if we see a political parallel to her aesthetic issues: "she would move the tree to the middle, and need never marry anybody" (p. 262). Why does moving the tree allow her to escape the "need" to marry? If we read her painting as a political map of society, with the tree marking the difference between the Left and the Right, moving the tree to the middle would provide more space for the "mass on the left"—the working class. This is not an image of eliminating classes, but only of moving toward greater equality, just as the Labour Party felt that it had to move toward socialism gradually. The movement of the boundary also would create a new space in the middle, a space neither fully working-class nor upper-class, a space that would allow blending together some qualities of the working class (such as allowing women to work) and of the upper classes (such as high culture). In such a space, Lily could be a working, unmarried, culturally upper-class woman. Being in the middle, she could take on the task of connecting the masses.

In *Ulysses*, Molly's final soliloquy also turns people into masses; the indefinite reference of all the "he's" makes us aware of men in general, of maleness, as contrasted to femaleness. Stephen and Bloom no longer appear to be individuals, but simply parts of the mass of men. As in *To the Lighthouse*, this loss of individuality is liberating. For one thing, it reduces all the great male heroes such as Odysseus and Telemachus to ordinary people like Stephen and Leopold and hence frees Stephen from the need to be a great, heroic male author, from the need to write like a god. Joyce neatly summarizes the change that Stephen needs to undergo in Bloom's misinterpretation of Stephen's mutterings at the end of "Circe." Stephen quotes Yeats, "Who . . . drive . . . Fergus now?": he is still dreaming of becoming the kind of author who could move a god. Bloom responds, "Ferguson, I think I caught. A girl. Some girl. Best thing could happen him" (15.4950). Turning the Irish legendary hero Fergus into "some girl" is precisely the transformation that could break Stephen out of his paralysis, his literary coma: he has to stop trying to drive Fergus about and instead go driving with, and start writing like, "some girl," becoming an anonymous part of the mass of females.

Pluralist Style

The change from representing individuals to representing masses was a change in artistic style as much as a change in politics. Critics who focus on artistic movements have made much of the stylistic innovations in *To the Lighthouse* and have connected them to Woolf's famous quote about human character changing, interpreting December 1910 as referring to the Postimpressionist exhibit organized by Roger Fry. I have suggested that the date refers to the demise of the Liberal Party and its replacement by the

Labour Party. These two interpretations may not be as contradictory as they seem: there are intriguing connections between Postimpressionism, the breakdown of cultural boundaries, and the demise of the Liberals. Fry's exhibition and his theories of art implied that the newest European art forms had resulted from the influence of non-European cultures; as Marianna Torgovnick comments, "Everything about the exhibition sent the signals, 'Modern!' and 'Primitive!' "[36] The poster for the exhibit portrayed a Gauguin painting of a "native" woman and a Tahitian statue. The exhibit thus raised the questions about the cultural origins of modernist innovations that I have been exploring in this chapter.

Furthermore, both Postimpressionism and collectivist politics insisted on the constructedness of all visions: representations of the world are never the result of an individual looking at the world alone, but are mediated by artistic conventions and political institutions. The breaking of conventions that is such a feature of modernist literature and Postimpressionist art was not a route to "truth" or an unmediated mirroring of the world, but rather a way of recognizing that all mirrors are broken. In Postimpressionist art, we look at the world constantly aware of the medium and the distortion. Woolf describes a similar breaking of the mirror in the dark of "Time Passes":

> Did Nature supplement what man advanced? Did she complete what he began? . . . That dream, of sharing, completing, of finding in solitude on the beach an answer, was then but a reflection in a mirror, and the mirror itself was but the surface glassiness which forms in quiescence when the nobler powers sleep beneath? Impatient, despairing yet loth to go (for beauty offers her lures, has her consolations), to pace the beach was impossible; contemplation was unendurable; the mirror was broken. (pp. 201–2)

The mirror breaking in this passage may seem a loss of religious or mystical solace having little to do with politics or the working class. But a passage in the novel connects mysticism directly with the working class, equating Mrs. McNab's singing while she works with the answers that mystics find on the beach.

> Some cleavage of the dark there must have been, some channel in the depths of obscurity through which light enough issued to twist [Mrs. McNab's] face grinning in the glass and make her, turning to her job again, mumble out the old music hall song. The mystic, the visionary, walking the beach on a fine night, stirring a puddle, looking at a stone, asking themselves "What am I," "What is this?" had suddenly an answer vouchsafed them: (they could not say what it was) so that they were warm in the frost and had comfort in the desert. But Mrs. McNab continued to drink and gossip as before. (pp. 197–98)

In the early drafts of the novel, this passage did not end with Mrs. McNab's drinking and gossiping, but with her giving a "message" that is described as "what great poets have said."[37] Woolf backed off from giving Mrs. McNab such stature, but the novel still credits Mrs. McNab's music-hall song, the epitome of low-class art, with providing what visionaries and mystics seek, even if this cannot be put into words. It can, however, be put into light, the light that issues from the lighthouse, from the working-class world.

Mrs. McNab thus restores some of the security that was lost in the period of broken mirrors. But this is a new kind of security, no longer created by looking in the mirror of nature and seeing oneself: instead one has to look at and listen to Mrs. McNab and accept answers one cannot express. The image of nature as a mirror refers back to the moment of unity that climaxes the dinner party. In that scene, Woolf shows the creation of the illusion that the upper class is "natural," is mirrored by nature: the windows surrounding the diners become mirrors when Mrs. Ramsay lights the candles at twilight:

> Now all the candles were lit up, and the faces on both sides of the table were brought nearer by the candle light, and composed, as they had not been in the twilight, into a party round a table, for the night was now shut off by panes of glass, which, far from giving any accurate view of the outside world, rippled it so strangely that here, inside the room, seemed to be order and dry land; there, outside, a reflection in which things wavered and vanished, waterily.
>
> Some change at once went through them all, as if this had really happened, and they were all conscious of making a party together in a hollow, on an island; had their common cause against that fluidity out there. (p. 147)

The act of lighting the candle creates a double illusion—that everyone inside is nearer to everyone else inside, united into a "party," and that outside there is nothing but water. Mrs. Ramsay's act of lighting the candles is not an act of illumination, but an act of self-blinding. Outside, of course, there is not only another house, the lighthouse, but the people in that house, the workers, who comprise another "party," the Labour Party. By emerging out of quiescence and gaining the vote, the workers destroyed the illusion that those in the dinner party, the upper classes, were the only natural rulers, the sole natural occupants of the houses of Parliament. They broke the mirrors by which the upper classes had created an illusion of looking into nature.

George Dangerfield used similar imagery to characterize the violent movements that emerged in the early twentieth century. After describing the illegal efforts of aristocrats such as Bonar Law and Edward Carson to stop Irish Home Rule, he summarizes the effect of such acts:

> For nearly a century men had discovered in the cautious phrase, in the respectable gesture, in the considered display of reasonable emotions, a haven against those irrational storms which threatened to sweep through them. And gradually the haven lost its charms; worse still, it lost its peace. Its waters, no longer unruffled by the wind, ceased to reflect, with complacent

ease, the settled skies, the untangled stars of accepted behavior and sensible conviction; and men, with a defiance they could not hope to understand, began to put forth upon little excursions into the vast, the dark, the driven seas beyond. When Mr. Bonar Law incited the army to mutiny, his boat was already out; when Sir Edward Carson played upon the fury of Orange Ulster, he had left the haven. (p. 141)

Between 1910 and 1914, Dangerfield says, politics changed style: it no longer was a world of "accepted behavior and sensible conviction," but rather one of acts of defiance that those performing "could not hope to understand," acts that seemed to be "excursions into the vast, the dark, the driven seas." The mirror that Dangerfield describes as breaking was the mirror of political representation: the violent political movements of the early twentieth century wrecked the idea that social issues can be settled in that mirror realm, Parliament, where calm speech replaces violent emotions. After 1914, politics expanded into the vast, dark region outside Parliament and outside consciousness.

Just as for Dangerfield this change in politics changed the conventions of ordinary behavior and the ways people dealt with their emotions, in Woolf's novel, the break in the mirror is clearly a change in the calm and settled world of upper-class family life. This change in family life, in turn, causes a change in the world of intellect, of philosophy, just as there has been a change in the world of visionaries and mystics. Mr. Ramsay's academic books were discovered on the beach; after the mirror breaks in the middle of this novel, Mr. Ramsay can no longer find his ideas on the beach. Woolf entwines the acts of seeking philosophical solace and seeking Mrs. Ramsay: in the dark middle of the book,

> no image with the semblance of serving and divine promptitude comes readily to hand bringing the night to order and making the world reflect the compass of the soul. . . . Almost it would appear that it is useless in such confusion to ask the night those questions . . . which tempt the sleeper from his bed to seek an answer.
> [Mr. Ramsay, stumbling along a passage one dark morning, stretched his arms out, but Mrs. Ramsay having died rather suddenly the night before, his arms, though stretched out, remained empty.] (pp. 193–94)

The parallel of the sleeper seeking a "serving and divine promptitude" with Mr. Ramsay seeking Mrs. Ramsay shows that what he was really seeking in nature was the wife as servant, Mrs. Ramsay. Though men like Mr. Ramsay think that they go "in search of some absolute good . . . something alien to the processes of domestic life" (p. 199), it is the processes of domestic life that produce the beliefs and security they find. Without Mrs. Ramsay, Mr. Ramsay has to take over the maternal role and actually travel to the lighthouse—to the working-class enclave—in order to restore his vision.

His trip to the lighthouse is unlike his earlier rambles along the beach, which were described as efforts to reach the North Pole. The trip to the lighthouse, a trip from the northernmost tip of England out to a rock off the coast, is not a journey into nature, but a journey to the edge of English culture. Thus—to return to the issue of what the lighthouse may be said to symbolize—it does not symbolize the light from outside England, but the light from one part of the social system that shines into another part. The novel suggests that what we can see of the world around us, when we look outside our little domestic enclave, is a product of the light produced by other domestic enclaves shining into this one. "Out there" is just "inside" some other part of the social system. When Mr. Ramsay leaps from his boat onto the lighthouse rock, he feels young again: he is leaping into a little domestic community, regaining some of what Mrs. Ramsay had provided, the solace and security to actively set out on explorations. Thus, the novel shows repeatedly that the working class and women provide the mirror, the semicomprehensible world, in which high culture sees itself.

When that mirror breaks, it is not the end of a structured world, but rather the replacement of a single mirror with many—the result of its breaking—replacing a vision of unity, wholeness, and comfort with pluralist discontinuity and uncertainty. The continuity of the first part of the novel, which built to an illusion of beautiful unity, is broken, and the novel moves on to a new kind of beauty, created by rupture and violence and loss, similar to the "terrible beauty" that Yeats, in "Easter, 1916," imagines being born in Ireland as a result of British massacres.[38] In the middle of "Time Passes," Woolf describes "flowers standing there . . . eyeless, and so terrible" (p. 203). The new "terrible beauty" is created by eliminating the "eyes," the "I's," the individual points of view that had been the basis of the old social order and of novel structure. Dangerfield similarly says that through the disruptions of the prewar years, "a new and terrible England took the place of the old"—an England of workers, women, Lords, and ex-colonials who, many feared, shared no point of view at all.[39]

Political pluralists envisioned a way to overcome the differences insisted on in this new England: not by trying to recreate a universal point of view, but rather by reconceiving of each individual as a part of many different groups and so capable of partial understanding of many points of view. The individual becomes, then, fragmented and even incoherent. Such a view of the self could seem a distortion of the "natural" individual who appears whole, but pluralists argued instead that the appearance of wholeness and coherence is the distortion. As Harold Laski put it in describing his proposed pluralist governmental structure, "because experience is many and not one the individual personality can not engulf itself in a single expression of one of its aspects . . . but that is to admit already breakage and ignorance in the world, to postulate discontinuity."[40] The relationship between political pluralism, "breakage," and "discontinuity" is important in understanding the fragmentation in modernist art. Woolf and Joyce both sought to break up the form of the novel in order to allow more voices to speak than their own. To do so was not merely to increase the voices, but to leave room for voices they could not even know about. As William James described pluralism, in a passage that Harold Laski quoted to justify his political system, "the pluralistic world is . . . more like a federal republic than an empire or a kingdom. However much may be collected, however much may report itself as present at any effective center of consciousness or action, something else is self-governed and absent and unreduced to unity."[41]

In both *Ulysses* and *To the Lighthouse*, there is an essential incompleteness. Woolf presents this not as a loss but as a miracle. Lily thinks: "Could things thrust their hands up and grip one; could the blade cut; the fist grasp? Was there no safety? No learning by heart of the ways of the world? No guide, no shelter, but all was miracle, and leaping from the pinnacle of a tower into the air?" (p. 268). Woolf wanted to leap off the tower into the waves, to give up the goal of security and authority. And this image of giving up shelter and safety immediately turns to an image of being connected to the "alien" class and culture surrounding the Ramsay vacation house. Immediately after Lily has the revelation of life as leaping from the pinnacle, there is a remarkable discontinuity in the text:

> For one moment she felt that if they . . . shouted loud enough Mrs. Ramsay would return. "Mrs. Ramsay!" she said aloud, "Mrs. Ramsay!" The tears ran down her face.
>
> VI
>
> [Macalister's boy took one of the fish and cut a square out of its side to bait his hook with. The mutilated body (it was still alive) was thrown back into the sea.]
>
> VII
>
> "Mrs. Ramsay!" Lily cried, "Mrs. Ramsay!" But nothing happened. (pp. 268–69)

The fish that appears while Lily paints has a square cut out of it; it is a creature in sections. And the image itself is doubly set off like no other passage in the book—inside its own section number and inside brackets. This jarring, disconnected image creates in the reader the sense of being jerked out of and then thrown back into the text, uncertain when the next tug will pull or where. This small insertion operates much as the entire "Time Passes" chapter does: it disrupts the tale to reveal characters who would seem to have no place in the unity of the novel and of the house—and it reveals that these are necessary to the structure of the group that excludes them. Just as a house may be constituted by those entirely outside it, so an individual is not a sealed entity: Lily is "curiously divided" as she paints, "as if one part of her were drawn out there" (p. 253). She is not an individual in control of her art or herself; one part of her and one part of her sketch are "drawn" by something "out there."

In the last part of the novel we see that there are no relationships that exist simply between two people: always there is a third, not even considered part of the relationship, who is necessary to maintain what seems the structure of the twosome. Every group is partly structured by something not in that group. The working class maintains the house that allows the family to feel securely sealed off from, among other things, the working class. Lily herself is created in this novel as a stranger who becomes a crucial part of the structure of the family. For Mr. Ramsay and his children to maintain their relationship in the last section, Lily must soothe him, support the rebellion of the children, and yet remain outside the family. Similarly, Paul and Minta's marriage is held together by his having an affair. The lighthouse is quite literally a governmental agency protecting the Ramsay household—and in the process it invades that house with its strange, alien light.

That Woolf would use as an image of liberation a voyage toward an agency of governmental protection mirrors the logic of collectivism. Jacques Donzelot finds a similar entwining of women's liberation and government protection and regulation—policing—of the family in his analysis of twentieth-century France: the government encouraged women's independent voices to justify intervention in the family.[42] In the postwar collectivist world, social units—classes, genders, cultures, the government, and the private house—are not isolated, discrete entities, but remain open, crisscrossing each other, depending on each other to even "be themselves," to maintain their own internal structure.

Under these conditions, art itself must give up hope of being an isolated cultural activity. Lily's painting is completed only when she gives up her hope of escaping from society into art; she has to allow the Ramsay family to invade the enclave of artists and she has to accept in some fashion the roles that are thrust upon her by that family. In the third section, Lily overcomes her desire to utterly withdraw and avoid the Ramsays. The first step is her praising Mr. Ramsay's boots, an act that causes her to feel emotionally drenched by the flood of his emotion, a drenching that seems necessary for her to overcome the "dryness" of her isolation. Then, as she paints, she recognizes that she is not in control of herself. An accidental flurry of air stirs "some flounce in the room" she is looking at, so that a triangular shadow appears that reminds her of Mrs. Ramsay and James sitting on the steps. At this image, Lily's

> heart leapt at her and seized her and tortured her.
> "Mrs. Ramsay! Mrs. Ramsay!" she cried, feeling the old horror come back—to want and want and not to have. Could she inflict that still? And then, quietly, as if she refrained, that too became part of ordinary experience, was on a level with the chair, with the table. . . .

> And as if she had something she must share, yet could hardly leave her easel, so full her mind was of what she was thinking, of what she was seeing, Lily went past Mr. Carmichael holding her brush to the edge of the lawn. Where was that boat now? And Mr. Ramsay? She wanted him. (p. 300)

Earlier, Woolf had spoken of Lily being "drawn" out across the water; we see that she is also drawn into the past to the dead Mrs. Ramsay. Part of her is attached by hook and line to Mrs. Ramsay, another to Mr. Ramsay. Lily is at first horrified at this feeling of wanting and not having, of incompleteness. But then she finds it is simply part of "ordinary experience." By accepting her incompleteness and her lack of control, Lily can step out of the enclave of artists and carry her brush with her as she seeks Mr. Ramsay. She gives up the security of either the family or the isolated world of art and accepts the jarring discontinuity of living in a world where all institutions intersect and yet cannot be harmoniously united: every step one takes through complex social spaces alters the balance of power of different institutions and so one constantly feels new tugs suddenly emerging into consciousness. This sense of uncertainty and instability may even be one of the goals of the new social order: George Dangerfield suggested that the "abandonment of security" was the "psychological motive" that lay "beneath the political and economic motives" for the "disintegration of Liberal England" (p. 145). The post-Liberal world was to be one in which everyone would prefer insecurity, instability, and disintegration. This novel, with its broken structure, like pluralist government and Postimpressionist art, exemplifies the new discontinuous structures of mind and politics that emerged as part of mass society. Such a breakup was necessary, Woolf implies, to overcome her own class, gender, and cultural biases.

Unfortunately, she ultimately fails in that project, just as she failed to envision what new kind of gift Mr. Ramsay could carry to the lighthouse. The others who speak in this novel are still constructed to satisfy the needs of the dominant groups, groups to which the author continued to belong. Woolf felt she could never fully identify with a working-class woman and so could never create believable fictional portraits of such women: "The imagination is largely the child of the flesh. One could not be Mrs. Giles of Durham because one's body had never stood at the wash-tub. Something was always creeping in from a world that was not their world and making the picture false."[43] Woolf struggled against the limitations of her imagination; she tried to write "Time Passes" as Mrs. McNab's internal monologue, but finally gave up. The workers in this novel end up expressing mostly admiration for the upper class.

Joyce similarly created working-class women who could criticize and even rebel against their treatment, but ultimately they, too, are controlled, contained in their dark town and made to speak their acceptance of that treatment. The last line a prostitute says to Stephen is, "He insulted me but I forgive him. I forgive him for insulting me" (15.4741–42); Joyce constructed his women to forgive his insults to them, to say "I forgive" (or "Yes") over and over again, perhaps soothing male guilt. Woolf too seems to need repeated forgiveness for what she and her class have asked of working-class women: Mrs. McNab's last lines are also repeated, and are the closest that a laborer comes to complaining about her treatment: "There was always plenty doing, people in the house, twenty staying sometimes, and washing up till long past midnight. . . . Twenty she dared say in all their jew-ellery, and she asked to help wash up, might be till after midnight" (p. 211). These lines hint at Mrs. McNab's resentment about her hours and her work, but her potential anger is overshadowed and stifled by her admiration for the glamour of the Ramsay parties her labor created.

Woolf makes the working class speak its acceptance of the unfair de-mands made on it, as Joyce makes the prostitutes speak their forgiveness of the insults of gentlemen. However, the simple fact that these last lines are repeated suggests something unresolved in the minds of Joyce and Woolf: the implied complaints of working-class women echo on and on, unan-swered, even after these novelists try to leave such women behind. Much in these two novels suggests that Joyce and Woolf never overcame their guilt about their relations to working-class women because these novelists never overcame their desire to be superior to and served by such women. And much outside these novels suggests the same conclusion: Joyce's guilt per-meates all his books; Woolf's fills her diaries, as Jane Marcus has pointed out.[44]

In Woolf, Joyce, and Dangerfield, we see authors struggling to represent people with whom they cannot fully identify. Woolf may have been more active in the movements for political liberation—feminism and social-ism—than Dangerfield or Joyce, but she shared their uncertainty about just what such liberation would mean. These writers supported the destruc-tion of stifling conformist Liberal England, and yet they were fearful of the strange mentality of mass movements that was replacing liberal, indi-vidualistic consciousness. Lily Briscoe finds both freedom to be herself and dissolution of that self in the transformation of her art into representa-tion of masses. Dangerfield ends his book declaring that in Liberal England "nothing was real" and yet rhapsodizes that "we could almost find it in our hearts to envy those who saw it, and who never lived to see the new world" (p. 442). Such contradictions do not reduce these authors to reactionaries. Rather, the ambivalences in these texts show how difficult it is to undergo social changes that alter one's own consciousness or that reveal alternative consciousnesses—and how difficult it is to write about such changes. The best that these writers could do was to interrupt their own works, leaving dark spaces within English literature and history to be filled with the words of others.

PART II

Fearing the Masses

CHAPTER 3

Leaving the Self at Home

'The Voyage Out'

Although writers in the 1920's and 1930's conceived of the emergence of a new mass collectivist consciousness as a sudden, explosive, almost incomprehensible event, forces that led to this explosion began battling against individualism long before those writers were born. The first historian of the transition, A. V. Dicey, claimed that "between 1830 and 1840 the issue between individualists and collectivists was fairly joined."[1] Most historians still follow Dicey's periodization of the history of the transition, seeing individualism dominating until around 1870, then a period of rapid change characterized by uncertain theorizing from 1870 to 1910, and finally a period in which collectivism became the dominant philosophy. This fits nicely with the periodization now current in literary history: roughly from 1830 to 1870 is generally regarded as the Victorian era, from 1910 to 1940 is recognized as the modernist era, and the period from 1870 to 1910 has given literary historians much trouble, possibly because it was an era in which two views of society, and, we might say, two master narratives concerning it, were in conflict. To understand the way literary and political history were entwined in the modern era, we need to examine briefly the changes during the nineteenth century that led up to the explosions of mass politics and of modernism.

The change in politics can be understood as a change in the way people explained and plotted their lives, particularly in the way they envisaged each life as tracing a relationship with the masses. In 1835, when de Tocqueville defined the term *individualism*, the goal of each person was understood to be to calmly leave the masses for the pleasures of private life: "Indi-

vidualism is a novel expression, to which a novel idea has given birth. . . .
Individualism is a mature and calm feeling, which disposes each member
of the community to sever himself from the mass of his fellow-creatures,
and to draw apart with his family and friends."[2] By the 1850's, however,
the step away from the masses was no longer a calm choice, because the
masses came to seem a coercive power, interfering with the moral freedom
of the individual. John Stuart Mill's classic 1859 essay "On Liberty" took
as its fundamental premise the need to end such interference:

> One very simple principle [is] entitled to govern absolutely the dealings of
> society with the individual in the way of compulsion and control, whether
> the means used be physical force in the form of legal penalties, or the moral
> coercion of public opinion. That principle is, that the sole end for which
> mankind are warranted, individually or collectively, in interfering with the
> liberty of action of any of their number, is self-protection. . . . The only
> purpose for which power can be rightfully exercised over any member of a
> civilized community, against his will, is to prevent harm to others.[3]

In Mill's essay, the relationship of the individual to society is no longer
the friendship of fellow creatures that de Tocqueville described, but has become a battleground, involving "compulsion," "control," "physical force,"
and "coercion." "Interference" became a key concept of individualism, with
its implication that people are strongest and happiest when left alone in
legally protected private spaces. The threat of interference meant that individuals had to be strong to maintain their right to privacy, often against the
government itself, and the process of growth from tutelage to independence
was fraught with dangers.

By the end of the century, the distinction between mass and individual
no longer was between whole and part, but rather between two distinct
classes. Individualism, as Charles Maier comments, "was narrowing into
a nostalgic defense of an uncontested bourgeois leadership."[4] The effort
to defend a bourgeois leadership that had become quite contested turned
the plot of individual liberation into a drama of righteous moral defense.
Instead of calmly retreating, liberals were shutting themselves into their
houses in fear of what was outside in society, declaring that any tampering
with privacy and with liberal political economy would destroy civilization.
In his history of liberalism, Anthony Arblaster labels the nineteenth century an era of "fear of democracy."[5] George Dangerfield defined the tone of
liberalism at the turn of the century as "the final expression of everything
which is respectable, God-fearing and frightened."[6]

The anxiety and fearfulness were in part a response to the perception
that the plot of individual liberation in the society's master narrative no
longer seemed possible or even desirable. The government's interference
in private life grew steadily during the nineteenth century in response to
political movements and even scientific discoveries such as the revelation

of invisible microbes that could invade all private spaces. By the end of the century, many people concluded that the individual could not sever connections with the public realm. A. V. Dicey devoted a section of his 1914 analysis of the decline of individualism to "The Existence of Patent Facts which impress upon ordinary Englishmen the Interdependence of Private and Public Interest."[7] We can detect Dicey's individualism in this phrase: he believed that the "patent facts" that impressed "ordinary Englishmen" were false. Even so, the term "interdependence" serves well to epitomize the collectivist view in contrast to Mill's emphasis on "interference" as the usual result of the contact of public and private spheres. Interdependence suggests that the contacts between people are mutually supporting; one thinks of people leaning on each other, propping each other up. An individual's ability to stand or move about is, in such a view, increased by his being connected to others. To leave a person in privacy, free of interference, as individualists proposed, would reduce his ability to accomplish his own goals.

Dicey gives two main examples of the "facts" that convinced ordinary people of their interdependence: First, "the whole course of trade tends rapidly to place the conduct of business in the hands of corporate or quasi-corporate bodies."[8] Contract negotiations changed from two individuals agreeing on shared interests to two "corporate bodies" (say, a stock company and a trade union) interacting. Individuals became parts of a system, not independent entities. Writers concluded that an individual who tries to negotiate on his own not only reduces his own power but also the power of all his fellow negotiators. Such a person would be less successful alone than in a group.

For a second example, Dicey says that collectivism was forwarded by "the advance . . . of human knowledge," which "has intensified the general conviction that even the apparently innocent action of an individual may injuriously affect the welfare of a whole community."[9] In particular, Dicey says, "science" has shown "that the health of a nation depends, or may depend, on the general observation of certain rules of health." The actions of a person in the most private parts of his private property, such as the bathroom, may end up affecting people who live far away. The private realm can never be sealed up: its borders are porous, and the individual can never even know what is leaking out or invading.

And just as the body could not be protected from germs by the individual acting alone, so the mind could not be isolated from hidden influences: Beatrice Webb described the spread of incest in crowded housing conditions as an example of "moral malaria"—immoral thoughts entering minds the way microbes enter bodies, without anyone even knowing it has happened.[10] The possibility of "unconscious" influence threatened the belief in truth itself. I quote a perhaps unlikely source, W. H. Auden, on the ways that the advance of knowledge was connected to the loss of a belief in universal truths and the demise of liberalism. In the introduction to *Poets of the English Language: Victorian and Edwardian Poets, Tennyson to Yeats*, Auden writes:

> The confidence of the liberal humanist was not seriously shaken by the natural sciences, which were based on the presupposition that whatever his origin, whatever the relation of his mind to matter, man was capable of a disinterested search for an objective truth which was universally valid. The dangerous assault came later from the half-sciences, like sociology, anthropology and psychology, which are concerned with man as an interested actor. Their exhibition of the mind's capacity for self-deception, of the unconscious effect upon its thinking of social status and sex, their demonstration that the customs and beliefs of other peoples could not be dismissed as merely savage, irrational and quaint but must be accepted as rival civilizations complete in themselves, cast doubts upon the finality of any truth. Again, in practical politics, the pure liberal doctrine of laissez-faire was proving unworkable.[11]

Auden's leap in the last sentence from the loss of all truth to the failure of the politics of laissez-faire may seem an odd change of subject, but the connection is not hard to see: if the individual cannot think on his own, but will "unconsciously" be affected by class and sex and nationality, then the logic of laissez-faire falls apart. The new "half-sciences" seemed to show that no person ever thinks without interference from the customs and traditions of other people, from unconscious forms of the coercion of public opinion. No person can ever be sure of just what is controlling her mind—or of what is her "own character." The mind, like the body and like the house, has porous boundaries, and tides of thoughts produced by various corporate bodies flow in and out.

One image that I find useful for summarizing the shift from individualist to collectivist theories is to imagine a person as suspended by strings pulling in various directions. Imagine that she is suspended at an angle and wants to straighten up. The individualist solution would be to teach her how to pull her own strings so as not to interfere with anyone else and then cut off all the strings tying her to other people, letting her straighten herself up. In the new views, cutting all the strings would produce a shapeless mass. Without social structure, a person couldn't maintain any definite personality at all. A person could make efforts to straighten herself, but only by interacting with the social forces (the strings) and trying to get them to have a different pattern so they pull her straight. And it may turn out that the desire to be straightened up was a product of the original state, so that the resultant new state may still appear undesirable.

I derive this image from a passage in Mill. Mill argues that various forms of control of one person over another—including even slavery, he says—are justified as long as they remain "leading strings" that function only until the person learns to walk on her own.[12] Mill invokes a plot of older guides (who could even be agents of the government) controlling a young person until that person becomes educated, strong, and moral enough to be autonomous. The demise of "Liberal England" was the demise of this plot: as we have seen, in George Dangerfield's 1935 history of that demise he describes fully adult political leaders—none other than the Liberal Cabinet—in just these terms, as "puppets" moved by vast, unconscious, collective entities.[13] In the postliberal world, leading strings never come off, and no one is ever sure what is the cause of what she is doing.

One other component needs to be added to this image: in most collectivist theories, the strings are constantly shifting no matter what the individual does, so the individual is herself constantly shifting. The individual is carried along as the whole social structure around her changes. A fully collectivist narrative plot would simply trace the flow of the currents carrying everyone along regardless of their individual personalities—as we see in a book like *The Waves*. At the turn of the century, though, there emerged texts that I categorize as transitional between individualist and collectivist narrative plots; these books show individuals striking out on their own but ending up surrounded by strange masses and either being swamped or finding a narrow and difficult way out. Often the masses are represented symbolically: Patrick Brantlinger has suggested the category "Imperial Gothic" for the numerous turn-of-the-century novels of British subjects facing alien monsters, either as a result of invasions or as a result of traveling to strange lands.[14] He includes both high-culture and low-culture novels in this category—both *Heart of Darkness* and *Tarzan*. But there were also "Domestic Gothics," books about the horrible monsters emerging from within England, such as C. F. G. Masterman's *From the Abyss*, which portrays the working classes as masses "emerging like rats from a drain."[15]

Michael Levenson has developed a related theory about *The Ambassadors* and *Heart of Darkness*, describing both as novels about the near impossibility of maintaining individuality in a postliberal world: "In *The Ambassadors* and *Heart of Darkness* it requires two cultures to construct an individual. There can be no self-definition through retreat to a strictly private region; there *is* no such region. . . . Faced with contending values, they choose one and then decide to live with the other. Only in this way can they preserve the *friction* that sustains the 'I' against the 'us.' "[16] Both these novels also trace voyages toward older and more collectivist cultures (from America to England, from England to Africa). These novels thus built on the anxieties surrounding the projected mass society of the future: the move beyond capitalist individualism appeared to be a return to a feudal or tribal past. The "us" that threatened the individual seemed to be an ancient communal social order that lay buried underneath the modern, liberal world, as England remained underneath American consciousness and Africa (in Conrad's view) lay deep inside the English psyche.

Some modernists continued to produce such novels all their lives, never

moving to the fully fragmented, multivoiced, fluid forms of high modernism. I would thus classify Joseph Conrad, D. H. Lawrence, and E. M. Forster
as holding to the transitional novel form into the 1920's and 1930's. These
authors developed a variety of methods of maintaining the individual in
fictional worlds represented as being without a private space. Lawrence
proposed, in *Women in Love*, the technique of having a liberated couple
constantly moving about. As Rupert Birkin says, "one should just live anywhere—not have a definite place. I don't want a definite place. —As soon as
you get a room, and it is *complete*, you want to run from it. It is a horrible
tyranny of a fixed milieu. . . . You must leave your surroundings sketchy, un-
finished, so that you are never contained, never confined, never dominated
from the outside."[17] The individual is preserved from social domination by
constantly changing the social influences.

In novels of this transitional form, there is always some way to step out
into the destructive element and yet not be overwhelmed or drowned by
it: after tracing the movement toward the mass mind, the unconscious, the
social, such novels find a way to return from the horror that is uncovered.
Forster's *Passage to India*, for example, confronts the question of collective
minds that are not located in any individual bodies directly by focusing
on the question of what to make of a "babble of voices" in a cave. But
the novel then retreats from that babble and from what that babble says—
that the relation of England and India is one of mutual violence and rape.
The novel switches from the cave of collective voices to a central locus of
individuality—the court—and establishes that individual testimony about
"the truth" is more important than the collective voice. So it restores individualism—at least as the ideal. When it ends on the question of whether
two men of different cultures can be friends and says they cannot for many
years, it presents a vision of individualism currently failing, but potentially
restorable: it ends in hope of private lives transcending cultures.[18]

Virginia Woolf, in *The Voyage Out*, followed much the same trajectory
as these other early modernist texts; the journey in this novel bears many
similarities to the journey in *Heart of Darkness*, but with quite a different outcome: her heroine finds no way back. Her "other world"—a strange
South America—is actually much less "foreign" than Conrad's Congo or
James's Europe, but perhaps for that reason it is much harder to escape its
hold. When Woolf's voyagers look at the jungle, they do not see an incomprehensible mystery, but rather the origins of Elizabethan style. Encoun-
tering a "native" village, they feel they have entered an English park. South
America is less an exotic place than the end of Rachel's development, the
extension of her education to its inevitable result. For half the novel, we
seem to be in a nineteenth-century *Bildungsroman*: Rachel Vinrace, helped
by her parental guides Helen Ambrose and St. John Hirst, voyages out of the
limited world of her childhood, beyond her father and even her nation. She
seems to become ready to take up her autonomous existence in the private
realm, ready to be married. But then she gets sick with a mysterious illness

and at the same time the text itself changes style. The illness is presented as a mysterious invasion of her body and mind that causes her to lose the ability for independent motion so that she becomes, in Woolf's description, merely an object at the "bottom of the sea," rolled about by passing waves.

Most criticism of the novel has focused on psychology, treating Rachel's voyage and her illness as movements into unclear, disturbing depths of the self: the bottom of the sea is then the unconscious. Harvena Richter has coined the phrase an "inward voyage" to describe this journey.[19] Like Kurz, according to Rosemary Pitt, Rachel travels "too far into unknown areas of the self and experience and has to pay through extinction."[20] But the comparison to Kurz is more exact than that, involving not only a similar psychology but a similar anthropology: in both *Heart of Darkness* and *The Voyage Out*, the movement into unknown areas of the self is presented overtly as a journey to the south into "dark," tribal cultures. The use of another continent presses us to consider Rachel's voyage in social terms, not merely in individual ones.

Critics who have treated this novel as commenting on social issues have mostly focused on gender and marriage: Rachel's death becomes, as one critic puts it, "the result of her desire to escape being written into the marriage plot."[21] Marianne DeKoven has examined class and race issues in this novel and *Heart of Darkness*: she sees both as journeys into the fluid world outside the rigid structures of patriarchy, capitalism, and imperialism.[22] But ultimately, DeKoven treats gender as the fundamental issue here: she shows how concerns about social revolution—the rising of the masses—are embodied in images of the feminine emerging, and thus engender different reactions in male and female authors. The two novels, in her view, are opposed versions of facing the repressed maternal: they are both "vaginal passages" toward the womb.

DeKoven's work postulates that the reaction to the feminine underlie reactions to the masses; I wish to consider the converse, that political rhetoric of the masses (of workers and colonials in particular) shapes images of the feminine. Instead of seeing Rachel's trip to South America as a voyage into the maternal, I want to examine how the issue of seeking to liberate or simply explore the repressed feminine becomes entwined with the necessity of joining the masses, conceived of both as lower classes (the sociological outside) and as "primitive" races (the anthropological outside).[23] I accept what most critics have argued, that Woolf started this novel seeking to explore her own depths, freed from English, bourgeois, and patriarchal restraints. This exploration, however, had unexpected results: it did not lead to a vision of a liberated self or to a distinctly female consciousness, but to a sense of the complete loss of self, because liberation seemed inextricably linked to the masses. Woolf's novels constantly lead to this same conclusion: liberation from the bourgeois patriarchy means liberation from being an individual; to leave the home is to leave the self behind.[24]

But what is this other thing that one becomes without a self? James

Naremore says that Rachel glimpses "an elemental terror . . . the primitive biological force of life itself."[25] The terror of facing the "primitive" was not merely a metaphysical experience: it was also part of the political rhetoric permeating early-twentieth-century England in reactions to collectivism. The possibility of becoming a mass society appeared to be a form of racial degeneration, a return to primitive or tribal existence. The question of racial degeneration permeates the novel, and is connected to issues of collectivism, individualism, and dependency: if independence were possible for Rachel, she would not degenerate through her mysterious disease into a creature at the bottom of the sea. The equation of dependence and degeneracy was a commonplace of early-twentieth-century arguments against government interference and often was invoked by medical authorities, as if degeneracy were a type of disease. For example, Sir James Barr, the head of the British Medical Association, in response to the 1906 Unemployment Insurance Act, said: "It will tend to reduce individual effort and increase the spirit of dependency that is the mark of degenerate races."[26] In the first draft of the novel, the issue of devolution was raised explicitly: Rachel comments that Darwin declared that women were "nearer the cow" than men.[27] If women are closer to lower species, the move away from the patriarchal, male world may lead women down the evolutionary ladder. Louise DeSalvo describes the early version of the novel as an "angry novel about how the power of women had eroded since the time of the Egyptians, since pre-Olympian Greece."[28] Thus, Woolf's desire to restore something that she imputed to prehistorical eras is an act of devolution. Gillian Beer argues that throughout her career, Woolf reframed Darwinian discourse, undermining metaphors of development and degeneration in her attack on imperialist and patriarchal discourse.[29] In this early novel, we can see Woolf struggling to break free of the claimed superiority of the English, but at the same time anxiously wondering what it means to adopt an image of herself as a "lower" race.

Sending Rachel to South America was part of that struggle. In early drafts, the voyage was to South Africa; Woolf inserted her heroine into the common turn-of-the-century plot of the traveler losing contact with English civilization and so undergoing mutation. Henry Stanley's 1891 journal, *In Darkest Africa*, provided the model for such stories. Conrad has made popular the image of "degeneration" as succumbing to the enticements of strange rituals and violence, but as William Atkinson points out, Stanley repeatedly claimed that on his expeditions, men "fell through inactivity and immobility."[30] Woolf's redoing of *Heart of Darkness* follows Stanley's vision more than Conrad's: when Rachel deteriorates, she becomes unable to move.

The mysterious region outside the familiar territory of upper-class England this novel is exploring is as much the lower classes as it is colonial worlds. Woolf's use of South America (or, originally, South Africa) to represent the world outside the upper classes is similar to numerous turn-of-the-century texts in which the lower depths of English society are equated with the "dark" of non-European continents such as Africa and South America, for example William Booth's book about the East End of London, whose title imitates Stanley's: *In Darkest England and the Way Out*. Woolf prepares us to think of the voyage to South America as a voyage into "darkest England" by opening the novel with a short domestic journey that parallels the larger voyage of the rest of the novel: Helen Ambrose and her husband move out of the West End into a "mass of streets" full of "innumerable poor people" (pp. 11–12). The crowds seem full of "small, agitated figures—for in comparison with this couple most people looked small" (p. 9). Noticing that "not one of the thousand men and women she saw was either a gentleman or a lady," Helen "understood that after all it is the ordinary thing to be poor" and is "startled by this discovery" (p. 12). She feels she is moving out of a small realm of wealth and beauty into a vast, dark continent: she visualizes the West End in relation to London as "a small golden tassel on the edge of a vast black cloak" (p. 12). The first "voyage out" in this novel is this walking tour through the East End. Around the turn of the century, numerous writers described the East End as an uncharted wilderness in which such a mass of people were breeding that they formed essentially a sea on which England floated. According to C. F. G. Masterman in 1900, "Below . . . England . . . stretches a huge and unexplored region which seems destined in the next half-century to progress toward articulate voice, and to demand an increasing power. . . . To most observers from the classes above this is the Deluge. . . . They see our civilisation as a little patch of redeemed land in the wilderness."[31] As Rachel grows in knowledge in this novel, she also discovers more and more about the region beneath England, and she and the novel "progress toward articulate voice" about that region—and hence toward the deluge. This deluge is the rising of the dark world and the sinking of enlightened England, just as Rachel's progress toward being able to articulate her sense of the world ends by sinking her to the bottom of the sea.

The novel is built around repeated "voyages out" into the wilderness similar to the Ambroses' walk from the West End into the East End: the ship going from shore to sea, the small group of friends leaving the colony to go up the Amazon, Rachel and Terence leaving the boat for a hike up the jungle, and finally, Rachel's passage into illness. All the journeys in this novel are movements from small realms of light out into vast darkness, and this opening scene sets up the possibility of interpreting all of them as metaphors for the movement from the upper classes into the masses.

In each of these moves, what had seemed the stable structure of the world comes apart. The black cloak of London appears, as the Ambroses enter it, a "great manufacturing place, where the people were engaged in making things, as though the West End . . . was the finished work" (p. 12).

Mrs. Ambrose's stroll reveals that what had seemed the "base" of her world—property itself and all the gold and lights of the upper classes—is built on and by the working class and hence could disappear if the working classes should change in any drastic way. Similarly, when the ship takes off, "a slight but perceptible wave seemed to roll beneath the floor," hinting at the departure from the stability of land, the first step away from the calm, liberal world of property. As they move out to sea, England appears to be a "shrinking island in which people were imprisoned" (p. 32). Liberal rhetoric is inverted: England with its system of private property is no longer the realm of freedom, but the realm of imprisonment, and the vast, dark waves around the island become the realm of freedom.

Woolf struggled to write a voyage out of the prison of England and into a realm of autonomy, but the problem was that the area outside was not a region of autonomous individuals, but a sea of humanity. William Booth's project in exploring "Darkest England" was to bring autonomy to those in the lower class, but he despaired because, he says, the poor had devolved into "pygmies . . . dwarfish de-humanized inhabitants" who cannot be turned into citizens: "no amount of assistance will give jellyfish a backbone. All material help from without is useful only in so far as it develops moral strength within."[32] Woolf evokes "pygmies" herself in describing the Ambroses as surrounded by masses of smaller people. The voyage out in search of autonomy threatens to turn Rachel into one of "them"; she is in danger of losing her shape, like a jellyfish. Jellyfish are a repeated symbol in this novel of the strange new world the travelers find. Terence says that from a cliff he "saw a sight that fairly took my breath away—about twenty jellyfish, semi-transparent, pink, with long streamers, floating on the top of the waves" (p. 204). Hirst asks in response, "Sure they weren't mermaids?," hinting at the possibility that there is some relationship between these jellyfish and an alternative species of women—a species that would be at home floating among waves. Woolf directly connects this vision of pink jellyfish to a vision of racial degeneration: when Rachel and Terence stand on "the cliff where, looking down into the sea, you might chance on jelly-fish," they look around:

> the vast expanse of land gave them a sensation which is given by no view, however extended, in England . . . earth widening and spreading away and away like the immense floor of the sea, earth chequered by day and by night, and partitioned into different lands, where famous cities were founded, and the races of men changed from dark savages to white civilised men, and back to dark savages again. Perhaps their English blood made this prospect uncomfortably impersonal and hostile to them, for having once turned their faces that way they next turned them to the sea, and for the rest of the time sat looking at the sea. (p. 210)

The English are more comfortable looking at the blank top of the sea and the pink jellyfish than at the lands and people of this new world that seems to be the deep floor of the sea itself. Rather oddly, the land seems "impersonal" while the sea is more comfortably personal. This land destroys their sense of personality, of individuality, and threatens to turn them into a dark, savage race, as the theories of degeneration were in fact predicting.

When Rachel and Terence eventually go into the jungle, they find themselves in effect journeying down through the sea: they feel they are "walking at the bottom of the sea" (p. 270). Terence begins to think of the world "not carved into hills and cities and fields, but heaped in great masses" (p. 291). He is terrified of a world without the "domesticated" spaces of hills, cities, and fields. Rachel is drawn to this alternative world of great masses outside domesticity: "she wanted many more things than the love of one human being—the sea, the sky" (p. 302).

The central problem with a world of great masses is that one cannot distinguish which great mass is the best. English politicians in the nineteenth century argued that what made England the greatest civilization was that the English system freed individuals from mass (feudal, tribal) existence into private life. John Stuart Mill defined the history of the world as the progress from "savage" life to individual autonomy.[33] What Rachel and Terence find in Woolf's South America is that the choice between individualist England and savage, uncivilized tribal existence is only a choice between two great masses, and history can move in either direction. The change from dark savages to white civilized men, Mill presumed, was irreversible, but in England in 1915 the whole world seemed to be moving along with the Ambroses in the other direction, from the golden tassel out onto the vast black cloak. As Rachel is educated in this novel, she also moves from light to dark, from personal to impersonal, from civilized to uncivilized, and eventually finds herself, in her illness, "under the Thames" (p. 331) and finally "at the bottom of the sea" (p. 341). Terence accompanies her part way, but finally holds himself back "on a little island by himself" and watches her die (p. 343).

There is a sense, then, that the world at the bottom of the sea is incompatible with the island of England. The creatures that live at the bottom of the sea are a different kind of "jellyfish" from those visible at the top: the deep-sea creatures are not simply beautiful and pink and mermaidlike. Early in the novel, Mr. Pepper speaks of "white, hairless, blind monsters lying curled on the ridges of sand at the bottom of the sea, which would explode if you brought them to the surface, their sides bursting asunder and scattering entrails to the wind when released from pressure" (p. 23). The whole novel is a journey into the realm of such monsters, the monsters buried under both the English empire and the English upper classes. These monsters can exist only in a tight relationship with their environment: they have no internal structure and cannot be separated from their world. These jellyfish are symbolic of the "lower orders" who William Booth said could never be given "backbone" and hence could never become autonomous citizens, never rise into the middle-class world and escape their exis-

tence as mass.[34] Pepper feels little threat from these monsters: they will
destroy themselves if they try to rise. Masterman's view of an impending
deluge suggests rather that the rising of the monsters of the deep will drown
England, converting the higher land into the bottom of the sea. Even in
Pepper's description, we can feel the threat deriving from the lower world,
a threat that could be defined as the question of who will determine the
medium in which we shall all live.

Rachel Vinrace is forced to confront that question because she is not
merely a visitor to the realm of monsters at the bottom of the sea: she
discovers that she herself is such a monster and after her discovery has to
plunge herself to the bottom of the sea to keep from exploding. The novel
implies that the world is divided into two kinds of people: those who live
in the depths, in the black, and those who live on the surface, in the light.
Neither can live in the other's realm. The unity that Richard Dalloway
defines as the goal of empire is brought about only by suppressing those
who live beneath the surface, keeping them in the dark. But the changes in
English society at the turn of the century were bringing people across the
boundaries, allowing, as Woolf observed, the "Victorian cook" to leave "the
lower depths" and change from a "leviathan" to a person reading the newspaper. In A Room of One's Own, Woolf similarly describes the new woman
who was just emerging in the early twentieth century as an "organism that
has been under the shadow of the rock these million years" and suddenly
"feels the light fall on it, and sees coming her way a piece of strange food—
knowledge, adventure, art . . . and has to devise some entirely new combination of her resources, so highly developed for other purposes, so as
to absorb the new into the old without disturbing the infinitely intricate
and elaborate balance of the whole."[35] In 1924, when she wrote A Room
of One's Own, Woolf may have felt that women could adapt to the new,
strange food, but in 1915 Rachel is an organism emerging from under a rock
who, in absorbing the strange food of knowledge and adventure, cannot
adapt to the light, but rather brings up her dark self from the depths and
threatens to darken all of England.

Much of Rachel's growth in her awareness of herself is entwined in this
novel with becoming aware of the darkness or immorality of the whole
English social system. Critics have focused on her discovery of the corruption of sexuality in the patriarchal system, but little has been said about
the ways that this novel presses us to see connections between Rachel's
growing sense of sexuality and her awareness of racial and class structures.
Woolf certainly signals that patriarchy is an abusive system: Mrs. Ambrose
suspects Rachel's father of "nameless atrocities with regard to his daughter, as indeed she had always suspected him of bullying the wife" (p. 24).
And similarly, Rachel's introduction to sexuality is by an act of aggression, a kiss imposed on her by Richard Dalloway. But if Willoughby and
Dalloway are representatives of patriarchy, they are at least as much rep-

resentatives of imperialism and the oppression of workers. Willoughby's "bullying" of his wife and daughter is repeatedly paralleled by his treatment of the South Americans and workers. Woolf reveals the man's essence in describing a letter from him: "there lay Willoughby, curt, inexpressive, perpetually jocular, robbing a whole continent of mystery, enquiring after his daughter's manners and morals . . . and then half a page about his own triumphs over wretched little natives who went on strike and refused to load his ships, until he roared English oaths at them" (p. 196). The novel struggles to undo the effects of Willoughby's kind of writing, to break out of the jocular and inexpressive world of English manners and morals and enter a mysterious land of "natives," women, and striking workers. Woolf sought to restore what Willoughby robbed from a continent, his daughter, and his employees.

To expose the crimes of the capitalist patriarchy is to move over to the side of the masses, and this move is embodied in Rachel's fearful reaction to Richard Dalloway's kiss. When he kisses her, she finds her mind full of terrifying images of being trapped in a long, damp tunnel that opens into a "vault" in which there is a "little deformed man" (p. 77). DeKoven and many other critics have seen this vault as vaginal, as representing the way Rachel has introjected the warped view of female sexuality held by the men around her, and as a reflection of Woolf's childhood abuse. But this image of descending beneath the surface and finding people in the dark who are smaller is more immediately an image of joining with the lower classes, those "dwarfish de-humanized inhabitants" whom William Booth found in "Darkest England," those people who were described as "smaller" than the Ambroses as they walked through the East End. It also resonates with the loss of barriers between the English and "lower" races; after her dream of the tunnel, Rachel has the feeling that "all night long barbarian men harassed the ship; they came scuffling down the passages and stopped to snuffle at her door" (p. 77). Louise DeSalvo has traced images of snuffling pigs to Woolf's experience of abuse as a child, and so this image is certainly an image of the emergence of horrible parts of Rachel's and Woolf's childhood.[36] But it is overtly an image of alien races attacking the ship, races that emerge from the vast sea of humanity to swamp the English ship of state.

Woolf sets up Dalloway's kiss as involving far more than sexuality by having it occur at the end of a conversation about imperialism. His kiss is an enactment of his imperialist methods of treating those who are not upper-class British males: he uses them, deforming them from equals into lesser (or smaller) people. Dalloway's kiss, as an act of violation of the rules of bourgeois marriage, is part of the process of leading Rachel out of the bourgeois world.

In Rachel's fever at the end of the novel, she returns to the image of a tunnel full of deformed, little people, but then identifies it as a "tunnel under the Thames," and the small person becomes a "little woman." In both these changes, the world in the tunnel is no longer as alien to her. Masses of workers were emerging each day in London from tunnels under the Thames. Consider, for example, the full context of the passage in which C. F. G. Masterman compared workers with rats in *From The Abyss*: "our streets have suddenly become congested with a weird and uncanny people. They have poured in as dense black masses. . . . they have been hurried up in incredible number through tubes sunk in the bowels of the earth, emerging like rats from a drain, blinking in the sunshine." Masterman's use of the term "black masses" neatly brings together multiple fears: those pouring into the streets and emerging from the tubes are unenlightened, undiffer-entiated, African, satanic. Masterman describes the masses as a "wave of humanity" sitting below the calm surface of England—but soon, he pre-dicts, the "tides of the great sea will pulsate through the little trim, clean, ordered pond and trouble the serenity of the surface."[37]

Becoming aware of the "lower" regions of England is equivalent to be-ginning to see threatening waves. Dalloway's kiss causes Rachel to feel "black waves across her eyes" (p. 76): his sexual aggression is an effort to sink her but has the unexpected effect of releasing something buried in her, the black waves that are the forces undermining upper-class English male power, undermining the empire, carrying everyone down to the bottom of the sea. Rachel's breaking out of convention is described throughout the novel as her entering such waves. When she revolts against religion, she reacts against a conventionally religious woman who seems to her "a lim-pet attached to a rock": Rachel is in contrast allowing herself to be carried by the tides. And this act of becoming unattached to the rock of society is equated with her becoming aware that "underneath" the everyday world "great things were happening—terrible things, because they were so great. Her sense of safety was shaken, as if beneath the twigs and dead leaves she had seen the movement of a snake" (p. 263). Rachel is beginning to see movements that threaten to upset the dead leaves of social conven-tions. This discovery is both exhilarating and horrifying, threatening to destroy her safe little world but also to reveal that her world was actually already "terrible" and full of snakes in the grass such as her father and Dalloway.

The "black waves" that accompany Dalloway's illicit kiss undermine his argument that the English are bringing unity to the world because they are "whiter than most men, their records cleaner" (p. 64). Even before the kiss dirties his own record, Rachel argues against Dalloway's vision of En-glish moral righteousness by saying that even within England, the minds of poor widows "remain untouched" by empire: she turns to an image of the repression of class and gender otherness as proof of the failure of empire. Dalloway responds that "a human being is not a set of compartments but an organism. . . . Use your imagination; that's where you young Liberals fail. Conceive the world as a whole" (p. 66). Dalloway explicitly equates the structure of the interior of the body and the structure of the world; the novel plays out the unexpected consequences of that equation: if the world is not a whole, with a distinctly unified leadership, then the body is not a whole under the direction of a unified mind, either. As Rachel breaks with Dalloway's vision of empire, she becomes aware of parts of her own interior that are alien in race and class to the self she has thought was her whole being.

The book more and more undermines the Conservative Party's vision of organic unity within each person and within the empire. Woolf sets Dalloway less against the Liberal Party he thinks he is opposing and more against the pluralists of the Labour Party. Rachel, by contrast, moves in the novel toward a vision of a pluralistic world that cannot be organically integrated into a single state or empire. In an argument with Terence about whether there is any universal human nature, she says that "human beings were as various as beasts at the Zoo, which had stripes and manes, and horns and humps" (p. 299). Her pluralism goes further than Harold Laski's: he thought mostly of a multiplicity of classes and industries; she thinks of different species or races. Her vision suggests it may be impossible to hold together a pluralistic society; there is a hint of horror in the vision of the human zoo.

The setting of the novel, with the English hotels surrounded by South Americans, emphasizes the issue of racial division. But even within the English colony, Woolf shows that there is no organic unity. The colony splits into "two houses, the big and the small . . . and the words 'the villa' and 'the hotel' called up the idea of two separate systems of life" (p. 220). As we've seen, the image of English society as divided into a big and a small house is central to Woolf's later novel of a "voyage out," *To the Lighthouse*. In *The Voyage Out*, though, the big and small houses of the colony are both upper-class houses, and people move easily between them: in effect, they set up an illusion of transcending class differences and uniting the empire.

However, there is a more mysterious barrier that Rachel crosses over, entering a normally invisible third part, a "wrong side" of the colony that does not even have a house:

> She looked down at the kitchen premises, the wrong side of hotel life, which was cut off from the right side by a maze of small bushes. The ground was bare, old tins were scattered about, and the bushes wore towels and aprons upon their heads to dry. Every now and then a waiter came out in a white apron and threw rubbish on to a heap. Two large women in cotton dresses were sitting on a bench with blood-smeared tin trays in front of them and yellow bodies across their knees. They were plucking the birds, and talking as they plucked. Suddenly a chicken came floundering . . . pursued by a third woman whose age could hardly be under eighty. Although wizened and unsteady on her legs she kept up the chase, egged on by the laughter of the others; her face was expressive of furious rage, and as she ran she swore in Spanish. Frightened by hand-clapping here, a napkin there, the

bird . . . finally fluttered straight at the old woman, who opened her scanty grey skirts to enclose it, dropped upon it in a bundle, and then, holding it out, cut its head off with an expression of vindictive energy and triumph combined. The blood and the ugly wriggling fascinated Rachel. (p. 252)

In this dark, hidden part of the colony, Rachel discovers the violence that the poor are required to perform to produce the elegant dinner parties of the upper classes, but she also discovers a strong, old woman who is able to express vindictive rage and whose image returns in Rachel's delirium: she sees "the old woman with the knife" (p. 333), and this vision transmutes into "an old woman slicing a man's head off with a knife" (p. 339). Rachel's fever, carrying her to a world in which women slice off men's heads, is carrying her through the "maze" set up to mystify and hide the "wrong side" of the English empire. She enters the dark world of racial, class, and gender violence—and begins to imagine possible violent acts of liberation.

Rachel is attracted to the blood she has never seen before. But Woolf does not simply carry Rachel to a violent rebellion against the bourgeois world, though the possibility is raised in the novel when another young woman, Evelyn, says she would "give all I have in the world to help on a revolution against the Russian government, and it's bound to come" (p. 321). The powerful mystery of Woolf's South America turns out to be not its violence, but rather its fluidity and softness. The "natives" that appear are not violent dart throwers such as Helen imagines in her embroidery, but rather "soft instinctive people" who seem "majestic" and who live in a place "like an English park" (pp. 284–85, 279). These soft people will draw Rachel in, include her. They are "far beyond the plunge of speech," and Rachel's illness will lead her to being "completely cut off, and unable to communicate with the rest of the world," thus sinking to "the bottom of the sea," where she sees again the old Spanish woman (pp. 284, 330, 341). In other words, her illness makes her one with the world she finds outside and underneath the English colony. She crosses the boundaries between the races and between the classes, the boundaries so important to preserving English homes from "interference." Once those boundaries are crossed, the world becomes a fluid place of nonindividuals.

Rachel is not the only one who finds that the boundaries that are supposed to protect English individualism do not work in Woolf's strange land: "Nothing was private in this country" (p. 100). One odd scene early in the book illustrates the problem. Rachel, thinking she is hiding, peeks through a window at Terence and St. John, only to discover later that they were in fact peeking out at her: two groups violating the boundaries of each other's privacy. Rachel has no internal sense of what should remain private, and so living with her is, as Helen puts it, "like having a puppy in the house . . . a puppy that brings one's underclothes down into the hall" (p. 145).

The danger is that Rachel's increasing awareness threatens to bring into visibility much more than the "underclothes" of the English: her expanding consciousness threatens to bring the deluge Masterman predicted would occur once those silenced under English rule had "progressed to articulate voice." One scene in the book symbolizes just such a possibility, though it is Susan who gives voice to the inarticulate masses. The English go on a hike to the top of a hill for a picnic until a woman screams that she is "covered by little creatures . . . large brown ants with polished bodies" (p. 133). The people then decide to "adopt the methods of modern warfare against an invading army." This scene encapsulates the attitude of the upper-class English against the various "little creatures"—workers, colonials, and women—threatening to overrun them. But one person refuses warfare: Susan "pronounced that that was cruel, and rewarded those brave spirits [the ants] with spoil in the shape of tongue" (p. 134). Susan's act undermines the warfare of the English against the invasion from beneath: given a tongue, the "brown bodies" that live in South America would no longer be "beyond the plunge of speech." Woolf was very strongly drawn toward Susan's act: condemning the war of the English against others and giving her tongue to those others, speaking for them.

But as we have seen, Woolf could not imitate Susan and provide a tongue or voice for the masses—working-class or colonial, "could not be Mrs. Giles of Durham because one's body had never stood at the wash-tub." The sense that working-class women (and similarly "native" South American women) have different kinds of bodies than "daughters of gentlemen" such as Woolf herself haunts this novel. From the beginning, when the Ambroses are larger than the masses they walk among, to the end, when Rachel feels trapped in a tunnel with little, deformed women, Woolf betrays her fears that the others she wishes to liberate politically are so different from her that they appear nonhuman, masses of brown ants overrunning her elegant body.

Rachel's illness may symbolize her body's changing so that it no longer fits in the world of bourgeois England. Such a view would explain the odd role of the two doctors at the end of the novel. At first, a Dr. Rodriguez treats Rachel and can find nothing much wrong with her. Eventually, he is replaced by an English doctor who reveals that she is dying and that it is too late to do much. The comparison of the doctors seems a bit of Anglocentrism in the novel: the Latino doctor is incompetent. But if we regard Rachel's mysterious illness as a change in her body that allows her to experience, as Woolf could not, the emotions that comprise the unconscious of those others who reside beneath the English empire, of the South Americans, then the action of the Latin American doctor in effect helps her in her transition, a transition that is tantamount to dying to the English world. The British doctor and the British colonists are horrified by such a possibility, and so, perhaps, was Woolf herself—changing into the small, brown body of the others around them would be racial degeneration, becoming an ant. But this book anxiously revolves around the possibility that it may be necessary to undergo something like a racial transformation if one is going to live in the coming world: Woolf may have to alter her body to write the lives of those who are going to replace the upper-class English. The mystification on which this book ends expresses Woolf's sense that she is torn between preserving her individuality—gaining a room of her own—and trying to speak for the masses. Liberating the masses may involve tearing the tongue out of her own mouth and giving it to them—or transforming herself into a different species in the human zoo. On the other hand, trying to preserve herself as she is may implicate her in the war being waged against the masses overrunning the West End of London and the whole British Empire.

The issues raised in this novel can have no satisfying ending: Woolf's prose and her main character simply dissolve and disappear. Early modernist works are full of such dissolutions: Prufrock drowns in a sea of human voices; Stephen Dedalus flies over the sea on Icarus's wings, and we expect him to fall; Lord Jim allows the leaders of Patusan to kill him. The sovereign self disappears, and we are left with no boundaries between ourselves and a world of alien masses, an undifferentiated sea of humanity.

CHAPTER 4

"The Mob Part of the Mind"

Sexuality and Immigrant Politics
in the Early Poems of T. S. Eliot

T o the British in the early twentieth century, the upwelling of a mass unconscious, a mass mind, appeared in several different guises: the "natives" throwing off colonial status, the workers rising into the largest domestic political party, and the women demonstrating for votes all seemed to threaten to swamp the old order. The anxieties I traced in *The Voyage Out*, that the only way out of women's oppression was through the elimination of class and national boundaries, were one product of this perception. In the United States there were similar concerns, but they were expressed in different terms because of yet a fourth kind of alien mass: immigrants. As a million immigrants entered the United States each year in the 1910's, "Americanization" became a central answer to the threat of the masses, and both workers and women adopted anti-immigrant positions as part of their own efforts to gain power. American women gained the vote within a year of British women, but in America that expansion of the vote was offset by a series of laws aimed at reducing the influx of new voters, first by taking the vote away from new immigrants and then by drastically reducing the number of immigrants. In America, the transformation into mass politics carried with it a rhetoric of "assimilation" and "purification"—the masses would be made like "us," and to do so would involve certain exclusions, not merely expansions. The contrast between English and American reactions to the threat of mass politics can be symbolized by the contrasting reactions to socialism after World War I. The Labour Party in England adopted a socialist charter in 1918, and that same year a Reform Bill greatly increased the number of working-class voters.

Rising socialist fervor in the United States led to the Red Scare of 1919 and to the deportation of hundreds of "alien subversives"; labor unions adopted stridently anti-immigrant rhetoric.

The contrast between the forms that mass politics took in America and in England is important in understanding T. S. Eliot's decision to resettle. The role of immigrant politics in Eliot's social projects and in his decision to move to England has been little noted because his preference has seemed explainable in terms of his later public stances in favor of monarchy and Catholicism. In retrospect, it has seemed clear that the United States was distasteful to Eliot as a Protestant, liberal, antimonarchical polity. Yet when he wrote directly on the topic of what was wrong with America, decades after settling in England, he did not focus on the country's founding acts of overthrowing monarchy and separating church and state. Instead, he focused on late-nineteenth-century events that climaxed in a dangerous tide of immigrants. According to *Notes Towards a Definition of Culture*, the events that truly separated American culture from English,

> the real revolution . . . was not what is called the Revolution in history books, but is a consequence of the Civil War; after which arose a plutocratic elite; after which the expansion and material development of the country was accelerated; after which was swollen that stream of mixed immigration, bringing (or rather multiplying) the danger of development into a *caste* system which has not yet been quite dispelled.[1]

Eliot added in a footnote, "I believe the essential difference between a caste and a class system is that the basis of the former is a difference such that the dominant class comes to consider itself a superior *race*." Eliot's comments, though published in 1948, reflect attitudes that were prevalent in America at the turn of the century.[2]

Eliot provided what was a common description of the antebellum era as the period when America lost its cultural authority, blaming the "plutocratic elite" such as J. P. Morgan and Andrew Carnegie for turning the nation from cultural to material goals. By dating the demise of America from the end of the Civil War, Eliot also suggested that the dangers of racial mixture resulted from the North's victory. Eliot viewed the South as remaining closer to American roots; he said in a speech given in Virginia, "The chances for the re-establishment of a native culture are perhaps better here than in New England. You are farther away from New York; you have been less industrialized and less invaded by foreign races; and you have a more opulent soil."[3] Eliot's use of the term "native culture" to describe what was in America before the era of industrialization was clearly borrowed from the nativist anti-immigration movement of the early twentieth century.[4] Eliot's view of the South as "less invaded by foreign races" suggests that he shared the nativist fear that the new immigration from southern and eastern Europe after the Civil War posed a far greater threat to "native culture" than the racial mixture in the South.

The center of nativist concern was the belief that the new "stream" of "foreign races" could swell forever and swamp the country. Henry Cabot Lodge in 1891 feared that "the immigration of those races which thus far built up the United States, and which are related to each other either by blood or language or both, was declining, while the immigration of races totally alien to them was increasing."[5] He concluded it was "madness to permit this stream to pour in without discrimination or selection." When Eliot came to Boston, he was exposed to such attitudes from family friends such as the Lodges and from his intellectual mentors. As Eric Sigg has written, "The suspicion and even hostility that Santayana, Adams, James and Eliot display toward urban immigrants is only one of a cluster of Mugwump responses typical of the educated Yankee classes."[6]

Eliot's fear of a swelling tide of mixed immigration also derived from his sense that when he searched for common American culture in immigrant neighborhoods, he found himself facing an alien world. In Boston, the wanderings in poor areas that produced poems such as "Preludes" and the beginning of "Prufrock" were basically trips through such neighborhoods. The "Preludes," for example, were written about his visits to North Cambridge and Roxbury, Italian and Jewish communities. Eliot did not believe that a "melting pot" could eventually blend disparate cultures together. To have a culture at all, he wrote in his 1932 Virginia lectures, "the population should be homogeneous; where two or more cultures exist in the same place they are likely either to be fiercely self-conscious or both to become adulterate." And no one could plan out a new culture to include several old ones, because culture is "the unconscious background of all planning . . . it is of the blood, as it were, rather than of the brain."[7] The problem with "mixed immigration" was its alteration of the "blood": the "swollen stream" would adulterate and dilute the biological fluid that is the basis of culture. Eliot left America because he concluded that the mixture of masses made it impossible to have a unified mass mind—a culture—in the pluralist United States. He traveled to England to find that mass mind.

Eliot's attribution of cultural adulteration and racial mixture to the policies of "a plutocratic elite" shows why Eliot felt less concern about the racial structure of the South than of the North. The system in the South seemed to Eliot to pose less danger of invasion and of mixture of races than the system in the North because of a difference in leadership, in the elites present in the two halves of the United States. Southern leaders agreed with Eliot on the importance of maintaining unity of race in the government and succeeded in "restoring" single-race government in the years from 1865 to 1900, eradicating African-American voting in the South through legal restrictions and intimidation. Northern leaders, in contrast, seemed, to critics such as Eliot, willing to allow mixtures at all levels and in all institutions. To him, they were plutocrats because they relied on economics to legitimate their leadership rather than on culture, understood as the bond of common blood.

T. Jackson Lears has shown that many Americans, like Eliot, reacted to the sense of a lack of cultural authority by turning to Catholicism, medievalism, and an emphasis on art as a saving discipline.[8] What made Eliot's position distinctive, and what drove him to the fragmented forms of modernism and to an aesthetic of extinguishing one's own personality, was his lifelong fear that he was himself a product of mixed immigration, that he had "mixed blood" in him and could not then be a cultural producer, an artist. His family had immigrated from England to New England and then to Missouri; he reversed those movements in his own life, but rather than unmixing his identity, his moves, he feared, left him even more mixed. He described this fear in a 1928 letter to Herbert Read:

> Someday I want to write an essay about the point of view of an American who wasn't an American, because he was born in the South and went to school in New England as a small boy with a nigger drawl, but who wasn't a southerner in the South because his people were northerners in a border state and looked down on all southerners and Virginians, and so was never anything anywhere.[9]

This Faulknerian sentence ends up creating a vision of the young artist as a white boy with a "nigger drawl." In America, Eliot felt that his own voice, out of which he sought to produce his poetry, was racially other to the traditions he wanted to speak. He needed to perform on himself the same operation that the South performed in the antebellum years: to silence the "nigger drawl" and restore a purely white voice to those who speak for "the culture."

The parallels between what Eliot said about himself and about the antebellum period suggest a parallel between the individual body and the social body: if culture dissociates into biologically disparate castes, the individual will find himself dissociated as well. Eliot's lifelong project to "regrow culture from old roots" can be understood as a project to restore his own bodily wholeness. He needed to reject America to find his own identity because he viewed America as having no identity: America had lost its blood, its traditions, its history, its very shape, at the end of the nineteenth century. Eliot, as a young man, felt infected by the shapelessness of America: he felt amorphous, "never anything anywhere." The mixed immigration that had swept over America had destroyed individual identity for people like Eliot.

Many writers saw the swelling immigrant tide as a call to battle but felt that there was no way for the "cultured few" to oppose the inhuman masses. As a letter in the *Nation* in 1903 put it,

> we shall be swamped by a gang of Poles, Hungarians and yawps that can't speak English, don't understand our system of government, and vote just as they are told by their boss. If the election were to be determined by the intelligent portion of the community, we would be there with both feet, but we don't care to waste our time in bucking against a lot of cattle whose vote is just as good as ours.[10]

The sense that the herd was about to overrun or swamp the "intelligent portion of the community" implies that there is a proper relationship between the herd and "intelligent" portions of society: the intelligent should speak while the herd defers. When this arrangement breaks down, chaos and rule by bosses—a caste system—takes over.

Eliot saw the problems created by immigration repeated in the intellectual realm. He criticized his Harvard mentor, Irving Babbitt, for having, in effect, allowed mixed immigration into the intellectual world of America. Babbitt proposed a curriculum of great works from all different cultures. Eliot wrote in response: "The great men whom he holds up for our admiration and example are torn from their contexts of race, place and time. And in consequence, Mr. Babbitt seems to tear himself from his own context."[11] Babbitt's pedagogy created just what Eliot feared, people who are "never anything anywhere." Eliot ultimately rejected Babbitt because he saw a strong connection not only between Babbitt's humanism and the mob going out of control, but between Babbitt's liberal individualism and the fear and bewilderment of elite intellectuals like Eliot himself. As we have seen, he declared that "all humanists—as humanists—have been individualists. As humanists, they have had nothing to offer the mob." But from Eliot's point of view, Babbitt's apostasy as a leader of the elite was worse than his failure as a leader able to control the masses. It was for this reason that he added, "they have usually left a place, not only for the mob, but . . . for the mob part of the mind in themselves."[12] The humanist ideal of creating individuals who can transcend their culture leads not just to mobs in the streets, but to a mob inside each individual, a horde of impulses released from any control by the cultured part of the psyche.

By equating the mob and the mob part of the mind, Eliot posited the need for a quite different kind of intellectual, one who did have something to offer the mob, something different than "the mob part of the mind" but also different than the dead end of liberal humanism. Such an intellectual could cure the rioting in the streets and, to that end, become a genuine leader, at the head of an intellectual elite in touch with the impulses represented by the emerging masses. Eliot's later emphasis on culture as the crucial basis of poetry and on the poet's need to extinguish his own personality derived from Eliot's desire to discover "something to offer" to the mob and to the mob part of his own mind.

That "something" is very close to what Freud called the "super-I" or I-ideal" and what we call the "super-ego." As we've seen, the development of Freud's ideas about the structure of the unconscious mind dovetail with other contemporary attempts to theorize the mentality of the mass and the mob and even with contemporary political rhetoric about it. Eliot's tripartite configuration, unruly "mob part" of the mind/humanist individualism/ "something" more, uncannily repeats the structure of id/ego/super-ego that Freud theorized. Freud says that joining in a group with an ego-ideal allows a return to primal feelings of unlimitedness, an "exaltation or intensification of emotion," especially feelings of love or, in Freudian terms, libido.[13] The super-ego satisfies the chaotic desires of the id, of the mob part of the mind. The individual and the social order are held together by sexual satisfaction. A society of mixed cultures, mixed bloods, must replace the passion that unites with sheer relations of power—a caste system—leaving everyone dissatisfied. Eliot, feeling himself dissatisfied with the prevailing caste system in just these terms, as a Yankee Brahmin in the South and a Southerner "with a nigger drawl" in the North, as "never anything any-where," devoted his life to searching for the ego-ideal, the super-human, as a way of finding satisfaction that, as Freud claimed, cannot be supplied by the ego, with its Eliotic feelings of inadequacy. The problem Eliot found in "mixed immigration" was the loss of the passion that holds a nation together and that provides the basis for sexuality.

The importance of a super-ego to produce national passion translated in early-twentieth-century theories into the need for powerful male leader-ship. Freud argued that "the super-ego of an epoch of civilization has an origin similar to that of an individual. It is based on the impression left behind by the personalities of great leaders—men of overwhelming force of mind."[14] The members of a culture so identify with the super-ego figure that they would never think of disobeying: they then feel free of constraints and able to love the leader with much of the joy of primary narcissism. One line in *The Waste Land* suggests the emotional complex generated by such a leader: "your heart would have responded / Gaily . . . beating obedient to controlling hands" (pp. 49–50). The equation of heartfelt delight and con-trolling hands, of pleasure and obedience, is the essence of the relationship of id to super-ego, of mob to idealized leader, of human to God. Freud was terrified of such an emotional complex, regarding it as part of the return to the primitive horde, but he recognized that the alternative was the repres-sion of passion in "civilized" social order, where the ego, the rational part of the psyche, dominates. Eliot regarded the rational, individualist social order as equivalent to a living death: in it, the absence of controlling hands, of some kind of superhuman image to which the individual can submit, leaves humans incapable of any real passion. The equation of liberalism, cultural deadness, and sexual sterility was both a reflection of Eliot's own psychol-ogy and a conservative version of the Freudian view of civilization, that modern rationality represses passion and leaves everyone discontented.

Eliot and turn-of-the-century writers connected together theories of sexuality, the failure of masculine leadership, and the horrors of immigra-tion. Eliot's "plutocratic elite" and humanists failed as men and as sexual figures in offering nothing to the mob: they were seen as impotent as cul-tural leaders; their economic and intellectual systems were condemned as passionless. The caste system they developed was judged to be horrible be-cause it silenced the mob instead of offering a form of love, the passion of surrender to a superhuman authority, an authority that Eliot found in Catholicism and monarchy.

Restoring masculinity to cultural leaders was frequently proposed as a solution to the problems posed by the the immigrant mobs. Many intellectuals promoted a cult of militarism in order to, as Lears puts it, "toughen a flabby bourgeoisie against the threat of anarchists, immigrants, strikes, tramps, and criminals."[15] The historian Frances Parkman, in an article entitled "The Failure of Universal Suffrage," argued that "Demos" had become a "beast" and that the "muddy tide" of immigration threatened to swamp American culture and government because of a disturbance inside upperclass males: the "hordes of native and foreign barbarians, all armed with the ballot, have so bewildered him [the well-educated man] that he begins to lose his wits and forget his kingcraft."[16] Parkman argued that "culture" needed to fight against the "morbid leveling of the times" and against the worship of "vulgar wealth"—against a plutocratic elite. He concluded with a call for a change in education:

> What we need most is a broad and masculine education, bearing on questions of society and government; not repelling from active life, but preparing for it and impelling toward it. . . . The low politician is not a noble foe, but he is strong and dangerous enough to make it manly to fight him. . . . The "literary feller" may yet make himself a practical force, and, in presence of the public opinion which he has evoked, the scurvy crew who delight to gibe at him may be compelled to disguise themselves in garments of unwonted decency.[17]

The upper-class intellectual has become emasculated, feminized, by the jeering masses and those who use them as a means to ascendancy; to restore him to potency, political and cultural, elite education has to become more "broad and masculine."

Irving Babbitt also argued for his great works curriculum as a way of restoring masculinity to culture. He railed against the industrialists for their materialism, which left culture as a purely "female" pursuit: "the great industrialist . . . bows down before his wife's superiority because she gets up at noon and plays a little Schumann on the piano. Men are . . . absorbed in utilitarian pursuits . . . and inclined to turn over to women the cultural values which have been a chief concern of the great civilizations of the past."[18]

Eliot shared Babbitt's and Parkman's views of the feminization of education and of culture. He wrote Pound in 1905 that all anyone learns in American universities is "how to appreciate the Hundred Best Paintings, the Maiden Aunt and the Social Worker. Something might be said (at another time) about the Evil Influence of Virginity on American Civilization. It might be pointed out again and again that literature has rights of its own which extend beyond Uplift and Recreation. Of course it is imprudent to sneer at the monopolisation of literature by women."[19] Eliot translates the female monopoly of culture into the "Evil Influence of Virginity": the loss of masculinity is the loss of sexuality entirely, the loss of passion.

Eliot's inclusion of social work in his criticism of women's monopolization of culture is a reference to his mother, Charlotte Stamps Eliot, who was quite active in the Humanity Society in St. Louis, a club devoted both to culture and to social work. She based her good works on the tenets of liberal Protestantism: her father was John Greenleaf Whittier, scion of the Unitarian Church, and she wrote a hagiography of his life. Peter Ackroyd describes her as "a Fabian of American life."[20] She advocated what Eliot and Parkman feared: the feminization of both cultural and political power. She argued that women's organizations such as the Humanity Society could become genuine agencies of political reform. In a poem, she wrote,

> Thus organized, what may not women do?
> What *will* not do, if only they be true
> To high ideals and if they unite
> With Noble purpose to achieve the right?

> Though culture may be our corner stone
> We cannot exist for culture alone
> In scholarly retreat.
>
> . . .
>
> For lo! grave problems press.
> The pleadings of distress
> Will follow the mind's sublimest flight.
> A voice from the depths disturb the height,
> When wrongs demand redress.[21]

In this poem, "culture" has provided women with the "corner stone" on which to construct an organization powerful enough to "disturb the height." Women can thus become the political representatives of the "depths," the "mob," and successfully challenge the ruling elite of upper-class men. T. S. Eliot devoted his life to resisting the methodology for social change advocated here. When the depths of society organize in order to disturb the heights, the class structure breaks down so that upper and lower become competing castes. His mother's poem is a recipe for cultural disintegration as Eliot defined it: "when two or more strata so separate that these become in effect distinct cultures."[22] Women and the depths alike must remain strata, layers arranged hierarchically under upper-class males, not separate, distinct, and disturbing organizations or cultures.

I have been seeking to weave together several strands in Eliot's social theories and in his personal life to reveal a pattern in which we can place Eliot's early poems. In Eliot's way of viewing the world, the raging tide of sexual impulses in his psyche, the swollen stream of mixed immigration, the conquest of culture by women, and the cowardice and impotence of upper-class male intellectuals were all connected: all were taken to be causes or effects of dissociation, of the separation of upper and lower into competing entities. Eliot's early poems are full of the fear of this dissociation, in America and in the psyche of the individual American male.

This dissociation is repeatedly attributed to two mobs: poor men (often located in immigrant neighborhoods) and upper-class women, the "lonely men in shirt sleeves" and the "women [who] come and go," the two groups that J. Alfred Prufrock visits in his attempt to write a love song (pp. 4–5). Since "Prufrock" has never been regarded as a poem having much to do with immigration or with politics, I will seek to make my interpretation of that poem clear by first examining poems that more obviously address such issues.

The threat of women's power in Eliot's early poems has drawn frequent comment.[23] As Carol Christ has shown, there is a common pattern of male voices "decomposing" in the presence of competing female voices.[24] Only equally threatening and ungentle males such as Sweeney with his razor can escape being terrified of the "oval O cropped out with teeth" or of women such as Clytemnestra with knives (pp. 25, 36). Women "are suspect, thought to be in league," perhaps united with the animal powers in a conspiracy to overthrow the cultural super-ego: in "Sweeney Among the Nightingales," the icon of masculine power, Agamemnon, lies dead, killed not merely by Clytemnestra but by a whole mob of nightingales, who drop "liquid siftings" on the shrouded corpse, an image of the triumph of the disgusting over the noble, of female over male, and of the amorphous liquid mass over the leader's body (pp. 35–36). The mob is out of control, silencing the male authority—and the male author.

The failure of male authority is not only a cultural disaster, it is also perverse. The contest between leader and mob is fraught with sexual tension. When Eliot visited in poor neighborhoods, it was in part to feel this sexual charge. Critics have commented on the sexuality that pervades his poems about such visits. Albert Gelpi suggests that the surroundings of urban squalor mirrored the "psychological world of the Eliot persona," particularly ambivalent masculinity.[25] Eliot portrays himself as in effect having to go through the lower classes to reach his own sexuality because he is so disconnected from it and so disgusted by it. This is especially clear in some unpublished poems, which present raw versions of his adolescent emotions.[26] In one, entitled "A Debate of Body and Soul," he views a poor man stirring leaves in the gutter as an image of "imagination's masturbations" and "imaginations's defecations." In a passage left out of "Prufrock," J. Alfred equates his "madness" with "a blind old drunken man who sings and mutters." As the drunk sings, the "world begins to fall apart."

In both these unpublished passages, Eliot created images of finding in urban squalor a way to recapture certain parts of his own imagination— the mob parts of his mind—that he had rejected and treated as excrement, as madness. The discovery of alienated parts of his psyche also served to develop his art: he found a form of aesthetic pleasure in poor areas that was unavailable in the cultured world. In "Second Caprice in North Cambridge," he writes that in a dirty, vacant lot he feels himself "far from our definitions / And our aesthetic laws," and yet he experiences a sense of "unexpected charm" and even "repose." Eliot strove to develop an art that would combine the slums and the elite in order to become the "literary feller" that Parkman dreamed of as able to tame the beast of democracy.

Eliot was not the only male modernist who sought in the lower classes forms of sexuality and of aesthetic pleasure unavailable in the upper or middle classes. Stephen Dedalus's search for "epiphanies" mixes together wandering into poor neighborhoods, masturbating, excreting, visiting prostitutes, and writing poetry, all presented as ways to escape from repressive and aesthetically ugly middle-class life. Many writers contrasted the weak, sexless bodies of the upper classes with lower-class potency. Pound's poem "The Garden" describes an elegant woman as so bodiless that she is "like a skein of loose silk" in her garden, but "round about there is a rabble / Of the filthy, sturdy, unkillable infants of the very poor."[27] The woman is bored and wishes the poet would speak to her, but is "almost afraid that I will commit that indiscretion." Here, the upper classes, afraid of passion, have let their bodies wither, while the very poor are breeding with such potency that their infants are born unkillable.

Pound's poem echoes eugenic arguments that were common at the turn of the century about the degeneration of humankind due to the much higher birth rates of the poor and of "lower races." Even without such "scientific" evidence, many writers felt an urgent need to restore a lost sexuality to the upper classes. Yeats's complaint in "The Second Coming" that the "best lack all conviction, while the worst / Are full of passionate intensity" carries, among its many meanings, the notion that the cultured few will be overwhelmed by the greater passion of the lower classes.[28] He eventually proposed measures to limit the fertility of the poor.[29] Stephen Dedalus postulates an artistic intervention in the sexual lives of the Irish as a way of stopping the degeneration of the race: he hopes to "cast his shadow over the imaginations" of Irish women "before their squires begat upon them, that they might breed a race less ignoble."[30] Stephen hopes that his mental insemination of Irish women will raise the quality of the stock. He thinks of this act while brooding on the fact that he has been unable to bring himself to speak to the girl of his class he really wants and has turned to prostitutes instead. R. B. Kershner has shown how Stephen's language draws on the eugenic theories of the day, which treated genius as a byproduct of the forces producing degeneration in the masses. Genetic alternations in the racial psyche lead to the subhuman and the superhuman: in other words, the mob part of the mind is the source both of riots and of artists.[31]

There thus seemed a general sense in the early twentieth century that the mob had access to something that artists needed, something the upper classes had lost—the basic motive force of sexual instincts. If the cultured few were going to be artists, leaders, or simply potent men, they would have to descend into what appeared to them as squalor. Yeats suggests such a conclusion in "Crazy Jane Talks with the Bishop," a debate between lower-class and upper-class voices about where to find love. Crazy Jane says "Love has pitched his mansion in / The place of excrement."[32] The place of excrement is a bodily location, but by having Crazy Jane, a poor woman, make this speech to a bishop who is advocating keeping love in a "high" region, separate from squalor, Yeats parallels anatomy and social geography: sexuality is located in the lower regions, and those of the highest status—even bishops—must descend to participate in love. D. H. Lawrence's *Lady Chatterley's Lover* is filled with social theories that purport to prove that the modern industrial system has destroyed the potency of upper-class men but not lower-class men.

All these male modernists thus speak of seeking a lost part of their own psyches among the lower classes. To find such a part of the mind would restore the dissociated sexual and social body. But what Eliot found in the poor neighborhoods he visited was not his lost sexuality; rather, it was a sexuality dispersed across masses, a sexuality that could not be made part of one body, as we can see in "Preludes," a poem collecting short pieces Eliot wrote about Jewish and Italian slums of Boston. The poem begins with two stanzas presenting visions of mass existence filling up minds:

> The morning comes to consciousness
>
> . . .
>
> From the sawdust-trampled street
> With all its muddy feet that press
>
> . . .
>
> One thinks of all the hands
> That are raising shades
> In a thousand dingy rooms.
>
> (p. 12)[33]

The poem shifts to a third stanza about "you," which would seem a move away from the mass scene to a private world, but "you" turns out to be simply the embodiment of the mass scene: the "thousand dingy rooms" turn into a "thousand sordid images / Of which your soul was constituted," the "muddy feet" and "hands" turn into "yellow soles of feet" and "soiled hands." Punning on "soul," "soles," and "soiled," Eliot suggests that there is little difference between the material and the spiritual parts of this person: everything in "you" is constituted by the dirt of slum life.

The poem switches again in the fourth stanza to an image of what is necessary to clean up the masses of dirty feet, hands, and images in this neighborhood: a heavenly male, "His soul stretched tight across the skies . . . The conscience of a blackened street" (p. 13). But "His soul" may not be able to remain in the sky above the crowd: via the ambiguous conjunction "or," the poem raises the possibility that "His soul" may instead be "trampled by insistent feet . . . And short square fingers stuff-

ing pipes" (p. 13). The insistent feet recall the "feet" in the earlier stanzas
and suggest that the ugliness of the urban world is due to the trampling of
the "soul," the conscience, the spiritual, by the quite material "soles" and
"short square fingers" that identify a distinctly immigrant mob. If the moving feet trample "His soul," then there will be no conscience to restrain the
"blackened street" in its "impatien[ce] to assume the world": everything
in America will be blackened, soiled, trampled, by the materialism of the
masses. The impatience to assume the world could represent either capitalist greed (the masses imitating the plutocratic leadership) or socialist
rebellion, the mob rising up to overthrow the plutocracy.

The speaker tries to revive a faint image of something that could move
people in a different way:

> I am moved by fancies that are curled
> Around these images, and cling:
> The notion of some infinitely gentle
> Infinitely suffering thing.
>
> (p. 13)

The speaker seeks a "notion" that is not quite an "image" of the infinite,
the superhuman, to place above the masses. But this notion cannot be of a
god, a super-ego, because the poem has already shown that a heavenly male
soul would not be able to transcend the trampling feet. So "I" can conceive
of the infinite only as a genderless "thing," hardly the stuff to inspire passion. Whatever this ambiguous "thing" is, it is immediately dismissed as
little more than a bad joke because the cosmos is distinctly feminine and
clearly associated with the forces represented by the lower classes:

> Wipe your hand across your mouth, and laugh;
> The worlds revolve like ancient women
> Gathering fuel in vacant lots.
>
> (p. 13)

These final lines are thoroughly ambiguous. Are they just an image
of hopelessness—worlds revolve with no real purpose? Or is the gathering of fuel a hopeful sign—something will be kept burning, perhaps some
passion? Or is there a hint of revolution in the revolving worlds, perhaps
fueled by the impatience of "ancient women," females from the "old world"
who threaten to burn the New World? Are these ancient women carriers of
the culture lost in industrial America, or are they immigrants whose fires
produce only soot that blackens the street?

All these interpretations of the ancient women redounded on Eliot himself. As he tried to gather poetic material in immigrant slums, he was himself like these women gathering fuel, and uncertain whether his efforts were
hopeless, mundane, or revolutionary. The ambiguity of the ancient women
mirrors the ambiguity throughout the poem created by the uncertain ref-

erences of "you" and "I." Eliot was unsure whether he was meeting in the ghetto part of himself or the other, whether he was masculine, feminine, or a "thing."

"Preludes" reveals Eliot's uncertain identity in 1909 and his uncertain evaluation of the social structure of America. By 1916, he became convinced that America was a nightmare he must escape and left for England. The poems he wrote at this time, collected in *Poems* (1920), contain some of his most horrifying and disturbing images: going far beyond the dirt and hints of perversity of "Preludes," he created worlds of half-human creatures, improper mixtures that are coded in the poems as both racial and sexual. Sweeney's neck seems more ape than human, his jaw spotted like a giraffe; Rachel's hands are "murderous paws"; Bleistein is "protozoic slime" (pp. 35, 24). The horror in these poems is connected quite strongly to the new immigration of Jews, Irish, and "dark" races from the southern parts of the world. Immigrant Jews include Rachel, who has changed her name from "Rabinovich," Bleistein, who is "Chicago Semite Viennese," the "owner" in "Gerontion," who has moved from Antwerp to Brussels to London, and Sir Ferdinand Klein, whose mixture of aristocrat and Jew is made more jarring by a stanza break that makes "Klein" follow "Sir Ferdinand" with a vengeance (p. 24). Sweeney is of course Irish but seems also to have some blood from African animals (ape and giraffe). Even the stars in "Sweeney Among the Nightingales" are from the Southern Hemisphere, "Death and the Raven" replacing "Orion and the Dog" (p. 35). The change of constellations marks the inversions of hierarchies in these poems: Orion and the Dog represent the ideal relation of god and animal, the animal serving the god, while Death and the Raven suggest only a dark, horrifying partnership between superhuman and subhuman. Sweeney guards Cape Horn, a gate in the traffic between the colonies and England, but he inverts the proper line of movement: the colonies have brought their blood and their heavens into the English Isles.

Eliot said he was simply trying to create a mood of unspecified horror in the Sweeney poems, not referring to anything in particular. But in "Sweeney Erect," Eliot digresses to suggest that the scene of horror he describes reveals something about how we ought to understand history:

> (The lengthened shadow of a man
> Is history, said Emerson
> Who had not seen the silhouette
> Of Sweeney straddled in the sun.)
> (p. 26)

We could interpret this parenthetical stanza to mean simply that Sweeney is not the kind of man who makes history; he is a minor figure in the world. But the sentence structure makes it seem rather that Sweeney's silhouette contradicts Emerson's dictum, as if history is not the impress of men on the

world, but something else. The opening of the poem, with its commands
to arrange the scene and place a god, Aeolus, "reviewing" it, suggests that
something else besides the characters is making history, some larger, ma-
levolent force. Similarly, in "Sweeney Among the Nightingales," the whole
atmosphere of ambiguous danger and the reduction of everyone to animals
imply that there are no men at all, but rather subhuman and superhuman
forces moving everything about. The sense that superhuman and subhuman
forces compete for domination was the essence of Eliot's fear of the caste
system. In these poems, history has been ruined because the superhuman
has lost the power to inspire the love of the subhuman: the cultural super-
ego has been reduced to one man among many. Instead of cultural heroes,
we have Sweeneys, men who gain power in a world of conspiracies and
razors and deceit—perhaps an Irish ward boss such as Eliot saw in Boston.

"Gerontion," too, presents history as distorted and distorting, full of
"cunning passages" and "supple confusions" (p. 22). In this poem we can
also see that what has twisted history are mixed races, plutocratic elites,
and an absence of "blood" and passion. The speaker is old, dried out, and
trapped inside his brain, unable to connect to tradition, which is "of the
blood, not of the brain." He cannot make contact with the blood that would
connect him to other people, the blood that would turn history into a tradition, a source of belief and of passion. The opening few lines associate
his dryness and even the lack of rain with his failure to be moved by hot
blood: he has not "fought in the warm rain / Nor knee deep in the salt
marsh" (p. 21). Having been unwilling to bloody himself, he has lost the ties
that blood provides. The blood and body of the past that would unite the
masses has instead been "divided" among Mr. Silvero, Hakagawa, Madame
de Tornquist, and Fräulein von Kulp (p. 22).

The world of the poem is invaded by foreign races, allowed in by "the
owner," a Jew of inhuman birth who does not identify with any country
("spawned in some estaminet of Antwerp, / Blistered in Brussels, patched
and peeled in London"; p. 21). All passion is, as the poem says, "adulterated"
(p. 23), full of impurities: the ties of blood that held the social body together
are lost—"I that was near your heart was removed therefrom"—and everyone ends up merely "fractured atoms" whirled about by dry winds (p. 23).
Instead of real passions, this society is full of false excitements provided
for profit, with the result that no one knows even what he or she really
wants. The artificial sources of excitement, like too many "pungent sauces"
put together, "multiply variety / In a wilderness of mirrors," so that people
do not recognize themselves (p. 23). They cannot identify themselves because they cannot identify with each other. Instead of being driven by the
blood that produces identity, this world is "driven by the Trades," winds
whose very name implies they are the medium of business, of the constant exchange that destroys identity (p. 23). At the end of the poem, the
speaker thinks of resisting, like a "gull against the wind," but concludes

that such gulls only end up "white feathers in the snow," an image of his own cowardice: he earned the white feather given to men who did not fight in World War I, and he will not fight the trades now. He suffers from weakened masculinity and from racial mixture, like so many others in Eliot's early poems.

The loss of history in "Gerontion" and in "Sweeney Erect" is the loss of men who can cast their shadows over history, the loss of men of good blood. Blood has degenerated; humans have devolved to the apelike Sweeney and even to "protozoic slime" such as Bleistein, who is "underneath the lot," even lower than "the rats." This lowest of the low is a Jew because Jews were the symbol of a cultureless people in their acceptance of Diaspora: they are the essence of "heterogeneity," of adulteration. Eliot argues in *After Strange Gods* that to keep a tradition from becoming "adulterate," "reasons of race and religion combine to make any large number of free-thinking Jews undesirable . . . and a spirit of excessive tolerance is to be deprecated."[34]

But in uncanny ways, Eliot identifies himself with the Jews in his poems. At the end of "Gerontion," the speaker calls his thoughts the "Tenants of the house," identifying himself as an absentee landlord just like the Jew, his own head not a house of "culture," but only a useless building that can contain anything. When Eliot wrote the volume published as *Poems*, he was himself an immigrant, working at the most stereotypic Jewish job: negotiating international loans for a English bank. Eliot became the essential plutocrat, the cosmopolitan financier, providing the kind of international funding that the Jew brings to the house that the speaker lives in. Eliot was at the center of what he viewed as the worst kind of economic system, one that destroyed all national or cultural integrity by passing money across borders, adulterating all ownership. Eliot's loans gave economic substance without spiritual substance: the corridors of the banks he inhabited, like the memories in the speaker's head, have "no ghosts," only streams of rootless money, like the streams of thoughts whirled about in a mind with no tradition. Eliot's most intensely racist poems and essays were in this sense outgrowths of his self-hatred.

Eliot also bears surprising similarities to the horrifying Jew in "Burbank with a Baedaker: Bleistein with a Cigar." If Burbank with his Baedaker is a prototypical Englishmen, Bleistein, with his Chicago roots and a Semite Vienna cultural mixture in his background, is a midwestern American of mixed heritage traveling around Europe—like Eliot. The similarity between Bleistein's and Eliot's backgrounds is rarely noted because Eliot sought to cover up his midwestern roots: he presented himself as a New Englander, effacing the immigration of his ancestors to St. Louis. In this effort to hide his past, Eliot was like the third Jew in these poems, "Rachel *née* Rabinovich." Eliot desperately wished to escape his "nigger drawl" and pass as a cultured Anglo-Saxon. Virginia Woolf mocked Eliot for his cover-up of his own past by naming a character based on Eliot in *The Waves*, "Louis," after St. Louis.[35] Woolf made the character a colonial in England, forever feeling inferior to others and trying to establish himself as an authority, but also forever feeling roots clutch that he would rather escape. This neatly inverts Eliot's common image of not having roots: instead, his loss of roots has to do with his rejection of his midwestern, middle-class, American childhood. Eliot would reply that his family was not rooted in St. Louis and that was why he felt he was "never anything anywhere." But it was precisely such a feeling that identified him with the immigrant Jews and led him toward modernist fragmentation: his intense animus against the other, the Jew, tore apart the self and the coherent voice of lyric poetry.

Now we can turn to "Prufrock," written between "Preludes" and the 1916 poems. We can place the fears of cowardice and sexual failure in this poem in the context of Eliot's concerns about the lack of a common blood to unite mob and intellectual in the United States. J. Alfred Prufrock is a prime example of a cultured Anglo-Saxon who has lost contact with his body, with his passion, and so cannot even begin to sing a love song to a woman. He needs to recover his id, the mob part of his mind, and so he goes to visit the slums, the mob. In the middle of the poem, Prufrock wonders if he should begin his love song by saying, "I have gone at dusk through narrow streets / And watched the smoke that rises from the pipes / Of lonely men in shirt-sleeves" (p. 5). These lines describe what would be a very strange beginning of a love song, and they also describe what is in fact the beginning of this poem, taking "us" into slums full of transients, people who stay in "one-night hotels." The beginning makes sense if we see Prufrock as seeking to break out of the "etherised" and ethereal upper-class world: he seeks to find his own lost desires, the mob part of his mind, among the lonely men in shirt sleeves.

There are hints in "Prufrock" that Eliot's difficulty in expressing his passions may have derived from repressed homoeroticism: he may have been drawn toward the lonely men. James E. Miller, Jr., has provided much evidence for such a theory, but argues it was not merely homosexual desires that Eliot could not accept: Eliot was a person "with deeply disabling inhibitions about sex, certain deeply ingrained revulsions and repressions," and so is J. Alfred Prufrock.[36] Prufrock is dissociated from his desires in all their polymorphous perversity; he is entrapped within his ego, the calculating part of the self that measures out his life, subjects every thought to infinite revisions, and can never act because it lacks impetus from the id. Unable to acknowledge his body, Prufrock grows thin and becomes prematurely old. Prufrock covers himself with a "rich and modest" tie to hide his body and his poor and immodest desires, which might be exposed if he took off that tie and could sit like the lonely men in shirt-sleeves (p. 4). He dreams of descending even lower than those poor men, of becoming "a pair of ragged claws at the bottom of the ocean," an image of aggressive, unconscious power living at the bottom of the world (p. 5). If he could become claws, he would be a part of the millions of lowly creatures in the sea; this is an image of entering the mob part of the mind and leaving the rich and modest self behind.

The sea in this poem thus carries, among many other possible meanings, a connotation of representing the mob and the mob part of the mind, which together comprise the social medium in which we float. To become part of the sea is to become part of the ragged world of urban squalor. Such a meaning for the sea could also be extended to the other image of a shapeless mass in "Prufrock," the fog. The fog certainly seems to represent urban squalor, since it pools around drains and lets "fall upon its back the soot that falls from chimneys" (p. 4). The ugliness of soot seems a complaint about industrialization, but the willingness of the fog to let the soot fall on its back resonates with comments made about immigrants: for example, the head of the Boston Anti-Immigrant League, Robert de Courcy Ward, wrote in 1910 that America was suffering from the "immigration of races which are able and content to live under wholly inferior conditions."[37] The poem itself suggests a connection between the fog and the poor men Prufrock has visited: he speaks of seeing the smoke from their pipes, and the fog is described at times as "smoke." The poem also connects the fog with the sea at the end of the poem through the repetition of the word "lingered." The fog "lingered upon the pools" just as "we," the Prufrocks of America, "have lingered in the chambers of the sea" (p. 7). But soon this lingering may be over, the fog may make another "sudden leap," to enter the house and turn the "room" into a foggy mass, and drown "us," in a "sea" of "human voices."

Threats of drowning in an anarchic sea of voices or of being engulfed in a dirty tide or fog permeated anti-immigrant literature at the time Eliot wrote "Prufrock." Senator Chauncey M. Depew called on Congress to "stop the reservoirs of European anarchy pouring into our country."[38] Frances Parkman described the new immigration as having changed from a fog to a sea: when the new immigration began in the 1850's, it was "a little cloud, no bigger than a man's hand," but then grew until a "muddy tide of ignorance rolled in upon us."[39] The fog in "Prufrock" seems to come out of the filthy "pools that stand in drains" in a reversal of the process of disposal of waste. Immigrants were frequently described as a stream of garbage being drained on American shores. General Frances Walker coined the term "Pipe Line Immigration," which was used in political cartoons, and in his explanation of the term he combined images of pools, drains, and tainted air: "So broad and smooth is the channel, there is no reason why every foul and stagnant pool of population in Europe, which no breath of intellectual or industrial life has stirred for ages, should not be decanted on our soil. . . . [We cannot go on] allowing its city slums and its vast stagnant reservoirs of degraded peasantry to be drained off on our soil."[40]

Though the fog and the sea in "Prufrock" may carry some hint of the fears of the alien mob swamping America, the poem also expresses a strange fondness for the fog and the sea: the fog is rather like a cat, and its leap might simply bring it into the lap of the people in the house, to be petted. Similarly, the sea is full of "sea-girls" and mermaids who promise a certain pleasurable relationship, if only they would speak to Prufrock. The problem is that Prufrock is the wrong person to deal with these new, mass creatures, as he is the wrong person to deal with the animal parts of the human psyche. What is needed is not this old man, but some new man.

Eliot, the twentysomething poet, clearly identified with the much older Prufrock, but the reason Eliot chose to project an older image of his "Prufrockian self" was that at least part of him hoped that this self would soon die. The mob is not simply threatening; it is necessary, providing the base, the blood, that could support and nourish the cultured brains that remain dry and windy without it. The ending of the poem could be read as enacting the merger of Prufrock and the mob: he becomes part of the sea, dying as an individual and perhaps assuming a new life as part of the collective. Other elements in the poem also suggest that Prufrock's problems have to do with his inability to deal with collectives: he cannot sing a love song to any one woman because he only meets "women" who "come and go," women who seem to exist not as single individuals at all but as a circulating collection of interchangeable bodies. The women in the poem, like the men in shirt sleeves, are collective entities, not individuals. The only people in this poem who are singular, who have names, are Michelangelo, Lazarus, Hamlet, and J. Alfred Prufrock, and Prufrock is the only one who is living in the twentieth century. Prufrock's singularity has much to do with why he eventually drowns in the sea of human voices. He cannot live in a plural or pluralistic world.

The ending is distinctly ambivalent: it is both a horrible death and an awakening. To try to be a Prufrock, a cultured gentleman, in America, was, Eliot concluded, to live in a dream: there was no culture possible in a nation of mixed races. Eliot awakened to the need to be surrounded by people who all share one culture. In pursuit of this goal, he moved to England, hoping there was enough common blood left to overcome the fragmentation within him. The ending of "Prufrock," a drowning, became a transition in the middle of The Waste Land—"Death by Water." In early drafts of The Waste Land, we can see quite clearly how that section began as a reworking of the ending of Prufrock: "Death by Water" was originally a long scene in which a ship is caught in a storm, during which

> the sea with many voices
> Moaned all about us.
>
>   .   .   .
>
>   no one dared
> To look into anothers face, or speak

> In the horror of the illimitable scream
> Of a whole world about us. One night
> On watch, I thought I saw in the fore cross-trees
> Three women leaning forward, with white hair
> Streaming behind, who sang above the wind
> A song that charmed my senses, while I was
> Frightened beyond fear, horrified past horror, calm,
> (Nothing was real) for, I thought, now, when
> I like, I can wake up and end the dream.[41]

The sea of voices, the singing women with white hair streaming behind them, the lack of daring, the inability to speak, and the act of waking up, all repeat the ending of "Prufrock," transformed into a scene of horror. In this draft, however, these lines do not mark an ending at all; immediately after, the draft goes on: "—Something which we knew must be a dawn— / A different darkness, flowed above the clouds." This drowning is a prelude to a new day, a new life, a new culture; it is a baptism.

In England, Eliot felt he could cease to be an American, an unstable product of mixed cultures, a person "never anything anywhere," and instead be reborn as part of a tradition. He could escape the nightmare of trying to speak against the howling voices of a sea of humanity because he could finally join the sea. To do so he had to give up the Prufrock persona, the very idea of being a single individual; in *The Waste Land* he let his own personality dissolve into the multiplicity of voices surrounding him, relying on the unconscious background buried beneath them to eventually bring his art together and restore his passion and his faith.

CHAPTER 5

A Portrait of the Artist
as a Young Fascist

Gabriele D'Annunzio's Political
Influence on James Joyce

In Ireland, the masses emerging into politics took the form of a nationalist movement seeking home rule. Mass movements did not appear, then, to pose the same threat that we have seen in English writer Woolf and the American writer Eliot. Most of the Irish writers who supported the nationalist movement at the end of the nineteenth century were not driven to modernist forms because the success of the masses did not involve the loss of home and individuality, but rather the release of both from domination by aliens, the British. The turn to modernism in Joyce and Yeats, in contrast, was foreshadowed by their early refusal to accept the dominant forms of nationalist literature. The modernism of these writers, particularly of Joyce, has seemed a result of their rejection of politics altogether. But if we look more closely, we can see that what they were rejecting was only one form of nationalism in favor of another. Yeats complained about the clear rhetoric of the Young Irish movement precisely because such rhetoric implied that the new nation could be understood in already familiar terms and hence would not be much of a change: the Young Irish in his view were middle-class revolutionaries who would merely make Ireland into another bourgeois state. Yeats did eventually join the nationalist movement, but only after the Easter 1916 massacre, when the movement no longer seemed to be seeking to preserve familiar worlds, but rather to be violently breaking through to something new through sacrifice of the self. It was at that same time that Yeats's writing turned toward modernist obscurity.

Joyce never joined any active political movement, so it is more difficult to equate his modernism with any political goals. Even when he wrote pamphlets as a young man, he focused on the need of the artist to resist all popular moments. In "The Day of the Rabblement," published in 1901, he begins by saying "no man . . . can be a lover of the true or the good unless he abhors the multitude." He goes on to condemn the Irish Literary Theatre for having pandered to the "trolls" and presents Ibsen as a model for playwrights to imitate and D'Annunzio as a model for novelists. It might seem that these writers provided a model of how to create an art free of all social influence, a purely aesthetic art: Joyce even says that D'Annunzio represented the culmination of the "tide" begun by Flaubert, "for two entire eras lie between *Madame Bovary* and *Il Fuoco.*"[1]

Dominic Manganiello has given one way of seeing political meaning in Joyce's resistance to the masses in this pamphlet, arguing quite forcefully that Joyce was an anarchist all his life.[2] It is not hard to see such views in Joyce's first novel: Stephen Dedalus's flight to escape the "nets" that hold individuals back seems a call for everyone to pursue such a similar freedom, "to kill the king and the priest" in our minds.[3] However, if we examine the novel by D'Annunzio that Joyce singled out for praise in the pamphlet, *Il Fuoco* (The flame) it is hard to see why Joyce would think of it as showing how to abhor the multitude at all. D'Annunzio tells the story of a young poet, Stelio Effrena, who decides to quit writing poetry and become an orator instead. The novel is partly autobiographical: D'Annunzio turned from writing to politics three years before he published this novel, entering the Italian parliament in 1897. He even put parts of his campaign speeches verbatim into Stelio's mouth.

Many critics have shown that Joyce was strongly influenced by D'Annunzio, but generally this influence has been seen as entirely focused on Joyce's imitation of aesthetic innovation.[4] But Joyce brings much more than D'Annunzio's aesthetics into *Portrait*: he also imitates D'Annunzio's presentation of how the artist can take a stance in the swirl of mass movements. Joyce's preferring D'Annunzio's novels to the productions of the Irish Literary Theatre was not a preference for art against politics, but a preference for one kind of political art against another.

To begin seeing the political implications of the aesthetic forms Joyce borrowed from D'Annunzio, let us consider how these two writers used epiphanies. The first half of *Il Fuoco* is entitled "The Epiphany of the Flame"; Corinna del Greco Lobner claims that "Stephen's epiphany [looking out to sea] in *A Portrait* is not greatly different from Stelio's epiphany in *Il Fuoco*, insofar as the veil of ignorance is torn from the eyes of the young artist, who is able to experience for the first time an uninhibited, mystical communion with natural beauty." Lobner cites as evidence Stephen's visionary cry, "To live, to err, to fall, to triumph, to create life out of life!" and argues that it has the "same cadence" and "rhythmic pattern" as the Italian version of Stelio's cry, "To create with joy! It is an attribute of Divinity!"[5]

Lobner emphasizes the purely formal structure and transcendental na-

ture of these aesthetic credos, making it seem that they have nothing to
do with politics. Yet Stelio's credo and his epiphany are directly presented
as wedding him to the masses. He discovers his credo in the middle of an
improvised speech in which the waves of response from the crowd stir him:

> Once more the soul of the multitude was in the poet's power, strained and
> vibrating like one only chord made of a thousand chords, that incalculably
> prolonged every resonance. That resonance awakened in it the sense of a
> truth that it had contained all along, but that the words of the poet were
> suddenly revealing in the form of a message never heard before. . . .
> In that sonorous silence the solitary voice reached its climax.
> "To create with joy!" It is the attribute of Divinity. (p. 73)[6]

The "resonance" of the crowd is what awakens the buried truth; the poet,
too, is being awakened by that resonance, by his relationship with the
crowd. He calls the moment a "time of communion between his own soul
and the soul of the crowd" and describes it as a transformation very much
of the sort Le Bon theorized, the individual personality disappearing into
the crowd mind: "an unknown power had seemed to converge within him,
abolishing the limits of his particular personality and conferring the harmony of a chorus to his solitary voice" (p. 124). At the end of the first half
of the novel, when he repeats his credo while looking out to sea, he is remembering the way that the crowd transformed him: "once more, he heard
the sound of his own voice and the crash of applause . . . and distinctly
saw himself oscillating above the multitude like a hollow, sonorous body
inhabited by some mysterious will. He was saying the words: 'To create
with joy! It is the attribute of Divinity' " (p. 140).

Even Stelio's relationships with women, which Lobner says are similar
to Stephen's, are ways to embrace the masses, not simply beauty. Stelio's
primary love is an actress, La Foscarina, who is important to him because
she has a powerful relationship with the masses: even in the folds of her
dress, she "seemed to carry the very frenzy of those distant multitudes"
(p. 58). Stelio needs La Foscarina to speak his words, to give him access to
the frenzy, the mass enthusiasm that can transform him into a sonorous
body inhabited by a will not his own, the will of the crowd.

Stelio's epiphany does not lead him to exile, as Stephen's does, but
rather to plans to form a national theater modeled on Wagner's theater at
Bayreuth. Wagner in fact plays a role in the novel: the last chapters show
Stelio meeting the dying Wagner and carrying the coffin at his funeral.
Wagner is also the topic of a long conversation early in the novel: Stelio says
Wagner "succeeded in inflaming the world . . . exalted his own image and
magnified his own dreams of dominating beauty; he, too, had been drawn
to the crowd as to the preferable prey" (p. 120). Here we can begin to see
how D'Annunzio's novel could seem to Joyce to reveal how a writer could
"abhor the multitude." The disdainful writer does not avoid the masses, but

uses them, building himself into a superhuman figure through their worship. Such use of the multitude could make the artist dependent on them. As one character puts it, "Richard Wagner affirms that the only creator of a work of art is the people . . . and that all the artist can do is to gather up and express the creation of the unconscious throng" (p. 124). Stelio, expanding on Wagner's ideas, defines the central task of the poet as igniting a hidden explosive power within the masses, an act that makes the writer similar to a military hero leading a charge. Charles Klopp points out that Stelio's definition of his artistic goal in fact repeats exactly a paragraph D'Annunzio used in an 1897 campaign speech:

> There must, therefore, be in the multitude some hidden beauty from which only the hero and the poet can draw a flash. Whenever that beauty revealed itself by a sudden clamour arising in theatre or entrenchment [in the trenches] or public place, a torrent of joy must swell the heart of him who had called it forth with his verse, his harangue, or the action of his sword. The word of the poet, when communicated to the crowd, must therefore, be an act like the deed of a hero.[7]

D'Annunzio claimed, then, that the way to resist surrendering to the trolls is to become their hero and lead them into battle. He pursued this goal all his life: in the Italian Parliament from 1897 to 1900 he stridently argued for building up the Italian military; during Italy's invasion of Abyssinia, he wrote poems glorifying the nation's military conquests, paralleling them to his own sexual conquests and presenting both as showing the racial superiority of Latins; in World War I, he became a military hero; in 1919, he led a march on Trieste to install himself as dictator, a feat Mussolini imitated later by marching on Rome. In politics, writing, and love, D'Annunzio claimed to be following the ideal of ancient Greece, which was, as he put it, "to exalt and glorify *above all things* Beauty, and the power of the pugnacious, dominating male."[8]

Stephen Dedalus is clearly incapable of such iron-man behavior, but there are hints throughout *Portrait* that he harbors dreams of being a D'Annunzian artist-hero-leader-lover whose epiphanies would ignite the masses into political movement. In the early draft of the novel, when Joyce followed D'Annunzio's vision of the poet-hero so closely as to give Stephen the last name "Hero," there are more than hints. Stephen Hero conceives of his writing in terms of violent acts that could create revolutionary movements. He writes an essay in school seeking "a maximum of explosive force. It seemed to him that the students might need only the word to enkindle them towards liberty or that, at least, his trumpet-call might bring to his side a certain minority of the elect." He calls himself a "fiery-hearted revolutionary," and when he gives his manuscript to a friend, he says, "This is the first of my explosives."[9]

Revolutionary explosives were the methods of anarchists and might

seem to point away from the D'Annunzian politics of strengthening the
Italian military and seeking to conquer other races. But the distinction
between Left and Right was not at all clear in prewar Italy, where Joyce
wrote most of *Portrait* while following D'Annunzio's career. Joyce had
little difficulty in admiring D'Annunzio and at the same time also supporting socialist syndicalists such as Arturo Labriola. D'Annunzio himself occasionally crossed the Italian Parliament to sit with the Left. When
D'Annunzio marched on Trieste, he started out with the fervent support
of the Right, then switched and tried to enlist the help of anarchist and
republican factions in an assault on mainland Italy.

The reason D'Annunzio could slide from calling for a strong nationalist government into seeking to lead an anarcho-syndicalist movement—
and then support Mussolini—was that all these tactics were ways of turning a disorganized, "liberal" Italian people into a fiery mass movement.
D'Annunzio and the syndicalists all sought to mobilize the Italians to resist the capitalist leadership: for this purpose, the workers could be organized into unions or into protomilitary cadres. The very word *Fascist*, derived from *fasces*, a bundle of sticks, referred to small, militant collections
of workers and emerged out of anarcho-syndicalist theorizing: Mussolini
began his career as a syndicalist. In a 1906 letter to his brother Stanislaus, Joyce describes himself in terms borrowed from both the Left and
the Right: he calls himself a "nationalist" who supports syndicalism (even
though syndicalism was a distinctly antistatist movement at that time).
He calls his exile in Italy a "virtual intellectual strike," suggesting that he
feels he is part of the active resistance; he even labels Gogarty, Colm, and
Yeats "the blacklegs of literature."[10] When Stephen similarly leaves Ireland,
the act is coded both as a strike and as an effort to mobilize the masses:
Stephen hopes exile will allow him to "forge in the smithy of [his] soul
the uncreated conscience of [his] race" (p. 253). Syndicalists postulated that
a general refusal to participate in the corrupt social order is the essential
act that would fire the hearts of the people and bring them together in a
revolutionary mass movement. The general strike, Georges Sorel argued,
"gives . . . high moral value" to the movement by making everyone impervi-
ous to seductive arguments: the strike instills a conscience in the people.[11]
Leaving, going on strike against Ireland, is Stephen's method of putting
himself in position to produce the cultural icons that will unite the race in
a disciplined mass movement.

Stephen Hero does not see himself ever becoming an orator like Stelio
or D'Annunzio, but even as he denies that possibility, he imagines his art
serving much the same political function: "though a taste for elegance and
detail unfitted him for the part of demagogue, from his general attitude he
might have been supposed not unjustly an ally of the collectivist politicians."[12] Collectivism was the politics of mass movements, and Stephen

Hero was seeking an art that could supplement the demagogues such as D'Annunzio in creating such movements.

In Joyce's revision of *Stephen Hero* into *Portrait*, almost all of Stephen's fiery revolutionary goals became muted and unclear. Critics divide on whether Stephen is admirable or foolish, on his way to being an artist-hero or on his way to a pathetic life of failure.[13] Joyce's ambivalence in this novel was in part the result of a transition in his politics, a transition defined particularly in terms of his relationship with the masses. *Stephen Hero* is a D'Annunzian novel, with an artist-hero seeking to inspire and dominate the masses through violent acts and speeches that seek to mobilize an elite leadership. When Joyce turned to *Ulysses* in 1918, he dropped his artist-hero and substituted the unheroic mass man, Leopold Bloom. By *Finnegans Wake*, Joyce seems to have concluded that individuals do not even exist, turning every character into a "mass" and giving the thoroughly anti-elitist name "Here Comes Everybody" to his antihero. Joyce thus underwent a remarkable shift, moving from a position on its way to Fascism to a position close to international socialist pluralism. *Portrait* was written in the middle of this transition, while Joyce struggled to overcome his abhorrence of the rabblement. Much has been made of the anarchist elements in *Portrait*; I want to examine the elements that suggest how close Joyce was to the D'Annunzian (or Fascist) belief that a great male leader was the only solution to the chaos of the masses.

Portrait repeatedly shows confrontations between potential male heroes and the masses, generally portrayed as female. In the opening children's story, Baby Tuckoo meets a moocow: a weak, immature, undeveloped male meets a representative of the herd. This tale may not seem to present a battle for domination, since the moocow appears friendly, even motherly. But this is a story told by Stephen's father, who will later stand in angry confrontation with the female herd—and lose. Repeatedly, Stephen tries to admire and imitate male leaders (Parnell, his father, the priests), and repeatedly he is disappointed as one after another is exposed as weak, ineffectual, surrendering to the herd and generally to women. We could diagram the novel as a series of rises and falls: potential heroes try to rise out of the sea of corrupt humanity into a position of leadership, but all fail. There are no Dedaluses any more, only Icaruses.

As Stephen watches men fall, his dream of heroic freedom transforms into a search for social control, for a way to stop the masses from dragging everyone down. This transformation is at the heart of the novel, so I want to trace it in detail. At first, Stephen believes that an artist-hero can stand apart from the corruption in society, so he searches for men untainted by the vulgarity of the masses, "intelligent ... athletic ... highspirited ... men who washed their bodies briskly with cold water and wore clean cold linen" (p. 156). But all who seem clean and "highspirited" turn out to be dirty and low-class, and so become indistinguishable from the masses around them. Potential heroes end up floating in the general cesspool, like all the "corks that lay bobbing on the surface of the water in a thick yellow scum" (p. 66). In reaction to these falls, Stephen's thoughts move from admiration for the independence of noble men to dreams of power.

The first such fall is Parnell's, and it provides the model for all the others. It enters the ten-year-old Stephen's consciousness entwined with images of waves of people swamping and drowning the hero. Stephen is in the infirmary watching a fire and thinks:

> The fire rose and fell on the wall. It was like waves. Someone had put coal on and he heard voices. They were talking. It was the noise of the waves. Or the waves were talking among themselves as they rose and fell.
>
> He saw the sea of waves . . . and he saw a multitude of people gathered by the waters' edge to see the ship that was entering their harbour. A tall man stood on the deck . . . and by the light at the pierhead he saw his face, the sorrowful face of Brother Michael . . . and heard him say in a loud voice of sorrow over the waters:
> —He is dead . . . Parnell! Parnell! He is dead! (p. 27)

In this passage, waves of voices announce the fall of the leader. The waves may be Parnell's followers mourning his death, but in the scene that follows, it seems that waves have killed Parnell, since his body is brought in on a ship. Brother Michael might be exulting in Parnell's death as a deserved fate meted out by God to the sexual sinner.

When Stephen later remembers this scene in the hospital, he thinks about how closely he had been identified with Parnell, so that the death seemed his own. But as he grows up, he slowly switches to identifying with those who defeated Parnell: the priests. The flame of power that was associated with thoughts of Parnell (derived from D'Annunzio's "Epiphany of the Flame") returns when a priest suggests that Stephen become a priest himself: "A flame began to flutter on Stephen's cheek as he heard in this proud address an echo of his own proud musings. How often had he seen himself as a priest wielding calmly and humbly the awful power" (p. 158). Parnell may have seemed a flame lighting the way for Ireland, but Stephen's attraction to such flames transfers to Parnell's enemies once they have won: Stephen is fascinated as much with power as with the true and the good.

Parnell's fall is implicated in the fall of the other central male figure in Stephen's young life—his father. Stephen sees his father reduced to tears at a Christmas dinner by an argument about Parnell. Joyce thus links the loss of leadership in politics with a loss of leadership in the family. Both Parnell's fall and the Christmas fiasco appear to be orchestrated by the same powerful female, Dante. Stephen's fantasy in the infirmary of Parnell's death ends, "And he [Stephen] saw Dante in a maroon velvet dress and with a green velvet mantle hanging from her shoulders walking proudly and silently past the people who knelt by the waters' edge" (p. 27). Dante's presence in this fantasy must be due to Stephen's sense that in his own small, familial world, she represents the force that would overthrow Parnell, the force of Catholic morality. But it is also significant that a female appears to be rising into leadership to replace Parnell. In the Christmas dinner scene, the anger of Stephen's father and uncle about the fall of Parnell is presented entirely in terms of a battle with women: they tell the story of spitting in the face of a young woman who attacked Parnell, and then Dante reduces Simon Dedalus to tears by almost "spitting in his face" (p. 39). Dante makes male firmness dissolve into watery flux, repeating the loss of manly independence that was enacted nationally in the fall of Parnell.

Stephen's father actually undergoes a whole series of falls: first he loses to Dante in the conversation, then he is exposed as sexually corrupt by the word "foetus" carved in a college desk (residue of a dirty joke Simon made in college), and finally he tumbles into poverty. Joyce explicitly blurs together the exposure of the corruption of the male body and the loss of economic status: they seem interchangeable forms of the descent into squalor. When the Dedalus family moves into a slum neighborhood, Stephen is "angry with himself for being young and the prey of restless foolish impulses, angry also with the change of fortune which was reshaping the world about him into a vision of squalor and insincerity" (p. 67). Later on, Stephen is "conscious of . . . the squalor of his own mind and home" (p. 79). The humiliation he feels about his father's decline mixes with his own humiliations, including being accused of "heresy" by his teachers and his schoolmates (pp. 79–81). Stephen's anger at the squalor around and inside him motivates his desire to leave Ireland and return as an avenging hero like the Count of Monte Cristo.

D'Annunzio's desire to become a dominating male artist derived from similar experiences. As Gregory Lucente puts it, D'Annunzio was "the self-conscious son of a middle-class *pescarese* bankrupt. In this regard, perhaps the most telling memory of D'Annunzio's early years was the protracted jeering of his fellow students upon his first recitation at the Collegio Cicognini in Prato [due to] his unmistakably provincial (and *meridionale*) accent."[14] Financial failure and provincial accents are mixed together in *Portrait* as well: Stephen's father, on the day he loses his property, travels around town telling everyone how he "had been trying for thirty years to get rid of his Cork accent up in Dublin" (p. 93). D'Annunzio's and Joyce's personal experiences of the failure of fathers mirrors their experience of the humiliating positions of Italy and Ireland in the world community. In political speeches, D'Annunzio constantly harped on the decline of Italy from former glory, equating loss of wealth, loss of military power, loss of masculinity, and loss of morality. The solution: powerful male leadership that could transform the nation from prey to predator.

It takes Stephen a long time to come to a similar conclusion. He first tries to escape the squalor that seems to have destroyed his household and

Irish politics by using the money he wins from writing an essay to organize his household into a "commonwealth." His main goal is to isolate part of the world from the general corruption, to establish a realm of "order and elegance." But the vulgar tides reappear, not only crashing over his barriers, but also emerging from inside his mini-elite realm and inside him: "He had tried to build a breakwater of order and elegance against the sordid tide of life without him and to dam up, by rules of conduct and active interests and new filial relations, the powerful recurrence of the tides within him. Useless. From without as from within the water had flowed over his barriers: their tides began once more to jostle fiercely above the crumbled mole" (p. 98). Stephen is becoming aware that there is no way for an individual to stand against the tides, because those tides are partly within him. To build castle walls is useless, because there is no distinction of inside and outside, no untainted nobility to be protected from the scum in the gutters.

Even Stephen's one apparently noble act, his protesting of his unfair pandying at school, is revealed as merely an illusion allowed by a system that actually has no place for noble heroes. Stephen's protest succeeds because it allows the priests to cover up a much more extensive unfairness, the fact that punishments are distributed according to the affection between boys and ruling priests. Because Corrigan has a homosexual relationship with Mr. Gleeson, he will not be much punished. The way Stephen's individual moral rebellion functions to maintain the whole unfair system is summarized in the image that ends the scene of his heroism. Standing alone, he hears the sound of the cricket bats "like drops of water in a fountain falling softly in the brimming bowl" (p. 59). Stephen himself has risen to stand alone, like a drop of water, but only for a moment, after which he will fall back into the mass, the pool of boys. The separation into drops is simply part of the working of the fountain, of the whole social system; individuals are lifted up, allowed to appear separate and heroic—superior—and then dropped back into the pool. The impression of heroic superiority is an illusion: the apparently elevated drop is always part of the lowly social tide.

With the weakness of individual morality revealed in the fall of Parnell, his father, and himself, Stephen begins trying out the D'Annunzian tactic of dominating women as the first step toward becoming able to control the tides swamping everything: "he wanted to sin with another of his kind, to force another being to sin with him and to exult with her in sin" (p. 99). He goes to a prostitute, where he can use money to buy the impression of imposing his desires on a woman. He dreams that a woman could make him "suddenly become strong and fearless and sure of himself," but in a real encounter he cannot even control his own body:

his lips would not bend to kiss her.

With a sudden movement she bowed his head and joined her lips to his and he read the meaning of her movements in her frank uplifted eyes. It was too much for him. He closed his eyes, surrendering himself to her, body and mind, conscious of nothing in the world but the dark pressure of her softly parting lips . . . and between them he felt an unknown and timid pressure. (p. 101)

Stephen's first physical encounter with a woman is an occasion not of gaining strength and control, but of surrendering. The encounter turns into an inversion of conventional sex roles, as the woman's tongue penetrates his lips. Stephen's attempt to find the most controllable women in society has revealed instead his own weakness. Instead of the rigid power he hoped to find in himself, he is overcome by a soft, timid, female pressure.

Stephen, of course, is horrified by his failure to become strong through sin and considers becoming a celibate priest. But that, too, fails when he sees the "pink tinges of suffocated anger" in the "shaven gills of the priests" (p. 161). They, too, are not superior, but rather self-repressed, self-hating. Their anger is very much the anger he had felt toward the squalor around and inside him. They are not, as he had thought, men who wear "clean cold linen" but men who tell dirty jokes about each other (p. 156).

Stephen finally gives up on finding anyone noble enough to save him and turns to art to recreate himself. He develops an aesthetic similar to his earlier politics, his fantasy of a commonwealth of order and elegance separated from all the social tides around him. He envisions the artist inhabiting a realm of divine "indifference" in which he can create an art that is not "kinetic" and hence not "improper" (p. 205). He wants an art that will not move others because he fears being moved by others. Through his art, he seeks a realm where nothing is moving, where "the mind is arrested," along with everything else (p. 205). Specifically, he seeks to liberate masculinity, to escape being controlled by the feminine. His poem consists almost entirely of a plea to a woman to stop moving him, to stop her "ardent ways," to stop producing "flame" and instead produce "smoke." Flame either draws an inflamed person or burns—it produces desire or loathing; smoke can curl around a person without moving him. In his desire to escape flame, Stephen for a time becomes quite unlike D'Annunzio: D'Annunzio's novel is titled *Il Fuoco* in part because Stelio's goal is eventually to inflame not only women but the whole nation. Stephen, for a while, is terrified of inflaming anything. But he cannot reach the calm stasis of floating in smoke and aesthetic "arrest" that he theorizes about because, of course, the flame he is trying to put out is inside him. He pleads with the woman to stop inflaming him, but it is his own mind that he is trying to cool.[15]

Soon after he has written his poem, he finds himself surrounded by images of E.C. that revive the flame and the scum that his poem sought to smother and to purge. He thinks about her eyes, asking himself "what was their shimmer but the shimmer of the scum that mantled the cesspool of the court of a slobbering Stuart?" (p. 233). He tries to deny and suppress these images: "They were secret and enflaming but her image was not entangled by them. That was not the way to think of her. It was not even the way in which he thought of her" (p. 233). In other words, to keep himself from being moved by his own images, to keep the pornography out of his sexuality, Stephen has to declare that certain of his thoughts are not even his own thoughts. The scum is deep inside him, hence there is no way to escape it.

Stephen is terrified that the cesspool inside him means he will never be able to control himself; he worries particularly about the effects of un-controllable impulses on his art. He asks Lynch, "If a man hacking in fury at a block of wood . . . make there an image of a cow, is that image a work of art? If not, why not?" (p. 214). In other words, can a person out of control be an artist? Similarly, he asks, "Can excrement or a child or a louse be a work of art?" In other words, can the body produce art when it is operating without conscious direction from the mind? This question is not merely rhetorical; Stephen describes his own thoughts, after he makes an error in remembering a line of poetry, as "lice born of the sweat of sloth" (p. 234).

The lice breeding in his mind and the swirling cesspool of inflaming images inside him are too powerful for Stephen to simply remain detached, as his aesthetic requires. When he tries to compose his poem, he finds that his art requires active methods of controlling the mob inside him. He chooses a highly structured poetic form, a villanelle, to keep the impulses he is drawing on from flowing out of control. Even so, in the middle of the composition of the villanelle, his own thoughts break up into a mob and threaten to destroy him as an author. In his reaction to the dissolution of his own mind we can see him beginning to develop the methods of crowd control that would bring him close to D'Annunzio's politics.

He starts to lose control of his process of composition when he remembers a moment when the model for his poem, E.C., flirted with a priest. His mind "broke up violently her fair image. . . . On all sides distorted reflections of her image started from his memory: the flowergirl in the ragged dress . . . the kitchengirl in the next house . . . a girl who had laughed gaily . . . a girl he had glanced at . . . as she passed out of Jacob's biscuit factory" (p. 220). Stephen loses control over the image in his mind, and he finds himself surrounded by a crowd of women, mostly lower-class.

He tries to say to himself that in conjuring up this crowd he is simply trying to "mock" E.C., but then he realizes that "his anger was also a form of homage. . . . perhaps the secret of her race lay behind those dark eyes. . . . she was a figure of the womanhood of her country, a batlike soul waking to the consciousness of itself" (pp. 220–21). In other words, his disdain of her as an individual has led him to "homage" of her as "figure" of the race. Her awakening sexuality is also the awakening Irish people. The question of whether she is attracted to the priest or to Stephen becomes the question of what kind of male will lead the newly awakened race. Stephen turns to competing with the priest, "railing at her paramour." He finally finds a way to imagine himself winning—by becoming a priest as well, "a priest of the eternal imagination," and by performing a ritual on his own mind: "The radiant image of the eucharist united again in an instant his bitter and despairing thoughts" (p. 221). He thus overcomes the threat that the mob of impulses in his own mind will flock to an attractive priest by borrowing the methods of the Church. The Eucharist is a ritual of placing part of the ideal male into the bodies and souls of everyone; performing Mass is a perfect way to reach the mass mind—and it works to unify even the mob inside Stephen's own mind.

An early D'Annunzio novel, *Il Piacere* (Child of pleasure), also tells of a young, irreligious poet creating an image of the Eucharist as a way of gaining control of himself. D'Annunzio's poet, like Stephen, feels chained to horrible lusts, but thinking of the Eucharist makes him feel "every foul stream dammed. . . . And quenched the flame of my impenitence."[16] Once that is done, the young man sees himself as a "king." The term "king" was more than a metaphor for D'Annunzio, who constantly employed traditional images of power—religious, military, classical—in his project of making himself a popular dictator.

The fear that the real mob, the batlike masses, are somehow identical to a mob of impulses inside the body of the male, according to Klaus Theweleit, was at the heart of the psychology of Fascism. Theweleit analyzed the writings of Nazi soldiers, concluding that when one of them reacts "negatively, with hatred, loathing, fear, disgust, of the mass (the human mass), it is not from any direct relation to the human masses themselves that his emotions spring; they arise in relation to the 'mass' that issues from his own body." The masses threaten to "undermine the internal dams of these men, as if their bodily boundaries might collapse under the pressure of the masses without." Joyce created in Stephen precisely this psychology: Stephen feels that he lives in a "cesspool" and cannot build walls to keep the scum out; as he says when his commonwealth collapses, "From without as from within the water had flowed over his barriers" (p. 98). Theweleit says that Fascism overcame the fear of the masses by substituting another kind of mass, of men marching: "The mass that is celebrated is strictly formed, poured into systems of dams. Above it there towers a leader (*Führer*). To the despised mass, by contrast, is attributed all that is flowing, slimy, teeming."[17] Stephen's poem and his aesthetic are devoted to creating the strict form, the system of dams, that will stop the flowing scum of the Irish masses from carrying him along. Since Stephen fails to find a leader who can accomplish this task, he seeks, as did D'Annunzio, to create within himself a towering image.

To do so, he not only borrows the trappings of the priesthood but also develops several other techniques of gaining power over the masses that are quite similar to D'Annunzio's. He dreams, as did D'Annunzio, of bringing into the modern world the glory of ancient Greece. But Stephen doubts whether a combination of Greek and Catholic imagery will be enough to give him power: there is something lacking in the unconscious of the masses that cannot be derived from ancient models. Stephen envisages himself as a Vulcan creating backbones for the vacillating, "batlike" Irish. This goal resonates with Stelio Effrena's ideal of the poet-hero "extracting thunderbolts" from the crowd. Stelio seeks through his art to create a racial will, modeling such a goal on what he sees as Wagner's success: "Like the will of the Iron Chancellor, like the blood of his soldiers, the Master's musical numbers had contributed toward the exalting and perpetuating the soul of his race."[18] D'Annunzio often talked of his own art as forging a new racial mind. In his most patriotic poems, the *Laudi*, he says he sought to forge a "new myth" from the

> holy material
> of the race, the deathless
> generative substance
> of the blood, the pristine
> force of the people
> turned red hot in the flames before us
> like a steely mass
> ready to be placed on the anvil.[19]

D'Annunzio wanted to turn the people into red-hot swords; Stephen's rhetoric may be less inflamed, but to describe a conscience emerging from a smithy's forge suggests that Stephen also dreams of creating an iron-willed people. Theweleit argues that Fascist soldiers had to see themselves as "figures of steel" and tried to convert the masses into similar figures to control the disgusting flow that threatened to disintegrate them.[20]

Underlying the fear of the masses is a fear of women, who are equated to "all that flows"; the Fascist man of steel, according to Theweleit, is only an extreme version of the "anti-female armor" that has been a part of male psychology for centuries.[21] D'Annunzio's novel *Il Fuoco* shows that the first step in forging a movement, in becoming a leader, is asserting power over women. Stelio is described as thus literally shaping the actress who passes his words to the public: near him she was drawn "into that atmosphere, as fiery as the encircling neighbourhood of a forge, she felt herself capable of suffering all the transfigurations that it should please the Life-Giver to work in her for the satisfaction of his own constant desire of poetry and beauty" (p. 11).

Stephen dreams at the end of the novel of using his art for a similar purpose. As we have seen, he proposes a kind of artistic eugenics: if he can insert his "seminal thoughts" into women's minds, they will produce more noble children, and he will thereby regenerate the race—also thereby creating some people who will admire him. The passage that begins with him wanting his art to "cast his shadow over the imaginations of their daughters, before their squires begat upon them, that they might breed a race less ignoble than their own" is also the one in which he broods on "the thoughts and desires of the race to which he belonged flitting like bats" (p. 238). Stephen wants to discipline and organize the thoughts and desires that flit around him, just as he wants to discipline and organize his own flitting thoughts. He wants to create an art that will "arrest the mind," stop all minds from flitting about, and force them to remain still, focused on moral, noble ideals. He wants to be the policeman and god of his race.

Stephen's idea that he can restore his race by casting women into the shadow of his imagination is just what Virginia Woolf said many male writers were in fact doing in response to the suffrage movement, increasing the presence of the letter *I* in their texts until it became a "straight dark bar" across the page.

> One began dodging this way and that to catch a glimpse of the landscape behind it . . . in the shadow of the letter "I" all is shapeless as mist. Is that a tree? No, it is a woman. But . . . she has not a bone in her body, I thought, watching Phoebe, for that was her name, coming across the beach. Then Alan got up and the shadow of Alan at once obliterated Phoebe. For Alan had views and Phoebe was quenched in the flood of his views.[22]

Stephen leaves Ireland hoping to construct a giant "I" to have exactly the effect Woolf describes—to put women in the shadow of his mind, to become the source and leader of the flood, the mass movement, that will swamp the nation. Woolf argued that the end result of such desires would be an entire nation based on "self-assertive virility," a result that she noted the Fascist regime in Italy had "already brought into being."[23]

When put in the context of this desire to eclipse other minds, Stephen's desire to forge a conscience for his race, a super-ego or super-I, becomes an act of self-glorification as much as an act of moral reformation of his people. It is a desire to create the impression of a man of overwhelming force, to forge a giant statue or image of himself to be inserted into everyone else's mind. Joyce expressed a somewhat similar goal while working on early drafts of *Portrait*: in a conversation with his brother Stanislaus, he said the only novels worth writing were those of "egomaniacs" such as D'Annunzio.[24]

One more element in Stephen's aesthetic goals echoes D'Annunzio: the repeated use of the term *race*. Stephen's desires to forge a racial conscience and to breed a less ignoble race are hard to reconcile with his rejection of the Irish nationalist movement. In *Stephen Hero*, though, he gives a precise explanation for not joining the Irish nationalists, and his explanation suggests that he is in fact seeking to join writers such as D'Annunzio and Wagner in a move toward racial unity that goes beyond national borders. Stephen Hero says that the fire "in his blood" that inspires his art derives not from Irish roots but from "some movement already proceeding out in Europe."

He prefers this "European" movement to the call for an "Irish Ireland" and therefore decides to write in English, which he considers the "medium for the Continent." In response to an accusation that he is supporting "English civilisation," he says, "the civilisation of which you speak is not English—it is Aryan. The modern notions are not English; they point the way of Aryan civilisation."[25] The term "Aryan" has of course become charged by its association with the Nazi regime, and I am deliberately drawing attention to Joyce's early use of this term to raise the question of where his fascination with D'Annunzio was leading him. The word had no connotations of Fascism when Joyce used it in *Stephen Hero*, but it did carry connotations of racial competition. The term emerged from nineteenth-century linguistic theory, describing a group of languages of Indo-European roots that were always contrasted with the "Semitic" group of languages and with a few tongues that seemed to stand alone, such as Hungarian and Basque. The term *anti-Semitism* derives from the theory of "Aryan" and "Semitic" linguistic groups, which might suggest how thoroughly the word *Aryan* was entwined with claims of racial dominance. Joyce's later decision to make Leopold Bloom both Jewish and Hungarian thus was a way to doubly define him as non-Aryan, a way to strongly mark Joyce's effort to repudiate the attitudes expressed by Stephen Hero. Bloom's Jewishness was also a rejection of D'Annunzio, who, like Wagner, spoke of "low-browed Hebrew[s] with greedy hands" as the people who would be thrown out of power if leaders could forge the racial consciences of all the European nations.[26]

The language of racial unity also emerges in *Stephen Hero* in a description of the poet's relationship with Ibsen: the "minds of the old Norse poet and of the perturbed young Celt met in a moment of radiant simultaneity."[27] Identifying Ibsen and Stephen as Norse and Celtic implies that their radiant simultaneity is mediated by an underlying racial unity.

The language of European racial unity was removed from Joyce's revision of *Stephen Hero* into *A Portrait of The Artist as a Young Man*: the word *Aryan* does not appear, nor does the merger of Norse and Celtic poets. In these alterations, Stephen's calls for racial reform become vague statements. Joyce similarly removed Stephen's claim to be pursuing the same goals as "collectivist politicians," leaving the politics of the novel also vague: the most prominent reference to politics left in the novel is as one of the terms that confuses the young Stephen.

But even though Joyce muted and diffused Stephen Dedalus's political and racial goals, we still see that the poet's search for a way to escape the "batlike souls" around him keeps slipping from a search for freedom into a desire for social control. If we combine the D'Annunzian elements in *Stephen Hero* and in *Portrait*, we see that Stephen dreams of using in his art most of the techniques of mass politics that were promulgated by D'Annunzio in the 1910's as methods of creating a nationalist movement: violently disrupting the social order to bring forth an elite, forging an iron will, reviving ancient glory, restoring racial nobility, using religious rituals for secular purposes, creating images of forceful male leaders, and putting women in the shadow.

As Joyce finished *Portrait*, the Left and the Right in Italy—the syndicalists and conservatives such as D'Annunzio—joined together to support Italy's role in World War I. All over Europe, socialist and nationalist movements began merging, and the result was not the liberation from capitalist and imperialist oppression that Joyce had hoped for: instead, nationalist socialism became the common form of the military dictatorships in Italy, Germany, and the USSR. Seeing the reality of Fascism may have been what led Joyce to alter his early views, to break with his own fascination with powerful leaders.

To make that break, Joyce had to change as well his view of his own psychology, to stop seeking to escape the cesspool of impulses within him. John Bishop has suggested in conversation that the letters Joyce wrote in 1909 to Nora about her relationship to Vincent Cosgrave might mark the beginning of such a transition in Joyce's sense of himself. Bishop says that these letters reveal a stylistic fluidity that could mark the loosening of the armor of rigid form that we see the young Stephen using to control the mob of impulses inside himself. Richard Ellman similarly sees in these letters Joyce's discovering how to build a new self out of a sense of ignobility.[28] Ellman says the character Richard in the play *Exiles* shows the attitude that grew out of Joyce's suspicions about Cosgrave and Nora. Discovering his friend and his wife have been together, Richard says, "in the very core of my ignoble heart I longed to be betrayed by you and by her . . . to be for ever a shameful creature and to build up my soul again out of the ruins of its shame."[29] Some of the ambivalence in *Portrait* may derive from Joyce's beginning to prefer "shame" to the dream of restored nobility. Recognizing and working with the shame, the social scum surrounding and within each person, was part of the transformation of the social order that Joyce saw as necessary to avoid Fascism. In *Ulysses*, Joyce thoroughly undermines the idea that anyone (leader, hero, fictional figure) is free of scum or excrement: when Bloom searches for statues with anatomically correct bottoms, Joyce is satirizing the ways artists create fraudulent images of ideal humanity. All minds are corks floating in scum, and it is thus far more important, if one wants to alter the way the mind works, to explore the scum than to restructure the cork. The impression that the cork could control the scum is absurd, an illusion. Joyce wrote *Ulysses* in collaboration with the scum.

In that novel Joyce mocks Stephen's heroic dreams of restored nobility. Stephen slinks back to Dublin to resume a very mundane life. Instead of inspiring a minority of the elect, he teaches lazy boys; instead of reviving ancient glory, he is trapped in the nightmare of history; instead of becoming a forceful male, he begins to believe that genius derives from being overborne by women. Only in his drunken stupor among prostitutes does he revive his Wagnerian dreams of forging a sword for his people, swinging his ashplant around and crying out "Nothung." Instead of putting women in the shadow and releasing thunderbolts, though, he slashes a prostitute's lamp shade and ends up in the dark himself, knocked out by a particularly loutish soldier. This soldier represents the actual result of the D'Annunzian dream of iron-willed masses organized behind a great male hero—namely, Fascist thugs. But the soldier also mirrors part of Stephen's own psychology: both are young men trying to build dams against the vulgarity that threatens to topple all noble leadership. The soldier perceives the flow of Stephen's words as a disgusting, incomprehensible tide of insults against royalty; in reaction, he says, "I'll wring the neck of any fucker that says a word against my fucking king."[30] The soldier's obscenities humorously undermine his words, but they also suggest that in attacking Stephen he is attempting to ward off the obscenity he feels welling up within himself: he is struggling to do with his fists much the same thing Stephen struggles to do with art. Putting Stephen in confrontation with the soldier is Joyce's way of trying to neutralize or cancel out all such efforts: the soldier's punch is in effect Joyce's way of finally punching through the rigid armor of elitism and aesthetics that he had erected as a young man to separate himself from the masses. As we shall see in the next four chapters, all the modernists I am studying overcame their own early attitudes toward the masses: as collectivism developed workable structures for continuing a recognizable social order while incorporating mass political structures, the modernists developed workable structures for speaking to and from the mass unconscious.

PART III

Joining the Masses

CHAPTER 6

"The Birth of a New Species of Man . . . from Terror"

Yeats's Poetics of Violence

Yeats's career serves well as a bridge between early and late periods of collectivism and modernism—between fearing and joining the masses. In Woolf, Eliot, and Joyce, the early period, as we have seen, was characterized by a desire to remain separate from the masses and by a horror at the inability to do so. Yeats sought all his life to write a poetry that would express or create a national mind. So the transition in his works has to be seen as a move from an individualist to a collectivist vision of a nation, from a sense that the individual can hold the essence of the nation within his mind to the sense that the only way to create the nation is to disrupt the individual mind. In his early career, Yeats believed that the best way to create a new Ireland was to resist current political movements: like D'Annunzio and the young Joyce, Yeats felt that the artist's vision was superior to anything offered by political movements. Drawing on William Morris, Yeats felt that politics was in its entirety too bourgeois.

Around the time of the Easter 1916 massacre, there was a change in his thinking that modified poetic form and political practice alike: he became convinced that certain political acts, particularly violent ones, could be sufficient, if timed properly, to bring about radical change in everything, including the mind of the artist. His admiration for James Connolly and Padraic Pearse in the poems of this period points to the political theories of violence that underlay Yeats's new poetic project. Connolly studied with Sorelian syndicalists in France, and much of Yeats's development paralleled developments occurring among syndicalists in France and Italy that transformed socialists into Fascists. Such parallels do not necessarily condemn Yeats or suggest that his early interest in socialism was fraudulent. Yeats and the syndicalists alike were led from socialism to Fascism at least as much by a remarkable willingness to hold to the tenet of letting their theory develop out of a dialectical relationship with practical results as by any values they held: they changed their theories in response to the shifting directions in which the masses seemed to be moving. The contradictory statements that Yeats made during his career do not therefore need to be resolved into a particular set of "true" beliefs; rather, they reflect a political methodology, a way of deriving beliefs from analyses of historical trends. I will not, then, seek to evaluate Yeats's politics as a whole, a subject of considerable critical debate; rather, I will try to understand why he kept changing his values.[1] The presumption that a person (or a nation) inherently has certain values that should be held onto no matter what situations arise is precisely the view that Yeats was forced to give up by the events of 1916.

In his later years, Yeats was preoccupied with the question of how to alter the fundamental values of one's own political philosophy in order to join with the tides of history, the currents of thought in the masses. Yeats shared this concern with Georges Sorel, who wrote, "the great preoccupation of my whole life [is] the historical genesis of moral values."[2] Violence and obscurity were, for both these writers, ways to embrace the complete historicity of all values. Their works thus have considerable relevance for recent critical theory, even if from our current viewpoint the political views they ultimately embraced seem monstrous. Their theories suggest that it is not at all easy to accept the tenet that values are historical products, especially if that tenet is connected to the advocacy of significant change in the current social system. If so, they imply, one is in effect advocating the destruction of the self and alteration of the values that underlie the desire for change in the first place. Such a view could dissolve into paradox—and critics often see in Yeats's aesthetic an abstract desire to "combine opposites" that removes the poems from any social consequences.[3] But Yeats did not become simply a supernatural mystic bridging cosmic opposites; rather, he developed an educational program for living with the terror of inevitable self-destruction as a way of avoiding the rigidity of character that separates individuals from the shifting currents deep in the nation's soul, the shifting spirit of the masses.

Sorel's analysis of how violence, images, and myths combine in the historical genesis of moral values provides a framework for understanding Yeats's use of these three elements in his later poems. Sorel's entire argument turns on the premise that the social system is "bound together by an iron law which cannot be evaded"; it forms "one block" that cannot change "except in a catastrophe which involves the whole." To bring about such a catastrophe, intellectual operations such as criticism, proof, argument, and analysis are useless, because through such operations the mind remains bound by the iron law and so reaches conclusions that are still part of the block. All conscious thought remains locked into "the bonds of habit" and rigid forms of "character." The only way out is through transformative violence and the use of unconscious images and myths, verbal structures that ignore intellectual operations and release the mind into "creative consciousness."[4] An individual cannot undergo such a process alone: just as the iron law is a social phenomenon, so are the images, myths, and forms of violence that break people out of their habits. Sorel says that no one can know what they are doing when they foment a revolution, but that does not mean that any act of violence is justified—only those that lead to the releasing of the power of myth and so cause a mass movement. Writers such as Sorel and Yeats who conceived of their work as seeking revolution faced a paradox: they had to disrupt their own character to release the unconscious, mythic elements in their own psyche. They therefore would not be able to understand what they produced, since their conscious thoughts would remain bound by the iron law of the social order.

Sorel theorized how it would be possible for a person to produce texts without understanding them. He says that "it is possible to distinguish in every body of knowledge a clear and an obscure region, and to say that the latter is perhaps the more important." Those who would bring about revolution have to delve into those obscure realms: Sorel created a list of examples of "clear" and "obscure" parts of knowledge that are important to the project of socialism, and his list is intriguingly close to concerns that fill Yeats's poetry: in the realm of ethics, the clear part is "equitable relations," while the obscure part is "sexual relationships"; in the realm of law, the clear part is "contracts," while the obscure part is "the family"; in the realm of economics, the clear part is "exchange," while the obscure part is "production." Sorel goes on to say that "socialism is necessarily very obscure, since it deals with production, with the most mysterious part of human activity, and since it proposes to bring about a radical transformation of that region which it is impossible to describe with clearness. . . . No effort of thought, no progress of knowledge, no rational induction will ever dispel the mystery which envelops socialism." Sorel's way of defining socialism suggests a very strange form of that philosophy: not as a theory of equality or fair distribution of wealth, and certainly not as a science of historical dialectics, but rather as a theory of the transformation of the acts of production (including production of humans through sexuality and the family), a transformation of the very process of "creation." Sorel hated capitalism not for its inequities, but for its method of creation of both objects and people. Capitalism is in Sorel's terms a system that runs on "clear" knowledge, on contracts, claims of equity, and on exchange; such a system turns most people into slaves of what is already known, already measured, rather than into explorers of what is unknown and obscure. His revolution consisted largely of making people passionate; once passionate, Sorel argued, people become completely disobedient, unwilling to follow any masters. Such disobedience is the source of the equality of socialism, not a precise system of equality in the distribution of goods. Sorel argued that the "enthusiasm" that then motivates people is like that of "great artists."[5] The whole point of myths is to release desires, to produce passion, not to provide intellectual bases for action.

Yeats turned to modernist poetics out of a desire to produce an effect much like the one Sorel described: Yeats sought in his later works to be actively involved with violence in order to participate in the sudden transformation of the mass mind. Embracing violence marks Yeats's late phase, but all his life he sought a social revolution. To understand the subtle shifts in his career, I am going to trace a narrow line, focusing on poems and essays that mark stages in his theories of how values exist in the world and how they can be modified; I will try to show that these stages are intertwined with views of what the masses are and of how history functions.

The Failure of Romantic Nationalism

As a young man, Yeats followed Percy Shelley, William Morris, and John O'Leary in an aesthetic politics in which one opposed the bourgeois social order by holding onto beautiful images. This early view was based on the conception that certain values are, in Yeats's words, "the norm," regardless of how far the social order moves away from them. The moral position is to hold to these values and resist compromise. As Yeats wrote about his early views, "If the men and women imagined by the poets were the norm, and if Morris had, in, let us say, 'News from Nowhere' . . . described such men and women, living under their natural conditions, or as they would desire to live, then those conditions themselves must be the norm and could we but get rid of certain institutions the world would turn from eccentricity." This is an anarchic view, but quite different from revolutionary syndicalism, because it is an anarchy based on believing one can know what is the ideal or "normal" social order. But one may not know how to get to the better world, so Morris refused to be involved in socialist political parties: "Morris had told us to have nothing to do with the parliamentary socialists, represented for men in general by the Fabian Society and Hyndman's Social Democratic Federation. . . . During the period of transition mistakes must be made, and the discredit of those mistakes must be left to 'the Bourgeoisie.'"[6] In other words, holding to idealized alternatives is more important than taking any actions that would lead to those alternatives. Beauty becomes the marker of revolutionary value, a marker that has no history, no limitation, and no relationship to any particular policies enacted by the current government.

Such a view put Yeats in conflict with more pragmatic movements seeking to use art for political change. During the 1880's and 1890's, Yeats fought against the Young Ireland movement over the relationship of art to politics.[7] The Young Ireland movement wanted art that supported active nationalist movements. Yeats believed art could do more. The Young Ireland movement, Yeats felt, aimed at producing an Irish nation that would still be imbued with bourgeois and English culture: this would be a free Ireland in legal terms only, an abstract Ireland. Yeats wanted to recover the social (and physical) "body" of Ireland. He wrote in his autobiography that in his youth

> I thought that in man and race alike there is something called "Unity of Being," using that term as Dante used it when he compared beauty in the *Convito* to a perfectly proportioned human body. My father, from whom I had learned the term, preferred a comparison to a musical instrument so strung that if we touch a string all the strings murmur faintly. . . . When I began, however, to apply this thought to the state and to argue for a law-made balance among trades and occupations my father displayed at once the violent free trader and propagandist of liberty.[8]

Yeats's vision of a law-made balance is a collectivism quite different from his later syndicalist views; it depends on the belief that one can see directly what is "perfectly proportioned," what is the ideal shape of the social body. Yeats constantly used metaphors of bodily wholeness: in criticizing the Young Ireland movement, he said they cultivated only "hatred as the one energy of their movement, a deprivation which is the intellectual equivalent to the removal of the genitals."[9] Yeats claimed the movement was "lower middle class"; equating the middle class with the breakup (or castration) of the body was a crucial element in collectivist views, whether socialist or aristocratic: the middle class was seen as inorganic.

By speaking of castration, Yeats implied that the Young Ireland movement was not inseminating the nation; they were a destructive and not a productive force. Their writing, in particular, seemed to Yeats inartistic: they wanted him to write what he called "rhetorical" poetry, fit only for "public speakers and journalists . . . din and bombast." Such poetry could become a political force within the utilitarian world of bourgeois Ireland, but it could never become a "spiritual force." Yeats favored another kind of literature, in which "life is being sung not for what can be proved or disproved, not for what men can be made do or not do, but for the sake of Beauty." Poetry should never be a "criticism of life," but rather a "revelation of a hidden life."[10]

Seeking to produce such poetry, Yeats's first two books were full of magical alternatives to ordinary life—voices from faery lands, from leaves, from the ancient past, from lovers, calling on people to "come away." Yeats valorized supernaturalism in the same terms that he valorized Morris's resistance to current institutions: "the seer of visions and hearer of voices [is] the normal and healthy man."[11] The call to follow a mysterious dream as the route to what is "normal" had a fairly clear political dimension: the Irish should break out of the dull, hopeless life of an oppressed colony and begin to believe in the dream of a restored Irish beauty, a restored culture. But there was no active route to realizing this dream: most of the poems showed that people who abandon their lives to follow strange voices end up wandering aimlessly, going insane, or simply dying. These poems seem to indicate that the less dreams lead to action, the more valuable they are. Yeats writes in "The Song of the Happy Shepherd" that there is no need to perform "dusty deeds" because "words alone are certain good" (p. 8).[12] Norman Jeffares has dismissed these poems as vague and lost in aestheticism, but Yeats was building on the politics of aesthetics he derived from Morris and Ruskin, the belief that beauty is the source of change and must remain whole in itself to function: for them, there could not be any in-between stages from this world to the world of beauty.[13]

In this political aesthetic, the ideal poet or politician is a person unaffected by history—in particular, uncorrupted by the current capitalist world. Yeats described William Morris in such terms, as a writer who always produced images of a world of fullness and plenty and beauty, of "the Green Tree and the goddess Habundia, and wells and enchanted waters." Yeats saw in Morris's work an artistic technique that fit the images produced: Morris was blessed with "the power to create beautiful things without labour, that he might honour the Green Tree." Morris demonstrated and advocated a process of work that was not "laborious," that had no history or process, but that derived from a Romantic overflow or abundance of feeling: he was one of those people "who turned everything into happiness because they have in them something of the abundance of the beechen boughs." All of Morris's poems, according to Yeats, are happy romances of the well found by "such a one as all women love," so that the "Dry Tree, the image of the ruined land, becomes green."[14]

In this image of the production of "green," we can see how Yeats could conceive of an identity between Morris's socialist revolution and the Irish national rebellion. Irish socialists and nationalists often joined together, viewing the British as their common enemy. Restoring natural man would restore Ireland economically and politically. In Italy, similar mergers produced theories of "Proletarian Italy" and images of socialist revolution leading to restored national glory or even imperial conquest. Arturo Labriola coined the phrase the "imperialism of a poor nation" to defend Italian conquests as part of the rise of the proletariat in the world.[15] In light of these parallels, Yeats's abandoning socialism for dreams of national glory and even aristocracy was essentially a change in methodology, another route toward the liberation of the people.

In Yeats's comments on Morris, we can glimpse how socialism could be conceived entirely as an alteration in the way production is carried out: Morris provided a theory of production without alienation, of labor that is not laborious. Yeats admired Morris for finding such a happy method of production but could not adapt it to his own work, or even fully appreciate the poetry that resulted: Morris's "poetry often wearies us as the unbroken green of July wearies us, for there is something in us, some bitterness because of the Fall, it may be, that takes a little from the sweetness of Eve's apple after the first mouthful; but he who did all things gladly and easily, who never knew the curse of labour, found it always as sweet as it was in Eve's mouth."[16] At the heart of the fall is a change in the nature of labor, the move from what we could call "organic" to alienated labor. Entwined with this fall is a change in artistic and bodily beauty, and with it a change in sexual relations. For Morris, beauty identifies the elements of the organic or natural world surviving within the alienated world of modern civilization. Hence the centrality of images of unearthly beauty and medieval painting techniques in Pre-Raphaelite art. But Yeats did not find the unending happiness and sweetness of Morris's works satisfying or even passionate. In Yeats's view, nothing was born from Morris's visions: even if they accomplished the revolution promised in them, it would bring to life only what had already been seen.

Yeats's dissatisfaction with Morris was a rejection of a "happy" poetry and a step toward Sorel. Sorel argued that his philosophy was deeply "pessimistic" and defined pessimism as never knowing what will come as one seeks change.[17] Sorel saw in the doctrine of original sin—of the curse that every person suffers after the fall—a version of his own pessimism. The fall in Sorel meant not merely the separation from a paradise that could be described, but the inability to see paradise and the necessity to destroy the current world and the current self to even gain a fleeting vision of it.

We can see the beginnings of such pessimism in Yeats in a poem that seems overtly to have little to do with politics but everything to do with the terms in which Yeats thought of William Morris: "Adam's Curse" (1904; pp. 80–81). The poem presents a man despairing because his love for a woman has worn out. His poetry, her appearance, and their love all seem illusions produced by hard labor that drains the soul and the body. Such complaints could have been made in any era, and we can read this poem purely as a complaint about old age and loss of passion. Yet Yeats uses historically specific metaphors that would seem more appropriate to an economic debate than to a love poem: contrasts between "labour" and "idle trade," between "pauper[s]" and "bankers." These metaphors add an odd resonance to the poem; on one level, they function to debunk love and aesthetics as no more magical than manual labor. At the same time, they also connect the issues of passion, love, and human relations with economics, particularly socialist economics. The opening stanza of "Adam's Curse" is built almost entirely around the effort of the poet to align himself with the working class against the middle class. He says his poetry is harder than scrubbing kitchen pavement or breaking stones "like an old pauper," and yet he is thought an "idler" by "the noisy set / Of bankers, schoolmasters, and clergymen." Yeats sets up a contrast between manual laborers and white-collar workers and places himself in the first group. In the list of white-collar workers, bankers are first, suggesting that the banks and the economic system are entwined with or even the cause of what is said in schools and churches. We can thus see hints of Morris's socialism. The valorization of labor against the middle class continues in the criticism of those who try to love according to books: such people are engaged in "idle trade." They have, in effect, tried to get by exchange what they should have labored to achieve. The poem seems to be supporting Morris's view that modern forms of labor are debilitating, while old, medieval forms ("the old high way") produced beautiful objects and beautiful people.

But in the last stanza, the poem undermines its valorization of an old way of love and labor by implying that all effort is wearying: there is no production without Adam's curse. Even nature, which had remained for the Romantic tradition and for Morris the model of a production endlessly beautiful and happy, has become a source of wearying strain: the moon is worn out. At the end of the poem, when the poet says that he and his love had "seemed happy" and yet had grown "weary-hearted," happiness itself becomes suspect, and the idea of a "happy poet" such as Yeats called Morris seems an illusion. The poem suggests that living for beauty finally produces weariness, just as it does in Yeats's essay about Morris. This weariness may be a result of strain, but it also may be a result of trying to hold onto a norm of beauty, a weariness due to the fact that such labor is not creative, even in its production of poetry.

In this poem, we cannot simply step out of the modern world into visions of what is normal and healthy or into ancient worlds. There is no eternal, changeless, "normal" world at all; everything is enmeshed within time, within history, including dreams, visions, and nature. The poem ends up despairing, but Yeats eventually turned to another way of understanding the necessity of giving up dreams of beautiful alternatives to this world: the possibility that dreams and beautiful images are in fact products of the current historical world, not alternatives at all. What seem ancient images have force only insofar as they are entwined with current historical forces. One then has to choose dreams based on how the current world is moving. Yeats felt forced to give up "the dream of [his] early manhood, that a modern nation can return to Unity of Culture."[18] The failure of the lovers in "Adam's Curse" resembles the failure of an ancient unity of culture: the lovers are trying to love in the "old high way," when they need instead to find a new way. Instead of hoping to rip up the "pavements grey" that in "The Lake Isle of Innisfree" (p. 39) separated him from ancient nature, Yeats turned to seeking dreams that could survive in a paved world, dreams that could inspire new kinds of movement across the new surfaces of the modern world.

Yeats's most direct efforts to bring about movement in the modern world were undertaken in the Abbey Theatre, where he sought to turn "the mob into a people"—in other words, to produce an organized mass movement. His early plays repeatedly turn on questions of what kind of leaders the people will follow. One play in particular, *Where There Is Nothing* (1903), focuses on the efforts of Paul Ruttledge, whom Yeats described as "a man like William Morris," to liberate the masses.[19] Paul leaves his upper-class friends, marries a poor woman, learns the trade of tinkers, and then conceives of what is in essence a general strike. He says: "Let us send messengers everywhere to tell the people to stop working, and then the world may come to an end."[20] Paul sees this general strike as the beginning of a process of violently destroying almost all institutions. The last part of the play turns Paul's syndicalism into a new religion, but one without any priesthood or leadership at all. Sorel had argued similarly that the "epic enthusiasm" that would follow the general strike would produce a world in which "there are no masters."[21] When one of Paul's followers asks him to act like a leader, to organize his followers into a movement, he responds, "To organize? That is to bring in law and number? Organize—organize—that is how all the mischief has been done." Instead, Paul says, "We must destroy the world . . . for where there is nothing there is God. . . . Jesus Christ . . . made a terrible joy, and sent it to overturn governments and all settled order."[22] But Paul dies, and nothing much changes. In this play, all efforts at radical reform end up turning back into the same old systems, particularly because the masses tend to become followers. The problem is similar to what Yeats speaks of in "Adam's Curse": the effort to produce or organize joy or beauty is destructive to that joy. Instead of an organized joy, Paul advocates a "terrible joy," an early version of the "terrible beauty" that Yeats discovered in the Easter 1916 massacre, a kind of beauty that eliminates "all settled order," all sense of the normal, and produces something utterly unknown.

Yeats's own experiences in the theater showed him how difficult it was to escape the problems of organizing. As he sought to transform "the mob into a people," he discovered that he turned into a leader of an institution not much different from the other capitalist institutions around him. In "The Fascination of What's Difficult" (p. 93), Yeats complains about the "theatre business, management of men," saying that it makes him feel like a "colt" that must "Shiver under the lash, strain, sweat and jolt / As though it dragged road metal." The theater, which was supposed to free the people from capitalism, becomes a form of extremely alienated and unnatural labor, a business indistinguishable from other forms of corporate management. Instead of liberating the nation, Yeats says, the theater "dried the sap out of my veins, and rent / Spontaneous joy and natural content / Out of my heart." The poem builds to what seems an anarchic escape, the speaker swearing he will go out at night, "find the stable and pull out the bolt."

This would seem to mean the destruction of the whole "business," releasing the natural horse from the mechanical structure of roads and metal. But it also implies giving up the effort to run a theater and returning to an art disconnected from any audience, an art that will not inspire any mass movement.

At this time, Yeats did consider a third possibility besides organizing the masses or ignoring them, but it was a possibility that he could not then embrace: that the masses were already moving and even making use of his poetry for inspiration, but moving in a direction that made no sense to Yeats. There was a nationalist movement that Yeats admired, but it was racing toward socialism. Yeats was stuck in the perplexing position of seeing the spirit he believed would reform the world seeking a reformation he hated. And at the core of his confusion was his relationship with Maud Gonne, who seemed in many ways the incarnation of that mythic and violent force that would transform the world in theories such as Sorel's. As a person and as a political leader, she inspired Yeats and focused his poetic power, and yet she refracted it, so that the movement it inspired was not what he intended. In his comments about her, we can see Yeats wrestling with the strange ways in which the power of myth and violence operates. In "No Second Troy" (p. 91), Yeats describes her as the reincarnation of the power celebrated in myth, the power of Helen to destroy institutions and create vast movements. Maud's beauty is described as a weapon,

> like a tightened bow, a kind
> That is not natural in an age like this,
> Being high and solitary and most stern.

But when she brings this ancient beauty into the modern world, it has quite different effects than it had in ancient Greece. Instead of inspiring the kind of movement that raises the masses to greatness, turning every soldier to an epic hero (as Sorel believed myths would),

> she would of late
> Have taught to ignorant men most violent ways,
> Or hurled the little streets upon the great.

In other words, her advocacy of a socialist revolution threatens to destroy the very "high and solitary" greatness that she embodies and that gives her power.

The title and the last line of the poem point to the problem: "Was there another Troy for her to burn?" The presence of mythic beauty, of a Helen reincarnated, did not simply destroy this world and restore ancient or eternal forms; it led instead to unpredictable social changes. Yeats oddly did not blame Maud Gonne for her own ideas, but rather saw the direction she was leading the people as resulting from the intersection of her ancient beauty and "an age like this." He concluded that her power may have been a projection of the crowd itself. In the *Autobiography*, Yeats writes that Gonne "looked as though she lived in an ancient civilisation where all superiorities whether of the mind or the body were a part of public ceremonial, were in some way the crowd's creation, as the entrance of the Pope into St. Peter's is the crowd's creation."[23] She then appeared to have ancient beauty because she embodied the desires of the crowds around her. It followed that she was not at all misguided: she was precisely what Sorel argued was necessary, the external embodiment of the unconscious desires of the crowd.

But Yeats had great difficulty accepting the conclusion that the masses were carrying leaders along. Until the 1916 massacre, he continued to believe that leaders and poets could and should resist the direction of mass movements. In the poems he collected in *Responsibilities* (1914), Yeats calls on the great to ignore the masses, the "Paudeens" who simply "play at pitch and toss" (p. 108). He also attacks the masses as "Eunuchs" who "rail and sweat" as they look at the great men with "sinewy thigh" like Synge, who create unpopular art (p. 111). But there is an implied doubt about the power of leadership in these poems. If Synge has such a sinewy thigh, why hasn't he simply won over the crowd, which is always conceived of as feminine? Why is it that "Romantic Ireland's dead and gone" (p. 108)? After the anxieties of the poems in *The Green Helmet* (1910) about the direction and power of the crowd, the angry assertions of the need to ignore and to dominate the crowd in *Responsibilities* reveal Yeats's uncertainty of his own or anyone else's power to do so.

At the end of the volume, several poems raise the possibility that the power of the crowd may be the natural, passionate, potent force in the world, while Yeats's own art and the kind of leadership he has been calling for may be artificial and weak—precisely because they seek to hold to visions of alternative, ancient worlds, as Morris did, rather than accepting the direction in which the masses are going. Particularly pointed in its critique of Yeats himself is "The Magi" (p. 126), a poem about wise old men in "stiff, painted clothes" who are "hoping to find once more . . . The uncontrollable mystery on the bestial floor." These are men who once were leaders, but who are now searching for direction from the "bestial" parts of society—from the lower classes. They are searching because they were "unsatisfied" by "Calvary's turbulence." Calvary ought to have been purely an ascent, a movement to heaven, toward divine leadership, the Son looking up and traveling toward the sun. But it was a turbulent scene, unsatisfying possibly because of the involvement of the mob in the crucifixion. The bestial floor is the movement down, God joining with the poor and passing through a woman, a scene where the wise men have to bow down to a baby and deny all their accumulated wisdom. Calling the birth an "uncontrollable mystery on the bestial floor" suggests a mystic, unpredictable power, a power that is difficult to worship or even look at because it inspires disgust as well as awe. Yeats's comments on Maud Gonne's power similarly reveal a mixture of awe and horror. Something about her invokes strange gods: "Her oratory, by its emotional temper, was an appeal to herself and also to something uncontrollable."[24] Yeats was a Magus carrying gifts to Maud Gonne, and he was terrified of her uncontrollable power, especially her attraction to the "bestial floor," to the lowly.[25]

In "The Magi," Yeats mocks his own early poetics based on reviving the spirit of the people through the use of ancient texts. The wise men are almost a comic image of ancient art, ancient texts, facing a new and "bestial" power in the world to which they have been led by their study of ancient magic. Yeats went on to a clearer mockery of his early belief in ancient myths in "The Circus Animals' Desertion" (pp. 346–48), and in that poem as in "The Magi," the alternative to those high myths is an image of lowliness that clearly disgusts Yeats: "the foul rag and bone shop" and the "slut / Who keeps the till." In "The Magi" and in succeeding poems, Yeats no longer presented the alternative to modern society in images of beauty: the other world was presented in images of ugliness, of mystery, of merging with animal bodies, and of speaking as a female—all images of descending, of joining with the lowly people, rather than simply looking up to heaven to find inspiration. Yeats moved from a belief in magical alternative worlds to mocking the Magi-cians who have created such illusions.

The Magi are disoriented, searching for a mystery, because they have been too devoted to artificial forms of beauty. Like the doll maker in "The Dolls" (pp. 126–27), they cannot appreciate babies, which seem "noisy and filthy," preferring mechanical beings or stiff, painted things. There is a connection in "The Magi" and in "The Dolls" between disgust at what is natural and the creation of illusion: Yeats was worried he was engaging in a worthless kind of artifice. In an essay, "The Galway Plain," Yeats argued against the kind of artificial aesthetic that disdains the common people's tastes as too vulgar:

> The poet must always prefer the community where the perfected minds express the people to a community that is vainly seeking to copy the perfected mind. To have even perfectly the thoughts that can be weighted, the knowledge that can be got from books, the precision that can be learned at school, to belong to any aristocracy, is to be a little pool that will soon dry up. A people alone are a great river.[26]

The poet who seeks precision by copying the perfected mind is like the doll maker who creates an art that treats the masses, the people, as noisy and filthy children. And the vision of a community seeking to copy the perfected mind is similar to Yeats's description of the followers of Morris: such a community ignores the living people for perfect visions of green worlds. Yeats's describing such people as an "aristocracy" might seem surprising, given his general advocacy of aristocracy, but it is not hard to see how he was using the term in this essay: a group of people who regard themselves as the ideal to be copied by the masses, rather than an elite who are devoted to the masses. In the essay, Yeats was clear which kind of elite he would create, but in his early poems, he was devoted to what "can be got from books" and disgusted with the masses. Yeats fought against himself when he tried to "express the people," continually haunted by the question of how one can join the great river of the masses without being drowned by it.

Modernist Violence

The 1916 massacre cut through Yeats's self-contradictions because it revealed to him a force that could radically alter his own mind, his own values. David Lloyd argues that the poem "Easter, 1916" initiated a period in which Yeats felt bereft of his bardic role because real political action and violence were doing what poetry was supposed to do—changing the images in people's minds.[27] I agree that "Easter, 1916" expresses Yeats's break with one traditional image of poetic power, but it replaces it with another that revives his poetry. Yeats realized a new way to write: in conjunction with violence. He clearly saw his poetry as having a powerful relationship to events. He realized that he really was prophetic and expressive of the mass mind and that part of the power of his poetry derived from the fact that he disliked what he was expressing and what the effect of his poetry was. He began to see himself as participating in the pessimistic Sorelian act of fomenting a catastrophe that could disrupt his own mind.

Sorel's theory implies two different kinds of historical time: the smooth flow of "progress" in any one era—which supports habits and hinders revolution—and catastrophe, sudden shifts of value that cannot be fit into the past as either progress or decline. Before writing *Reflections on Violence*, Sorel wrote a series of articles on the concept of progress, arguing that it was a prop of bourgeois ideology.[28] All his life, Yeats dismissed the concept of progress in favor of cycles and broken rings, but only after the events of Easter 1916 did Yeats become convinced that he could be and was involved in a radical and sudden change, a catastrophe that was altering the structure of history and the flow of time.

The poem "Easter, 1916" (pp. 180–82) is built around the contrast between these two kinds of time, progress and catastrophe. It begins with a description of the slow, private time within which Yeats and the Irish had been living. The opening line, "I have met them at close of day," has a double meaning: it partly indicates a world of individuals meeting in private talk, living their lives day by day, and it partly indicates the final "close of day," the end of this daily kind of life and the start of another chronology, of eras and masses. Those who live the daily life have "vivid faces"—they are distinct individuals—and reside in "eighteenth-century houses" while spending their time telling tales to "companion[s] around the fire at the club." They are living in a world of outdated liberalism. Yeats twice describes the language of these companionable people as "polite meaningless words"; in the companion poem, "The Rose Tree" (p. 182), Yeats similarly critiques the light banter that has dominated everyday language as "a breath of politic words." Polite and politic words keep people isolated and divided; they make up the language of the world "where motley is worn" (p. 180), a world that cannot come together in mass movements or in large-scale change.

The second stanza of "Easter, 1916" continues to explore the old worldview, presenting a series of descriptions of individuals from a single point of view, presumably Yeats's: this is a stanza of nineteenth-century novelpoetry; it assumes that the best way to make sense of history is to carefully specify individual characters. The mass death of these people destroys the importance of their distinct characters, their vivid faces, and changes the form of poetry and novels, leading to a "terrible beauty" that effaces individuals, inspires mass movements, and alters the flow of history. As Sorel argues, if the pessimistic view of the social order as a single block is "admitted, it then becomes absurd to make certain wicked men responsible for the evils from which society suffers."[29] "Easter, 1916" is a poem showing Yeats struggling to give up his personal values, his sense that certain people are evil and others good. The middle of the poem is devoted to listing his judgments and then dismissing them, replacing them with a "terrible beauty," a passion that alters his own values and disrupts his own mind.

The companion poem, "The Rose Tree," represents Yeats's final rejection of Morris's and O'Leary's Romantic politics in favor of the theories of James Connolly and Padraic Pearse, in which violence and myth are the agents of social change. Yeats had viewed Morris as a man who would always know how to find the well to revive the dying tree of the modern world. But in "The Rose Tree," "all the wells are parched away," and it takes more than a happy man to restore them. In fact, it takes the destruction of the individual who has remained separate from the current world, wrapped up in his dreams. The use of "our own red blood" is a call to violence and sacrifice, but it is also a call to stop thinking of the individual body and the individual mind as elements that must be held separate from the corrupt social system. Shedding "our" blood is violating the boundaries of "our" individual bodies, destroying "us" as individuals to release the social medium, the blood. It is giving one's body over to the flow of history in the most complete way.

In "The Rose Tree," violence seems intended to restore the cycles of nature, to allow the tree to turn green. In "Easter, 1916," Yeats has a more complex vision of what violence will do: it will alter nature itself, or rather move people from living within one kind of nature to living within another. In this poem, the rebels who have given their lives are compared to a stone, in contrast to the "living stream" that changes "minute by minute" (p. 181). The stone might seem to represent unchanging eternity and even unnaturalness; people whose hearts are "enchanted to stone" would seem to have lost contact with nature. However, stones are as natural as streams or clouds. The contrast between streams and stones is a contrast between two time scales of natural change: the immediate and the geological. Humans are capable of acting in both time scales: the individual lives minute by minute, but the society and the race live by geological eras.

Yeats was seeking to bring about "geological" (or we might say sociological) change and hence to disrupt the minute-by-minute lives most people live. In our minute-by-minute lives, we cannot see changes of eras, just as we cannot see stones changing. The goal of Connolly's syndicalist theory of mass movements was to bring about mass change, and the method was to "enchant" hearts to "one purpose alone," to make them like "stones" so they would not respond to the immediate changes or to the politic words of reason.

The stone that syndicalists wished to become is the stone that would "trouble the living stream," disrupting the bubbling flow of daily life, changing the channel in which the stream runs. A few sacrifice their daily lives in order to alter everyone's lives permanently. Sometimes, though, the sacrifice takes "too long": some stones sit in the stream without changing it. One can create mass movements that fail, movements that do not produce vast social change, but merely are run over and worn down by the continuing flow of the old ways. The key element is timing: one has to sacrifice one's individual life only when such resistance to the movement of society will turn the social tide. Yeats describes the result of inopportune sacrifice by using the same image that defines the firm resolve of resistance: a heart turned to stone. There is a difference between a heart "enchanted to stone" and a heart that "too long a sacrifice makes a stone": the enchanted heart "troubles the living stream"; the heart made a stone is withdrawn, having no effect, while the stream runs over it. When Yeats asks, "O when may it suffice?" he is asking when the stones will be strong enough to move the living stream into a new channel, replacing the motley world of British individuals with the green world of a restored Ireland and replacing the separated bodies with a feeling of common blood carrying everyone along.

There is another element besides timing that is important in transforming violence into social revolution: myth, the distinctive contribution of the poet. A myth takes the emotions released by violence and makes them cohere—turns them into passion, into a collective emotion that unites the masses in something like love. The only evidence that a particular set of images form a myth is that it brings those who are released from daily life by catastrophe into a new unity. In the poems that followed "Easter, 1916," Yeats wrestled with the question of his role in various moments of violence or of peace: had he contributed to the transformative forces? Once he had given up on the idea that he could know ahead of time what values or images to use, and once he knew that the images he created were going to have effects, he was then faced with the problem that generated his poetry: how to allow his mind to join with the shifting tides, how to generate the myth that would make violence revolutionary and passionate, not merely chaotic.

The difference between riotous emotions and passion underlies the poems Yeats wrote during the civil war, which suggest that the problem of those monstrously violent years was a lack of passion in the people committing violent acts. The truly despairing civil war poem, "I See Phantoms of Hatred and of the Heart's Fullness and of the Coming Emptiness" (pp. 205–6), says the masses are rioting because they are "rage-hungry," desperately wishing for a genuinely bloody emotion. Lacking passionate desires, each "plunges towards nothing, arms and fingers spreading wide / For the embrace of nothing." These masses are driven by a chaotic stream of "monstrous familiar images [that] swim to the mind's eye," appearing and disappearing too rapidly, so that nobody can embrace them fully. Yeats feels himself almost drawn into joining in their cry for "vengeance on the murderers of Jacques Molay." His refusal to join in the call for vengeance was a difficult act in the time of the civil war, when each Irish party felt betrayed by the other. In some ways, Yeats did support the vengeance of one side: he was a Free Stater, accepting the treaty with England that ended the Anglo-Irish War and allowed Ireland to rule itself within the limits of an oath of loyalty to England. He was serving in Parliament, supporting government policy to put down the revolt of the Republicans, who refused to accept anything other than complete independence. Yeats's party argued that the violence should end because a workable Irish state had emerged and a peaceful process would eventually sever the last legal ties to England. Yeats believed his party could overcome the hatred that divided the Irish. In his poem, though, he has little hope that the passion that should unite the Irish—love for the nation—will replace the hatreds that divide them. The problem is that the only images of love and unity that poets such as Yeats can produce are ones that have no appeal. There are only phantoms in Ireland, ephemeral images that do not coalesce into a myth of national unity.

The poem is structured around the failure of fantasy, of imagination: the three stanzas together trace the results of projecting false images of love into a situation of violence. In the first stanza, the violence has a potential of bringing people together: the poet himself feels drawn into the crowd, and there is a common cry on everyone's lips, "Vengeance for Jacques Molay." There is some possibility of unifying passion left. By the third stanza, though, there is no unifying emotion at all, no passion, rage, or even hatred. The masses then become an "indifferent multitude," losing all trace of the "eyes that rage has brightened, arms it has made lean."

The people even lose their cohesion as a mob, becoming merely "brazen hawks," birds of prey glutting themselves, lacking any general motive at all: "Nor self-delighting reverie / Nor hate of what's to come," just "eye's complacency" and "innumerable clanging wings."

The stanza between hatred and emptiness presents the poet's effort to create images of the "heart's fullness," to extract the kernel of unity and love buried in the hatred of the first stanza. But the image seems far more a retreat from the emotions surrounding the poet than an expression of their deep core. Unicorns who "bear ladies on their backs" while "the ladies close their musing eyes" is unquestionably an image of unity, peace, and love, but it seems to bear very little relationship to the parties warring with each other. It is precisely because the image of the "heart's fullness" is irrelevant to the violence engulfing the world that the rage-hungry troops are going to turn into an indifferent multitude. The image of fullness does not feed the rage-hungry troops. It is merely an outdated image from the past, a thoroughly "poetic" image, much like the images in so many of Yeats's earlier poems.

The speaker in this poem is aware that he bears some responsibility for the horrors surrounding him; he ends by evaluating his own actions, raising the question of whether he should have created different images. He admits he has an uneasy conscience because he did not produce "something that all others understand or share." He excuses his writing by saying that if he had written something that had "drawn forth / A company of friends," it would have "but made us pine the more"—the love and unity that he could have created only would have made the general disunity more painful.

There are hints, though, that the speaker feels the need to explain and justify his acts because he cannot fully forgive himself. He says he has settled for "the half-read wisdom of daemonic images" and that will "suffice" for him. It sounds as if he has had to settle for only half-read wisdom because the images have been too obscure to read fully. But it may also be that he has been willing to read only half the daemonic images that have arisen in him. He writes out an image of unicorns and ladies, but does not write out the "monstrous familiar images" that in the first stanza he says are swimming about in his mind. The speaker explains why he does not focus on those images: when he does, he is swept up in the riotous feelings of the crowd, leading his "wits astray." In other words, he is keeping himself separate from contact with the social whole in order to preserve the discreteness of his own mind. His images of unity and "heart's fullness" are false because he has "shut the door" on the chaos around him to preserve his individual integrity,, preferring "the abstract joy" he can find in isolation, and the result is that the entire social order becomes abstract, impersonal, emotionless, indifferent.

In the *Autobiography*, Yeats argues that poets must not seek thus to preserve themselves if they are to produce the greatest poetry, the poetry

that alters mankind: they must endanger their own wits, or, in effect, ter-
rorize themselves. He says that when we examine poets such as Dante and
Villon,

> We gaze at such men in awe, because we gaze not at a work of art, but at the
> re-creation of the man through that art, the birth of a new species of man,
> and, it may even seem that the hairs of our heads stand up, because that
> birth, that re-creation, is from terror. Had not Dante and Villon understood
> that their fate wrecked what life could not rebuild, had they lacked their
> Vision of Evil, had they cherished any species of optimism, they could but
> have found a false beauty . . . and suffered no change at all.[30]

The birth of a new species is the birth of a new mass. Yeats pursued this
goal throughout all his later poems, seeking to find that particular conjunction of image and cataclysm, of myth and terror, that would unite and
mutate the Irish people. In "I See Phantoms," however, Yeats shows a poet
unwilling to wreck what life could not rebuild, unwilling to give up his
cherished optimism, his pretty visions of unicorns and ladies, the hope of
the happiness of William Morris. The speaker in this poem does not have
the strength to create a "Vision of Evil": he is suffering from a touch of
cowardice.

In "Nineteen Hundred and Nineteen" (pp. 206–10), Yeats directly con-
demns himself for such cowardice and then moves on to overcome it, to
face the images in his mind that frighten him: he begins to create a ter-
rorist poetry, a poetry that is truly postcolonial because it goes beyond the
entire colonial world that formed the mind of Yeats himself. In this poem,
he shows how he finally was driven by the winds of change to break with
himself, his own values, his own sense of good and evil.

He begins by speaking of the "pretty toys" such as "law" and "philosophy" that Yeats and his cohorts had at one time believed would bring peace
to the world. But "a levelling wind" has destroyed these toys, and his group,
who "planned to bring the world under a rule," are reduced to "weasels
fighting in a hole." He had been part of a leadership that had thought it
could stand above the world, but this group is now hiding from the social
movements outside, bickering with each other about what went wrong.
The young Yeats and those he joined were out of touch with the real tides of
history and so dreamed of the wrong ideals: universal law rather than ties
of blood, abstract truths rather than passions. This group has lost control
not only of the winds of change but of the mob part of their own minds.

The poet severely criticizes his own cowardice, saying that as a poet
he ought to be a "swan" who could "play, or . . . ride / Those winds that
clamour of approaching night." He contrasts such a poet with a man who
retreats into a hole in the ground or in his own mind: "A man in his own
secret meditation / Is lost amid the labyrinth that he has made / In art or
politics." The whole poem is about whether Yeats will remain withdrawn,
hiding in a hole, or will try to fly on winds that appear simply destructive.

What is needed is a paradoxical act: joining in the destruction in order to stop it; or, we might say, giving up hope in order to initiate a new hope. The next-to-last section enacts the process of joining and thereby overcoming the nihilistic winds. The poet for three stanzas calls out "Come let us mock at the great," the "wise," and the "good," thus becoming the voice of the destructive wind. But then he turns the destructive force against itself:

> Mock mockers after that
> That would not lift a hand maybe
> To help good, wise or great
> To bar that foul storm out, for we
> Traffic in mockery.

Yeats realizes that even when he is hiding in a hole, and even when he is condemning himself as a "weasel," he is in fact part of the destructive wind and trafficking in mockery himself. By condemning everything great, good, and wise, including his own earlier dreams, he has in effect joined in the process that Le Bon talks about whereby the crowd unconsciously rises up to drag one generation of leaders down to prepare the ground for growing new ones. That Yeats was one of the old generation of leaders makes his willingness to join in such an act of "levelling" poignant.

The description of the wind as "levelling" suggests that it represents the democratic movement—not a rejection of the dreams of law and peace that began the poem, but the result of those dreams. As Yeats specifies in *A Vision*, the historical transition he saw coming was a move from democratic to aristocratic, or, in his terms, from "primary" to "antithetical." The primary phase of history is "dogmatic, levelling, unifying, feminine, humane, peace its means and end; an *antithetical* dispensation . . . is expressive, hierarchical, multiple, masculine, harsh, surgical."[31] The poem ends with an image of such a new age arriving, an age of masculine, harsh, surgical social order. The "wind drops," and "there lurches past, his great eyes without thought . . . that insolent fiend Robert Artisson." This is an image similar to the beast in "The Second Coming," a creature with a point of view that is so alien to ours that it seems devoid of thought (as the beast has "blank" eyes). The fiend's name suggests that he is the "artist's son," that he represents the artist's or poet's success in giving birth to a new leader, a new age. Robert Artisson's first effect is to inspire the love of "Lady Kyteler": the cure for social disorder is a male who can inspire passion, replacing the abstract love of law and philosophy that is bloodless. The last image in the poem is a description of what Lady Kyteler brings to Robert Artisson: "red combs of her cocks," the red blood that fills the glorious crown of the great leader.

We might read "Nineteen Hundred and Nineteen" as saying that only the emergence of a leader will calm the chaotic winds, but that would invert the sequence of the poem: the winds die down and then Artisson emerges. The leader is part of a cycle that involves periods of chaos and periods of calm. The artist's role is not to predict the future, but to make conscious the current state of the social order, to ride the wind, to prepare the way for something neither the artist nor anyone else can understand. Yeats here disclaims the creation of images of timeless beauty or eternal values; his art is to function only in conjunction with specific social tides. He even speculates that great works that outlast the violent spirit that gave birth to them get in the way of social change. In "Ancestral Houses" (pp. 200–201), Yeats wonders whether aristocratic great houses can destroy the greatness of the families in them by replacing the "violence" and "bitterness" that built them with "sweetness" and "gentleness" and thereby "take our greatness with our violence . . . [and] our bitterness." A great house, or similarly, a great poem, is merely an

> empty sea-shell flung
> Out of the obscure dark of the rich streams,
> And not a fountain.

Cultural products lose their value when they are separated from the rich streams that flung them up. Houses, poems, societies created by violence become empty shells in times of peace.

For Yeats to argue during the chaos of the civil war that there may be something wrong with peace seems very strange. However, in those years when he participated in the violent formation of a new society, he was profoundly aware of what is often obscured in times of peace—the violence that makes peace possible. Dreams of peace, gentleness, and sweetness may be merely efforts to forget the origins of those dreams, to forget what gives them power. Dreams of peace may then be part of what eventually destroys every peaceful social order by sapping the "bitterness" that makes people feel that violence is necessary. Yeats accepted that history would consist of cycles of partial peace followed by great violence. His late poems can be read as a challenge to live without forgetting that violence will always return.

The necessity for violence is directly tied in to the importance of the masses as creators of the social system. The "rich streams" that fling up great houses, great poems, and great leaders are, ultimately, the masses. As Yeats writes, "Whatever existence we think of, a Civilisation's or an individual's, it arises from the general mass, wins its victory & returns."[32] The process of creating order is in effect the process of a part of the mass gaining power over the rest. In a much later poem, "Blood and the Moon" (pp. 237–39), Yeats speaks of this process as it occurred when Ireland long ago became a great empire:

> A bloody, arrogant power
> Rose out of the race
> Uttering, mastering it.

This equation of uttering and mastering puts together the literary and ruling functions. Literature can achieve its richness only in conjunction with the power that produces great leaders, great houses. When the race has no such utterance and no such masters, it becomes "half dead at the top," and Yeats fears that "every modern nation" is in that state. The half-dead top, like the drowsy emperor in "Byzantium," leaves the race both unconscious and leaderless, caught in the sensual music of mass chaos, not the passion of mass movements.

"The Second Coming" (p. 187) traces the process of a "bloody, arrogant power" emerging out of mass movements and shows the role of the poet in this process. The poem is not a mere abstract meditation, but an effort to come to grips with and influence the history happening around him, as Yeats indicated by placing it at the end of a brief history of Western civilization in his *Autobiography*. After tracing the increasing fragmentation of the social order up to its present moment of "growing murderousness," he inserted the first stanza of "The Second Coming": the widening gyre that separates and isolates the falcon and the falconer.[33] Thus, it is the fragmentation of the social order that is turning people into unleashed falcons, uncontrollable birds of prey, like the "brazen hawks" in "I See Phantoms" that make up the "indifferent multitude." The falconers, in this reading, are the leaders of the current, corrupt social order, the capitalists who encourage people to be hunters and then take for themselves the prey that the people have accumulated. The falcons who do not listen to the falconer are doing just what capitalism tells workers to do, breaking with bosses and becoming entrepreneurs, self-centered hunters. This process of separation and fragmentation ironically produces a "blood-dimmed tide" sweeping over the nation because it destroys leadership and sets people against each other in competition for prey. "Blood-dimmed" may seem to suggest a bloody tide, but the phrase seems more to imply a lack of blood: these masses, like the "rage-hungry troop" in "I See Phantoms," are murderous because they have lost contact with their common blood, so they are willing to tear the social body apart.

The beast is a contrast to the chaos of the early stanza, though not necessarily a happy alternative. What is particularly changed is the separate bodies of falcons and falconers. The leader, the human falconer, is reduced to a head, unable to stand or move on its own; the serving forces, the animal falcons, are transformed into a lion's thigh, united animal force, unable to direct itself. The different "species" within Ireland (classes, religions, etc.) can no longer be separated without doing obvious violence to all of them. The shadows of birds that circle indignantly are all that is left of separate bodies—the empty illusion of individual existence, all real substance now revealed as part of the social body.[34]

Yeats himself used the term "the second coming" to label a coming form of the state that he directly connected with the development of modernist literature. In the introduction to "Fighting the Waves," as we have seen, he says that nineteenth-century realism produced a view of man as "dry sticks," while *Ulysses*, *The Waves*, and Pound's *Cantos* presented man as "a swimmer in the waves, or the waves themselves." Yeats then goes on to argue that the "revolution in thought" that produced this new vision is part of a "second coming, Plato's Republic, not the Siege of Troy."[35] The second coming, then, is the goal of modernist literature and will be accomplished by the creation of a new republic, built out of waves, and not merely by acts of destruction, by another Siege of Troy.

But as this poem suggests, Yeats was ambivalent about this future social order. He clearly hoped that the new age would reunite the fragmented parts of society and so accomplish in some form his childhood dream of "unity of culture." But by the time of "The Second Coming," he had radically altered that dream. When he was young, as he says in the *Autobiography*, he thought that art could bring the warring classes and nations of Europe together, producing a beautiful mix of different species:

> I thought that all art should be a Centaur finding in the popular lore its back and strong legs. I got great pleasure . . . from that tale of Dante hearing a common man sing some stanza from *The Divine Comedy*, and from Don Quixote's meeting with some common man that sang Ariosto. Morris had never seemed to care greatly for any poet later than Chaucer and though I preferred Shakespeare to Chaucer I begrudged my own preference. Had not Europe shared one mind and heart . . . until a little before Shakespeare's birth?[36]

The centaur is an image of a beautiful unity bringing upper and lower classes together; it is an image from the aesthetic of Morris. But Yeats goes on to say that he was simply mistaken in dreaming of such unity because he did not "understand as yet how little that Unity, however wisely sought, is possible without a Unity of Culture in class or people that is no longer possible at all."[37] Yeats's later poems pursue the thoroughly pessimistic and Sorelian goal of advocating what seems no longer possible, of creating images of catastrophic change. The beast in "The Second Coming" is a terrible version of the centaur, an image of the mixing of lower and upper classes that is no longer beautiful but terrifying, involving the destruction of the present age and of the poet himself.

The history of the reception of this poem suggests further that Yeats succeeded in contacting deep social tides of which he was unaware, tides he would probably have opposed. "The Second Coming" has become famous partly because of its Egyptian imagery, its Latin words, and its vagueness, so it can be adapted to non-Irish contexts. Poems such as "I See Phantoms" and "Nineteen Hundred and Nineteen" present much the same scenario as "The Second Coming," but use images of the new leadership taken from Irish traditions, not Egyptian. None has become as famous as "The Second

Coming": we might speculate that Yeats in fact tapped into a much larger gyre in "The Second Coming" than he recognized: not merely a change to conservative, aristocratic rule within Ireland or Europe, but a change to a multicultural world order. Eliot similarly used images from India to represent the new hierarchy in his most famous poem, *The Waste Land*, and then went on to write many considerably less famous poems that present Catholicism as the tradition that needs to be revived. Yeats's and Eliot's poetry has served to inspire writers in Africa and India: conservative hopes of overthrowing capitalism and restoring "culture" easily translate into anticolonial sentiments (and sometimes into neocolonial sentiments), and Egyptian and Indian images may easily be interpreted as part of the process of breaking free of a Eurocentric tradition. Yeats often interpreted the change he saw coming as far more than the overthrow of democracy: as "The Second Coming" implies, it would be the overthrow of Christianity as well. He would even have accepted the idea that his poems could be part of social movements he himself would have opposed: he presented his poetry as having been written by the social medium, not by him.

Yeats did not flinch from fully exploring the consequences of letting violent social forces he did not understand or control shape his actions and his poetry. His later poems are frequently about the terror poets experience as they write, the terror Yeats had to inflict upon himself to accept the role of violence in the world. In "The Second Coming," we see the poet finding a "revelation" coming into his mind that is clearly derived from a book of horrors. The poet does nothing; the image is itself the agent of its emergence as it "troubles" the poet's "sight." The passivity of the poet as herald of a new age is important in Yeats's vision of history. He described the process of a new era emerging as a version of a minority being inseminated by a "force": "When the new era comes bringing its stream of irrational force it will, as did Christianity, find its philosophy already impressed upon the minority who have, true to phase, turned away at the last gyre. . . . And it must awake into life . . . organic groups, *covens* of physical or intellectual kin melted out of the frozen mass. I imagine new races, as it were, seeking domination."[38] The frozen mass waits until the hot stream of irrational force strikes it, and then new groups are melted out of it: this is indeed a second coming, a violent sexual act that produces a new minority. Yeats imagined himself part of the "coven," the group of witches awakened by the force of what appeared to be Satan but would become the new God. Yeats hoped himself to be one of those giving birth to the new age. But as such, he was going to be subjected to the "stream of irrational force": the act of creation is in effect an act of being raped. The greatest poetry is not only an act of "giving birth" through "terror," but an act of being inseminated involuntarily by a "species" quite unlike one's own.

Yeats's poem about the "annunciation" of a new age, "Leda and the Swan," (p. 214), presents such an act of rape. Part of the power of this poem is the unsettling lack of a coherent point of view: Yeats seems to identify as much with Leda as with Zeus. The question that ends the poem might be one Leda would ask herself: has she put on Zeus's knowledge with his power? Has she replaced Zeus? If so, does she know what to do with her awesome power? Yeats feels himself like Leda: he feels within him a god-like power, an awesome responsibility, but he does not know what to do with it. By expressing the images arising in him, he may usher in a new age against his will. The enigmatic last lines suggest that the result of Zeus's rape is to turn Leda into an active part of the creation of the future, and possibly into an agent who will turn things in a direction quite different from that intended by Zeus. If she has taken on his power but not his knowledge, she will perhaps rely on her own knowledge, her own mind, to direct the use of Zeus's power. The word that Yeats uses to indicate the transformation of an act between two individuals into a vast social change is "engendered," as if what is happening in these social events is a change in gender itself. Central to what Yeats says is "engendered" is "Agamemnon dead," an act of revenge by a woman, as if the ultimate result of this rape is to initiate an age of women's violence against men.

In another poem, "The Mother of God" (p. 249), Yeats writes from the first-person perspective of a woman discovering a god growing within her. Yeats alludes to Leda in this poem about Mary by describing the "terror of love" in terms of "wings beating about the room." The poem turns the "terrible beauty" of "Easter, 1916" inward, expressing what we might call a syndicalist theory of poetic inspiration: inspiration by terror. Yeats shows that to give birth to the new age, one has to be taken by the force of the age, by the images from the new gyre beginning to develop.

Altering the Gender of the Unconscious

The relation of terror to a change of gender—why Zeus "engenders" a new age—is that terror serves to break apart the unconscious background of the poet and hence gives the poet another unconscious, or, we might say, the unconscious of the other. Yeats pursued this literally: he based all his later poems on automatic, supposedly unconscious writings by his wife. For Yeats, it was not enough to use metaphors of giving birth or being impregnated in his poetic practice: he wanted to actually gain access to a female's unconscious.

Yeats did not merely use his wife as a therapeutic device to handle his own neuroses, and he was not merely engaging in obscure occult practices. In seeking to tap his wife's unconscious, he sought to understand what was driving the unconscious of the West, the same thing that, as we have seen, George Dangerfield believed he had to do to understand the unconscious motives of all the violent mass movements of prewar England—and indeed, to understand what had caused World War I. Dangerfield turned to a study of the women's movement in order to reveal the hidden, unconscious, mass forces driving all the male-dominated events and institutions he examined. By studying women, Dangerfield claimed, "we may get some notion of other forces then sweeping through England; until at last we may even catch a glimpse, fleeting but complete, of that new energy which rose like a phoenix from the strange death of the pre-war world and rushed headlong onto the battlefields of Flanders and the blood-stained beaches of Gallipoli."[39] Like Yeats, Dangerfield described the violent, savage energy transforming Europe as the result of "unconscious desires" that no one, male or female, actually recognized. Yeats examined what his wife wrote while she was supposedly unaware of what she was doing in order, like Dangerfield, to use those writings to provide him with a theory explaining the violent transformations of history.

Yeats needed to study the female mind because, he believed, it has a different relationship to violence than the male mind has. In "Among School Children" (pp. 215–17), Yeats proposes modifying the entire educational system in order to base it on the female way of using violence rather than on the male way. In this poem, Yeats identifies men, particularly old men, with social institutions that are deadening, that cause the deepest desires to be condemned to unconsciousness. Old men have done this by developing abstract philosophies and "neat" systems of schooling: Plato's and Pythagoras's otherworldly philosophies of eternal verities and the music of the stars are much the same as Aristotle's educational system of disciplining a young conqueror: all are efforts to overcome the violence and constant change in the world, to develop philosophies and politics based on a goal of eventually uniting the whole world into one peaceful whole. But such philosophies and such educational systems are nothing more than "old clothes" to cover up the reality of the aging bodies of the old men, the bodies that are going to undermine their philosophies. These old men like to believe that the mind can escape or conquer the body, can transform the untidy natural world into ghostly paradigms that are eternal. The children in the modern school are similarly being trained to be quiet, neat, unemotional, philosophical—nonviolent.

Sorel argued similarly that the modern, bourgeois social order is based on the tenet that "violence will disappear when popular education becomes more advanced." The modern world is a result of a "transition from violence to cunning."[40] Sorel sought to restore violence to a central role in the social order and to eliminate the dishonorable and deceitful world of cunning capitalists. Yeats's poem expresses a similar critique, but finds in the experiences of women a survival of the function of violence.

The poem begins by showing that Yeats has been cast in the role of comfortable old man, supporting the philosophies of other old men. By a series of shocks, though, he finds himself thrust out of that comfortable role. The shocks that carry him are the rage felt by a young girl, the screaming pain of birth, and the broken hearts of mothers and nuns. These are the emotions left out of the school system, and they become the basis of an alternative education. Yeats wants schools based on the suffering of women rather than on the illusions of eternal beauty that old men create. Yeats's own visit to the classroom was supposed to support the authority of old men: he was supposed to show the students what they could become if they tamed their wild emotions to the contours of abstract philosophy. But after one stanza, the situation reverses, so a young girl in the room becomes a figure who teaches and transforms him. Instead of the poet taking the children into their adulthood, they take him into his youth. Instead of the old man teaching the children about the importance of disciplining their passions, they remind him of the importance of being driven wild.

But this poem is not simply a glorification of youthful exuberance against old, dry philosophy: it is not a carpe diem poem, and Yeats is not trying to recapture his own "pretty plumage." The poem undermines the glorification of youth by making us uncomfortable at the sight of an old man getting excited when he looks at a young girl. There is a genuine danger in an educational system that would unleash passions. Teachers would not be "comfortable," sexless "scarecrows"; they would be frightening figures, because they would have their own desires, which would pose a threat to the children.

Yeats then turns to disrupting the power of beauty to seduce—or rather to using that power to do something other than to propel people into sexual relations. He turns directly to the painful experience of birth and takes us into a woman's point of view. He thinks about his own mother, wondering whether she would regard him, a wrinkled old man, as what she had dreamed of in giving birth—and he concludes that she would be disappointed. This stanza takes us out of the classroom, and out of Yeats's sexual fantasies, into women's failed dreams, a move that is repeated in the next two stanzas as Yeats again contrasts male fantasies that pass as philosophy with the female dreams that lead to mothers' and nuns' broken hearts. Yeats repeatedly valorizes women's dreams because they are entwined with loss, with undergoing painful transformations, while men's fantasies are efforts to avoid losses. This poem is about Yeats's effort to understand the experience of undergoing violent transformations such as labor pains. Yeats was in effect making literal the metaphor that he used in his *Autobiography* to describe the greatest poets: causing the "birth of a new species of man" through "terror."

Yeats highlights the moment of a body breaking open when he "alter[s] Plato's parable" of male and female as two halves of one perfect whole by emphasizing the "one shell," and not the "one egg," as what the "yolk and white" comprise. He wants us to think of the moment of breakage, of the thinness of the shell, not of the wholeness of the united egg. Communions, sexual and social, exist as fragile shells that are continually broken. The poem is about how to live in a world that inflicts birth pangs on all, a world where all see what they have produced become distorted and altered— bodies, children, poems, and nations. To do this requires the use of something that women still understand but supposedly wise old men do not: images. The image is the verbal equivalent of a violent transformation: unlike Platonic philosophy, the image creates discontinuity. Though the image keeps a "marble or bronze repose" and so seems as outside of time as Plato's philosophy, it inevitably breaks hearts. The image does not smooth over change as the eternal seems to do; it enforces change, and it appears out of time precisely because it so powerfully alters history. "Among School Children" reveals the need for images that will engender radical change, that will crack open current social forms.

In the last stanza, Yeats seeks to transfer to sociopolitical theory what he has found in the images that mothers and nuns worship, and he does so through the double meaning of the word "labour." He signals that he is switching to the economic use of the term rather than the reproductive meaning by ending stanza 7 with the word "enterprise" and beginning stanza 8 with "Labour." As we read the last stanza, we are tempted to see an ideal of labor as something free of pain—"blossoming" and "dancing" seem gentle processes. But after the intense description of labor as painful birth, this last stanza seems an oddly willful insistence on an illusion. Yeats is forcing us to see that blossoming is not as gentle a process as it seems: a trunk or bole is split open, losing its own integrity and shape, to produce something unlike itself, a blossom. If humans are going to blossom, they will similarly lose their own bodily and mental integrity.

In this poem, Yeats is not trying to hold onto beauty; instead, he proposes a redefinition of the self and of the social order as processes that repeatedly erupt into momentary beauty and then break down into ugliness. The labor that is blossoming is not, then, simply a process of endlessly producing beauty, but rather a labor that is passionate, and so breaks hearts. Yeats is precise about what is wrong with current forms of labor: the impossibility of pleasure, the despair, the tedium. He wants instead a labor that would be a violent transformation connected to intense pleasures such as he conceives of women undergoing in the cycle of sexuality, birth, parenting, and aging.

Yeats wants people to feel their bodies are not neat, contained entities but things that continually change and eventually fail to function, becoming ugly and decayed. And he wants people to feel that the best use of the body as of the mind is to give up its own "definition" in the process of producing other people, other generations, as a mother feels her body losing its definition in the process of giving birth. The only way to accept such a vision is to be part of a social order beyond the individual body, to lose the distinction between the self and the social dance. The overall social order enters this poem in the image of the tree. By asking whether the tree is the leaf, the blossom, or the bole, Yeats wants to escape the idea of a single beauty, an ideal form, a progressive goal at which to aim. If we reframe the question in terms of the stages of humanity presented in the poem, we might ask, "Is humanity a young girl, an asexual embryo, or an old man?" Each of these shapes destroys itself in producing another.

The images of the tree and of the dance show that Yeats wants to emphasize an acceptance of history, not an escape from time. In this poem he is revising "Adam's Curse" by valuing the wearing down of the shell, the process of becoming weary and old, even as he feels disgust and horror at his decaying body. Similarly, Yeats believes that a decayed and corrupt state must be seen as part of the process of continual transformation, not as the absence of social perfection. The state always exists as a part of a historical process, and it gains its legitimacy from that process; as Yeats wrote in a diary entry from 1930, when he was wrestling with the question of violent opposition to the government, "A state is organic and has its childhood and maturity and, as Swift saw and Burke did not, its decline. We owe allegiance to the government of our day in so far as it embodies that historical being."[41]

The emphasis on cycles in this poem suggests that it, too, be read as a cyclic array of stanzas. The vision of beauty that ends the poem is then but a momentary part of the process of violent transformation. The last stanza is the blossom of this poem, a beautiful flower that emerges from the painful labor of the earlier stanzas. This beautiful image functions to propel us into further heartbreak. Yeats ends with such an image to draw us into the dance and in effect seduce us into the next transformation. He creates a terrible beauty, a beauty emerging from terror and propelling us into terror.

The Byzantium poems serve the same function as the last stanza of "Among School Children": they present Byzantium as a flower of social beauty in order to force us to recognize change and destruction. "Sailing to Byzantium" (pp. 193–94) may seem to be about stepping out of the current order of things to some moment of perfect beauty, but such a dream is belied by the last words: the poem is seeking to find a way to speak of "what is past, or passing, or to come," to speak of history. The metal bird is only an "artifice of eternity," and if the speaker could become that bird he would sing to the beautiful people of Byzantium what he knows is "to come" after them: he would tell them the story of their disappearance. Similarly, this poem is a song to the current world that throws the flower of Byzantium like a wrench into the apparatus of day-to-day life, disrupting the "sensual music" that has lulled everyone into dull routines. Yeats is using beauty to draw us out of everyday life and to reveal the process of history, a constant series of disruptions.

The later poem, "Byzantium" (pp. 248–49), focuses intently on the moment of social disruption and its relationship to images. Yeats places us in the moment when Byzantium is about to collapse: the emperor is drowsy, his soldiers drunk, and images of fire and flood, of impending catastrophic events, are in the air. The transformation to come will either sink everyone in unconsciousness and chaos, in "fury" and "mire," or some new social order will emerge. The crucial question at such a moment is whether or not a new image accompanies the destruction of the old order. The military defense of the current, drowsy emperor is useless—the soldiers are drunk and sleepy—and so the survival of civilization depends on "the golden smithies" who will have to forge a new empire out of the unconscious of the race.

This poem is obscure because it is about obscurity itself, about the process by which obliteration of meaning produces new meaning. In the Ireland of 1930, Yeats faced a world of fury and mire, a world of violent movements that did very little except create more and more ruins, more and more garbage. Yeats felt he had no direct access to the images that would bring the wonderful, unified flow of a restored culture. So the poem is in effect about the impenetrability of the moment. It is a prayer for "images that yet / Fresh images beget." He knows the basis of any new civilization will arise from the "general mass." In this poem, the sea represents that general mass, "dolphin-torn, gong-tormented," unlikely to coalesce into a unified social tide.

Yeats at first hopes for the "superhuman" who could escape such a world, but concludes that without fury and mire, the superhuman cannot alter anything; its flames "cannot singe a sleeve." Instead, Yeats celebrates the smithies who let themselves be carried by what terrifies and disgusts them, by the fury and mire: such smithies could "break the flood," perhaps adding to the torment for the moment, but perhaps also starting the process of images emerging that will eventually reshape the chaos. R. P. Blackmur argues that Yeats's goal in many of his later poems was to create a sense of terror in his readers, to make us feel the fury and mire within us.[42] Only out of such violence directed against the self, Yeats believed, can the images emerge that will transform the world.

In "Byzantium," the smithies who could create a new myth are connected with an aristocratic government—they are the "Emperor's" smithies. But as Yeats watched Ireland settle into a form that seemed to him simply to recreate the bland daily life before the break from England, he finally lost hope that a ruling class could be restored. With the Republicans in power, threatening to kill him as well as all the Protestant upper classes, he gave up all images of aristocracy, concluding in the third of "Three Songs to the Same Tune" (pp. 568–91), "When nations are empty up there at the top . . . Time for us all to pick out a good tune, / Take to the roads and go marching along": he wrote marching songs for the Irish Fascists.[43] Instead of holding to any ideal at all, he chose simply to march: "O any old words to a tune." In an era without leadership, Yeats saw no function for high art: the goal then was not to break the flood but to start the flood moving. In effect, Yeats was seeking the chaos he had decried earlier in his life. This did not make him a hypocrite: when the violence was there, the nation had the raw emotion of hate, the turbulence of the masses, but needed an image to turn that hatred into a unifying love, something that could survive as passion after the battles. In a time of false peace, he felt the need for turbulence, for the marching feet. By bringing the masses to march, he sought to revive the roots of the state, to start the sap flowing. In this poem, he called for "strong blows," for direct engagement with the lowest parts of society and of the human psyche.

In "The Circus Animals' Desertion" (pp. 346–48), Yeats speaks similarly of ending his worship of "masterful images" and seeking instead engagement with the unconscious bodies of the masses. He calls the ancient myths he had tried to resurrect "circus animals," thereby placing himself entirely within a world of lower-class institutions: the upper classes are now simply circus shows, entertainment for the masses. His earlier poems themselves are nothing more than mass entertainment, not so much because appreciative highbrows no longer exist, but because he sees such people as having no power to alter society. He needs to enter the lower-class world in order to prepare for a new civilization emerging. He must let down a ladder to where images "began," into

> A mound of refuse or the sweepings of a street
> Old kettles, old bottles, and a broken can,
> Old iron, old bones, old rags, that raving slut
> Who keeps the till.

Yeats turns to the dirty sections of town and to lower-class women for the alternatives to a political system and an art that seem worthless. This poem could seem a return to Romanticism because the "ladder" on which he will raise up his new poetry starts in "the heart." But this heart is not at all a mirror of what is outside society, in nature, but rather is a mirror of one of the most disgusting and most capitalist parts of society, a shop run by a prostitute, a shop in which body parts are bought and sold. He seeks not his own heart, but the dark heart of the social order, those people destroyed by capitalism, because such people have the passion to destroy capitalism. His "Crazy Jane" poems also turn to a lower-class woman to break through the rigidity of the social order. Jane's claim that "Love has pitched his mansion in / The place of excrement" identifies the locus in which Yeats felt he must search for the passion that could create another great house, another mansion, for Ireland—among the refuse, the lowliest people who so often disgusted him (pp. 259–60). He also feared the passion that lives in the valley of excrement, feared that it would simply reproduce more rubbish—and so he also contemplated eugenic limits on Ireland's lower classes.

The contradiction in his last works continues the contradiction that runs throughout his poems from "Easter, 1916" on: throughout, he hopes for the very force he fears the most, the force that will destroy him. Yeats was willing to turn loose a force that he could not comprehend. His willingness to do so does not reveal despair, but rather a remarkable faith in the deep core of the unconscious culture, a faith in the masses.

CHAPTER 7

Movements Unconscious of Their Destiny

The Culture of the Masses in 'The Waste Land'

T he Waste Land has become an icon of modernism's sense of the incomprehensibility of modern life and of impending apocalypse. Like "The Second Coming," it is read as a poem revealing the twentieth century as a disordered era full of violent forces out of control. It has been used to describe varied social phenomena that seem incomprehensible, destructive, or simply wasteful, such as world war, urban crime, and even television. And like "The Second Coming," much of its power derives from this adaptability: it serves as an emblem of almost any form of cultural disintegration. Nonetheless, there is still value in trying to recover the specific historical situation to which Eliot, like Yeats, was reacting. Images in The Waste Land that seem to us to refer to generalized sexual anxieties, for example, also carried for Eliot connotations of specific political anxieties (loss of potency of leaders, of the nation). In what follows, as in the preceding reading of Yeats's poems, I again want to trace out a narrow line. I do not intend to reduce Eliot's great poem simply to the contemporary social and historical movements and concerns that appear within it; I do, however, wish to show what is too often denied—the degree to which those movements and concerns inform the poem and helped motivate the poetics that underlie it.

Just as Yeats, in his later poems, embraced violence in order to break through the decayed mentality of bourgeois English culture and to release a genuine Irish culture, Eliot saw English culture as in need of an equally radical political aesthetic in order to reverse bourgeois decay and reestablish any culture at all. We can begin to specify the historical and political context that contributed to Eliot's construction of *The Waste Land* by recalling the peculiar way he defined "cultural disintegration": "Cultural disintegration is present when two or more strata so separate that these become in effect distinct cultures; and also when culture at the upper group level breaks into fragments each of which represents one cultural activity alone."[1] Eliot did not focus on those elements usually brought up in interpretations of *The Waste Land* as a poem about disintegration: he did not speak of sterility, absence of meaning, loss of morality, psychological turmoil, or the death of God. Instead, he focused on what was happening to "strata" and to "culture at the upper group level": he was concerned about changes in the great social hierarchies.

Eliot had left the United States, as we have seen, to escape a culture that seemed to him undergoing irreparable disintegration as a result of mixed immigration. In England, he soon faced another kind of disintegration as the orderly strata of gender and class threatened to be swamped by the tides of workers and women sweeping into the world of politics.[2] Before the war, there had been considerable violent agitation by these groups—Dangerfield notes that in the first seven months of 1914 alone women set more than one hundred fires in London and there were more than nine hundred strikes.[3] The war interrupted such actions, but they threatened to begin again after the armistice; violence was avoided by the passage of the Reform Bill of 1918, which vastly expanded the franchise and seemed at the time to radically transform the nation. To understand the anxieties, hopes, and fears generated by that bill, consider that from 1910 to 1922 the number of voters in England tripled. In 1910, seven million men were eligible to vote and five million did; in 1922, twenty-one million people were eligible and fourteen and one-half million voted, 40 percent of them women; two-thirds of all the parliamentary districts had 80 percent working-class majorities.[4] In 1921, the year that saw so many of the canonical high modernist works written, these new voters were enfranchised, but most had not yet voted in a major election: England seemed on the verge of a revolution.

Eliot hoped that the underlying cultural unity of England could keep the country from disintegrating as the United States had. Everything depended on leadership; however, the second half of Eliot's definition identified a serious problem with the culture of the upper group as well: it had broken into separate cultural activities (or, we might say, disciplines). Modernism is often praised for doing exactly what Eliot was criticizing here, for treating each cultural activity, each art, as isolated from all others: painting is about color, poetry about language, and so on. Such a view is decidedly incorrect about the modernists I am discussing. They certainly drew great attention to the artistic medium they worked in, but they did so because they believed that by focusing on the medium and not on the things portrayed in that medium they had the best chance of changing the social whole. Such an interpretation might seem to contradict Eliot's dictum in "Tradition and the Individual Talent" that poets should "express" a "medium," but the contradiction disappears if we note that what he contrasts to expressing a medium is expressing personality. The reason for emphasizing the medium is to break the artist out of his egotism, his limited individuality, his personality, and immerse him in a cultural medium, not merely an artistic one.[5]

If we put the two halves of Eliot's definition of cultural disintegration together, we can see that Eliot's prime goal was to have the cultural activities of the upper group become forces for unifying the strata. Culture could offer something to both the mob and the intellectuals: what Eliot called "myth." He saw, for example, Communism and Catholicism both possessing this ingredient: "The great merit of Communism is the same as the one merit of the Catholic church, that there is something in which minds at every level can grasp. . . . Communism has what is now called a 'myth.'"[6] Eliot feared that he and most people in America and in England had been separated from such unifying myths by liberal Protestantism (and by nationalism) and hence were incapable of uniting Europe, restoring the cultural whole that was present before capitalism. *The Waste Land* is a poem aimed at producing a myth, a belief that can be grasped by people of every social level. It may seem strange to produce an obscure poem as part of such an effort, but Eliot's point was precisely that different groups do not understand things the same way and cannot be unified by a single idea. He did not want the average, common language of the nineteenth-century novel; rather he wanted something that would be interpretable in quite different ways by different groups. For everyone to speak and understand the same kind of words, they would have to all be the same kind of person and belong to the same group: there would then be no strata at all and no need for leadership, but merely a collection of individual members of a single, homogeneous society united by articulated ideals and rational goals, the liberal, individualist, humanist vision of unity that Eliot, the poet who was so well versed in class and cultural difference that he was "never anything anywhere," set out to oppose. The unity to be created by what he called myth was not a unity of shared conscious ideas: rather, it was a mysterious unity that would work unconsciously, just as "culture" does.

In discussing his poetics, Eliot referred repeatedly to Sorel's idea of myth. As we have seen, Sorel argued that myths must be "necessarily very obscure"; they do not function the way ordinary language does. A myth is "a body of images [that] by intuition alone, before any considered analyses are made, is capable of evoking as an undivided whole the mass of sentiments" that unify the masses.[7] Eliot defended the difficulty of modern poetry for much the same reason: difficulty is necessary to express an "obscure impulse" that has never been expressed before.[8] The relation of poem and emotion is direct, not requiring analysis. Eliot has generally been taken to be speaking about impulses in the individual psyche, but that is hard to square with his view that the poet must be "aware that the mind of Europe—the mind of his own country—is . . . much more important than his own private mind."[9] Eliot was in fact seeking in his poetry to reveal hitherto unexpressed impulses in the national or European mind—as a way of creating a new myth. Myth provides, according to Eliot, "a way of controlling, of ordering, of giving a shape and a significance to the immense panorama of futility and anarchy, which is contemporary history."[10] Controlling and giving a shape to anarchy is a political goal: providing direction for the chaotic masses.

It was in this sense that Eliot viewed futility and anarchy as the symptoms of cultural disintegration, the separation into distinct quasi-cultures, each of which lacked what is necessary to be a complete culture: the masses had become mobs without direction, leadership, or coherent voices, and the leaders had become deadened, self-centered people with no contact with either the mob or the mob part of their own minds. The problem of anarchy was thus for him equally a problem of leaders, and Eliot's focus in *The Waste Land* was consequently on transforming leadership. The poem is a critique of high culture for having lost touch with the mob and the mob part of the mind—having lost touch with the roots of culture. The poem's references to "roots" blur together the ancient past, the lower classes, and the sexual. The importance of the past is that it was a time when there was a connection between lower and upper in society and in bodies: the reason Eliot advocated rereading pre-seventeenth-century literature (before "sensibility dissociated") was that he believed writers then wrote for and from the entire society and the entire mind. Such writers had roots in the lower classes and in their own bodies. The need for "roots that clutch" is a need for something from below, from the dirt of society and from the lower depths of the body, to reach up and grab the upper levels of the society and of the mind and provide the sustenance that will allow culture to flower. The painful "touch" of rain on deadened roots that begins the poem is at once an image of the stirrings of "obscure impulses" in the body, of the revival of "memory and desire," and of the stirrings of the mob in the social order.

The poem is a critique of a certain kind of personality and of a certain kind of class—isolated, self-interested, uncaring about those who seem basically different.[11] It is particularly aimed at the culture workers who have failed at their basic task, which is to make icons that express some part of the culture that underlies all classes. To overcome the fragmentation of culture, someone will have to break out of the limited view of the current upper groups to begin to speak what lies in the unconscious of all groups.

On the surface, it hardly seems that Eliot is advocating looking at and caring about the lower classes and women, because the images in the poem of those groups are generally disdainful if not grotesque. But in his search for the culture buried inside everyone, the most important task Eliot had was to look at those parts of society he himself most wished to ignore and escape. We can even say that Eliot's disdain for the masses was the motive force that drove him to seek a connection, an identification, with the masses. This might be easier to understand as a psychological trait: in these terms, as we have seen at some length, Eliot was disgusted with part of himself, and as a result of his disgust he broke himself apart in order to reclaim the part of himself that he found disgusting. Eliot also applied such a psychological theory to the social body, seeking to stop the society from rejecting part of itself, to stop the upper and lower classes from trying to destroy each other, because he felt that neither could exist alone.

In "Prufrock," the masses are presented as drowning the upper-class poet. *The Waste Land* suggests that by 1919 Eliot had developed some idea of how to survive the rampaging tides unleashed by mass movements. The poem traces for three sections the horrifying effects of the chaotic tides, which alternately swamp the land or leave vast sections parched. Then Eliot presents a transformation, a passage through death that would allow leaders (himself included) to overcome their fears of the mob and of the mob parts of their own minds and thus reconnect the parts of the social body.

The poem is full of images of mobs and crowds, often equated with water or tides. Early in the poem is the pair of lines, "Fear death by water. / I see crowds of people, walking round in a ring" (lines 55–56).[12] These crowds of people walking in circles, foreseen by "Madame Sosostris, famous clairvoyante" and associated with death by drowning, are similar to the circling falcons in the beginning of "The Second Coming": the masses, without leadership, moving like dead people. Two lines further on, the poet invokes the "Unreal City" in which a "crowd flowed over London Bridge." The speaker says, "I had not thought death had undone so many," making it seem this is a supernatural vision of the many dead of World War I. That reading is not inconsistent with a broader one, however. The crowd undone by death encompasses all of postwar society, including soldiers returning from the war, the "demobbed" persons who comprise an organized, working-class army that threatens to become a mob. Later in the poem, the flowing crowds come back as the "hooded hordes swarming / Over endless plains" that bring "falling towers" and that are footnoted via Hesse's *Blick ins Chaos* as the uprisings in eastern Europe, particularly the Russian Revolution (lines 369–70). Falling and upside-down towers symbolically represent the failure of the cultural centers, the failure of the tower of culture, of academia, and of all forms of upper-class male authority.

Besides being an image of the masses, water also seems to serve in this poem to represent female responses to male advances: either women are unresponsive, indifferent, remaining dry and unstimulated sexually (e.g., the typist), or they are too excited and exciting, too wet, taking control and engulfing the male, as the woman in the game of chess drowns the male in her synthetic perfumes. The poem suggests that these women are involved in mysterious ways in the emergence of anarchic mobs. Soon after the image of the hooded hordes, there appears a woman who

> drew her long black hair out tight
> And fiddled whisper music on those strings
> And bats with baby faces in the violet light
> Whistled, and beat their wings
> And crawled head downward down a blackened wall
> And upside down in air were towers.
>
> (lines 378–83)

This woman making music on her hair calls forth bats who whistle in response and move blindly to topple towers, very much as the "hooded hordes" do. The woman seems to be providing the music to which the hordes dance—or the music that conjures up the hordes. The breakup of the body of the Fisher King, the leader, has eliminated the voice that could calm the raging social tides. Eerie, uncanny voices emerge from the vacuum of leadership, "voices singing out of empty cisterns and exhausted wells" (line 385). Without leadership, everyone becomes hollow: the center of society is what provides the center of every person's mind and body. And if everyone becomes hollow, then in some sense everyone becomes female, or at least loses the possibility of being masculine (as we shall see in more detail in "The Hollow Men"). If, as Gustave Le Bon claimed, "crowds are everywhere distinguished by feminine characteristics," when the crowd takes over society, the feminine is in charge.[13]

The Waste Land is full of images of strange, unearthly women's voices. The woman in "A Game of Chess" also has hair that speaks: after having "drowned the sense in odours," the woman turns to her own toilette:

> under the brush, her hair
> Spread out in fiery points
> Glowed into words, then would be savagely still.
>
> (lines 108–10)

As in the description of the mermaids in Prufrock, woman's speech here is connected with their entangling, enticing hair, and this speech is dangerous; even when it is silent, it is savage. This upper-class woman who overwhelms men (lines 88–89) is followed by a lower-class woman whose mouth—and hence voice—repels, her bad teeth the emblem of her poverty (lines 139–72). Lil's ugly mouth and her body, exhausted by childbirth and abortion, will greet the soldiers who have been demobbed and who threaten to turn into a mob if they are angry at what they find when they get home. Like the power to drown that Eliot associated with both upper-class women and the social mass, images of the disgusting bodies of the masses were commonplaces in conservative critiques of industrial development. Anthony Ludovici described lower-class England in terms quite close to Eliot's in a 1921 political tract, *The False Assumptions of Democracy*: England was on its way to becoming "one long ugly street, full of ugly toothless people, pretending that their clammy urban passions are more exalted than the rut of rats."[14]

The image of a mouth full of bad teeth returns in the poem immediately after another image of rioting workers: "after the torchlight red on sweaty faces," the poet tries to escape into the hills, but finds only a "dead mountain mouth of carious teeth that cannot spit" (lines 322, 339). Mother nature has an infected mouth very much like Lil's. Even if one tries to escape the feminine crowd that is destroying the palaces in society, one cannot; the mountains, the retreat from society, have been invaded as well: "There is not even solitude in the mountains / But red sullen faces sneer and snarl" (lines 343–44). There is no private space anywhere; the distorted mouths are everywhere.

Though he portrays women and workers in such horrifying ways, Eliot does not indite them as the source of the horror of society. Rather, he blames the capitalist leadership who have altered women and workers, leaving them none of the "natural beauty" that the working class and women supposedly had before industrialization. Even if Lil had gotten herself teeth instead of squandering the money Albert gave her to do so, it would have done little good: she would merely have been covering up the horrors industrialization had already wrought on her. The distorted mouths Eliot sees about him are not the true voices of workers and women: these are the distorted, carrion mouths produced by the action of money and technology. If organic social relations could be restored, nature would be cured; women and men, workers and aristocrats would be bound together, not attempting to kill each other.

Eliot's images of distorted female mouths express his ambivalence about having women be the ones who speak the horrors in society. When Philomel cries "Jug Jug," it is a disguised speech attempting to accuse male leaders—gods even—of rape. Eliot wants to make this accusation himself, and so could be seen as agreeing with Virginia Woolf that men had turned to virile assertion, to rape, precisely because they had lost any real authority. Woolf described a Mr. A. who wrote sex scenes not for pleasure, but "in protest . . . protesting against the equality of the other sex by asserting his own superiority."[15] Eliot, like Woolf, combined images of women's rising power and images of rapes.

However, in Eliot's works, the rapes are the cause of women's gaining voice, not the result. He was not so much seeking the liberation of women's voices as the return of males who did not use women (and workers) but took care of them and expressed women's concerns for women. Eliot was also identifying with the women and seeking to find a male leader figure who could take care of him and express his concerns better than he could.

As Wayne Koestenbaum has argued, Ezra Pound fulfilled this function, serving to "exorcise the male poet's own identification with the hysterical women he purports merely to describe."[16] The psychoanalytic cure for hysteria, as Freud himself described it, involved discovering a "mass of psychogenic material" that has been "cut up, as it were into pieces or strips. It is the psychoanalyst's business to put these together once more into the organization which he presumes to have existed."[17] Koestenbaum argues that Pound's editing served such a function for Eliot, so that Eliot's "hysterical discourse suffers a sea change into masculinity."[18] Eliot and Freud both equated the "mass" or "mob" of impulses inside the individual with the masses; Freud's description of the cure for hysteria is an intrapsychic version of the social restoration that culture is supposed to accomplish, to give back to the "masses" the form they originally had before they were fragmented by the corrupt leadership. A male leader could edit women, the masses, and Eliot himself back into order.

The poem points particularly to capitalism as the source of mistreatment of women and of the masses. In the central scene of rape, the scene of the typist and the carbuncular young man, Eliot describes the rapist as acting like a capitalist—like a "Bradford millionaire," a man whose money came from industry (line 234). The scene is full of metaphors of machinery, implying that the system is in effect "raping" both men and women by turning the culture into a machine and transforming relationships between genders into the merging of cogs. A millionaire capitalist does not care what the masses feel: even when physically entwined with his employees, his individualist "vanity requires no response" (lines 241–42). The capitalist method of control, in Eliot's view, has no heart, and produces only a mechanical subject, a woman worker of gramophone voice who may repeat male words but who does not put her heart into them.

Eliot wanted a different kind of response from the masses, from women, and from himself, a response to a different kind of leader, a Tiresias who understands what these others feel and even conceives of himself as sharing a body with those who are led. And just as the indifference of leaders and workers can be imaged by a sexual encounter between a young man and a typist, so a satisfying relationship of social classes can be imaged as a response of one person's heart to another's hands. As we have already noted, he poem includes an image of such a passionate response to leadership:

> The boat responded
> Gaily, to the hand expert with sail and oar
> The sea was calm, your heart would have responded
> Gaily, when invited, beating obedient
> To controlling hands.
>
> (lines 419–23)

There are a number of ways in which this passage can be interpreted, aspects of the passage that are copresent in it. It can of course be read as a scene of two persons responding to each other, the sea representing the naturalness of the response as the gramophone represented the artificiality of the typist's response in the earlier scene. The passage also codes the response as one of deference to authority, accepting control by an expert. The passage thus could also be read as Eliot speaking to himself, describing the response in his own heart he hoped to derive from accepting the authority of religion and monarchy. Finally, if we see the water imagery as referring to the social tides, the scene presents an image of how the masses would respond if there were expert leaders. The parallel between "the boat" and "your heart" then implies that leading a social institution (the ship of state) is analogous to being a lover of a particular kind: one who is expert at touching the body of the beloved, knowing how to bring the heart to beat gaily by physical contact. In addition to the more frequently recognized senses of this passage, Eliot is also advocating intimate contact between leaders and the masses—as between priests and supplicants—in order to satisfy the desires buried in the mob and in the mob part of the self.

The "expert" leader is a person who has devoted his intellect to studying the sea of mass society, who understands how to use the deep currents he cannot control to move where he wants the ship of state to go. The poem traces the process that carries a person from utter revulsion at feeling his "roots" below him to extending his hands into the lower depths of the body and of the social order. We can see Eliot's struggle to achieve "expertise" in understanding the mob, in some lines he left out of the poem. In the manuscript of "The Fire Sermon," Eliot defined the task of the artist as looking very closely at the masses to discover the "unconscious" motives that they were trying but failing to express:

> London, the swarming life you kill and breed,
> Huddled between the concrete and the sky,
> Responsive to the momentary need,
> Vibrates unconscious to its formal destiny,
>
> Knowing neither how to think, nor how to feel,
> But lives in the awareness of the observing eye.
> London, your people is bound upon the wheel!
> Phantasmal gnomes, burrowing in brick and stone and steel!
> Some minds, aberrant from the normal equipoise
> (London, your people is bound upon the wheel!)
> Record the motion of these pavement toys
> And trace the cryptogram that may be curled
> Within these faint perceptions of the noise
> Of the movement, and the lights! [19]

The masses are swarming insects, gnomes, phantasmal, lacking in humanity, knowing neither how to think nor how to feel. But it is only by observing these creatures, recording their motions, tracing the "cryptogram" that is "curled within" their strange motions, that the artist can reach the "formal destiny" that is not only theirs but his. In another draft, instead of the phrase "trace the cryptogram that may be curled" within the masses, Eliot wrote "trace the painful, ideal meaning which they spell."[20] These drafts command the study of the movements of the masses as a way of discovering the ideal meaning or the mysterious cryptogram that lies at the heart of the culture. Eliot repeatedly advocated such a process of education: in 1931, for example, he wrote that "unrestrained industrialism . . . destroys the upper classes first," so that a person seeking what was left of the culture necessarily had to study the workers.[21] Eliot's wandering in slums was his effort to make himself a Tiresias, not the hollowed-out Southerner in New England and New Englander in the South, but a prophetic voice "throbbing between two lives," providing a living connection between the separated strata of society, linking female and male, workers and rulers, those destroyed by capitalism and those who could restore the culture. The "two lives" that Tiresias crosses can also be read as a split inside each person: the unconscious has become a "hooded horde," incomprehensible to the well-educated consciousness, and Tiresias has to speak from both the dark and the enlightened parts of the soul. Reconnecting social strata is equivalent to reconnecting the individual psyche.

Tiresias has to cross not only class, but even the split between mechanical and human in order to create a culture that can survive in the industrial world. Eliot parallels the "throbbing" inside Tiresias and the mechanical "throbbing" in society at large: Tiresias's vision comes

> At the violet hour, when the eyes and back
> Turn upward from the desk, when the human engine waits
> Like a taxi throbbing waiting.
>
> (lines 216–17)

If the social order has made every one of us into a machine "throbbing" like a taxi, then the artist who desperately wishes to escape this machine life must first allow himself to reconnect with them and hence live "throbbing" between the mechanical and the human. Those who refuse to allow themselves to experience the degradation visited on the poor, on factory workers, and on women end up feeling nothing, separated from the "roots," the culture that lies under every class and gender. The poem is thus directed at those who "turn the wheel" and bind the masses to it, those who seek to make humans but part of the machine: the capitalists who are going to undergo "death by water" one way or another, either by drowning in a mass revolution or by dissolving their greedy egos in the sea of culture. Some part of the upper class will have to break out of the prison of the self to become a new, noncapitalist, nonindividualist, nonmaterialist leadership.

At the end of the poem, the voice of thunder prepares the way for this new leadership. The three commands of the thunder are guides to transforming those leaders who have accepted the rule of money and technology and so have produced mobs and distorted women and workers. *"Datta"*—"give"—is a command to give up "prudence," to stop gathering money that can be counted up by "solicitors," to no longer hold one's property and one's self apart from others. Instead, the new leaders must dare to "surrender," as lovers surrender to passion. This surrender is a collective, not an individual act, as Calvin Bedient has argued: Eliot focuses on a collective surrender by saying that it is that "by which *we* exist." Bedient defines this collective act as the communion that causes all participating to give up their selves to an "Absolute," a selfless God.[22] I see no contradiction between such a religious interpretation and a political one: Eliot regarded religion as the basis of the myth that would unite the classes and the genders.

The second command, *"Dayadhvam"*—"sympathize"—thrusts people out of private lives: sympathy would turn the key and unlock the room that is a "prison" for each person. Instead of these separate, private people, "ethereal rumours revive for a moment a broken Coriolanus," a creature larger than an individual, a creature who exists not in a private room but in a public hall, a ruler. Coriolanus was of course a leader who was "broken" because of his egoism, because he failed to sacrifice himself to the social whole. His revival involves such self-sacrifice.[23]

Finally, *"Damyata"*: the revived leader can take "control." If one has broken free of the trap of individualism, surrendered to the duty of the governing class, one can then take control of the social tide and cause the masses and women to respond. The masses will accept "expert" leadership because their hearts will beat in response to the words of these leaders: such responses are not based on precisely understanding the words of the upper class, but on a response in the underlying social medium that produces the bodily emotions of all classes, the dedication of leaders and the beating hearts of followers. Usually the word *damyata* is translated as "self-control"; Eliot altered the translation in the gloss he supplied to line 402 because he wished to escape the focus on the self and on controlling only one individual's body: the disembodied voice of thunder speaks of control of the entire social body at once, all the hearts beating in response to expert hands. At the same time, the restoration of such awe-inspiring leadership in religion and in government would result in far better control of individuals than the liberal advocacy of self-control.

After the three commands, Eliot presents a man fishing on the shore, a perfect image of the restored relationship of leader and social tide (and of the restored relationship of conscious and unconscious in each person): connected together by a line, but each existing in a separate medium. Those on land and those in the water may not even speak the same language, but they are connected. The leader draws things up from the mass unconscious, making conscious symbols of culture, and thereby reconstructs the cultural order that calms the rioting social tides. Eliot shows metaphorically how this process works: the materials fished up are used to create the shore on which the Fisher King sits, as Eliot indicates by repeating the word "shore" in two different lines: "I sat upon the shore" and "These fragments I have shored against my ruins." The fragments are "shored" in the sense of becoming part of that shore on which he sits. The process of fishing things up from the water and using them to create new areas of land is a process of constructing new borderlands between upper and lower groups in society. These borderlands provide spaces for the leadership to survive in close proximity to the masses, and they also serve to control and direct the masses: the tides again run between shores in an orderly, peaceful manner. In other words, the leader has to get from the masses the very matter that then controls and directs those masses. Instead of parched land and swamping tides, the new social order has a shore and a peaceful sea, two disparate strata that are united in a harmonious, organic relationship. Similarly, the restoration of kingship would allow the individual to regain a relationship to his or her own unconscious, to let a line down into the sea inside the soul without being drowned.

Among the many things suggested by the end of this poem is thus a distinct strategy for achieving political power, a strategy that was at work in the Conservative Party's claim that Conservative leaders could express the deep desires of the masses and take care of them better than the Labour Party could. Conservatives presented themselves as "paternalistic socialists," loving patriarchs of the working classes who knew that workers wanted more than money.[24] They also carefully studied the masses and the unconscious and were willing to use irrational, vague myths of national and imperial glory that had mass and unconscious appeal and that at the same time could be elaborated into complex intellectual theories, thereby appealing to all classes. Finally, and most importantly, they proposed a social system in which everyone, leader and follower alike, would submit to the whole. They glorified the leader, but only as the spokesperson for the greater glory of the nation or empire. The Conservative Party's version of the leader should be deferential to the disembodied voice of thunder, the culturally produced symbol of the whole, just as the workers should.

The last stanza suggests that the currently broken-apart sections of society must all participate in creating the voice of thunder and resurrecting the Fisher King: the new culture must be fished up out of the desires of the masses, not flung down on them. The stanza presents a list of "fragments" that must be reunited if culture is to survive. First, the nursery rhyme of destruction, "London Bridge is falling down," seems a representation of the anger of the masses, the desire to destroy the bridges that connect disparate parts of society. Such destruction will occur if the lower classes deny the value of all high culture: nursery rhymes will be all that will be left. A reinvigorated monarchy must become the embodiment of that anger: a renewed aristocracy must grow out of the destruction of the current system.

The stanza continues with references to male cultural producers who

need help from females to achieve their ends: Dante, led through purga-
tory by Beatrice; then a Latin poet who has been unable to write, wishing
himself to turn into a swallow in imitation of Philomel. The restoration of
culture requires the help of women.

Finally, there are the references to Kyd's *Spanish Tragedy*, a play about
restoring a broken-up culture. The climax of Kyd's work is a play within the
play performed in "sundry languages"; this play initiates a massacre that
results in restoring a "dead" leader. Eliot's poem functions much the same
way: through chaotic multiplicity of tongues it seeks to initiate a process
that will restore a buried leader and a buried culture. Frank Ardolino has
argued that Kyd's play draws on the tradition of mystery rituals, a tradition that makes use of the same vegetation gods that Eliot refers to in *The
Waste Land*. Kyd's drama defines Eliot's role in creating an obscure poem:
Eliot is Hieronymo, a character whose name represents his "hierophantic
role" as interpreter of mysteries; as Ardolino argues, Hieronymo represents
the "mystagogue who performed the ritual initiation in conjunction with a
priestess and provided the initiates with a symbolic reenactment of the res-
urrection of the hanged god."[25] In Kyd's work, Hieronymo claims to be able
to interpret the sundry languages of the climactic play and reveal a truth
"in our vulgar tongue."[26] But we never hear the truth expressed. Kyd's play
thus performs the same function that mystery rituals always performed:
it brings the society together in a shared experience, a shared sense of the
availability of a common truth, but it does not reveal this truth. The rituals in effect pointed to the inexpressible "unconscious background" of all
thought, the shared truth that cannot be stated. Eliot's poem is in itself a
mystery ritual for the twentieth century.

The Sanskrit benediction at the end of the poem represents the end of
the ritual of orchestrated incomprehensibility. The word "Shantih," according to Eliot's footnote, declares that peace does not require understanding;
it requires only what the three "DA's" command, the acceptance of nonindividual, supernatural authority. The "DA's" are simultaneously childish
sounds and symbols to be interpreted in complex, intellectual ways. The
disembodied voice saying "DA . . . DA . . . DA" brings together all of Eliot's
concerns: the dream of a restoration of a dead father; the hope of finding
some greater, mystic whole in which the self and the individual body can
be dissolved; the need for a mythic image that can speak to all social strata;
and the desire to find the deep Sanskrit roots of Indo-European culture and
thereby create a social whole that Eliot, the American living in Britain,
could join. Eliot was in effect telling the myth of the restoration of myth,
the discovery in a surprising location (India) of words that can speak to all
levels of Western culture.

The ending presents itself as a benediction and a calming of the un-
ruliness of the rest of the poem: the waste land is restored by religious
reunification. However, this ending has never been convincing to readers

and probably felt unconvincing to Eliot. The poem fails in part because when Eliot wrote it he still had not found a way to actually join the masses. He did believe that a unifying culture lay deep beneath England, but he would not trust the masses to spell it out: instead, he went all the way to Sanskrit for the letters to represent it. Paradoxically, the poem has still functioned as a mystery ritual, as revealing in some mysterious way the essence of the twentieth century. The poem has provided icons that can be carried about by everyone, even as they declare they do not understand them—most notably, the title phrase, "the waste land," which has taken on a life of its own as a kind of mantra. The twentieth century has developed an almost religious belief in itself as a wasteland.

Eliot's difficult scholarship operates like Marx's difficult economic treatises, as a necessary intellectual density that backs up and makes credible various slogans and rallying cries that seem transparently meaningful to everyone without having to read the dense texts. But instead of producing a return to the old religious forms of the mystery rituals, Eliot's works have instead contributed to a new form of appreciation of mysteries—the notion that our society requires constant reform or even revolutionary change, that it has no center and must eternally devote itself to searching for a center. To the extent that we all remain modernists, we periodically remind ourselves of the absence of meaning or center, and this serves to cleanse the soul in a thoroughly religious way. The claim that the center is rotten has become so commonplace that political candidates jockey to position themselves as more "outside the system" than their opponents, more marginal, and hence less corrupt.

Eliot wrote *The Waste Land* just before the elections of 1922: the poem partly expresses his doubt that there was any way that English culture would hold together with a vastly expanded electorate. That election, however, initiated a long period of Conservative Party rule. There was, it seemed, enough power left in English myths to hold the culture together, and Eliot turned to embracing what he saw as the essential myth in English culture, the Anglican Church. "The Hollow Men" marks this transition: in it, he repeats much of the imagery of cultural deadness in *The Waste Land*, but he does not turn to India to find the revivifying roots. Instead, by 1925 he believed he had found in Christianity a myth that could speak to all levels, to the mob part of his mind as well as to the intellectual part. The grounds of his turning to Christianity were that the masses embraced it, not that the people whose intellect he most admired shared it. In "The Humanism of Irving Babbitt," Eliot declared that he chose religion over humanism because "the religious habit is still very strong, in all places, at all times, and for all people," while humanism is "merely the state of mind of a few persons in a few places at a few times."[27]

"The Hollow Men" is a poem about such humanists, about well-educated men who have disconnected themselves from the masses. The poem is a continuation of "Prufrock," but the cultured men who comprise the "we" have managed to escape being drowned in human voices because they have withdrawn completely from contact with all voices unlike their own. To escape drowning, they have retreated into a desert. These men will not admit that their roots need the "water" available in the masses and in women. There is no substance within the group itself, nothing inside them except dry straw, but they are so afraid of contact with the others who could fill them that they are simply withering away. These men are so afraid of being overwhelmed by others that they "dare not meet" anyone's "eyes," particularly "in dreams," in the unconscious, where individuals dissolve, replaced by the mob of impulses (p. 57). Their fear of dreams, of the id, deprives these men of their potency: they "grope together . . . Gathered on this beach of the tumid river" (p. 58). They will not take the plunge into otherness. By refusing to do so, they lose their masculinity, their violence, their "bang," and become instead passive objects, "stuffed men," whimpering figures who refrain from intimate contact with anyone outside their own group. Their loss of potency is tied to the loss of their position as rulers: the hollow men live in a "hollow valley / The broken jaw of our lost kingdoms" (p. 58). These men have lost their voices and their kingdoms; others are ruling and are speaking. The "stone images" (p. 57) to which these men pray are the dead symbols that no longer serve to unify the culture, that no longer bring the hearts of everyone to beat together. These men stand back from the living symbols that they would have to embrace to rejoin the culture. At night,

> At the hour when we are
> Trembling with tenderness
> Lips that would kiss
> Form prayers to broken stone.
>   (pp. 57–58)

The poem moves, as does *The Waste Land*, to an image of a restoration of a central authority, a restoration of the eyes that these hollow men have lost:

> The eyes reappear
> As the perpetual star
> Multifoliate rose
> Of death's twilight kingdom.
>   (p. 58)

Clearly, the rose and star are images of Christianity, but they are also images of the bridging of the gap between the kingdom of the other and "our lost kingdoms," creating instead a "twilight" kingdom, a place of multiplicity (p. 58). The new shape of eyes is singular and plural at once, both single star and multifoliate rose, mixing sky and earth, high and low, male and female (in a body still identified as male, the Lord of Christian tradition). These reappearing eyes represent a common culture that Eliot came to believe resided in Christianity, which he now believed could serve both to inspire the highest and lowest strata of society, both upper and lower classes, male and female.

After this vision of unity, the poem tries to complete the direct address, the love song, that failed in "Prufrock," to retrace Prufrock in reverse and move from "we" speaking to no one in particular to a speech directed at a particular "you." But instead of addressing an equal (who could be joined to "I" in the phrase "you and I" in "Prufrock"), the poem seeks to address a capitalized "Thine," a God who is both singular and plural: "Thine is the kingdom," not merely one body. The hollow men are trying to address the social whole, the "kingdom," and at the same time to address the single "Lord" who is that kingdom. But this address breaks down at the same time that the poem breaks apart into disparate high and low styles; the disconnection and inability to complete the phrases addressing God leave the speakers incapable of uniting upper and lower classes. The key word cut off in the prayer of the speakers is "kingdom": the hollow men do not want to devote themselves to someone else's kingdom, they want a God who will restore their kingdom. They do not want a God who speaks for the whole kingdom, but one that is their own private deity. To reach God through the kingdom, through culture, through the masses, is something these men are unwilling to do. So the voice of the masses appears as a separate style: in nursery rhymes, this new voice dances around the great intellectual men who have tried so hard to separate themselves: the hollow men *are* the prickly pears, the cactus men, who refuse to be connected to the childlike nursery-rhyme masses. The failure of these men to love the masses is identical to their failure to love God, their failure to attach themselves to the basis of culture (in Eliot's view, religion). Their erudition is useless because

> Between the essence
> And the descent
> Falls the Shadow.
>   (p. 59)

The essence, the culture, is inside everyone, but it becomes potent to hold society together only when those in the elite are willing to descend. These men are blocked: the shadow falls and stops them from descending, as it also stops them from being sexual, falling between "desire" and "spasm." Unwilling to pass through shadow, to enter dark realms, these men are left hollow, easily mocked and destroyed by nursery rhymes, by the lower forms of culture and the lower parts of their minds that they will not embrace.

The upper classes who refuse connection with the mob also lose their position as aristocrats: they become isolated individuals and not a class at all. Only the lower classes retain the potential for restoring class structure. Eliot's hope for a renewal emerging from the lower classes appears strikingly in his use of a chorus of working-class women in his 1935 play, *Murder in the Cathedral*. The play enacts the death of a spiritual aristocracy in the death of Thomas Becket, killed by knights who justify their act as promoting the "just subordination of the pretensions of the Church to the welfare of the State." But state welfare is no way to care for the masses, who need a church: the charwomen end the play speaking of the survival of the spiritual in the margins of the secular state: "There is holy ground, and the sanctity shall not depart from it / Though armies trample over it, though sightseers come with guide-books looking over it." There will always be "prayer in forgotten places by the broken imperial column," and from such prayer and such holy ground "springs that which forever renews the earth / Though it is forever denied." The charwomen are in themselves a version of "holy ground," a part of society trampled on by the modern state, but the part that holds the potential for renewal. If the prayers of those who pray in forgotten places succeed, they will rebuild the "broken imperial column" and restore the spiritual empire. The last line is "Blessed Thomas, pray for us": the working-class women believe they need a male religious leader to care for them; the welfare state will never be a substitute.[28] Eliot thus turned to the masses for the voice to express his desire for an alternative to his own middle-class world. To find hope for a new leadership, a new voice (we might even say a new poet), Eliot turned to charwomen, just as Yeats turned to the "slut who runs the till," to provide the base from which to build a new poetry.

CHAPTER 8

Social(ist) Institutions
in 'Ulysses'

Before World War I, Joyce shared the dream of a great artist-leader who could stand firm against the current tides of politics and yet express the deep desires of the masses, the dream that also motivated much of Eliot's and Yeats's poetry. Joyce was fascinated by heroic nationalism and anarcho-syndicalism. He dreamed of an artist who could create the myth to foment a Sorelian general strike in Ireland, freeing the nation from England and at the same time freeing the Irish proletariat from capitalist domination—without requiring a military movement. As we have seen, he conceived of his act of leaving Ireland as an "intellectual strike" and found in Italy political leaders who seemed to be dreaming of the same kind of revolution that he was. But when the war broke out and the masses showed more enthusiasm for war than they ever had for a general strike, Joyce watched in horror as the leaders he had admired, D'Annunzio and the Italian syndicalists, joined together to convert syndicalism into a militaristic nationalist movement that eventually became Fascism. Joyce's letters show considerably less enthusiasm for any political movement after 1914, and some critics have interpreted his later works as a rejection of politics entirely. But Joyce did not reject politics; he rejected only a specific political orientation—the politics of proto-Fascism. Joyce struggled to find a way out of the political logic that turned the refusal to serve anyone—a general strike—into militaristic obedience. *Ulysses* is one monument to that struggle. Joyce sought to revise the theory of myths and revolutionary violence that underlay syndicalism so that the power of myth to inspire acts of resistance did not lead directly to militarism.

In Georges Sorel's theory, the necessity of violence derived from the need for a general rejection of the social order as the only way to disrupt the "iron law" that "bound" society together into "one block." Anarcho-syndicalist violence, therefore, was supposed to disrupt the whole without forming another whole. But that was not what Joyce saw emerging in Italy from 1906 to 1918: syndicalists gradually became backers of a disciplined national unity, abandoning anarchism, internationalism, and anti-militarism in response to what seemed the fervent support of the masses for nationalist violence. The first major syndicalist move away from international anarchism came as a result of the 1911 war between Italy and the Turks, when many syndicalists became advocates of Italian expansion, theorized by writers such as Roberto Michels as "proletarian nationalism."[1] When World War I broke out and socialist parties across Europe backed their various national armies, a few syndicalists (including Mussolini) held out for neutrality, but by the end of 1914, nearly all came around to backing the nationalist, interventionist movement organized into *Fasci*, militant collectives. Mussolini became a leading propagandist for the movement, and after the war it turned into a political party espousing "nationalist socialism." Drawing on Michel's "iron law of oligarchies," which supposedly proved that resistance movements as well as states require an elite leadership, the national socialists proposed that a military dictatorship replace Italian democracy.[2] Violence in Italy had not then led to a breakup of the iron law of the state but rather to the creation of the far more rigid iron will of Fascism.[3]

To escape that conclusion, Joyce rejected the Sorelian theory of a monolithic social order, and that rejection is clear in his fiction. *Ulysses* is a novel that presents society as radically pluralistic, formed of myriad blocks that are bound together by myriad conflicting "laws" that are constantly shifting.

Such a vision was an integral part of some early forms of syndicalism, particularly the theories of Arturo Labriola, one of the few syndicalists who rejected the move into Fascism. Labriola, too, sought to eliminate the idea of a unified movement or a unified social order, before or after the revolution. He advocated a multiplicity of governing bodies (syndicates) rather than a unified leadership in the belief that unified leadership always represses some of the voices of the masses and hence would hinder the revolution. As a 1913 English translation of one of Labriola's treatises put it, "in industrial organization . . . nothing could be more repugnant than too much conformity." Labriola even saw capitalists as having distinctive "industrial" skills; they would be useful in their "directive and administrative capacity" after the revolution and would have a role like any other trade in the syndicates.[4] Joyce praised Labriola's willingness to include diverse groups in his movement; he wrote his brother, "Labriola . . . wishes to hasten *directly* the emergence of the proletariat. And to do this he would include in his ranks Catholics and Jews, liberals and conservatives."[5] Joyce's effort in *Ulysses* to bring together a Jew and a Catholic without producing any particularly unified consciousness is in part a version of Labriola's strange reasoning that the proletariat would emerge directly, the masses would replace the capitalists, if only multiple different groups could join together.

Labriola's desire for a direct emergence of the proletariat translated into a rejection of leadership and of conventional political power. As Joyce wrote in a letter to Stanislaus in 1906, syndicalists "do not desire the conquest of public powers which, they say, only serve in the end to support middle-class government." Instead, he said, they seek to take control of the actual institutions that keep the bourgeois in power. They "assert that they are the true socialists because they wish the future order to proceed equally from the overthrow of the entire present social organisation and from the automatic emergence of the proletariat in trade-unions and guilds and the like." As he pointed out, "It is strange that Italian socialism in its latest stage should approach so closely the English variety."[6]

Joyce's mention of guilds and his comparison of English and Italian varieties of socialism suggest Joyce felt that Labriola's philosophy was close to "Guild Socialism." Joyce's politics developed in the direction that the English Guild Socialists took syndicalism: to a nonviolent pluralism based on the elimination of any general system or action. As we have seen, Harold Laski and G. D. H. Cole developed pluralism as an attack on the very concept of "sovereignty," the concept of an underlying, unified power at the heart of the social order, and hence on the notion of a single, reductive form of political representation. *Ulysses* developed a new method of literary representation that paralleled Laski's and Cole's vision of a new kind of pluralist political representation.

Just as in Guild Socialist pluralism, where "a person requires as many forms of representation as he has distinct organisable interests or points of view,"[7] in *Ulysses*, each distinct style and chapter in the book represents a group or social institution. Within each of them, what we see of an individual is the part of his personality that emerges in that group or institution (or would emerge, since some of the "styles" place characters in groups they have never entered). Here, as in Cole's political theory, the autonomous, individual subject of classical liberalism is indeed "fundamentally incapable of being represented."[8] Cole and Laski saw socialist pluralism as the only way to escape the oppression of "sovereignty," the belief that ultimately there must be one highest power and one set of basic principles within the state and within each citizen. Sovereignty, Laski wrote, inevitably ends up serving that part of the state "which dominates the economic life."[9] Socialist pluralism was an effort to disperse and diffuse leadership; Joyce's novel was an effort to disperse and diffuse authorship.

In "Wandering Rocks," Joyce presents an allegorical version of the early syndicalist view that leadership and control of public powers are worthless as a method for accomplishing radical social change. Many critics have described the chapter as providing an overview of Joyce's project in this novel, but few readers have noted how much this chapter labels that project as political. Joyce said in his chart that the symbol of "Wandering Rocks" is "citizens," suggesting the chapter is about the role people play in the state. Further, Joyce included his only direct portrayal of high government officials, the vice-regal cavalcade. After eighteen sections showing all sorts of people moving about in a complex, intertwining social system, the cavalcade takes center stage, moving past all who have appeared earlier. One might see this last section as a representation of the unifying power of government: the cavalcade is stitching together the disconnected scenes presented earlier, uniting all the citizens in the state (perhaps in resistance to these invaders). However, the "unity" that the last section provides is quite peculiar. We see a sequence of "salutes" to the royal procession, but these salutes are neither reverential recognitions of the majesty of government nor direct acts of rebellion: some are salutes by not noticing, some by inanimate objects (the river salutes with sludge), and the last is a salute by the back of a pair of pants. The sovereign, which is supposed to represent everyone, is reduced to a passing perception, something seen by all, but only one among many sights, and a sight that produces quite disparate responses: it is not the basis of the unity of the whole nation, but merely one institution that intersects other institutions in many ways.

Resistance, as well, need not take the form of creating an alternative sovereignty: Joyce indicates that the social changes he was seeking in writing his novel had little to do with changing the people in power. If the Irish were to replace the governor-general with an Irish president or king, that would merely change the figure inside the carriage that nobody can quite see, and everyone would still be moved about in the streets in much the same way they were before. If the Irish were to seek to produce a unified nationalist movement, they would be essentially transforming themselves into a political organization, installing leaders and turning the nation into another "cavalcade." Joyce refused to simply take sides in the Anglo-Irish war going on as he wrote his novel: he refused to accept that joining one or the other movement would change the fundamental problem of the social order, which is sovereignty itself. Society is and always has been a world of "wandering rocks," of chaotic tides, and all efforts to claim that it can be a unified movement are illusory and result only in temporary and violently destructive distortions. The temporary creation of a unified movement may alter leadership, but it will do nothing to change those permanent forces that are moving everyone about in mechanical, disjointed ways (as Joyce indicated by labeling the technique of this section "mechanics"). Changing those forces means changing all those institutions and institutional sites that are arrayed along the streets—houses, stores, hospitals—and not merely changing the elected officials or the laws those officials write and enforce.

This novel is about those institutions, as Joyce indicated by the oft-noted parallel between the number of sections in "Wandering Rocks" and in the entire novel. The novel has eighteen chapters; "Wandering Rocks" has eighteen sections, plus the final parade. The eighteen chapters offer a detailed examination of the social system that mechanically moves people about; as we shall see, these chapters detail the ways various institutions shape people's thoughts and behaviors. The nineteenth section of "Wandering Rocks" is a depiction of what is excluded from the novel and what was irrelevant to Joyce's social politics—government and leaders. As Joyce wrote in his notes for "The Cyclops," "Why add government to moral and material forces existing?"[10] Joyce was not therefore writing a nonpolitical novel: rather, he was extending politics into every part of society.

Joyce dubbed the "organ" of this chapter the "blood," which, combined with his use of "citizens" as its symbol, suggests he is taking up a conservative metaphor and one invoked by nationalist movements everywhere. But this chapter makes us think of the circulation of the blood in all its numerous different veins, not of the unity produced by people of "one blood" joining together. Indeed, throughout the novel, Joyce twists biological metaphors to subvert the oppressive and essentially conservative results of nationalist essentialism. He assigns an organ to each chapter, which roughly translates into assigning each institution in the novel an organ, suggesting that this novel presents a view of society as an organic whole. But his presentation of organs emphasizes that each organ is radically different from the others. Joyce thus subverts the most common political uses of the metaphor of an organic nation as distortions. In the name of organic wholeness, politicians argue that institutions must be subordinated to a central leadership, but the head does not try to take conscious control of the other organs of the body. As Harold Laski pointed out, a recognition of "breakage" and "discontinuities" in both the body and the mind leads politics in the opposite direction—to radically discontinuous structures as the most representative of human organization.[11] The breakage and discontinuity in this novel are efforts to render this multiplicity of experience and to show the relationship of that personal multiplicity to the institutional multiplicity of any social order.

If we view *Ulysses* as a pluralistic work that attempts to express in terms of structure the facts of both personality and social complexity, and thus as a break with individualism, we have to read it in what may seem a strange way: instead of focusing on characters, we should focus on the various institutions in the novel. Instead of extracting what is said about Stephen in each chapter and meditating on how to unify all the varied things into one character, we should treat Stephen and Bloom and Molly and everyone else in the novel as devices that are exposed to a variety of institutions to register the effects of those institutions.

A number of critics have recently begun examining *Ulysses* in this way, as a novel about institutions rather than about characters. Cheryl Herr shows that all of Joyce's works form an "anatomy of culture," a dissection of the forms and particularly "institutional discourses" that comprise a social body. She argues that books from any period can be treated in this way, as "texts of culture," and that there is no particular political stance involved in creating such texts.[12] But as I have already begun to show, Joyce's anatomies, in all the contradictoriness that Herr demonstrates, are a powerful response to a particular political stance—the conservative anatomy of culture, the anatomy based on blood and organicity that justified, in the name of restoring social wholeness, the excising of parts of the social body through war and racial exclusion.

A number of critics writing new kinds of formal analysis—Karen Lawrence, John Paul Riquelme, and Perry Meisel—also have begun showing the peculiar status of this novel in its representation of cultural voices not embodied in individual characters or credited as original creations of individual authors.[13] The novel presents itself and its styles as institutional products, undoing what Michel Foucault called the "author-function."[14] Recently, critical focus on Joyce's use of popular culture and on his presentation of gender roles has shown that Joyce was at least as interested in cultural constructs as in psychological or aesthetic structures.[15]

Though reading this novel for institutions rather than characters may seem strange, it is in fact what most people do anyway: we keep losing track of the characters and their concerns; "style" and general topics of conversation take over the text and obliterate differences between characters. Joyce is blunt in his efforts to cause such effects. The book has a decidedly artificial structure that emphasizes the dominance of institutional forces over individual concerns: in chapter after chapter, Joyce shows that people's thoughts and conversations—in both style and content—are largely determined by the particular institutions into which they wander: in a maternity hospital, people think about birth; in a butcher shop, about meat; in a cemetery, about death; in a brothel, about illicit sex; in a concert room, about music; in a newspaper office, about stories and rhetoric; in a library, about literature. The city forms a spatial arrangement of consciousnesses: people entering a given area will find certain images and ideas in their minds. Further, Joyce shows that more than one institution can simultaneously contribute to forming a person's thoughts. In some chapters the characters' thoughts and speeches (and the narration) derive their content from the institutions in which scenes are set but derive their styles from various forms of socially created discourse such as headlines, legal documents, or romance novels. These styles function much like institutions in shaping the characters: within one style, only certain kinds of roles are available, and characters assuming those roles will also assume certain values and personality traits. Thus, Bloom becomes a Romantic hero, leader of a reform movement, Leop. Bloom of *Crawford's Journal*, and Herr Blumenduft, and is either loving, crude, practical, heroic, or cowardly depending on the conventions of the type of discourse in which his acts are being reported. The characters are of course usually unaware that they are being described as if they were assuming roles or as if their speech were changing styles (though sometimes they are assuming roles and know it), but our experience is one of seeing, as we almost never see in our daily lives, the overlapping of group influences. A sentence in the text seems to derive not just from Joyce's brain or from a character's brain, but from institutions that shape both characters and author. As Cheryl Herr puts it, "in *Ulysses*, culture makes culture," so that what may appear an individual is something "fashioned of cultural threads."[16]

The way Joyce shows particular institutions impinging on his characters emphasizes that people are being molded into socially useful forms and then distributed throughout the city every day. He focuses on two sets of institutions or locations where the functioning of institutions is clear—those that produce, maintain, and dispose of bodies: maternity hospital, restaurant, butcher shop, outhouse, and cemetery; and those that produce, distribute, and dispose of words: school, newspaper, advertising, booksellers, libraries, pubs (where words are produced and distributed as songs and political discourse), and gutters and outhouses (where papers end up). These two sets reflect the common socialist and anarchist distinction, "workers of hand and brain." But Joyce does not so much focus on the work people do as on the work done in such locations by social institutions in producing people. By paralleling the cycling of carefully packaged food and words, Joyce suggests that thoughts enter minds the way foods enter bodies; as Bloom says, "Never know whose thoughts you're chewing" (8.717).[17]

We also see, in "Wandering Rocks," the way these institutions and institutional locations are arranged in an overall structure by the grid of streets, a grid that does not make the city a unified whole by providing common thoughts for everyone; rather, in the streets, people continue thinking as they have in the various institutions. In "Eumaeus," Joyce does show one "universal institution" that anyone can enter—a cab—and one form of discourse available to all—clichés, but these are merely empty vehicles and forms. "Eumaeus" repeats on a lowly scale the issue raised in "Wandering Rocks" of what it means for a single vehicle to be able to pass across all the different social spaces of Dublin. The royal coach and the cab are quite similar in being boxes that create the illusion of a space of universality. We can distinguish these two illusory universalities as two important political images that Joyce sought to undermine: the image of an aristocracy, a royalty, an Irish king who could be restored, and the image of the "common man." The book also explores the institutional structuring of what seems "free space" (the beach) and what seems illicit and hence "outside" the system (Nighttown). As we shall see, the novel shows that even the "forbidden," the "abnormal," and the "unconscious" are institutionally structured.

Finally, the book begins and ends in houses. Bloom's house, the beach, and the streets are the only institutional locations that people enter in more than one chapter in this novel. These places might seem to be places of refuge from institutions and their operation, places to which people can escape and "be themselves." In particular, the importance of the house in this novel might make it seem quite similar to Victorian novels: the ending could be taken to portray the standard Victorian retreat from social interaction into the private house. Joyce was continuing to work within the tradition of the Victorian novel, but he also was revising the image of the house. Instead of being a realm of autonomy, a realm that allows the individual to be secure from social manipulation, the house in *Ulysses* is a social institution, one that is structured by many other institutions that intersect with it and connect it with the circulation through institutions that comprises the world of the novel.

The opening scenes in both Stephen's apartment and Bloom's house show food and words (mail) carried into these habitations and waste products carried out. In "Ithaca," Joyce has a lengthy description of the way houses are connected to "natural" water supplies by the social system of pipes and pumps. Water assumes symbolic import in this novel, representing the social medium surrounding and filling every body and mind. Further, inside each house, we see people who are not united at all by a common consciousness, but rather who have quite disparate, even antagonistic wills. The "Yes" that ends this novel is quite different from the agreements to marry that end Victorian novels. In nineteenth-century novels, the two main characters marry at the point when they have both broken free of all other social bonds, when they have achieved autonomy and know the true values by which they should live; the ideal marriages that end Victorian novels are perfect contracts signed by two fully autonomous people, each of whom is sure that both of them have sufficient self-control to keep the terms of the contract. In *Ulysses*, Leopold and Molly marry without knowing themselves or each other very well, and the marriage changes them in unexpected ways. They enter and stay in the marriage not as a result of autonomous choice, but as a result of intertwining social forces. The final result of such a union is not two persons joined in the perfect agreement of a "Yes," but rather a new, complex social unit: a couple lying head to foot at the end of a day in which each was unfaithful, both full of all the thoughts from their day and from their whole lives, ("Ithaca" showing all that Bloom brings to bed, "Penelope" all that Molly brings).

Their house and their connubial bed thus are institutional locations that are invaded and crisscrossed by others—other relationships, other social structures. By the time we reach the "yes I will Yes" that seems the essence of an act of individual will, the novel has so diffused the individual that we cannot even tell what is being agreed to or who is being agreed with. The agreement is not between Molly and Bloom, but between "I" and "him," two pronouns rather than two individuals. Molly is agreeing to a relationship with maleness, with the mass of men in the world, not with one particular person. The transforming of our understanding of people from distinct individuals and bodies into pronouns that blur together many people is perhaps the fundamental project of the novel.

The two main characters in most of the novel, Stephen and Bloom, are introduced largely by their ways of interacting with housing. Stephen's extreme desire to escape all social bonds leads him to refuse to settle any-where. In the first few chapters, he makes the decision that he cannot even stay in the relatively unrestricted realm of a temporary apartment shared with two other unattached males. In contrast, Bloom's first chapter shows him venturing away from his home into the streets and feeling cold, frightened, and lonely, and so rushing back for a warm, safe haven. Each is frightened by the world in which the other wants to live.

Their complementary fears represent opposed reactions to social insti-tutions: Stephen dreams of escaping; Bloom, of becoming accepted. The move from Stephen to Bloom represents a shift Joyce underwent from try-ing to rise out of the social cesspool to realizing he needed to work with institutions—and that he would have to struggle against his own back-ground and training to find a way to fit into institutions. *Ulysses* is in many ways an investigation of how it was possible for Joyce to change from thinking of himself as the semi-aristocratic Stephen to allowing the "mass culture" parts of his psyche to Bloom. If institutions constitute the thoughts and actions of individuals, how can a person switch from one defi-nition of himself to another? The first six chapters of the book are haunted by this question: there, we see Stephen and Bloom as two distinct, con-sistent personalities, but Joyce strongly marks those first six chapters to show that social forces are maintaining the difference between the two. In other words, the first six chapters show that the entities that appear to be individuals are actually complex products of a constant process of social construction and reconstruction. The "self" then is no longer located inside the individual but becomes something maintained by outside forces. Joyce goes to great lengths to define the two men as products of differing cultural backgrounds—the well-educated, Catholic, Irish Greek, Stephen Dedalus, and the mass-educated, Jewish, Irish Hungarian, Bloom. To bring these two together would be to merge disparate social institutions, and such a merger seems almost impossible due to the social forces keeping groups in society apart.

In chapter 7, we are introduced to the idea that those forces are not simply implacable, unchanging barriers: Joyce brings in the flow of history, represented by the shifting style of headlines. In most of the succeeding chapters, Joyce shows how institutions are changing, and this changing tide carries the characters along, moving them into new institutions, altering the old institutions, and changing individuals' personalities along the way.

Joyce was not merely chronicling institutional change: he was seeking to influence it. Much of the book examines the ways that literature is intertwined with various institutions: through those intersections, transforming literature could transform the social order. In particular, Joyce undermines the presentations of character and authorship by showing that they are products of multiple nonliterary institutions, and hence there are actually no unified or autonomous characters or authors. In the first six chapters, the consciousness of a character determines the limits of narration, as if there were such a thing as a distinct, individual consciousness, but the excessive parallelism of Stephen's and Bloom's lives undermines the appearance of autonomy. In the later chapters, the book enacts the breakup of these illusions of unity and autonomy, in people and in texts. In particular, the varied forms of writing produced by Stephen Dedalus, who above all wants to be an autonomous genius, reveal that his texts are actually products of the institutions in which he writes.

Chapters 11 through 15 take us through the contrast between consciousness and the unconscious as public realms. In "Sirens," "Cyclops," and "Oxen of the Sun," Joyce explores the ideological processes that create the conscious appearance of unity (of individuals, of families, of nations, of texts). These are chapters of group formation. In "Nausicaa" and in "Circe," Joyce explores what is left out—we might want to say what is "suppressed," but Joyce suggests that what does not fit in one institution is not so much suppressed as shunted off to some other location. Joyce focuses particularly in "Sirens," "Cyclops," and "Oxen" on the construction of legitimating public texts (including political speeches, music, and literature), and then in "Nausicaa" and "Circe" he shows that such construction depends on the complementary construction of "illegitimate" texts such as sexual fantasies.

"Circe" also appears to break up all the cultural constructions that appear everywhere else in the novel. But Joyce is not taking his readers into a revolutionary space outside institutions: Stephen's effort to escape all space and time in "Circe" leads nowhere at all. Instead, the novel circles back after "Circe" to the structures of the first three chapters, as Joyce's chart indicates. The entire journey of the novel consists not of a break with institutional forms, but rather a re-presentation of those forms, showing the contradictions and interstices between them, suggesting, as early syndicalist theory claimed, that the "automatic emergence" of new institutional forms can be brought about only by highlighting and increasing tensions already existing within and between institutions, by making use of processes of change already operating. The novel is most radical in its avoidance and rejection of complete revolution, its denial of any "outside" from which to criticize society as "one block." Everything in this novel remains packaged, institutionalized, and yet constantly changing. A closer examination of the novel will show in detail how Joyce was able to reconcile the constitutive effect of existing institutions with a radical change in how people must be regarded in an era of mass mind and mass politics.

Recycling Bodies

The first six chapters of *Ulysses* carefully look at the operation of the most mundane parts of everyday life to show how actively the social system functions to produce, or more precisely, reproduce, bodies and minds. These chapters show people waking up, beginning a day, shaving, eating breakfast, bathing, and going to the bathroom. Joyce portrays these actions not to sketch out an insignificant background against which independent minds boldly work, but rather to reveal those processes that maintain reality, processes of recycling, of filling living persons with packaged matter removed from other, usually dead bodies and of channeling socially useless by-products into a system of waste removal. In turn, this intricate process of shaping bodies is repeatedly paralleled with the process of shaping minds: the distribution and use of food is very much like the distribution and use of words. The early chapters of the novel could be characterized as a recapitulation, a beginning that consists of bringing into the novel and into the characters, physically and mentally, bits and pieces of previous people, books, and cultures. Even the style of these chapters is familiar; the novel begins by incorporating within itself the most recent style of novels, the structure of characters and narrator.

The book opens with Buck Mulligan shaving, shaping his appearance by removing what society has deemed waste. This act of self-shaping resonates with Stephen's question later in the chapter, "Who chose this face for me?" (1.137). After removing the wastes their own bodies have produced while they slept, these men take in what society has prepared for them: the chapter continues with a thoroughly symbolic scene of an old Irish woman bringing milk for them to drink. Stephen first thinks of this woman as a possible sign of a new beginning, imagining that she comes "from a morning world, maybe a messenger" (1.399). However, she does not bring messages from the future, but rather from a "mourning world," the world of his dead mother. Stephen believes he has left home, but he still drinks milk, still recreates himself every day from the body (and soul) of the "motherland" he wishes to escape, Ireland. Along with the milk, the old woman brings thoughts of the lack of individual autonomy that pervades Irish culture: the woman is "serving her conqueror and her gay betrayer" (1.405)—Haines, a Britisher representing the conquerors of Ire-

land, and Mulligan. Stephen feels himself being recreated as an Irish artist
into the same kind of servant he sees in the woman; he describes Irish
art as "the cracked lookingglass of a servant" (1.146). The mirror in which
the artist looks to see himself, to paint his own private soul, is owned by
others, by the masters, by the conquerors and the gay betrayers who work
for those conquerors. The use of such a looking glass makes art a form of
cosmetics, like shaving.

The looking glass also refers back to the opening sentence: Mulligan
carried a mirror crossed by a razor and turned shaving into a mock religious
ritual. Mulligan mocks all of Irish society and religion, but his mockery
does not lead him to alter the system; he merely classifies all challenges to
the system, including his mockery and Stephen's rebellious art, as silly play
or as waste products. Hence, as he cleans his razor with Stephen's hand-
kerchief, he says, "The bard's noserag. A new art colour for our Irish poets:
snotgreen" (1.74). Mulligan's mockery seems to match Joyce's assessment
of Stephen's efforts as well: Stephen's attempts at revolt are repeatedly
shown as simply leaving him disgusted with himself and tied to the system.

Stephen's initial symbolic effort to assert his autonomy was his refusal
to show obeisance to his mother: he would not kneel at her bed as she died.
However, his efforts to escape end up haunting him; when he thinks of his
refusal to kneel, he labels himself a "chewer of corpses," a person who feeds
off the deadly pain he caused his mother and who is therefore metaphorically eating and incorporating into his body exactly what he wants to avoid.
Stephen would like to escape his mother, all mothers, all the past that has
produced him, "history" in all forms, the "nightmare" from which he is
"trying to awake" (2.377). But the opening scenes show the only awakening
possible—the awakening he undergoes every day, which is always followed
by being recreated by the social system into the same person with the same
past he was when he went to sleep. He is physically a product of all those
things he wishes to escape, so his production of new things, his art, is limited to two choices: either he reproduces the culture that has fed him, or
he withdraws into starvation and dryness, as he seems to be doing.

Joyce goes to great lengths to emphasize that each person ingests his
dead past with his food every day. He violates his principle of presenting
a factually accurate portrayal of Dublin of 1904 to allow Bloom to buy his
breakfast from an eastern European Jewish butcher, Dlugascz, who did not
exist, but who is clearly a symbolic representative of Bloom's renounced
cultural heritage as a Hungarian Jew. The butcher literally wraps Bloom's
breakfast kidney in messages about their shared culture—in a flyer about
investing in land in Palestine. Bloom, like Stephen, has tried to escape his
past, but for precisely the opposite reason: Bloom wants to become an accepted member of Irish society. Unfortunately, his body and his tastes in
food are enough to keep him a cultural outsider, as Stephen's body and
tastes keep him an Irishman, no matter how hard they resist.

Stephen and Bloom not only are social products, they are active participants in the labor of constantly reconstructing society. They are shown as
workers whose own social constructions slot them into particular places
in the overall project of constructing the social order. Stephen, a product of a classical, Catholic education, is a teacher of history in a Catholic
school; Bloom, out of a lower-middle-class public education, sells advertising. Stephen hopes to move to another occupation, author, but Joyce shows
that would only move him to another part of the whole institutional process of cultural recycling. Indeed, his literary efforts bring him even closer
to Bloom; both of them are shown spending their time keeping the material
in books in the library in active circulation, Bloom transferring old texts
and images to ads, Stephen to literature and critical theories.

Work also provides another means for society to fill individuals: paying them. Money carries messages just as food does, as Stephen realizes
when he enters Deasy's office to be paid. As Deasy puts coins on the desk,
Stephen thinks: "symbols . . . of beauty and of power . . . symbols soiled by
greed and misery" (2.238). Stephen also takes, along with his pay, Deasy's
words, both some anti-Semitic ravings and an absurd letter to the newspaper about cattle diseases. Money carries outside influences into Bloom's
private life, as well: Boylan's body enters Bloom's household along with
Molly's income.

The contrast between Dedalus and Bloom is symbolized by what seem
to be decisions each makes this day: Dedalus to not go back to Martello;
Bloom to remain in his home. Both these decisions are responses to the
recognition of usurpers in their homes and hence symbolize the question
of what to do when one recognizes that one is not in control of one's own
private space—indeed one's own mind. Stephen struggles to be free, but
his very struggle identifies him completely with the past. The idea of freedom was already outdated, a part of the liberal heritage, though it may have
seemed "new" in an Ireland that, Joyce felt, was still in the feudal age. And
even more important, the social order already has developed institutional
structures that channel the desire for freedom, and Stephen simply falls
right into them. The end of his role in the first six chapters is his stroll
on the beach, where he dreams of Romantic freedom, wondering "Am I
walking into eternity along Sandymount Strand?" (3.18). All he can think
of on the beach, however, is his inability to break free of the hold of Irish
society and of his family on him—his inability to plunge into those waters
outside the social order. He equates his inability with weakness, lack of
heroism, and contrasts himself in this to, of all people, Buck Mulligan, who
can dive in and swim. It is Stephen's constant equation of freedom with
heroism that makes his escapes so fruitless. His entrapment seems the failure of his masculinity; he is entangled in the "strandentwining cable of
all flesh" (3.37) that leads to his mother's belly. He dreams of the ancient
Lochlanns: if he could revive their blood, he could become potent, free of

the entwining social order: "Their blood is in me, their lusts my waves. I moved among them on the frozen Liffey, that I, a changeling" (3.308). But "that I" is different from "this I," because "this I" is terrified of his own lusts and of the waves that move him, fearing that the tides around him are not those that moved great heroes, but simply mass movements of batlike souls, and in some way controlled by females: a woman walking is "a tide, westering, moondrawn, in her wake. Tides, myriad-islanded, within her, blood not mine" (3.394). Stephen is terrified of writing because it threatens to draw him into the female-controlled waters. He parallels his own efforts to use his lips to make words with a man's kissing a woman on the beach, imagining the man as a vampire feeding on the female—and then being engulfed by her: "[Stephen's] lips lipped and mouthed fleshless lips of air: mouth to her womb. Ooomb, allwombing tomb. His mouth moulded issuing breath, unspeeched: ooeeehah" (3.401–3). To Stephen, forming words or sounds is, like a kiss, an act that can entrap him. All contact with any otherness, especially with females, threatens to engulf him, to suck his soul out of him and seal it into a womb or a tomb.

Stephen ends his sojourn on the beach disgusted; even though he has composed a poem, he concludes that all he has done is participate in the recycling of waste products from the past: "Dead breaths I living breathe, tread dead dust, devour a urinous offal from all dead" (3.479–80). His poem is undoubtedly a dead breath he is breathing again because it is plagiarized from Douglas Hyde. Stephen's last gesture is symbolic of such "creation" that is little more than rearranging leftovers and waste products: he lays "the dry snot picked from his nostril on a ledge of rock, carefully" (3.500–501), carrying out the useless act of a poet whose "art colour" is "snotgreen."

Stephen's horror and disgust may seem insurmountable, given that a corrupt society controls both proper bodies and waste products, both licit and illicit thoughts. But there is an alternative, and it is not achieved by trying to escape taking in dead matter and excrement. Joyce shows this alternative strikingly in the first sentence of the chapter after Stephen's walk on the beach. Leopold Bloom is introduced as one who gets pleasure from precisely what horrifies Stephen, the eating of "urinous offal": "Mr. Leopold Bloom ate with relish the inner organs of beasts and fowls. He liked thick giblet soup, nutty gizzards, a stuffed roast heart, liverslices fried with crustcrumbs, fried hencods' roes. Most of all he liked grilled mutton kidneys which gave to his palate a fine tang of faintly scented urine" (4.5). One does not have to be bitterly disgusted by the eating of dead things: properly packaged and prepared, even urinous offal can add a fine tang to one's life. Bloom can see the usefulness of excrement: "All soil" is "scabby . . . without dung. . . . Mulch of dung. Best thing to clean ladies' kid gloves. Dirty cleans. Ashes too. Reclaim the whole place" (4.477–81). Bloom knows how to reclaim the past, to use dead and smelly waste products to clean and to make things grow. The difference between Bloom's attitude and Stephen's

can be attributed to temperament or taste, but it seems as much a difference of the locales and institutions in which they get the dead things they
feed on: Stephen, rejecting completely the corrupt institutions around him,
ends up in the junk pile on the beach, taking in what is not packaged for
use and adding his own waste products to the heap. Bloom gets his kidney
with its urine scent from a butcher shop, prepares and eats it in the kitchen,
a place set aside (in his home) for eating. Bloom seeks within society for
useful bits of the dead past, bringing both meat and words (books and mail)
into his house, all neatly packaged.

Bloom also knows how to dispose of the waste products of both mind
and body. In the outhouse, "quietly he read, restraining himself. . . . Mid-
way, his last resistance yielding, he allowed his bowels to ease themselves
as he read," and finally he "tore away half the prize story sharply and wiped
himself with it" (4.509–11, 537). The final use of words on a page, like
the final use of food, is to fill the outhouse, to become excrement, and to
keep neat and clean the whole system of carefully moving packages of food
and words. Bloom feels fine throughout the whole cycle of ingestion and
excretion that gives Stephen such difficulty.

Bloom also can happily play in the literal and figurative tides that
Stephen fears, as we see in the fifth chapter. Bloom enters institutions
such as the Church that "hypnotize" people into feeling they are part of
the social tide "like one family party, same in the theatre, all in the same
swim" (5.362). Joyce, through Bloom's comments, exposes the mindlessness of people who join such institutions and the cunning of those who
stage the shows that hypnotize: "Squareheaded chaps those must be in
Rome: they work the whole show" (5.434). However, Joyce also is showing Bloom easily slipping into the "swim," allowing himself to lazily pass
through this morning with nothing much pressing on him. Bloom recognizes the ways that social institutions hypnotize people, but can enjoy that
hypnotism precisely because he recognizes the limits of such institutions.
He can enter a church, be carried away by the music, and leave; he can
take a bath and leave. For him, mindlessness is a necessary part of life; one
eats the lotus every day, letting the mind be taken over by the body, letting
oneself float in the tide of history, sexuality, generation. The chapter ends
with Bloom thinking of settling into a bath, a "womb of warmth" (5.568)—a
striking contrast to Stephen, who has not washed for eight months. Bloom
sees water in much the same symbolic terms as Stephen, as something
feminine and womblike that makes individuals give up the conscious, directed self in favor of the body. But while Stephen finds water terrifying,
threatening to drown him and to turn the womb into a tomb, Bloom sees
water as warm and supportive, making him feel one with his body. The difference between the two attitudes is due to the social source of the water
they think about: Stephen thinks of entering the water outside of society
(the sea), while Bloom enters water institutionally packaged so as to be

safe and usable (the baths). Bloom does not mistake any part of Dublin as providing access to the world outside of society. He does not feel the need to step outside of society to be himself and even seems quite comfortable with the possibility that he never is himself. Stephen must escape all social illusions, all stage shows, and so finds himself backstage among the salvage of the shows and out at sea in danger of drowning because he refuses to use the containers society provides for packaging the various parts of the self or its world. Wombs and tombs are all mixed together in Stephen's mind and impossible to separate. Bloom, accepting social packaging, is free to think without unduly terrifying himself.

The sixth chapter, the last that still seems to be following a single consciousness in fairly conventional form, ties together the concerns of the first part of the book by presenting a funeral. We have watched Stephen and Bloom wake up, be reborn, and take in leftover dead pieces and waste products of the past. The process of reconstituting human bodies in this book is completed by the interring of a dead body. This might seem the end of the useful cycling of flesh; as Bloom says," a corpse is meat gone bad" (6.982). But society has a use for such bad meat by making a ritual of its disposal. The funeral provides support for social institutions; the government and the Church gain power from their role in the drama of death: the ceremony shows that all is kept in order, kept structured, even though a person has died. In this chapter, the particular individual who is lost does not matter, as Joyce indicates by presenting the funeral of an all but anonymous acquaintance of Bloom's; what is of importance is the social experience of death itself.

Institutionalizing Authors

The death of an anonymous man marks a crucial transition in the novel—away from the individual as the focus of the process of social construction. The first six chapters are structured to make us view Stephen and Bloom as distinct individuals and yet to make us vividly aware of how porous these individuals are, how much they are merely a nexus through which social tides flow. It is hard, however, to visualize these tides, because the two streams are so completely presented as located inside two distinct bodies. Bodies are the boundaries of individuals; when we think of bodies, we have difficulty seeing the way group forces act across many bodies and many minds. Joyce portrays, in "Hades," the burying of the body, and from then on the book shifts to showing mass consciousness, aspects of mind that derive not from any individual intention or bodily peculiarity, but from structures of language that have developed without anyone precisely directing their development, what Karen Lawrence calls "anonymous, collective discourse" such as newspaper headlines, romance novels, and legal and scientific styles.[18]

Joyce takes us through these different styles, and at each change we are jarred. Joyce provides a striking image for this process in the description of what Stephen hears when he is too groggy to make out the meaning of the words said by those about him (so that he can only perceive the general style of speech): "He could hear, of course, all kinds of words changing colour like those crabs about Ringsend in the morning, burrowing quickly into all colours of different sorts of the same sand where they had a home somewhere beneath or seemed to" (16.1146). Words—and ideas—assume different colors when they are embedded in different kinds of "the same sand"; as in "Proteus," sand is a metaphor for language as a repository of all the styles of the past that are silted together in current society. There may be a "home" for words beneath the sand, a place where they can show their "true meanings," but Joyce finally shows that there is no clear access to meaning or reality outside conventions. Even though there is no "true" or "home" meaning, we can still tell that conventions distort, if only by comparing them with each other, and we can still modify them for various social ends, including what could be called "greater truth, "though I do not think that was Joyce's goal. Rather, like Woolf, Joyce was seeking to reduce some of the pain that is produced by social structures.

The first step in this process is to make us stop looking at bodies and minds and focus on the sand in which every body and every mind is embedded. "Aeolus" marks this transition. The first word of the chapter, like all the headlines in it, cannot be traced to any particular mind: it introduces us to words generated by collective discourse. The first scenes in the chapter also provide a brief overview of the social system that we have been watching in operation in the first six chapters, where it shaped the "personal lives" of Stephen and Bloom. Now we see the overall circulation of bodies and substances used to fill bodies: trams moving people to various places, mail cars carrying letters, and draymen moving barrels of beer about. We begin to see that the Stephen and Bloom may be blown about the streets of Dublin by forces that have little to do with what is inside their minds.

The shift from individual consciousness to systems of circulation is a version of the shift from individualist to mass or collectivist social systems. Joyce provides a metaphor for this process in the chapter: the chopping up of the body and mind into separate pieces by institutions. From this chapter on, we no longer have the illusion that we will be able to assemble everything we see of each character into a unified whole. The point is made quite clear in the headline for Dignam's funeral: "DISSOLUTION OF A MOST RESPECTED DUBLIN BURGESS" (7.79). Joyce is presenting in this chapter the breakup of the universal individual, the respectable burgess, that the liberal social order claimed to create. Bloom's thoughts while reading this headline imply that the presses themselves are responsible for the breakup of the individual: "Thumping thump. . . . This morning the remains of the late Mr. Patrick Dignam. Machines. Smash a man to atoms if they got him caught. Rule the world today" (7.81). The reporting of the funeral smashes Dignam's body to atoms, to bits and pieces of stories produced by the functioning of the institution of the press. When Bloom finally reads the report on the funeral, we see that the dead man is not the only one being chopped up by the press: Bloom himself is in a sense blown up by being transformed in the obituary into Mr. L. Boom.

Joyce focuses not only on the breakup of the physical body but on the breakup or dissolution of the "literary body," the coherent, unified text produced by an author. As part of the introductory passages showing the overall system of production of works, Joyce presents the machinery that Bloom fears, the machinery that produces text: the presses, clanking away in "threefour time" (7.101). Newspaper stories are not shaped by individual minds, but by the rhythms of the presses, the constant, repeated mechanical processes that chop up events and people into little pieces that can be printed, distributed, and consumed quickly. Joyce makes us experience the effects of newspaper production and distribution on texts by cutting up the chapter into short sections, each with a headline. No particular logic seems to dictate the nature of the sections, except that they all are roughly the length of a newspaper story. The conditions of circulation and printing—and the kind of reading that newspapers encourage—determine the structure of the "atoms" into which newspapers turn texts and people.

If the move to mass media and mass social institutions breaks up bodies and texts, authorship is no longer an individual act. The shifting styles throughout the whole novel undermine the idea that an author is a single, unified mind identified by certain stylistic features and suggest instead that the author is a conglomerate of institutionally produced writing styles. Joyce highlights the breakup of the author in "Aeolus" by including two different samples of Stephen's writing: the poem he wrote earlier and "A Pisgah Sight of Palestine." The differences between these two small works point to a basic tenet of this novel: writing changes depending on the institutions in which it is produced. Stephen himself changes: in "Aeolus" he is not the bitter, self-destructive person he was in the opening chapters. Instead of projecting himself as a vampire haunting Ireland, he adopts the whimsical point of view of poor women on vacation. We might attribute the differences to Stephen's variable mood, but if we compare all of the texts that Stephen produces within this novel, we can see how completely Joyce recast authorship as an institutional and not an individual act.

Stephen's first act of writing—composing his poem—occurs on the beach, a place that may not seem to constitute an institution. Thomas Richards, however, has analyzed brilliantly how beaches were minutely constructed at the turn of the century, and his work, along with that of Garry Leonard and Suzette Henke, shows that Joyce in his beach chapters has, in Cheryl Herr's term, "anatomized" the cultural construction of this apparently free space.[19] Though Sandymount Strand is a barren place, people there still act, as Leonard puts it, "in accordance with the heavily mediated atmosphere of the British beach resort."[20] Critics have focused mostly on issues of gender and on Gerty's complicity in or resistance to the cultural pressures of the beach. But Joyce is also anatomizing the ways that the institutional structure of the beach crosses gender roles. Stephen, Bloom, and Gerty all perform the same acts on the beach: they compose imaginary scenes in their minds while being involved in voyeuristic acts of gazing at and thinking about what is underneath people's clothing. In the two scenes set at Sandymount Strand, Joyce shows that society has ways to indulge the desire to uncover what is hidden or repressed: society has distinct ways to allow people to, for a time, evade the barriers limiting their supposedly proper social roles. Those who desire to escape social limits are shunted to a carefully circumscribed region that is left apparently unstructured by man, a beach or a park, where they can have small breaks, vacations, replete with sexual fantasies, after which they must return home ready to conform. As Michel Foucault has argued, desire for rebellion becomes, in the modern world, desire for sex.[21]

Males are not the only ones to use the beach as an outlet for illicit fantasies. Gerty MacDowell also thinks about the limitations of her position and turns to erotic fantasy. Gerty's fantasies may seem far more clearly social products than Stephen's, and they have generated far more critical discussion of their social construction; the very language of her stream of consciousness derives from cheap fiction and underwear advertising. But Stephen, too, follows popular literary images and clothing styles in his fantasies, even when he acts out his dream of escaping Ireland. On the beach, he remembers his trip to Paris, where he felt he "must dress the character" in his "Latin Quarter hat" (3.174). Gerty tries to live out popular love stories; Stephen tries to live out the popular image of the Romantic artist. Both go to the beach to pursue their romances, Gerty dreaming of escaping in the arms of a foreigner, Stephen dreaming of walking into eternity. Such fantasies are contained by the beach and turned into nothing more than midday breaks. By 1904, Romantic escapes from society into nature or into exotic foreign lands were thoroughly institutionalized. The guilt that accompanies these pseudo-escapes is a crucial part of the institutional structure: it maintains the repression of the illicit dreams that underlie vacations.

Stephen's guilt is revealed in the small alterations he makes to the Irish poem he plagiarizes on the beach. Hyde writes of a man and a woman kissing, glued together; Stephen turns the man into a vampire coming on "bat sails" to feed on the female, as Stephen is guiltily feeding on the erotic couple on the beach and on Hyde's love poems. The vampire and bat images refer back to *Portrait*, to Stephen's definition of the goal of his art as bringing order to the "batlike" thoughts and desires of the Irish masses by casting the shadow of his imagination over women. A vampire is a creature who has the powers to perform these tasks, to mysteriously control women's minds and to provide consciousness to flitting bats. On the beach in *Ulysses*, however, Stephen imagines that the attempt to exercise such powers will result only in the vampire's own entrapment: to become a vampire is to be "glued" to women. Instead of shaping and controlling women's passions by creating literature, Stephen fears that any contact with Irish women will turn him into a part of the batlike masses, attached to the motherland and controlled by it. Furthermore, Joyce implies that both Stephen and Hyde end up "glued" to old literary forms rather than gaining power from their contact with the world of "the dead," as vampires do. The only way Stephen can be "original" is by "issuing breath unspeeched," by making sounds that are not words (3.403). Seeking Romantic transcendence on the beach leads only to babbling.

Stephen's second bit of creative writing is in striking contrast to his poem: in a newspaper office, he adopts the low style of contemporary hack newspapers. Joyce makes us aware that Stephen is adopting a new institutional style by including in the chapter the recent history of newspaper formats. The chapter is punctuated by headlines that change style in a way that parodies changes that occurred in newspapers from the nineteenth century to early in the twentieth. The early newspaper headlines are quite formal and suggest a world of great, independent men performing great deeds (even Dignam becomes a "distinguished burgess"). But by the end, the headlines are salacious and silly, marking a change in the reading audience (as literacy became universal) and a consequent change in the image of the individual, who was no longer assumed to be a respectable man of property. The men Stephen converses with in this chapter all praise the old rhetoric that is embodied in the older headlines, rhetoric that presented itself as produced by great men speaking about other great men. The prime example is Stephen Bushe, a great lawyer who praised the great artist, Michelangelo, who made a sculpture of a great leader, Moses. The discussion of Bushe shows how the institutions of law, art, and religion all support each other, and have in the past supported the belief that great individuals are responsible for all achievement. The rhetoric of the men talking about Bushe, however, fails miserably to equal what they praise and even seems quite out of their control: rhetorical devices proliferate cancerously in the chapter. The old, high rhetoric no longer has much of a function in the current institution of journalism; these men, shaped by the changing institutions, only imitate the old rhetoric, and they imitate it badly—just as Stephen on the beach can only imitate Romantic poetry with a bad, faux-Romantic poem.

In the newspaper office, though, Stephen for once joins the tide of institutional change, making use of the newest, lowly newspaper style, creating a short feature story complete with a headline that mocks the images of the great men Moses and Nelson. Instead of adopting the point of view of such great men, Stephen's story looks through the eyes of working-class women, who gaze up Nelson's pants to expose the "onehandled adulterer" while at the same time exposing their own drawers to the people passing below (7.1072). Stephen's story, like the newspaper headlines, descends in class, in gender, and into the lower parts of the human anatomy, examining what is underneath the respectable gentlemen who dominated newspaper headlines in the nineteenth century.

We can be sure that Stephen would not regard his little tale as part of his Art with a capital *A*, but his tale is much more like the writing in *Ulysses* than is his vampire poem. The tale is a humorous anecdote about ordinary people that resonates with possible symbolic meaning largely because of the Biblical parallels highlighted by Stephen's Biblical title for the tale, "A Pisgah Sight of Palestine," much as *Ulysses* is a humorous novel about an ordinary day that resonates with possible symbolic meaning because of the Homeric parallels highlighted by its Homeric title (7.1057). Joyce even indicates that the tale Stephen writes is a step toward *Ulysses* by putting "Dubliners" in the text as an odd bit of narration immediately before Stephen talks (7.921). If Stephen is to move from being a plagiarizing poet to being the writer who could produce *Dubliners* and *Ulysses*, he needs to make use of the nonartistic parts of himself that emerge when he is in lowly institutions such as the newspaper office and not merely accept as his vision of himself the Romantic image of the artist who writes while looking out to sea.

Stephen produces one other piece of writing that he could possibly publish, his theory of Shakespeare, delivered in a library. Joyce shows in fine detail that the library as an institution is structuring Stephen's theory. Like universities, libraries at that period were changing from places where gentlemen read the classics to research institutions. This shift produced a change in the treatment of literature.[22] In the old view, epitomized by the urbane librarian in *Ulysses*, literature consists of "priceless pages" produced by "great poet[s]" that reveal the eternal truths of "real life" (9.2–4). Since the only other texts we might need for interpreting a great poet are the words of "great brother poet[s]," literature is properly separated from all other texts. In the new view, great authors and great books do not exist in a realm separate from the rest of society, but are social products that can be explained by research into the culture, the period, and the groups surrounding the author.

At first, Stephen seems to be joining the new view: he shocks the literary gentlemen in the library by basing an interpretation of Shakespeare's plays on obscure and somewhat salacious evidence about Shakespeare's family taken from late-nineteenth-century histories. But as his theory progresses, Stephen tries to recover the old view of Shakespeare and reconcile it with the new, to make Shakespeare both a self-generating genius and a product of his culture. If that is to happen, Shakespeare must in essence create the culture that creates him, or, as Stephen says, become "the father of all his race, the father of his own grandfather" (9.869). Stephen's theory twists into absurdity in a vain effort to resolve the dialectic that is changing the library.

Stephen solves in just as summary a fashion the problem of impure, erroneous, unintended bits of excrement being part of every body and every art work: he says that, to the genius, errors are the portals of discovery. The genius takes everything, his culture, his parents, the errors he finds himself making, and turns them into his "own" creation. Stephen had sought as his aesthetic in *Portrait* a new type of "conception, gestation, and procreation"—a new form of generation other than the mixing of male and female—and in *Ulysses* he claims to have found it, and so his theory ends with a vision of "heaven" where "there are no more marriages, glorified man, an androgynous angel, being a wife unto himself" (9.1051–52). Mulligan's mockery of this as masturbation is appropriate: Stephen is trying to remove all otherness from literature and so reduces writing to involvement with self alone. Stephen's attempt to produce aesthetic theories is in itself an effort to keep his writing from making contact with any others; he wants to control and structure the codes of reading as well as his own writing, to make the readers copies of himself. Stephen wants to escape the limitations of social structures, to escape king and priest and mother, but all he does is retreat to the realms of nonsocial existence, dry and desiccated regions in which excrement does not fertilize and ejaculation does not impregnate.

The role of the library in creating Stephen's theory of artistic genius is underscored by the differing ways Stephen conceives of Shakespeare in other institutions. In the library, Stephen clearly is identifying himself with Shakespeare, presenting both as geniuses. Stephen even considers his theory of Shakespeare a product of genius, original, and thus worth money. In "Circe," however, Shakespeare appears in a mirror when Stephen and Bloom look, and Bloom has thoughts that describe Shakespeare in words identical to Stephen's. Ralph Rader describes this common image of Shakespeare as Joyce's way of indicating the identity of Bloom, Stephen, and Shakespeare with Joyce.[23] But Bloom is not a genius of literary studies; what he shares with Stephen is only what is generated by their common social institutions. In "Circe," a place of illicit sexuality, what Stephen, Bloom, and Shakespeare share is a common sexuality: all three have been overborne by women who then "betrayed" them with other men (in Stephen's case, a prostitute), and all three are as ridiculous as they are tragic for brooding about such betrayals. Thus, Shakespeare appears in the brothel mirror to Stephen and Bloom as a beardless man wearing a hat rack on his head, castrated, cuckolded, and silly-looking. This reduction of Shakespeare to a common social product is completed in "Eumaeus," when Stephen, in that most common place of all, the cabman's shelter, says, "Shakespeares were as common as Murphies" (16.364). Stephen's Shakespeare changes from being a particular, unique genius to being a common male, depending on the institution in which Stephen thinks of him.

The institutional multiplicity within every author in most literary texts is generally overshadowed by the presumption of individual coherence. Readers are trained in imagining an authorial genius underlying the most diverse elements in a text. To make readers alter this fundamental convention of reading, Joyce has to reveal literary authorship itself as a particular, limited institutional structure. He does so by throwing together in one chapter, "Oxen of the Sun," all the authors who would be united in the "Literature" section of the library. The chapter is constructed to undermine in several ways the very idea of an author standing outside of social determinants—the very idea of originality. The dominant metaphor of the chapter, embryonic development leading from one great male author to another, in itself reduces the autonomy of any of the authors presented; they become stages in the development of an institution, literature. Joyce makes claims of originality by each author seem about as plausible as claims by a developing child that he is autonomously creating a new body for himself. Moreover, as we have seen in Chapter 2, Joyce structured "Oxen" to draw considerable attention to the influence of other voices inside the supposedly autonomous author; the chapter makes us aware that the construction of an authorial voice involves suppression of part of the author's own mind. The chapter also implies that it is no longer possible to construct authors in that way: as we also have seen, its history of styles ends in an explosion that dissolves the coherent authorial presence into a conglomeration of commonwealth slangs and propels the characters into the "woman-city" of Nighttown. Joyce thus suggests that in the twentieth century, the lower-class, "foreign," and female parts of the author's own consciousness cannot be suppressed. The whole novel supports such an interpretation by showing that if Stephen is going to escape paralysis and plagiarism, he will have to give up thinking of himself as a great male genius writing in the company of other male geniuses; he will have to accept as well the hack author he becomes in the newspaper office, the clichés he mouths in the cabman's shelter, and the femaleness within him that emerges when he is in the maternity hospital and the brothel. His book will be written by these various social institutions, by the city, not by himself.

As the Homeric parallel with the chapter "Oxen of the Sun" implies, no one can fully digest and incorporate others into a single body: Odysseus's men cut up Zeus's cattle, but find to their horror that the cut-up pieces of cattle come back to life and begin lowing. Homer's tale is a nightmare about people of one culture being unable to take control of cultural others, even after killing those others and slicing them into small pieces. The myth becomes a commentary on modernist art: the artist does not have control over the fragments he collects, no matter how small he slices them. It is impossible to incorporate others, to create a corporate or collective voice

for a social order or for a single text: male English Catholics cannot incorporate women, Irishmen, and Jews by taking them into the body of the
British Empire or into the body of English novels. Though women are supposedly contained inside houses, the Irish inside the English Parliament,
and Jewish Bloom inside the Christian church and inside a Catholic author's novel, these others keep making noises, so no institution, whether
house, Parliament, religion, or novel, can speak with a single voice.

Creating Illusions of Autonomy

Joyce repeatedly in this novel shows that the effort to create a unified
voice is identical to the effort to suppress other voices. This issue extends
far beyond literature, to the whole system of cultural production. In the
two linked pub chapters, Joyce explores the way that the forms of "mass
culture"—song, newspaper columns, and such—also participate in the creation of images of unity and the suppression of alternative voices. In both
chapters, Joyce follows as Bloom is first drawn into a group and then expelled from it. The effort to incorporate Bloom creates tension and ultimately violence because he is labeled by the processes of group creation
as a contaminant. In both chapters, he is identified with excrement—his
"instrument" to add to the harmony of the musical pub is the fart, and he
is described as "cute as a shithouse rat" in "Cyclops" (12.1761). When the
citizen drives Bloom out with a biscuit tin, he is in effect seeking to box up
and ship away the excremental. These chapters lend themselves to a fairly
straightforward political interpretation: Joyce objected to the kind of purifying politics exemplified by the citizen and to the kind of purifying songs
of love and loss found in "Sirens." The two chapters are linked: the end of
"Sirens" turns to political rhetoric as the unity of everyone in a moment of
sexual communion, the cry "come" that brings "youmehimher" together,
turns easily into the song "The Croppy Boy" and the call for violence and
expulsion of the English. The chapter ends with Robert Emmett's epitaph,
which equates the act of expelling the English with restoring the Irish
"home." Sexual purity and national autonomy are mixed together; violence
is entwined with visions of perfect love. The citizen seeks to remove the
invaders that have broken up the Irish family and the Irish nation.

Joyce is at his most clearly ironic in these chapters, setting Bloom's fart
and the barmaid's lascivious gestures against the songs of idealized love
and exposing the citizen's rage as misdirected by having it turned against
poor Bloom. The citizen is condemned as a "Cyclops," a one-eyed, one-
dimensional person, the essential product of the system of ideology that
turns everyone into subjects who line up and march behind banners of
idealized homes, nations, and heroes.

In both chapters, we tend to feel Joyce's sympathies are with Bloom the
excluded, the repressed. Bloom's response to the citizen, though, suggests

that Joyce is not merely seeking to reverse the citizen's condemnation of Bloom by condemning the citizen. Bloom's response to the citizen is essentially that everyone is a Jew—suggesting that what the citizen is raging against is a part of himself. As Klaus Theweleit has discovered in Fascist writings, the violent politics of removing contamination exemplified by the citizen derives from a sense of contamination within—of a liquid, racially other beast inside that must be kept down.[24]

Joyce represents the unconscious not just as a part of the psyche, but also as a part of the social order, and we enter this realm by entering Nighttown. In "Circe," Joyce shows men confronting what is inside them, what they armor themselves against: the liquid, disgusting, female nonself. Stephen confronts his mother and her green bile, the disgusting liquid that he fears is inside him as well. Joyce shows that Stephen is unable to accept this part of himself: immediately after seeing the vision of his mother, Stephen strikes out to destroy the whole world. But the act of destruction simply unleashes a mob of lower-class people chasing him, a mob that parallels the mob of impulses released in the act of entering Nighttown. Stephen's only defense, finally, is to return what has arisen in his mind to unconsciousness: he has to be knocked out by a figure from the mob chasing him, a British soldier who seems as loutish as the citizen. The soldier and the citizen are the militaristic figures created by the social order to suppress the monsters created by that same order. Stephen maintains the opposition between himself and the soldier, and so his rebellion is easily snuffed out. Bloom's counter to the citizen is to suggest an underlying unity between the two of them, and that is far more subversive an act, one that allows Bloom to escape. At the end of his encounter with the citizen, Bloom moves at an angle of "forty-five degrees," an angle of neither resistance nor compliance, and thereby ends up setting against each other the social institutions that would control him.

But Bloom is not merely Joyce's new hero, a figure free of the ugliness inside everyone else. Rather, Joyce shows that Bloom, too, has to face what he has rejected in himself. There is in "Circe" a key event that marks the release of the repressed, and that event is the cracking of the nymph: the manufactured image of purity breaks apart. This very small event allows Bloom for awhile to circumvent the cycle of impulses welling up and being violently suppressed, the cycle that maintains the rigidity of masculine psychology.

To emphasize the political significance of this event, Joyce intertwines sexuality and politics throughout the chapter. The early part of the chapter consists of accusations against Bloom of sexual crimes: "unlawfully watching and besetting" (15.732), interfering with the clothing of a scullery maid (15.889), and even being a "plagiarist" of a pornographic novel (15.822). Gradually, accusations switch to political crimes: he is accused of being "a well-known dynamiter, forger, bigamist, bawd and cuckold and a public nuisance to the citizens of Dublin" (15.1160). He is condemned to hang, is saved at the last moment, and then is accused of sexual crimes again, culminating in his admission of his worst crime: "rerererepugnan[ce]"— anal intercourse (15.3058)—being excited by the excremental, by what is repugnant.

Bloom defends himself largely by trying to build an image of himself as the ideal political hero: at first he says he "did all a white man could" and that he is "as staunch a Britisher" as anyone (15.794, 797). Then he generates images of himself as "the world's greatest reformer" (15.1459) and even as a judge in "The Court of Conscience" (15.1629). It might seem odd that Bloom would end up thinking about becoming a political leader in a brothel, but this is not merely an idiosyncratic reaction: Stephen does much the same thing, generating images of himself as cardinal and king. The political rhetoric of racial (white) supremacy and social perfection is in part the product of a feeling of internal contamination, of guilt: Stephen and Bloom turn themselves into cardinals and judges in reaction to this guilt. They turn to the socially provided images of virtuous, strong, heroic males, images of males who would not succumb to low impulses. Political, legal, and religious systems depend on such images of heroic perfection for their existence. These systems provide antidotes for the guilts and weaknesses that everyone feels: trust in the men who are not suffering from such imperfections and define yourself as divided into two parts, one like these heroic leaders and one like the people they oppose. Admit only to the heroic side and hide as best you can the low, base side. And, as this chapter suggests, the guilt one feels comes from a female voice: the accusations against Stephen come from his mother, those against Bloom from various women. But these voices are parts of these men's psyches: the male is once again armored against a sliminess within that is identified as female.

Bloom undergoes a complex process of dealing with the accusatory female voices from within him. He tries admitting his guilt and at the same time transmuting into a female: in other words, he tries to become the accusatory voices themselves. This transformation into a female and the subsequent punishment by a female who has become male might seem a breakdown of the social machinery that makes males have the personalities they do and so might seem part of a process of escaping the system. Some critics have read Bloom's becoming a "womanly man" in this chapter as Joyce's image of an androgynous ideal. I do think Joyce was seeking to develop a new image of masculinity, but in this scene, Bloom's transformation into a female is a way of rejecting his guilt: if he is a female, his seeing down women's dresses or interfering with their clothing is not a crime. Moreover, Bloom is declared a "womanly man" by a doctor analyzing Bloom's anatomy, so that the source of his "problems" becomes his particular body. The doctor equates Bloom's womanliness with being a "Mongolian idiot"; in other words, Bloom is a freak who cannot help himself. If Bloom were to accept this diagnosis, he would be accepting all the racial insults flung at him for his Jewishness: he would be a person of inferior consciousness due to racial and bodily traits that justify his being ostracized.

The first part of this chapter, then, from the opening accusations to Bloom's confession and punishment by Bello, maintains the distinctions of proper/improper, moral/criminal, and male/female. If the chapter were to end at this point, with Bloom leaving the brothel after his masochistic fantasies, he would feel with renewed force the need to condemn the otherness within him—the womanliness, the Jewishness. However, something happens that breaks through his own sense of disgust with himself and so breaks the corresponding idealization of masculine heroism. This transformation takes the form of a change in the image of femaleness that he has actively incorporated inside his private world and in effect inside himself: a change in the picture of a nymph he has cut out of the newspaper and hung on the wall of his bedroom. Joyce emphasizes that the nymph is a socially manufactured device for constructing one's sexuality. The nymph describes her "origin": "I was surrounded by the stale smut of clubmen, stories to disturb callow youths, ads for transparencies, truedup dice and bustpads, proprietary articles and why wear a truss with testimonial from ruptured gentleman. Useful hints to the married. . . . Rubber goods. Neverrip brand as supplied to the aristocracy" (15.3248–54).

By cutting the nymph out of this environment, Bloom is separating the image of a female from the institutions that have created it and thus constructing his sexuality by effacing its social origin. He desires this picture, a goddess, a creature that would be "supplied to the aristocracy." She is what Theweleit calls the "white nurse," the image of the sexless female.[25] But by incorporating such an image of femaleness within his private world, Bloom renders sex impossible: the image requires that he suppress his desires. The nymph immediately joins in castigating Bloom, appalled at the sexual crimes she has "seen" from her position on the wall of Bloom's marital "chamber" (15.3285). Bloom farts, perhaps trying the method of undermining idealized images that seemed to work in "Sirens," but the nymph says "We immortals, as you saw today, have not such a place and no hair there either. We are stonecold and pure. We eat electric light" (15.3392). Bloom, accepting his degradation, responds, "Oh, I have been a perfect pig."

The nymph demands that Bloom feel "no more desire. . . . Only the ethereal" (15.3437). But then something changes, signaled by the button on his pants popping, an image of excess swelling that could refer either to eating too much or to getting an erection; in either case, Bloom's bodily desires are breaking their proper container. Bloom turns on the nymph, saying, "You have broken the spell. The last straw. If there were only ethereal, where would you all be, postulants and novices?" (15.3450). Bloom is experiencing the unreality of the images he has incorporated: creatures who do not eat, do not excrete, and have no sexual desires are not alive and cannot reproduce; they are man-made illusions, creations of advertising, and run on electricity. At Bloom's challenge, the nymph's claim to have no sexual or excretory organs is belied by "a large moist stain [that] appears on her robe." In Theweleit's terms, the "red flood" is breaking through the armor of the "white nurse."[26] In a last effort to regain purity, the nymph "strikes at his loins" with a "poniard," saying, "You are not fit to touch the garment of a pure woman" (15.4358–60). But Bloom grabs the knife and "clutches her veil," so that "with a cry [the nymph] flees from him unveiled, her plaster cast cracking, a cloud of stench escaping from the cracks" (15.3470).

This scene shows that Bloom's sense of self-hatred is entwined with socially produced illusions of the sexless feminine that are incorporated into male psychology. In the face of such images of women, a male is simply disgusting for having any desire at all, and male desire is turned into a desire for what is disgusting or repugnant. But when Bloom denies that only the ethereal exists and unveils the nymph as merely a socially produced image denying the actual workings of the female body, the statue breaks open. The focus on women having an anus and smelly gasses, not merely on genitals, is important because it is the acceptance of what appears disgusting that is most important, not the elimination of the disgusting in a redefinition, say of the body as thoroughly "natural."

The breaking of the statue does not, however, free Bloom from sexual problems: it only brings into his consciousness that there is no purity anywhere. The breakup of the image of purity releases into his mind the image he has been struggling to repress all day: Molly and Blazes together. Bloom fantasizes watching them and even cheering them on. But simply trying to enter an amoral world, to declare that all sex is wonderful, will not work either, because such a view itself is socially produced: the images of Molly's and Bloom's "improper" sex acts are taken from pornography: Bloom's scene with Bella from *Venus in Furs*, Molly's scene with Blazes from *The Sweets of Sin*. In these fantasies, Molly and Bloom end up unequal to the sexuality they imagine: they are rendered small, reduced to objects to be used by others. Both are slapped and ridden by the larger-than-life creatures they fantasize about (Bello, Blazes). In "Circe," then, there is no resolution of the problems created by the available definitions of sexuality: accepting the "proper" definition, Bloom and Molly both feel guilty for their desires; accepting the "improper" (pornographic) definition, both are reduced to objects, to less than human.

It might seem odd that Joyce so thoroughly codes the various possible images of sexuality as taken from other works: he does not even include fantasies that could be considered distinctively his own. But in doing so Joyce brings out the paradoxes of struggling against social forms that have created the person who struggles: even the images of opposition are part of the social system. Joyce's method of trying to alter the social system consists entirely of rearranging the pieces, the social stereotypes, he has been given. Critics who have criticized Joyce for his extensive use of stereotypes (particularly of women) fail to see what he was trying to do. Such criticism is based on the individualist assumption that high art escapes social determination to portray individuals while low art portrays types. Joyce's text reveals instead that everyone lives in a world of stereotypes. When men look at women or at themselves as males, all they can do is choose which stereotype to invoke. Joyce sought not to replace stereotype with reality, but only to present his "types" in "stereo," to make his images overlap, mix together, and create disturbing parallax effects in those who view them.

The old stereotypes provided a way to create perfect identity of wills in marriage: the male was the only one who had any desire at all, the female was compliant, and the contradictions in that system were dealt with by suppression in both male and female psychology. Joyce was struggling to imagine both husband and wife having desires, sexual and economic, that go beyond what their spouses can provide; neither becomes merely a mirror image of the other. The male becomes partly feminized in his awareness that he is not a self-determining entity, that his desires and acts are a product of other peoples' desires, and the female becomes partly masculinized in having desires of her own. Both become "dirty." Joyce was exploring the need for a new conception of desire—not a single, willful tendency in one person, but something that is always contradictory and multiple, already partly other. In each person there are in a sense two (or more) males, two or more sources of desire that conflict and can even have complex relations with each other, as Joyce suggests by referring throughout *Ulysses* to a homosexual relationship between Stephen and Bloom and by implication between two selves inside Joyce himself. Joyce was particularly struggling to develop a more complex vision of masculinity, to accept both his Stephen self and his Bloom self. One might say that developing a relationship between Stephen and Bloom is a prerequisite for bringing Stephen into relationship with a woman (and with the woman inside himself). Bloom is a transitional figure between Stephen and all the otherness inside and around Stephen. So after the disruptions in stereotypic masculinity in "Circe," Bloom and Stephen spend time together.

The problem remains, though, that Bloom is "strange flesh" to Stephen and to Joyce. Within the alternative world of "Circe," this is not much of a problem: in this entirely strange world, the barriers that separate the two so completely in the first six chapters break down, and they share bits of internal monologue, memories, and even marks on their bodies: Stephen seems to feel on his hand a cut that occurred to Bloom. But these crossovers remain strange, unsettling: Joyce simply could not imagine merging two such disparate persons, products of such disparate cultures.

Returning to an Unfamiliar Home

After the visit to Nighttown, the characters try to return to the familiar territory of the day world and try to reassemble the coherent characters they had at the beginning of the novel. But they carry with them social influences that do not allow them to return completely. The effect they have on each other has little to do with persuasion or personal interaction; rather, it is a result of each entering an institutional setting he had not known before. Bloom goes further away from home than he had previously gone, following Stephen to Nighttown, and Bloom draws Stephen into Bloom's house and tries to convince Stephen to stay there. Bloom carries home what he has gained from the brothel—some sense of how society has shaped and makes use of the illicit desires of males and females and hence some inkling of how to integrate illicit desires into a marriage. And Stephen carries into the streets thoughts from Bloom's house that are important in preparing him to be able to accept the Molly he will soon meet. As many critics have pointed out, the book is set on a date when Joyce first became involved with Nora Barnacle/Molly. But Joyce does not show Stephen meeting a lover; in fact, Stephen never even sees Molly. All Stephen sees is the home that Bloom and Molly have made; it is his first contact with this unusual kind of home and his first sense of the value of being involved with "strange flesh" that allows him to see that accepting involvement with a female need not press him into being identical to the husbands and fathers he saw as he grew up.

The two characters at the end are back where they started: Stephen with no place to sleep, Bloom in the bedroom. The narrative itself moves in a similar manner, returning after "Circe" to the techniques of the first three chapters, but with a significant difference. In Joyce's chart of *Ulysses*, the last three chapters repeat the sequence of "techniques" of the first three (narrative, catechism, monologue), but with a change, from young to old, personal to impersonal, and male to female. The young, personal, male techniques of the first section fit the heroes of D'Annunzian novels—they lead to the idea that society will be saved by the "artist as a young man" who can stand outside society and create the omniscient conscience for the race. The old, impersonal, female techniques at the end of the novel are what is left of the omniscient narrator after we have recognized that no person acts, speaks, or writes as an individual: nothing is young (new), nothing is "personal" (private), and nothing is what used to be male (dominant).

The search for an omniscient perspective, one that could unite Stephen and Bloom, takes the form of an investigation of possible "universal institutions," places where every person could be merely human. Joyce had already shown, in "Wandering Rocks," that the overall structure of the city is merely a physical arrangement, a grid of streets that does not provide a common perspective that all can share. In "Eumaeus," Joyce explores an institution that can move all over that grid and remain intact, a structure anyone can enter: a cab, and by extension, the cabman's shelter. Early in the book, Bloom says, "Curious the life of drifting cabbies: All weathers, all places, times or setdown, no will of their own" (5.224). Having no will of their own, cabbies can share part of the wills of everyone else. They are the "murphies" that Bloom, Stephen, and everyone else turn into when seen as merely another anonymous human. And in this chapter a Mr. D. B. Murphy is introduced, a strange, wraithlike figure. Ralph Rader points out that Murphy seems the embodiment of the description of Shakespeare that appears in the thoughts of both Stephen and Bloom. Stephen even makes the comment in this chapter that "Shakespeares were as common as Murphies" (16.364). Rader concludes that Murphy, standing between Dedalus and Bloom, is Joyce's way of indicating that both characters—and Shakespeare—are actually parts of himself (as Murphy's name indicates: Dedalus Bloom Murphy).[27] Murphy indeed represents what is common to Dedalus, Bloom, and Shakespeare, but that is not something unique to Joyce, but rather something common to everyone. The reduction of Dedalus and Bloom to initials emphasizes "Murphy" and shows how Joyce thinks of himself in this chapter—as partly fabulous artificer, Dedalus, partly involuntary exile, Bloom, but mostly common social product, Murphy.

The style of this chapter is constructed out of the "murphies" of language: clichés, linguistic cabs in which any ideas may travel. This common language is not, as in Victorian novels, a unifying perspective that provides the basis for a mutual understanding of everyone. In contrast to Matthew Arnold's belief that inside each person is a "best self" that transcends all social groups, Joyce shows that it is only the least self inside each person that transcends all groups. The chapter is written in the speech that everyone uses in chance encounters among people who do not share any group ties. In other chapters, Joyce shows how an institution generates a language that becomes a medium of communication among those in that institution. But those who do not share any common institutions have essentially no common language—or rather have only these clichés, these bits of language that have come loose from particular institutions and circulate everywhere—small particles of linguistic sand that provide a commonality across and between all institutions. In this chapter we see words buried in the "same sand" that can take "all colours of different sorts" in particular institutions, but that takes no distinct color here (16.1145). The cabman's shelter is the one place where Bloom and Dedalus converse with total strangers, with people not even from Dublin—especially with Mr. Murphy. We could say that the style of "Eumaeus" is what is left of a Victorian omniscient narrator in the new, collectivist ontology in which every mind is generated entirely by the groups of which it is part. This chapter employs "anonymous narration," the narration of Anonymous, that person with no personality whatsoever because he is not actively involved in any group whatsoever.

After "Eumaeus," Joyce explores one other "universal narrator" who might unite Stephen and Bloom: the voice of omni-science. In "Ithaca," we get "scientific" analyses of just about everything. But unfortunately, the perspective still shifts drastically—from the molecular to the astronomical. The chapter is obsessed with the relationship between Bloom and Stephen, but can neither settle into any definitive difference nor unite them; there are mathematical analyses that make the "proportion" between them anything from zero to sixteen through a million to one. Science can reach a perspective that includes everyone—by viewing people from astronomical distance. But this impersonal view is, much like the clichés of "Eumaeus," the view of no person, an empty view. This is also the view of a person utterly alone: when Stephen leaves, Bloom feels the kind of aloneness he has felt when other friends have left forever, "the cold of interstellar space" (17.1246). Everything that provides real content for the human mind, everything that can actually tie two people together, is created by social groups and is neither universal nor scientifically true. Bloom finally decides to quit the interstellar cold to return to be with Molly, to continue living as part of that relationship, a decision that he has made thousands of times and that each time is less and less an actual decision and more and more a part of the "self" that the situation itself has built.

Stephen leaves in an "exodus from the house of bondage to the wilderness of inhabitation" (17.1022), seeking to remain free. Bloom considers following him, but instead accepts bondage, accepts being in part a slave, because the pursuit of autonomy leads only to loneliness, coldness, and sterility. Bloom enters his house and his marriage bed neither an originator nor a free man, but he is warm. The final few pages of "Ithaca" refer to Bloom and Molly as "narrator" and "listener"; as Bloom goes to sleep, the "narrator" is enveloped by the "listener," Bloom becoming "the manchild in the womb" (17.2318). As Bloom accepts his warm bed and rejects Stephen's quest for independence, Joyce gives up the ideal of the adult male narrator who can impose himself on the childlike or female listener. The narrator instead merges with or marries the listener, giving up the illusion that one person writes or tells a story that other people hear.

In the last chapter, Joyce explores the very beginnings of a social unit, a subinstitution forming within an institution; Molly thinks back to try to understand how she and Bloom have become entwined. Her thoughts reveal that no person has a relationship with only one other distinct person: even in the moment of lying in bed together, Molly finds her mind full of all the other moments when she interacted with someone as an "I" with a "he." What society classifies as the most private place becomes a place where people lose their proper names and adopt generalized roles. We do not by any means see everything in Molly's life; we learn only as much about her as affects her relationship with Bloom in bed at night. In other places she would have quite different thoughts.

The last chapter provides a perspective that finally blurs Stephen and Bloom together. Molly's "he's" cross the boundaries that made the two men so strange to each other. And given that Molly is based on Nora Barnacle, the "he's" also refer to Joyce himself, so even the boundary between author and characters becomes blurred. By seeing Stephen, Bloom, and Joyce as vague and generalized others in Molly's life (or Nora Barnacle's), we see the men all together. But of course Molly is as much a version of Joyce as the men are, so what we are seeing in the last chapter is an author attempting to see himself as an other, attempting to give up the privileged perspective of narrator. The last chapter presses us to admit that the self is already full of otherness: there is no self-presence, no unmediated or purely internal relationship inside a single body. Molly is thinking about herself by thinking about "he's"; Joyce is thinking about himself by thinking about Molly. The self is made of parts that are derived from social groups (some parts coded as male, some female, for example), and one must think through those social groups to even see the self.

Reconstructing the self is an act of rearranging the relationships of these parts, and can be accomplished only by changes in the social environment. The book moves at its end back to the moment when Joyce began accepting the otherness within and around him, the moment of metempsychosis when he began changing from thinking of himself as a literary genius to thinking of himself as a hack producer of clichés, from thinking of himself as masculine to thinking of himself as womanly—in other words, the moment when he started changing from being Stephen to being both Stephen and Bloom. This was the moment when Nora/Molly said "Yes" to Joyce's/Bloom's proposal sixteen years earlier, a moment that effaced the differences between Stephen/Joyce/Bloom by reducing them all to simply something other, a vague "he" that can then become something else as part of a new relationship. The book ends on Molly's saying "Yes," not on Bloom's asking, to emphasize that one cannot change one's self alone; it was not Joyce's decision to enter a marriage that changed him, but the joint creation of a new institution.

To cause such a change, marriage had to become a new kind of institution, a kind Joyce was particularly interested in developing throughout society, namely, an institution that does not hide its mixed form, that does not repress signs of external influence. In this final scene with Bloom and Molly, Joyce provides an image of such a new social unit. Their bed, their house, are places invaded and crisscrossed by other people, other relationships, other social structures. The couple also exemplify the only way to develop new institutions: juxtapose socially structured pieces of various institutions and see what emerges. Bloom and Molly do not combine into a unit, and cannot completely merge (or completely have intercourse). The marriage incompletely merges cultures as much as genders: Bloom, a Hungarian Irish Jew, marries Molly, a Spanish Irish woman. The last chapter takes us to Molly's childhood on Gibraltar partly because Gibraltar is a place not on any continent, but a place between them, between cultures. Joyce was making an effort to turn Ireland, and his novel, into such a place—to actually construct a mixture of cultures. He had to marry texts from many cultures to do this, since he could not, as those in the nineteenth century thought they could, carry us to the perspective of a universal man as a way of bridging cultures. In *Ulysses*, Joyce intertwined elements of Irish, English, and European cultures, literary and nonliterary forms of prose, male and female parts of himself, to see if the crisscrossed structures thereby created could become functional in a new way. He needed and continues to need the collaboration of his readers to succeed in his efforts to change society: they have to say "Yes" to his proposed new structures—which does not mean that they have to accept his ideas, but rather that they have to live with his text, to entwine it in the social structures surrounding them, thereby creating something Joyce never envisioned.

CHAPTER 9

Ideology and Literary Form in 'The Waves'

In the 1930's, the Depression, challenges to British imperialism, Fascism, and impending war caused many writers to feel a need to confront political issues more directly than they had before. Writers such as W. H. Auden, Stephen Spender, and C. Day Lewis adopted a "coolly clinical tone" of social analysis in preference to modernism.[1] But the modernists, too, became more politically active: T. S. Eliot became a prolific essayist and turned to the more public and rhetorical art of drama, Ezra Pound became a propagandist for Mussolini, and Virginia Woolf published *Three Guineas*, an antiwar manifesto in which she excoriated imperialism and capitalism, accusing the leaders of England of having "For God and Empire . . . written, like the address on a dog collar, round [their] necks" and of circling "like caterpillars head to tail, round and round the mulberry tree, the sacred tree, of property."[2]

Woolf also wrote her most aesthetic work, *The Waves*, a work critics have almost unanimously declared unpolitical. There has thus seemed to be a split between her literary and her political sides, a split that has been mirrored in the way critics have dealt with *The Waves*. The novel is often entirely left out of political analyses of Woolf's works, and it is always highlighted in aesthetic analyses.[3] In an essay published in 1992, Jane Marcus summarizes the history of criticism of this novel (including her own work) by saying "*The Waves* simply does not exist as a cultural icon of the 1930s, as part of the discourse about the rise of . . . fascism, war, and imperialism"—the political discourse so important to the writers who came of age in the 1930's. Marcus has begun the process of "re-placing" this novel into the context of such discourses.[4] In continuing that project, I do not seek to reclassify *The Waves* as a political rather than an aesthetic work. Rather, I hope to show that aesthetic and political analyses of the novel can reinforce each other, that we can reunite the two sides of Virginia Woolf. What I have shown to be the case for other high modernist work pertains here as well: the elaborate aesthetic structures of this novel that make most readers think the book is transcending the "real world" are actually carefully designed responses to political issues and events.

Readers searching for the kind of hard facts that are supposed to characterize political novels usually criticize *The Waves* for the very qualities that readers seeking aesthetic experiences find wonderfully satisfying: the poetic prose, the rhythms, the mystical visions. The novel is ethereal, and that seems clear evidence that it is not political. The characters do not wrestle with social issues or even face any important personal decisions; mostly, they just observe what happens, reacting with vivid descriptions and intense feelings but with very little action. The usual vicissitudes of life—marriages, births, deaths—occur off-stage and are noted very briefly, with almost no details given—no names for spouses or children, no addresses, no precise job descriptions. Readers feel either exhilarated or drained after spending three hundred pages in a world where normal physical reality and the usual important questions are obscured in a beautiful fog. And whether the experience seems wonderful or tiring, it hardly seems likely to lead anyone to political action.

However, if we consider the novel's strange shape from the perspective of the contest between collectivism and individualism, we begin to see the outlines of a political interpretation. It is fairly common to consider this novel as presenting a communal or collectivist vision. The simple fact that it is at times hard to tell the characters apart suggests that individual differences are unimportant. As M. Keith Booker comments, the commonality of style of all the monologues "tends to undermine any focus on the 'egotistical self'" and suggests the novel aims at a "positive reconstruction of the self along alternative, communal lines."[5]

The novel goes further, though, than simply reconstructing the self: in it, the world is not even made of selves, but rather of groups. By leaving out physical descriptions and by having the most private thoughts (such as Rhoda's dreams) apparently known to everyone in the group, the novel ignores or violates the boundaries that usually define individuals. And by evenly rotating through the voices in the novel, Woolf seems to be suggesting that all six are parts of some one thing she is trying to reveal. The novel in effect presents only one character, a six-lobed creature that consists, not of physical bodies, but of the emotional interconnections between people. Such a creature could never be an individual because it does not have any precise boundaries, though it is located in space; it can expand as its six lobes move apart across the country or it can contract with them into one room; it can also gain and lose lobes.

Conceiving of the novel as the story of this one creature rather than six intertwined tales allows us to make sense of many of the odd features of the text. It explains, for example, why we never see the husbands, wives, children, or parents of any of the six people in the novel or any of the poetry or books they write. All these things may be important in individual lives, but they are largely distractions from the common life of the group. Probably the most striking elements left out of the book are the parents of the six members. For those critics who see the book as tracing the development of six individuals, Woolf must seem a very strange psychologist, leaving out familial influence entirely. But the parents serve only to influence and structure the six separate people who come together to form the group; the novel is tracing what grows out of those six already-formed pieces.

Woolf may blur individual psychology, but she marks with sharp edges the shifting structures of the group consciousness. To see these sharp edges, we have to stop looking through the text at the characters; instead, we have to view the mass of words in the text as a whole, because the array of words physically represents the shifting social structure of the group. For example, when the children are sent to school, the creature is divided quite sharply into two parts, a male and a female part. During the two sections showing the six at school, the text in the book is arranged into two large sections separated by white space, with all the male voices in one and all the female voices in the other. In other words, the group is split into two subgroups, a division that has effects throughout the book. (The males repeatedly speak of career, income, and writing, ways of making their mark on the world; the females speak of giving, attracting, love, and becoming part of places around them, never of career and never of writing.) The speeches in the school sections are not heard by all six; each gender remains ignorant of what the other gender is thinking at this time.

Percival emerges here: he is a creation of school, the image of the ideal male leader who will hold this group together. Woolf uses Percival to show how the belief in individualism can emerge from within group consciousness. Leaders allow those who are in a group to think of the group as embodied by a single individual. The six lobes can feel united, not by a group consciousness, but by the fact that each of them separately identifies with this single, individual leader. The fact that Percival never speaks suggests further that he does not in fact exist: he is a projection of the six, an image created by the social order, by schooling, as an icon of group identity in the form of an individual.

The most important event in the novel is Percival's death, and its importance is that it destroys the group, at least temporarily. We see this destruction in the fact that the six-lobed consciousness is completely broken in half in the two sections following the death. Every previous section had all six voices, but in the section immediately after it, only three voices are heard, and the other three are heard in the next section. These two sections are roughly half as long as the others in the novel: they are half chapters, broken chapters. For many years, the group is bereft of its basic structure and drifts in pieces. However, it eventually comes together again, as represented by the second dinner party, and it reconstitutes itself in a new form, without a leader, and for a moment sees itself without reference to individuals: as Bernard puts it during this second dinner, "This difference we make so much of, this identity we so feverishly cherish, was overcome" (pp. 288–89).

During that dinner, Woolf marks off a conversation between Louis and Rhoda by putting it in parentheses; at just about that point in the text, we discover that Louis and Rhoda have become lovers. It is the forming of a distinct subgroup, a fairly stable social relationship, that separates off the speeches of Louis and Rhoda from the others. Woolf is not portraying particular conversations that might actually occur between two people in a group without others hearing, but rather using the speeches to indicate the developing and relatively permanent qualities of the group's consciousness. Woolf also provides an explanation of why Louis and Rhoda would form a subgroup: because they both feel they are not a part of the even larger group, British society. Louis feels slighted because he is from Brisbane, and Rhoda never feels she can develop a proper self to interact in social situations. Both have a desire to rebel against social forces; they cannot escape, but their rebellion does have an effect: it creates a division within society, makes the social structure, even of this small group of six, more complicated. Woolf thus shows within the novel why individual rebellion is not an effective way to alter a social structure. Actually, we cannot even see the rebellion of these two as individual acts: both derive their feelings of not fitting from their families, specifically from their fathers. Rhoda has no father, and that seems to translate into having no identity. Louis's envy and hatred of British society derives from the fact that his father is a Brisbane banker. Thus, these rebellious and nonconforming individuals, too, are the result of the groups they come from, and the complex structure of the group portrayed in the novel derives from its intersection with these other groups.

The final chapter points to the possible emergence of a group voice, a voice that cannot identify itself with a single name. As Bernard says of himself, "I am not one person; I am many people; I do not altogether know who I am—Jinny, Susan, Neville, Rhoda, or Louis: or how to distinguish my life from theirs" (p. 276). Bernard tries to imagine "the world seen without a self," but he finds "there are no words" (p. 287). Bernard's conclusion may be a confession of the failure of this novel, the failure to get beyond the self—or it may be only an expression of Bernard's limitations. Woolf does find a way here to use words to let us see a world without selves. Woolf's use of white space, parentheses, chapter divisions, and length to mark off group structures is diagrammed in the illustration on page 222 as a series of pictures of the amoeba that is the group consciousness. There are nine drawings, one for each of the nine sections of the novel, but these represent only eight stages of the group's life cycle, because the fifth and sixth sections represent the group broken in half; as I argued earlier, these two sections are halves of one chapter.[6]

But how does tracing the shifting structure of a group make this novel political? Part of the answer is that Woolf was developing a psychology of particular value to socialist theory, a nonindividualist, collectivist psychology. Harold Laski argued that authors and scientists needed to "extend the concept of personality to th[e] incorporeal sphere" of group consciousness. Laski wrote that "as a corporation is distinct from its members, so too, we have to recognize that its mind is distinct from their minds."[7] Woolf attempted to create a corporate personality that did not reside in any corporeal body. But to understand how the particular forms of corporate personality shown in this novel were relevant to Laski's politics and to Woolf's—to the British Labour Party and to socialism—we have to look more closely at the events in the novel.

The event around which the novel revolves is Percival's death. That death, of the ideal British schoolboy by falling off a horse in India, is coded within the novel as representing a particular political development that is often considered quite separately from the rise of socialism: the decline of British imperialism. But if we examine the way this book addresses imperialism, we will see that Woolf was presenting a particularly socialist interpretation of why the British empire was falling apart.

Percival's mission to India is described by the characters in quite general terms: it promises to solve the "Oriental problem." As the six send Percival off, Bernard imagines what will happen,

> I see India. . . . I see the tortuous lanes of stamped mud that lead in and out among ramshackle pagodas; I see the gilt and crenellated buildings which have an air of fragility and decay as if they were temporarily run up buildings in some Oriental exhibition. I see a pair of bullocks who drag a low cart along the sun-baked road. The cart sways incompetently from side to side. Now one wheel sticks in the rut, and at once innumerable natives in loin-cloths swarm round it, chattering excitedly. But they do nothing. Time seems endless, ambition vain. Over all broods a sense of the uselessness of human exertion. . . . But now, behold, Percival advances; Percival rides a flea-bitten mare, and wears a sun-helmet. By applying the standards of the West, by using the violent language that is natural to him, the bullock-cart is righted in less than five minutes. The Oriental problem is solved. He rides on; the multitude cluster round him, regarding him as if he were—what indeed he is—a God. (pp. 135–36)

The oriental problem is a problem of bad roads and bad language: the application of the right kind of language rights the bullock cart and gets everything moving again. Percival is in effect rewriting the story of India, changing it from a timeless tale of a meditative people who cannot build

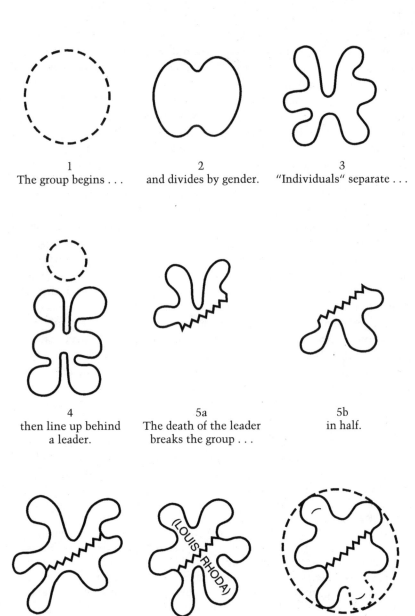

1
The group begins . . .

2
and divides by gender.

3
"Individuals" separate . . .

4
then line up behind
a leader.

5a
The death of the leader
breaks the group . . .

5b
in half.

6
It reunites . . .

7
a subgroup forms . . .

8
and a possible group
voice emerges.

Shifting group structure in *The Waves*.

anything but ramshackle huts into a story of progress, of good roads and a fast-moving people. Once they begin moving, they will then come to share the attitude that Bernard has toward Percival—they will worship him as a god, an emperor. And what kind of god is this? According to Bernard, Percival "is conventional; he is a hero" (p. 123). In other words, the solution of the oriental problem is to teach the Indians to worship the conventional heroes of Western culture. Percival's "violent language" accomplishes this task, compelling people to accept English conventions and to move faster on better roads.

Bernard's vision of Percival's triumph is clearly being mocked by Woolf as a compilation of clichés he has been told about India: Bernard is obviously repeating what he has seen at "Oriental exhibitions." Percival's mission is to teach the Indians this conventional vision of themselves, to bring them to leave their oriental selves behind.

Woolf very precisely made the failure of Percival's mission the exact center of her novel. If we conceive of the fifth and sixth sections of the novel as half chapters, as I have argued, then the center of this eight-chapter novel is between sections four and five, where Percival dies off-stage. Woolf also carefully arranged the lengths of the sections so that, in the first edition, the chapters before Percival dies take 161 pages out of the 320. Woolf also metaphorically labeled the spot between four and five as the middle: the sections of the book are identified with stages of the sun's progress across the sky; in the fourth section, the sun is high, while the fifth begins with the sun starting to sink into darkness. Woolf thus centered her novel on a moment marking the failure of the grand cliché of imperialism, "the sun never sets on the British Empire." Percival's death signals the breakup of the empire, the breakup of the group of characters, and even the breakup of the chapters in the novel.

Percival's mission of conventional heroism is connected in the novel to certain literary forms, so that his fall can also emblematize Woolf's project of breaking certain literary conventions. In another passage, a conventional form of storytelling—biography—is described in terms oddly similar to those used for Percival's mission: Bernard says that biographers lay "Roman roads across the tumult of our lives" (p. 259). Biography, like Percival's mission, imposes forms on people that do not fit those people and is thus the literary equivalent of imperialism. The way Bernard describes biography points neatly to just those elements that Woolf left out of this novel, such as marriages, births, and incomes:

> Once I had a biographer, dead long since, but if he still followed my footsteps with his old flattering intensity he would here say, 'About this time Bernard married and bought a house. . . . His friends observed in him a growing tendency to domesticity. . . . The birth of children made it highly desirable that he should augment his income.' That is the biographic style,

and it does to tack together torn bits of stuff, stuff with raw edges. After all, one cannot find fault with the biographic style if one begins letters 'Dear Sir,' ends them 'yours faithfully'; one cannot despise these phrases laid like Roman roads across the tumult of our lives, since they compel us to walk in step like civilised people with the slow and measured tred of policemen though one may be humming any nonsense under one's breath at the same time. (p. 259)[8]

Clearly Bernard—and Woolf as well—is mocking the "biographic" style. But Woolf is not merely saying that this style creates illusions; she is also criticizing it for being coercive, for making people "walk in step," police themselves, and stay within the confines of "Roman roads"—within, we might say, imperial ways of thinking. Imperialism is even more directly invoked when Bernard goes on to describe a time when his life seemed to perfectly embody the "phrases" that make up biographies. He focuses on a scene "at breakfast with my wife" when "the unconscious hum of the engine . . . functioned superbly" (p. 260). At such a moment, he says, he could have adjusted to anything "with ease," even a sudden telephone call asking him "to assume command of the British Empire" (p. 261). The conventional domestic life presented in biographies is preparation for imperial leadership.

Woolf also criticizes the political underpinnings of conventional biography in *Three Guineas*, where she says that "almost every biography we read of professional men . . . is largely concerned with war."[9] Woolf may have had a particular reason for attacking biography, since her father, Leslie Stephen, was the most famous biographer in England at the turn of the century through the "English Men of Letters" series. Stephen declared that the goal of biography was to increase the power of males: "The impression made upon his contemporaries by a man of strong and noble character is something which cannot be precisely estimated, but which we often feel to be invaluable. The best justification of biography in general is that it may strengthen and diffuse that impression."[10] Woolf wrote her novels and her essays to undermine such influence, particularly attacking the connection between the cult of manliness and imperialism. As Booker has commented, the presentation of Percival in *The Waves* is, in part, a way of undoing "the male bravado underlying the ideology of imperialism."[11]

The themes of recording one's life (biography), building roads, and subjugating the world are connected in the dinner party when the group sends Percival on his way. At the end of his farewell party in section four, Bernard says,

We have proved, sitting eating, sitting talking, that we can add to the treasury of moments. We are not slaves bound to suffer incessantly unrecorded petty blows on our bent backs. We are not sheep either, following a master. We are creators. We too have made something that will join the innumer-

able congregations of past time. We too, as we put on our hats and push
open the door, stride not into chaos, but into a world that our own force
can subjugate and make part of the illumined and everlasting road. (p. 146)

The ability to subjugate the world and make roads is equated here with
being able to record what is going on—to write—and with escaping from
slavery. Those who cannot subjugate the world and cannot record their own
lives merely suffer blows from others: slaves have their own lives written
on their backs by others. By uniting under Percival's leadership, the English
escape from slavery into a form of authorship, much as the Indians should
be lifted by Percival's violent language out of "the uselessness of human
exertion."

There are problems with the freedom achieved by the six at this party:
their escape from slavery involves their uniting to create exactly one road—
the illumined and everlasting road. In other words, they have to all be creating the same thing; they are free only if they make identical use of their
freedom. They may learn to record their own lives, but all their separate
biographies are simply part of the one grand biography of personified England. And English glory is created by treating the world as a place that
"our force can subjugate."

Before these people can police the world, they have to police themselves, to become soldiers under Percival's command, as is made clear in
Bernard's description of the effect of Percival's first entrance into the party:

> Here is Percival . . . smoothing his hair, not from vanity (he does not look
> in the glass), but to propitiate the god of decency. He is conventional; he
> is a hero. The little boys trooped after him across the playing-fields. They
> blew their noses as he blew his nose, but unsuccessfully, for he is Percival.
> Now, when he is about to leave us, to go to India, all these trifles come
> together. He is a hero. Oh, yes, that is not to be denied, and when he takes
> his seat by Susan, whom he loves, the occasion is crowned. We who yelped
> like jackals biting at each other's heels now assume the sober and confident
> air of soldiers in the presence of their captain. (p. 122–23)

Percival tames these jackals by giving them all, male and female, a common object to worship and a common goal: militaristic glory to be achieved
in India. In effect, by following Percival, these people accept the metaphorical "dog collar[s]" Woolf described in *Three Guineas*, letting "For God and
Empire" be written around their necks. By imitating Percival's perfect con-
ventionality and decency, the six characters learn to police themselves, to
organize their lives in the biographic style, to build roads. The reward of this
conformity is, paradoxically, that they feel themselves creators, writers of
their own lives, gaining their authorship from his authority as the conventional hero. Even the "biographic" goal of augmenting one's own income
is part of Percival's mission": Susan, whom everyone imagines Percival
will marry, says that after his mission, "he will come home, bringing me

trophies to be laid at my feet. He will increase my possessions" (p. 172).
Imperialism promises to increase everyone's possessions: people stop competing within the nation because they are promised more if they compete
against other nations (a theme we will see more of later). As Susan's statement suggests, Percival also brings everyone to assume their proper gender
roles: all the women love him and expect to be supported by him, and all
the men imitate him.

Woolf compressed into Percival all the political concerns she devoted
her life to opposing: militarism, imperialism, male chauvinism, and acquisitive individualism. Moreover, Percival is connected with a certain
kind of writing—is, in fact, the product of a certain kind of writing. The
fact that he never speaks in this novel but is only spoken of suggests that
he is entirely a product of other people's words. Percival represents a central part of the ideological system of England at the turn of the century.
His effect on the six is what Louis Althusser calls "interpellation": Percival "hails" and "recruits" everyone else as subjects who freely submit to
his leadership. Althusser argues that in the early twentieth century, the
school was in the process of replacing the church as the dominant ideological apparatus. In the religious system, according to Althusser, it could
be clearly seen that "the interpellation of individuals as subjects presup-
poses the 'existence' of a Unique and central Other Subject": people felt a
part of a religion because they believed that God hailed and recruited each
one of them as individuals.[12] In this novel, we see the alteration of ideology resulting from schools replacing churches: instead of an image of God,
an image of an ideal schoolboy such as Percival becomes the unique and
central subject, the most important thing taught in school.

Woolf does much to suggest that Percival has taken over the role that
God played in the feudal social order: his name suggests the English religious tradition, the six characters see him as "a God," and all define themselves in relation to him. When they submit to Percival's leadership, they
feel as if they are being released from slavery: Althusser describes such a
process as the essential act of ideology: "*the individual is interpellated as a
(free) subject in order that he shall submit freely to the commandment of
the Subject,* i.e. in order that he shall make the gestures and actions of his
subjection 'all by himself.' "[13] Note that Percival assumes command in the
section of the novel when the students are released from school to begin
living on their own.

Woolf was particularly concerned about the role of literature in contrib-
uting to the ideological effect, to the creation of subjects who will freely
march behind Percival into India. To undermine that effect, Woolf altered
the form of the nineteenth-century novel. It is fairly easy to see that Woolf
avoids in this novel the conventional, biographical details of nineteenth-
century novels—marriages and incomes and births—but it may not be apparent why Woolf would conceive of nineteenth-century novels as leading

people to police themselves, to build roads, or to become imperialists. But note that she uses the same terms and images in her depiction of the nineteenth century in the history of English literature described by the pageant in *Between the Acts*. In that novel, Woolf creates little playlets representing the Elizabethan, restoration, nineteenth-century, and modern literary periods. The playlet "The Nineteenth Century" begins with a speech by a policeman, who begins by describing his function: "It ain't an easy job, directing the traffic at 'Yde Park Corner. . . . At Piccadilly Circus . . . directing the traffic of 'Er Majesty's Empire. The Shah of Persia; Sultan of Morocco; or it may be 'Er Majesty in person; or Cook's tourists; black men; white men; sailors, soldiers; crossing the ocean; to proclaim her Empire; all of 'em Obey the Rule of my truncheon."[14] In this speech, as in *The Waves*, Woolf equates directing traffic (making roads work well), obeying the police, and imperialism.

This policeman is also a version of the omniscient narrator: "But my job don't end there. . . . Over thought and religion; drink; dress; manners; marriage too, I wield my truncheon. Prosperity and respectability always go, as we know, 'and in 'and. The ruler of an Empire must keep his eye on the cot; spy too in the kitchen; drawing room; library; wherever one or two, me and you, come together. Purity our watchword; prosperity and respectability." Woolf is, of course, parodying and exaggerating, but it isn't hard to see many Victorian omniscient narrators as moral authorities spying on people, rooting out the disreputable ones in order to ensure prosperity. As David Miller has argued in *The Novel and The Police*, omniscient narration is in itself a version of policing that disguises itself as liberation, just as Woolf's policeman and Percival's violent language present themselves as liberators freeing people from corruption and ruts.[15]

Besides producing better roads, the nineteenth-century policeman and Percival are also involved in creating certain kinds of houses. In *Between the Acts*, the depiction of the nineteenth century continues after the policeman's monologue to show a tale of a young couple deciding to marry and devote their lives to seeking to "convert the heathen" and "to help our fellow man";[16] the playlet ends with a panegyric to home and the singing of "Home Sweet Home." Building roads, making a home, converting the heathen—all these are nineteenth-century projects, all part of the imperial project to eliminate foreign policy by eliminating foreignness, bringing all people to recognize English domestic space as the universal arena in which humans should live. Creating homes and families to live in them are certainly central projects of numerous Victorian novels. In disrupting the "biographic style," with its focus on family, Woolf sought in *The Waves* to contribute to the ending of the nineteenth-century project of domesticating the world.

Many readers would agree that in this novel Woolf sought to escape conventional bourgeois notions of success and national expansion, but would claim that she did so in order to find a metaphysical alternative, not a political one. In this reading, the communal spirit of the book is taken as showing that everyone is united as a part of a natural, or supernatural, mystical whole. The interludes, especially, contribute to such a view: as events in the characters' lives are paralleled by the passage of the sun from dawn to dusk, by the life of flowers from budding to withering, by the repeated rhythms of waves, and by a sequence of changes in the behavior of birds, it seems of little concern what happens in the world of politics. The naturalism of the interludes thus would seem to undercut the argument that the novel addresses political issues: if we are to understand the world as a place where beauty and horror are simply natural phenomena that occur in never-ending cycles, politics matters very little.

However, Woolf does some very strange things in the interludes that suggest that the cycles she is presenting are not natural at all. For example, the actions of the birds, which parallel the behavior and feelings of the characters more closely than any other part of the interludes, show changes in social relationships that are distinctly unnatural, at least for birds. The birds start off chirping randomly, then move through stages of singing in chorus, competing with each other, and finally living in isolation. Woolf seems to have designed the "natural cycle" of the birds' actions to match the social development of the human characters. She was not merely using the birds symbolically to represent the natural sequence of social relations that humans go through; she was raising the larger question of what causes social relations of individuals in small groups to change: is it a cultural phenomenon or a natural one? We actually have more than two choices here. Saying the changes are cultural phenomena could mean (1) that the sequence simply grows out of the interactions within a particular group; (2) that there is a programmed sequence of social relations set by the surrounding culture, say a sequence of behaviors for people of various ages; or (3) that the culture as a whole is changing and the group is part of that history. And saying the changes are natural could mean the sequence derives from changes in the biology of each individual person or that groups themselves have a natural life cycle.

Woolf complicates this question immeasurably because she shows in the interludes that our sense of what is "natural" and what is "cultural" is itself something that changes. The interludes are all structured around a division between realms of culture and nature, and the point of division keeps changing. The first three interludes show the sea, a garden, and a house, in that order. The fourth and fifth interludes, though, bring in rivers, woods, and hills between the sea and the garden, and the fifth brings in a desert, a mosque, and a ship on the sea. The sequence of interludes up to this point seems to reflect the changes in the perception of the world as a child grows: at first, home and garden are the only recognizable areas, and everything else is just "out there" and undifferentiated—sea. At some point, a child recognizes the countryside that separates various houses. Finally, the child begins to conceive of other cultures (mosques) and other kinds of nature (desert) besides those that make up the English homeland.

The very possibility of such changes in perception undermines hope of knowing for certain that anything is "natural" or "cultural"—unless we can establish one stage as presenting the true view. We might say that the fifth interlude, with its awareness of foreign cultures and deserts, is the true one, the view of an educated adult. However, what happens after the fifth interlude calls any such claim into question. The sixth and seventh interludes return to the world of the fourth—all foreign lands disappear, and we have only woods and rivers again between sea and garden. In the eighth interlude, yet another view of the world emerges, a view from so far away that "no shining roof or glittering window could be any longer seen. The tremendous weight of the shadowed earth had engulfed such frail fetters, such snail-shell encumbrances. Now there was only the liquid shadow of the cloud, the buffeting of the rain" (p. 208). Human structures become mere snail shells as everything becomes liquid nature or sea. Furthermore, the birds, which have seemed to be in the interludes a representation of human social life, change into wild species: in the early sections, the birds seemed garden species, but in this eighth interlude they are identified as hawk, wild plover, and owl. This section suggests an alternative to the seemingly mature view of the world in the fifth interlude: man, in all his civilizations, is still a wild animal, not really distinguishable from hawks and owls. In this eighth interlude, culture seems almost nonexistent, in direct opposition to the fifth interlude, where culture seems to have spread almost everywhere.

The interludes themselves, then, undermine the naturalism they would seem to represent. Jane Marcus has argued that the interludes derive from Indian religious texts and present an alternative literary form that Woolf inserted into the British narrative in order to disrupt ethnocentrism.[17] But there is a problem with taking the interludes as representing any sort of alternative, cultural or natural, to British life: they are quite artificially constructed to mirror the events in the lives of the characters, in other words, to mirror British life. The changes in the interludes derive from specific social events presented in the speeches, not from extrinsic literary forms. If this is so, the interludes do not explain the natural cause of the events in the chapters and they are not an alternative to the British social system; rather, they are themselves products of the social stages shown in the text. The visions of nature and culture in each interlude are projections of the attitudes and worldviews—the ideologies—shared by the six characters at various stages of their lives.

Woolf was seeking to reveal how ideologies function, how they are constructed, and how can be changed by historical events. The drawing of a line between culture and nature is essential to ideology: by classifying some things as cultural and others as natural, ideology naturalizes power relations.[18] In the interludes, Woolf presents ideology as a collection of images that precede experience and provide metaphors for interpreting events and for constructing narratives. By presenting the British private house as the central image of culture, the interludes suggest that the conventions for dividing culture from nature support the ideological project of creating certain kinds of subjects (British homeowners) and denying subject status to other kinds of individuals (such as Indians). In this novel, we see in minute detail how ideology is constructed—namely, people develop visions of what is natural and what is not as a result of the social structures of everyday life.

To see how social structure influences the interludes, we have to look closely at the shifts between sections of the book. The shift from the first to the second interlude, from randomly chirping birds to a chorus, marks a change from isolation to being united in a group. This parallels the children's lives, the transition from living in their separate homes to being united in school. In school, the children live together—and thus the common life of the group begins and the children's voices become an orchestrated chorus. Some of the descriptions of the birds in the second interlude directly evoke the behavior of children at school: "The birds . . . now sang a strain or two together, wildly, like skaters rollicking arm-in-arm, and were suddenly silent, breaking asunder" (p. 29). In the third interlude, where school continues, mackerel are described as having "massed themselves" in "shoals" (schools) of fish, and birds begin moving in flocks, "swerv[ing] all in one flight" (p. 73). In the fourth section of the book, the six characters are sent out of school to live and work in separate sections of the country, to begin competing as individuals in the workplace. And in the fourth interlude, the animals stop acting in unified groups: each bird sings "with passion, with vehemence, as if to let the song burst out of it, no matter if it shattered the song of another bird with harsh discord" (p. 108). The change from school to work also can explain the emergence of hills and countryside in this fourth interlude: since the six characters now travel from city to city, their vision of the world now includes hills and countryside. The language of work, of engines and muscular effort, invades the descriptions of the countryside and the sea in this interlude: the waves "drew in and out with the energy, the muscularity of an engine"; the hills "curved and controlled, seemed bound back by thongs, as a limb is laced by muscles; and the woods which bristled proudly on their flanks were like the curt, clipped mane on the neck of a horse" (p. 108). Nature actually splits into three different kinds of realms in this interlude: the garden, where nature is merely a place for play; the countryside, where nature is something one conquers and labors on; and the sea, where nature remains unknown and undifferentiated.

The central event of the novel, Percival's death, occurs immediately after the fourth section, after the children have been inserted into the world of labor. In the fourth interlude, labor is presented as transforming nature into culture—tying the hills with thongs, turning the motion of the waves into a muscular engine—a process of gradually expanding the cultural space. Because all the fully acculturated or domesticated spaces are defined as centered on individual houses, the project of converting nature into culture is a competitive project—each person seeks through labor to expand his or her own realm. Thus, we see the birds in the fourth interlude become competitive just as the people go to work.

There is, nonetheless, a project that unifies the birds and keeps competition from destroying their community, and a similar project unifies the six equally competitive characters. The birds join together in opening a snail shell: "They tapped furiously, methodically, until the shell broke and something slimy oozed from the crack." The birds find common cause in their desire to destroy and eat a form of life different from their own. The waves provide the rhythm for a unified military action: the "sea beat like a drum that raises a regiment of plumed and turbaned soldiers" (p. 109). The event that unifies the six in this section is the sending of Percival to India, the project of imperialism, which brings together the competitive individuals in a common promise of gain for all. They form a military unit, no longer "yelp[ing] at each other's heels" but rather becoming "soldiers in the presence of their captain." Birds attacking a snail is a perfect "natural" image of Percival's job in India: he goes to destroy the slow-moving Indian vehicle, the cart stuck in the rut, and release the energy encased in useless traditions to feed the quick-moving birds of English industrialism. He will replace the snail/cart dragging through the slime with cars and planes flying by. The project of imperialism is an extension of the capitalist project of conquering nature and expanding domestic space.

Between the fourth and fifth sections, Percival's imperial mission fails; in the fifth interlude, a mosque appears, and the countryside and house in the previous interludes are identified as "English." We might have expected this division of the world into differing cultures to appear in the previous interlude, when Percival was being sent to India. But Virginia and Leonard Woolf believed that the essence of imperialism lay in not recognizing other cultures at all. As Leonard wrote in *Imperialism and Civilization*, imperialists simply saw "an imaginary international vacuum" when they looked beyond their own culture.[19] India in this novel is a vacuum that sucks up human effort: even the basic attempt to keep moving is overwhelmed by nature, by the ruts in the road. India is like an untilled field, a land that is uncultivated, uncultured. In the party that sends Percival off to India, the group of friends comes together in a perfect unity against this uncultivated world: they feel "walled in here. But India lies outside" (p. 135). The group sends Percival to subjugate the dangerous natural world outside, to build a road along which they can construct further walled spaces, expanding their empire.

The death of Percival breaks through the illusion that everything in the world is either English or a cultural vacuum; it is the destruction of this illusion that reveals mosques and deserts, alternative walled structures and alternative natures that may not be convertible into English houses and English gardens. This shift is a real historical shift that occurred around the turn of the century. We can see it vividly in the changing meaning of the word *culture*. In the middle of the nineteenth century, *culture* usually referred to what Matthew Arnold wanted it to mean—the best of all that humans produce, a universal kind of cultivation available to people of any nationality, but of course epitomized by English life. From 1870 on another use of the word appeared: the anthropological, first truly noticeable in print in England in E. B. Tylor's book *Primitive Culture* (a title that Arnold must have regarded as an oxymoron). When English culture is only one among many, the act of turning Indians into Englishmen becomes an act of coercion of one group by another. Woolf embodied in the sequence of interludes precisely this shift in Western consciousness, a shift that is hardly a natural development for all humans or all groups, but a particular social and historical event.

Woolf was not claiming that the six characters in her novel, or the English in general, had no awareness of foreign cultures until the end of the nineteenth century. But people utilize different kinds of awareness in different social contexts. People can have a textbook awareness of other cultures and yet go through their daily lives never thinking of any other culture than their own. To switch to living the awareness of other cultures—say, having actual decisions one makes during the day affected by what happens in other cultures—requires shocking events, such as the death of an idealized friend in a foreign land, the tarnishing of the image of the ideal, conventional hero, or the failure of a policy such as imperialism that has become thoroughly entangled in one's domestic life.

But even such strong shocks do not last long: Woolf did not see the failure of imperialism as changing the English worldview as much as she hoped it would. Woolf shows only one interlude in which other cultures appear with any definiteness; in the sixth interlude, she shows the English returning to the single-culture, ethnocentric view of the world divided into home/garden/countryside/sea. However, as the sense of decline hanging over the novel after Percival's death shows, this retreat to ethnocentrism is not the same as the ethnocentrism that prevailed before Percival's death. This is the sadness of the novel, this vision of life as declining, never achieving its former glory, that most of the characters seem to share. It is easy to interpret this as something that enters everyone's life after middle age, but this novel is tracing specific changes brought about by social structures and social events around the turn of the century, not universal patterns of individual lives. It is not because Percival happens to die as these characters enter middle age that the sun switches from rising to setting across his death; rather, it is because his death has so completely changed their sense of their lives that they conceive of his death as marking "noon," the turning point of their existence. This view of their lives as shaped into rising and sinking portions was not the group's invention, but was a topos of political and cultural discourse in England during the period of the novel; the image of post-empire England as a time of the setting sun pervaded English thought and writing in the early twentieth century, and perhaps continues today. The characters sink into the dark side of the dream of imperialism: the vacuum wins, rather than the single culture, and all becomes meaningless nature.

However, Woolf provides hints of a countermovement to this sad sinking, suggestions that a new system is replacing imperialism. To identify this new system, we can turn to Leonard Woolf's 1928 socialist analysis of imperialism:

> There are two opposite and contradictory systems by which international relations may be regulated and adjusted, and we happen to be living in a transition age in which the world has not yet made up its mind to choose the one or the other of these systems. The first is the respectable and time-honoured system of individualism. The world of nations is a world of sovereign and independent States, individual and omnipotent units of Statehood, each pursuing through an imaginary international vacuum its own sacred interests. Unfortunately the real world is not an international vacuum, and when from time to time the paths of two of these omnipotent units cross, the question whose interests are to prevail is settled ultimately by the question of whose omnipotence is more omnipotent. The system is therefore individualistic, and under it the ultimate arbiter is power and force. It is the system under which imperialism attempted to regulate the relations between Europe and the rest of the world. Each European State pursued its own interests in Asia and Africa, as an isolated unit, up to the point at which it could no longer impose its will upon the subject peoples and the other States of Europe.
>
> The other system is based upon a completely different conception of the world of nations. It is no longer a world of isolated units moving majestically in their own orbits; it is a world of States, nations, and peoples, all closely interrelated parts of a vast international society with its own economic and political organization. No part of this whole has either the right or in fact the power to pursue its own interests without reference to the interest and will of the other parts. . . . This system is, of course, not yet in existence. The observant eye can discern it beginning to grow in shadowy and distorted growths all through the nineteenth century.[20]

Leonard Woolf's description of individualism/imperialism as a system in which each European state conceives of itself as facing an "international vacuum" devoid of other states matches the vision of the world in the first four interludes in *The Waves*, a world in which civilization (the one house) is gradually taking over a natural world devoid of human culture, spreading gardens and industries across the wild landscape. Leonard Woolf says that this vision of the world will fall apart and another arise after each European nation begins to lose its faith in its omnipotence. *The Waves* shows this moment in the fall of Percival; the invincible hero fails to triumph.

By referring to imperialism as individualist, Leonard was explicitly paralleling foreign and domestic policy. Such parallels were commonplace in Labour Party tracts. R. H. Tawney wrote in 1920: "Nationalism is the counterpart among nations of what individualism is within them. . . . the perversion of nationalism is imperialism."[21] The alternative to individualism in domestic policy was recognized by Tawney, Woolf, and anyone else in the early twentieth century as collectivism: in its foreign policy, the Labour Party similarly advocated a form of socialism for nations. The parallel of foreign and domestic issues also appears as a central tenet of this novel, that a change in the domestic structure of nations, the shift away from individualism toward collectivism occurring all over Europe, was part of what was causing imperialism to fall. The parallel problems of imperialism and domestic oppression thus had the same solution: individual people had to begin thinking of themselves as parts of a vast international society, no longer seeing themselves as independent entities. The novel seeks to develop such a view, and in such terms we can understand how the strange, ethereal style of the novel serves a political purpose: it forces readers to stop looking at individual entities (people, nations) and instead to see that "shadowy" network of "interrelated" parts that Leonard Woolf described as starting to replace empires.

Woolf's novel appears to create an ethereal world because we are so used to looking at a world of discrete bodies, of isolated units. Instead, *The Waves* demands that we refocus on the structure that emerges as a group of people interact over many decades, a structure that is fluid and changeable, an ether that exists within and around the people in a group. The novel presses for an alternative vision and an alternative structure of domestic life, a change away from the nineteenth-century distinction, so important to capitalism, between private and public worlds, between realms in which people were individual and realms in which they had to interact as parts of large crowds. Woolf struggled to break with the fundamental feature of ideology, as Althusser described it: "the belief that you and I are always already subjects . . . concrete, individual, distinguishable."[22]

Bringing together all the formal features of the novel that I have been describing—the blurring of boundaries between characters, the precise lengths of chapters, the arrangements of white space and parentheses to trace shifting group structure, the careful design of the interludes to show shifting boundaries between nature and culture, the parallels between interludes and human events—we can summarize the unconventional plot of the novel. The first half shows how the social system creates the illusion that each person is an individual or a subject who defines his or her life by the biographic style, jealously competing with every other individual and uniting only under the leadership of the ideal individual, Percival, in pursuit of gain from the joint enterprise of imperialism, the conquering of the part of the world that the English have classified as uncultivated or natural. When the horse throws Percival in India, what has seemed the natural part of the world throws off the cultured part. Or, to switch to the novel's own dominant metaphor, waves of humanity overthrow imperial rule in India as Woolf hopes waves of humanity will overthrow class and gender rule within England.

Even more important than her encouragement of those outside her own social group, then, was Woolf's effort to show that there was a change occurring in the British upper class itself, a collapse of its own ideology, and that upper-class British were in the process of reconceiving of their society and themselves as waves, as collectivities, not as individuals. If they underwent this change while holding onto their outdated conceptions, they would conceive of their culture in the way so many conservative, upper-class English already had, as disappearing into wild, chaotic waves. But if they could adjust their own institutions—schools, workplaces, military organizations—they could live through the change in something other than depression. Representing this as a possibility is the political work that the novel employs aesthetic means to achieve.

Woolf shows the characters in the novel beginning this process. The first step out of individualism is replacing the leader of the group—on the way toward eliminating leaders altogether. The British Labour Party struggled in the first few decades of the twentieth century to run elections and party conferences without empowering individual leaders: at each party session, they would elect a "chairman." It was the sense of the party that, as Philip Snowden wrote, "the Sessional Chairman should not be the 'Leader.' It was considered undemocratic. The party must not permit one man to dictate policy."[23] In 1922, however, Ramsay MacDonald was elected "Chairman and Leader" and began referring to himself as the "Leader of the Labour Party."[24] Debates ensued about how much power MacDonald should have, and these debates exploded in 1931, the year Woolf published *The Waves*, because MacDonald bolted to join Conservatives in a "National Party." It seemed horrifying to Labour M.P.'s such as Leonard Woolf that workers would line up behind MacDonald no matter what party or principles he represented. In the novel, Percival has the charismatic appeal of a MacDonald, and his death, like the loss of MacDonald, brings to the fore the question of whether a group can remain together without such an individual with whom to identify. Bernard in part replaces Percival, but with a different kind of leadership: instead of inspiring everyone to line up behind him, moving in a clear direction, Bernard finds himself in effect letting those in the group lead him: he is always "streaming away mixed with Susan, Jinny, Neville, Rhoda, Louis" (p. 279); he cannot even stick to the group, finding himself also "mixed with an unknown Italian waiter" (p. 118)—a delightful image of crossing class and national boundaries. Bernard is an image of the kind of pluralist, nonindividual leadership the Labour Party hoped they could have.

Bernard is a rather ineffective leader, and he never becomes comfortable giving up his individuality or his dominant role as British male. Woolf suggests, thus, that in her world there was little hope of a successful democratic, leaderless movement such as the Labour Party for a time tried to be. If Althusser is correct, it may be impossible to even imagine a social order without an ideology of subjects. But Woolf resisted the notion that ideology forms every person into an identical subject. All the six fail in different ways to become fully interpellated. Bernard and Jinny in particular are not as fully individualized as the others—and for that reason they escape certain politicizing effects of that process. Bernard describes himself as escaping the militarizing effects of education precisely because he always sees himself as a relatively indistinct part of a crowd:

> We suffered terribly as we became separate bodies.
> Yet I was preserved from these excesses and have survived many of my friends, am a little stout, grey, rubbed on the thorax as it were, because it is the panorama of life, seen not from the roof, but from the third story window that delights me, not what one woman says to one man, even if that man is myself. How could I be bullied at school therefore? How could they make things hot for me? There was the Doctor lurching into chapel, as if he trod a battleship in a gale of wind, shouting out his commands through a megaphone, since people in authority always become melodramatic—I did not hate him like Neville, or revere him like Louis." (p. 242)

Bernard does not revere or hate authority, and thereby escapes being bullied because he chooses the perspective of a "third-story window," where people are slightly blurred, neither reduced to an undifferentiated sea, as they would be from the roof, nor perfectly defined as individuals, as they would be in a relationship of one man and one woman. He prefers the perspective of the crowd.[25]

In Bernard's statement of how he escaped being bullied, he suggests a tripartite division of perspectives. In another passage, he makes this schema clearer, and from it we can see why Woolf felt it necessary to create exactly six characters. "The truth is that I am not one of those who find their satisfaction in one person, or in infinity. The private room bores me, also the sky. My being only glitters when all its facets are exposed to many people" (pp. 185–86). The private room and the sky represent two realms in which people seek wholeness and individuality: the home and nature. These are the ideological possibilities advocated by Victorian novels and Romantic poetry—either retreat to a little house in which everyone has one-to-one, loving relationships or climb a mountain and reach an omniscient view, becoming the voice of humanity in its entirety. Individualists often equated the two realms: by retreating into a private house, one could achieve the freedom of thought to mentally escape into universal truths; or, conversely, by standing outside society one achieved the kind of love for all mankind that is most embodied in familial relations. In this novel, Woolf comes close to setting up a neat tripartite division of the characters based on the three possibilities implied by Bernard's speech: Rhoda and Louis pursue universal truths, the sky; Susan and Neville pursue "satisfaction in one person" and life in the private room; Jinny and Bernard both glitter when all their facets are exposed to many people in crowds. Rhoda, Louis, Neville, and Susan are trying to maintain nineteenth-century social ideas, even in their seeming rebellion against society, while Bernard and Jinny, in their existence as shifting products of crowds, are the ones actually breaking with the past—but only because they are early products of the collectivist social system that the Woolfs hoped would replace individualism.

Rhoda and Louis would seem to be the characters most in rebellion against the social order. But as Bernard suggests, reverence for authority and hatred of it are essentially identical. In an individualist order, hatred of society ties people to the system quite as well as reverence for leaders. Individualism promises an escape from society, from social conventions, and so is a system based on rebellion (as American worship of the Founding Fathers suggests). Percival is both the ideal leader and the ideal rebel: if he had lived, he would have "done justice" and "shocked the authorities" (p. 243).

Thus, when Rhoda and Louis feel oppressed by conventions, their desire to escape leads them to the most conventional way of understanding their lives: they become identified in this novel with nineteenth-century fiction. As Neville describes their rebellions:

> But then Rhoda, or it may be Louis, some fasting and anguished spirit, passed through and out again. They want a plot, do they? They want a reason? It is not enough for them, this ordinary scene. It is not enough to wait for the thing to be said as if it were written; to see the sentence lay its dab of clay precisely on the right place, making character; to perceive, suddenly, some group in outline against the sky. (p. 197)

Rhoda and Louis seek in the world what art has led them to expect—plots, reasons, virtues, and truth, all that would make them into stable characters in a coherent narrative. Instead, the ordinary scene involves the constant making and remaking of character, not by any individual acts, but by the flow of conversation that carries all the minds in a group along without anyone particularly directing it. The only outline that is possible is neither individual nor eternal, neither one person nor sky, but a group against the sky. To seek more is to fail to accept the sentences being written by groups every day in ordinary scenes and to become violent, to claim one group's ideas are true and thus to suppress some other group's.

There is another conventional way to transcend group differences: entering the private home. Within the home, the individual could escape social pressures and could also experience familial bonds that could become the model for political relationships between classes, nationalities, and, of course, genders (after women gained the vote). Woolf plays on the various contradictions that socialists saw within this system: she shows as a crucial step in the development of individualism the production of males and females separately—an educational system that tries to convince people that they fit into only two roles, which then can mesh perfectly in the private home. Woolf plays on individualist sexual ideology by having the person most in love with Percival be Neville, a homosexual, and by presenting the woman most suited for Percival as Susan, who finds the entire educational process painful. Neville sees in Percival's death the end of the romantic image of love, which is a crucial part of individualism. Love promises the perfect relationship, one entered utterly freely, one in which two whole people become in some sense identical (though of course not sexually identical, as Neville and Percival would be), allowing escape from partiality and alienation and forming the basis of the home. Yet the one person who seems to live a traditional home life, Susan, does so only by resisting the ideology presented in school. The role Susan chooses, as earth mother in a country home, may be stereotypical, but it is outdated in the urban, industrial age, so the schooling that is supposed to train her in her "natural" female role produces only a pain in her side. Here, even the ideology of the private home shifts, and cannot be regarded as in any way natural.

Unlike Susan, Neville, Louis, and Rhoda, who all wish to escape the social realm and become individuals, Jinny and Bernard feel most themselves in crowds. Bernard's pen and Jinny's body both come alive and glitter when they are surrounded by many people; they represent the possibility of reconceiving words and bodies as products of the crowd, not parts of individuals. But neither Bernard nor Jinny can fully live in the crowd: too much of their lives has been devoted to training them to believe in individuals. They do not escape the biographic style, they just remain suspended in the beginning of their conventional biographies, Jinny repeatedly living out the first stages of a romance, Bernard repeatedly beginning the process of writing, of becoming a narrator—a role he finally adopts in the last chapter.

Bernard in particular depends on Percival's stability; when Percival dies, the ensuing sense of chaos inspires Bernard to try to borrow Percival's methods of making order: "was there no sword, nothing with which to batter down these walls, this protection, this begetting of children and living behind curtains, and becoming daily more involved and committed, with books and pictures" (p. 266). Bernard imagines a sword would allow him to reach the truth, to break through ideology, but he is copying the imperialist belief that truth and order could be created by breaking through all alternative snail shells to bring everyone into the one house. He eventually calms down and begins considering alternative ways to make sense of the world—perhaps there is no single story, no final truth, and, most important, no individual. It is then that he decides "I am not one person; I am many people; I do not altogether know who I am" (p. 276).

Bernard describes how all in the group undergo a similar transition in their sense of themselves at their second meeting, years after Percival's death. That meeting marks their attempt to reform the group without Percival, to overcome the seeming destruction of what held them together. At the beginning of this meeting, all they can think about is the loss of Percival, of the wholeness promised by individualism: "We saw for a moment laid out among us the body of the complete human being whom we have failed to be, but at the same time, cannot forget. All that we might have been we saw; all that we had missed, and we grudged for a moment the other's claim, as children when the cake is cut, the one cake, the only cake, watch their slice diminishing" (p. 277). These characters feel incomplete and envious of what anyone else has—otherness reduces each one. The sense that there is one cake in the world for which everyone competes is the dangerous driving force of individualism. Imperialism stilled the domestic competition within English society (especially workers' uprisings) by promising to increase the size of the whole cake and thereby increase each person's slice. Imperialist rhetoric sought to make everyone feel larger: identify with the hero going off to India and you will become greater than you are.

As this meeting progresses, Woolf shows the six people achieving a very different sense of themselves, escaping at the end of the novel the individuality they had been trained in all their lives. Immediately after the passage about feeling the one cake diminishing, Bernard goes on to say: "However, we had our bottle of wine, and under that seduction lost our enmity, and stopped comparing. And, half-way through dinner, we felt enlarge itself round us the huge blackness of what is outside us, of what we are not. . . . And who were we? We were extinguished for a moment, went out like sparks in burnt paper and the blackness roared" (p. 277). Once they stop competing with each other, they feel both extinguished and vastly enlarged, for a moment seeing themselves as part of all that is outside their group, their class, their nation. The unity created by eating and drinking together extracts them from all the shells the social order has created. As Bernard says, looking back at all the dinners they shared, "I have lost in the process of eating and drinking and rubbing my eyes along surfaces that thin, hard shell which cases the soul, which, in youth, shuts one in—hence the fierceness, and the tap, tap, tap of the remorseless beaks of the young. . . . This difference we make so much of, this identity we so feverishly cherish, was overcome" (p. 288). Breaking through a snail shell, which during the novel represented the effort to take from others, here becomes an image of overcoming selfishness, of merging with others, and hence of the demise of individualism and imperialism. The logic of imperialism, which believed that all snail shells of "others" should be cracked to fill the snail shell of the one imperial individual, had the result of cracking its own shell.

The novel does not show the end result of this process, the replacement of the system of individual and national shells with some other system that would allow group differences without setting up the intense desire to bring everyone together in one shell. Indeed, the group reforms and eventually achieves even greater identity, coalescing into one voice, Bernard's. But there are hints of what would happen if the old system did disappear. In the two broken chapters after Percival's death, and only in those two chapters, someone other than Bernard begins the speeches: there, Neville and Louis speak first. While the group is cracked open, its internal hierarchy breaks down and other voices can be first. It is only a small step, allowing other males to be first, but these other males are not quite as canonical as Bernard, not heterosexual, not purely British.

At the end of the novel, there is also a brief moment when Bernard himself is driven beyond individualism. He calls upon his self: "This self . . . made no answer. . . . His fist did not form. . . . No fin breaks the waste of this immeasurable sea" (p. 284). By losing for a moment the conquering self denoted by a fist and a shark, he sees "in a dust dance the groups we had made" (p. 284). Then he finds the self again, taking up Percival's lance: he becomes militaristic in fearful reaction to the destruction of the familiar social order that has made him and that has forced everyone else to be militaristic. But before he takes up his lance, he sees for a moment a new kind of social order, one in which all the separate, little groups join together in a dance like dust or waves, passing through each other: a vision of a constantly shifting, fluid social structure, a pluralist mass society. Woolf dreamed of the disappearance of the kind of group identity and stability provided by a silent, militaristic leader or a single spokesperson; instead, in the multinational world after the dismantling of the capitalist empires, she imagined masses that would speak in many voices and move in many directions at once.

Epilogue

By the end of the 1930's, modernism and collectivism both became uncertain of themselves. Mass movements succeeded and yet did not bring utopia or even much in the way of revolution. The vast expansion of the voting population in England had the paradoxical result of causing the Conservative Party to win most of the elections from 1922 to 1940. Ireland gained its independence and developed a government that seemed distressingly bourgeois to those who had hoped for more complete change. At the same time, the examples of Stalin and Hitler suggested that collectivism could lead to something even worse than capitalism.

In the works of modernists (and other writers) in the late thirties, there was a sense of doubt that any revolution was ever going to occur. Joyce's and Woolf's last works are radical, perhaps desperate arguments against the rhetoric of cultural unity that brought Fascists to power in Europe and Conservatives to power in England. In Woolf's *Between the Acts*, the writer La Trobe tries to show the people in a small English village that they are "orts, scraps and fragments"; La Trobe and Woolf want to counter the "Merry England" rhetoric of village unity, of England as an ancient, unified race ready to go to war against other unified races such as the Germans.[1] This novel directly opposes Yeats's 1938 poem "Under Ben Bulben," which expresses an equally desperate desire for war to get rid of the distracting fragmentation of the modern mind:

> Send war in our time, O Lord!
> Know that when all words are said

> And a man is fighting mad,
> Something drops from eyes long blind
> He completes his partial mind,
> For an instant stands at ease.[2]

Woolf and Yeats were still presenting collective events—village pageants, war—as the vehicle for change, but they also imbued these later works with a strong sense of hopelessness: Yeats's prayer for war is part of a poem telling where he should be buried; Woolf committed suicide before her novel was published.

Such despair may have derived in part from a realization that bourgeois capitalism would survive the challenges of left-wing and right-wing collectivism. One of the ironies of the history of modernism is that it gained canonical stature as "the" literature of the twentieth century in the 1950's, when collectivism was not only degraded but had become the main enemy of the Left and the Right in the English-speaking world, with the obsessive hunting down of Communists and Fascists. Modernism may have gained its stature as canonical for the same reasons it became labeled apolitical: the transformation of the dream of collectivism into the nightmares of Stalin and Hitler. Since modernism was connected with those nightmares, but did not quite embrace them, the modernist could be turned into the hero tempted by the darkness of modern politics but finally rejecting the temptations.

Modernism became separated from its anticapitalist politics because capitalism changed, giving up its individualist, liberal core in the development of the welfare state; the modernist period was mostly a period of such adjustment. The sense that the masses—as folk or as proletariat—represented an alternative to capitalism disappeared because yet another image of the masses emerged: as consumers. The women's, worker's, nationalist, and aristocratic movements did not then lead to revolution at all, because they could all be satisfied as "market segments": the discovery of alternative mentalities and the demise of the universal individual translated not into the demise of capitalism, but into alternative sets of objects to buy. As Chris Waters argues in *British Socialists and the Politics of Popular Culture: 1884–1914*, socialists and conservatives alike sought an authentic culture to replace capitalism while capitalism itself constructed the new mass culture of leisure that leaves permanently unsettled what is in the "mass unconscious."

Thus, neither side ever won the political debates of the interwar years: the mixed economies and partially pluralist political systems that became the norm in Europe had neither the unified cultural center of the Right nor the pluralist equality of the Left. We could say that capitalism won, but it did so by using the language of the mass mind developed by modernism, which bears similarities to advertising, as numerous critics have suggested.[3] The pluralism of the Left transformed into the panoply of styles for sale; the dream of castles to which the masses could feel they belong transmuted into the immense sports emporiums and shopping malls. The modernist critique of capitalism no longer seemed to press for political change or even to imply an alternative social order: it seemed, rather, an inherent part of capitalism itself, a ritual of plunging beneath the surface, seeking the mass unconscious and failing to find it, a ritual of admitting there is no meaning to it all, no coherence, a corollary of a system so adaptable that it could incorporate all dreams of political change.

The recent collapse of Communist regimes (and the end of the last overtly Fascist regime in Spain) has seemed to some to represent the final triumph of capitalism over all alternatives, but it may instead revive interest in some early-twentieth-century collectivist ideas—and partly explains why it is now possible to see once again the relationship between modernism and collectivism. No longer needing to obsessively avoid collectivism as something alien to us, we may no longer need be terrified of the political dreams embodied in modernist works. Those dreams now seem outdated rather than nightmarish: T. S. Eliot's and Charles Maurras's hope of restored monarchies throughout Europe; Harold Laski's and Virginia Woolf's visions of societies operating without any central sovereignty. Many of the issues these dreams addressed have returned in the questions of how to define social ideals without relying on the ideologies of capitalism and Marxism. As we ask again what a culture is and whether a multicultural society is possible, we return to visions of the social unconscious, of various mass minds that may or may not be able to coexist. Recent debates about how to build a social order out of people with differing backgrounds suggest that it has become politically important to understand how deep, underground mass structures create consciousnesses and communities. Similar concerns underlay the political debates of early-twentieth-century collectivism and modernism. The turn toward "the postmodern" in critical and political contexts suggests that we are once again undergoing a version of the modern(ist) alternation of the social order. As capitalism once again seems the universal social order threatening to become a wasteland, and both the Left and the Right argue that the solution is to restore suppressed sources of culture (though disagreeing on what those sources are), we may find that the political dimensions of modernism once again become visible and relevant.

Reference Matter

Notes

INTRODUCTION

1. William McDougall wrote the most popular psychology text in England during this era, *Social Psychology*, in 1908; in 1920 he published a theory of mass mentality, *The Group Mind*. Sorel published *Reflections on Violence* in 1906; Wallas, *Human Nature in Politics* in 1908; Trotter, *Instincts of the Herd in Peace and War* in 1921; and Freud, *Group Psychology and the Analysis of the Ego*, in 1921.

2. Le Bon, *The Crowd*, p. 21.

3. Ibid., p. 22.

4. Sorel, *Reflections on Violence*, pp. 48–49.

5. Perloff argues that many of the innovations of modernism were first developed by avant-garde artists who had an "urge to communicate directly with the masses, to play to the crowd." *The Futurist Moment*, p. 10. For other recent views of the relationship between modernism and mass culture, see Huyssen, "Mass Culture as Woman: Modernism's Other," in *After the Great Divide*, and Moretti, "From The Waste Land to the Artificial Paradise," in *Signs Taken for Wonders*.

6. Richard Poirier has suggested that modernism, though a "snob's game," is also a "colonialist protest" against the nineteenth-century literary forms that claimed to "cater to the ethos of the so-called common man or common reader"—in other words, a protest against the claim of nineteenth-century literary forms to represent the mass mind. "The Difficulties of Modernism," pp. 272–73.

7. Eliot, "The Humanism of Irving Babbitt," in *Essays*, pp. 81–82.

8. Eliot, "Tradition and the Individual Talent," in *Selected Prose*, pp. 39–40.

9. Yeats, "The Philosophy of Shelley's Poetry," in *Essays and Introductions,* p. 87.

10. Woolf, *A Room of One's Own,* p. 68.

11. Woolf, *The Waves,* p. 288.

12. Lukács, *The Meaning of Contemporary Realism,* p. 20; Maurice Beebe, "*Ulysses* and the Age of Modernism," in Staley, ed., *Ulysses: Fifty Years,* p. 175.

13. Dicey, *Lectures;* Beer, *Modern British Politics;* Maier, *Recasting Bourgeois Europe;* Lowi, *The End of Liberalism.*

14. Critics who present modernism as the breakup of the individual include Calverton, "T. S. Eliot: An Inverted Marxian"; West, *Crisis and Criticism;* Sypher, *Loss of Self in Modern Literature;* Langbaum, *The Mysteries of Identity;* Brown, *The Modernist Self;* Levenson, *Modernism and the Fate of Individuality;* and Cixous, *The Exile of James Joyce.* Critics who have described modernism as a rejection of middle-class liberalism include Trilling, *Beyond Culture;* Easthope, "Why Most Contemporary Poetry Is So Bad"; and Moretti, "The Long Goodbye," in *Signs Taken for Wonders.*

15. Wilson, *Axel's Castle,* p. 268.

16. For example, Ross argues modernism is an effort to escape subjectivity, one that can never succeed because "language, as a medium, resists . . . and reaffirms its *irreducible* share of subjectivity." *The Failure of Modernism,* p. xvi.

17. Calverton, "T. S. Eliot," p. 372.

18. DuPlessis, *Writing Beyond the Ending,* p. 163.

19. Allen McLaurin, "Consciousness and Group Consciousness in Virginia Woolf," in Warner, ed., *Virginia Woolf: A Centenary Perspective,* p. 39.

20. Riquelme, *Teller and Tale,* p. xv.

21. Bernstein, *The Tale of the Tribe.*

22. Critics who have placed modernism in the context of popular culture have been quite useful in developing this book. See Herr, *Joyce's Anatomy of Culture;* Kershner, *Joyce, Bakhtin, and Popular Literature;* Wicke, *Advertising Fictions;* and Moretti, *Signs Taken for Wonders.*

23. M. H. Abrams et al., eds., *Norton Anthology of English Literature* (1993), 2: 2261–62.

24. M. H. Abrams et al., eds, *Norton Anthology of English Literature* (1962), 2: 1597.

25. M. H. Abrams et al., eds., *Norton Anthology of English Literature* (1993), 2: 1916.

26. Jane Marcus, "No More Horses," p. 273.

27. Ibid., p. 271.

28. My view is similar to that expressed by Catherine Gallagher in describing discourses as existing "between and within ideologies, thereby creating the coherence and legibility of ideological conflict." Gallagher, *The Industrial Reformation of the Novel,* p. xiii.

29. Beer, *Modern British Politics,* pp. 69–104.

30. Wilson, *Axel's Castle,* p. 286.

31. Maier notes that in the 1920's, "commentators began to suggest that sovereignty was dissolving in a new feudalism." *Recasting Bourgeois Europe,* p. 355.

32. The *Oxford English Dictionary* (1989) gives the following dates for the

first appearance of these words in English: *individualism*, 1827; *collectivism*, 1880; *liberalism*, 1819; *socialism*, 1832–37 (uncertain); and *communism*, 1843.

33. Cited in the *Oxford English Dictionary* (1989) s.v. *individualism*.

34. T. H. Green, *Prolegomena to Ethics*, p. 210; quoted in Milne, *The Social Philosophy of English Idealism*, p. 105.

35. Trotter, *Instincts of the Herd*, p. 42.

36. Bradley, *Ethical Studies*, p. 158.

37. Eliot, *Notes Towards the Definition of Culture*, p. 94.

38. Dangerfield, *The Strange Death of Liberal England*, p. 185.

39. Woolf, "A Sketch of the Past," in *Moments of Being*, p. 80.

40. Irigaray is quoted in Theweleit, *Male Fantasies*, 1: 432.

41. Jardine, *Gynesis*, p. 25. Many critics have seen modernism or the works of particular writers as creating a feminine aesthetic or revealing the emergence of the feminine: DuPlessis, *Writing Beyond the Ending*; Henke, *James Joyce and the Politics of Desire*; Friedman and Fuchs, eds., *Breaking the Sequence*; MacCabe, *James Joyce and the Revolution of the Word*; and Minow-Pinkney, *Virginia Woolf and the Problem of the Subject*.

42. Julia Kristeva, "Oscillation Between Power and Denial," trans. Marilyn A. August, in Marks and Courtivron, eds., *New French Feminisms*, p. 165. Hélène Cixous, in "Sorties" and "The Laugh of the Medusa," in the same volume, also interprets the disruptions of modernism and deconstruction as breakthroughs of the feminine.

43. Huyssen, *After the Great Divide*, p. 47.

44. Theweleit, *Male Fantasies*, 1: 229–300.

45. Torgovnick comments that the familiar tropes for primitives always end up "conventionally used for women." *Gone Primitive*, p. 17.

46. I have drawn upon many political analyses of individual authors, including Manganiello, *Joyce's Politics*; Jane Marcus, *Virginia Woolf and the Languages of Patriarchy*, and "Brittania Rules *The Waves*," in Karen Lawrence, ed., *Decolonizing Tradition*, pp. 136–64; Zwerdling, *Virginia Woolf and the Real World*; Cullingford, *Yeats, Ireland, and Fascism*; and Cooper, *T. S. Eliot and the Politics of Voice*.

47. See, for example, Craig, *Yeats, Eliot, Pound, and the Politics of Poetry*; and North, *The Political Aesthetic of Yeats, Eliot, and Pound*.

48. See, for example, Kristeva, "Oscillations Between Power and Denial," in Marks and Courtivron, eds., *New French Feminisms*, p. 166. Manganiello, in *Joyce's Politics*, and Jane Marcus, in "No More Horses," as well as in other essays, have argued convincingly for the relationship of Joyce and Woolf, respectively, to socialism.

49. North, *The Political Aesthetic of Yeats, Eliot, and Pound*, p. viii.

50. Craig points to the importance of reading Le Bon and Sorel if we are to understand why the conservative modernist poets were attracted to Fascism. Craig argues that "associationist" psychology underlies Le Bon's and Sorel's theories of mass mind and also underlies the poetics of Yeats, Eliot, and Pound. But he also claims "There is no obvious correlation between modernist novelists—Joyce, Woolf, Faulkner—and the kinds of politics we find in Yeats, Eliot, and Pound." The politics of these modernists, he contends, "flows directly from

their conception of—or the very nature of—poetry itself." Though I am indebted to Craig for suggesting the importance of Le Bon and Sorel and for his careful analysis of relationships of the poetics of three modernists and their politics, I cannot fully accept his theory: as I argue at the end of Chapter 1, the move into collectivism seems connected to the development of new psychological theories that replaced associationism. I also find Craig's limitation of his analysis to poetry troubling. *Yeats, Eliot, Pound,* pp. 22, 266–71.

51. Berman notes that "modernist anti-liberalism was regularly directed at the failures of a progressive liberal project, leading in turn either to a rejection of that project (fascist modernism) or its radicalization on the left." *Modern Culture and Critical Theory,* p. 121.

52. Jameson, "Modernism and Imperialism," in Eagleton, Jameson, and Said, *Nationalism, Colonialism, and Literature,* pp. 50–51.

53. Perry Anderson, "Modernity and Revolution," in Nelson and Grossberg, eds., *Marxism and the Interpretation of Culture,* pp. 317–33.

54. Eliot, *The Idea of a Christian Society,* p. 19.

55. Eliot, *After Strange Gods,* p. 30.

56. Harold Macmillan, *Reconstruction: A Plea for a National Policy* (London: Macmillan, 1934), pp. 127–28; quoted in Beer, *Modern British Politics,* p. 296.

57. Disraeli is quoted in Briggs, *Victorian People,* p. 278.

58. Harold Macmillan, interview, *London Star,* June 25, 1926; quoted in Beer, *Modern British Politics,* p. 271.

59. Cole, *Guild Socialism Re-Stated,* p. 33.

60. Ibid., p. 95 n.

61. Anthony Ludovici, *The False Assumptions of Democracy* (London: Heath Cranston, 1921); quoted in Webber, *The Ideology of the British Right,* p. 66.

62. Ibid., p. 59.

63. Sorel, *Reflections on Violence,* pp. 48–49.

64. Woolf, *Three Guineas,* p. 106.

65. Levenson, *Modernism and the Fate of Individuality,* pp. 1–77, esp. pp. 74–77; Pecora, *Self and Form in the Modern Narrative,* pp. 176–213.

66. Jameson argues that Lewis experimented with "the representation of a collective or postindividualistic content," but quit these experiments because "the exploration of this narrative option would by its own inner logic and momentum have ended up positioning Lewis squarely on the Left." *Fables of Aggression,* p. 108. Lewis retreated to liberalism: in *Self Condemned* (Chicago: Henry Regnery, 1965), the historian-hero declares the "liberal idealism" would have produced a "new age of social justice, had it not been for the intervention of the Marxist ideology" (p. 91). I find Jameson's analysis of Lewis's shifting politics convincing, but disagree with Jameson's belief that collectivism existed only on the Left. Instead, I would argue that both left-wing and right-wing collectivism involved accepting the masses as the basis of the social order, and that is what Lewis could not accept. Lewis's admiration for Fascism was congruent with his liberalism because he focused on Hitler, believing the Fascist claim to free the strong individual from the mediocre masses and ignoring the Fascist use of the masses as the basis of power. Jameson in effect repeats Lewis's views in denying Fascism the status of a collectivist social order. In

any case, Jameson's analysis of Lewis supports my argument, because he shows that Lewis's literary styles and politics shifted together: when Lewis had most faith in the masses, his prose became most modernist, most fragmented and multiple-voiced. When Lewis rejected modernism, in *Time and Western Man*, he did so by returning to individualism, to the "formally fixed self," the "eye."

    67. Beer, *Modern British Politics*, p. 71.

CHAPTER 1

    1. Moretti, *The Way of the World*, pp. 79, 77, 228.

    2. DuPlessis, *Writing Beyond the Ending*, p. 163.

    3. Woolf, *The Years*, p. 190.

    4. Karen Lawrence, *The Odyssey of Styles in 'Ulysses,'* p. 64.

    5. Yeats, "What Is Popular Poetry?" in *Essays and Introductions*, pp. 5, 8.

    6. Ibid., pp. 10–11.

    7. Yeats, "Fighting the Waves," in *Explorations*, p. 373.

    8. Ibid., p. 377.

    9. Yeats, *Autobiography*, pp. 158–59.

    10. Ibid., p. 159.

    11. Woolf, "A Sketch of the Past," in *Moments of Being*, p. 80.

    12. Yeats, *Autobiography*, p. 242.

    13. Pound, *Personae*, p. 111.

    14. Yeats, *Autobiography*, p. 119.

    15. Beer speaks of a "vast, untidy system" of extraparliamentary representation. *Modern British Politics*, p. 337. Maier speaks of "the bleeding away of parliamentary authority." *Recasting Bourgeois Europe*, p. 353.

    16. Joyce, *Letters*, 2: 174.

    17. MacCabe, *James Joyce and the Revolution of the Word*.

    18. Ruotolo, *The Interrupted Moment*, discusses interruptions in the introduction (pp. 1–18) and anarchy in the conclusion (pp. 231–38).

    19. Kermode, *The Sense of an Ending*, p. 100–112. Kermode's analysis is worth looking at in some detail, because in it we can see the way that postwar anticollectivism sought to undo Sorel's arguments. Kermode recognizes that modernism was involved in the development of political myths, but he asserts that this was basically a mistake, an erroneous extension of the act of creating fictions: "Fictions, notably the fiction of apocalypse, turn easily into myths: people will live by that which was designed only to know by" (p. 112). Kermode is in effect denying Sorel's and Le Bon's claims that in the collective mind no one can distinguish fictions from real descriptions or myths. Kermode also inverts Sorel's claim that myths produce change: "Myths are the agents of stability, fictions the agents of change" (p. 39). Kermode tries to restore the liberal belief that the individual, in day-to-day life, can escape totalizing myths: he argues that there is a "common language, the vernacular, by means of which from day to day we deal with reality" (p. 107). Change is, in Kermode's view, due to doubt and challenges posed by "reality," not to passionate belief and mass movements. In such a view, the modernist's search for the springs of mass thinking and of communal passions must seem extremely dangerous.

    20. Eliot, "*Ulysses*, Order and Myth," in *Selected Prose*, p. 177.

21. Margolis, *T. S. Eliot's Intellectual Development*, p. 43 n.
22. Gregor, *Italian Fascism*, p. 25.
23. Ibid., p. 100.
24. Roberto Michels, *Political Parties*, trans. E. Paul and C. Paul (New York: Dover, 1915), p. 53; quoted in Gregor, *Italian Fascism*, p. 217.
25. Margolis, *T. S. Eliot's Intellectual Development*, p. 11.
26. Sorel says that socialism should bring workers to an "enthusiasm similar to that which we find in the lives of certain great artists." *Reflections on Violence*, p. 271.
27. See, for example, Chadwick, "Violence in Yeats's Later Politics and Poetry"; Freyer, *W. B. Yeats and the Anti-Democratic Tradition*, p. 72; Suheil Badi Bushrui, "The Rhetoric of Terror in the Poetry of W. B. Yeats," in Bramsback and Crogham, eds., *Anglo-Irish and Irish Literature*, pp. 19–38; G. J. Watson, "The Politics of Ulysses," in Newman and Thornton, eds., *Joyce's 'Ulysses': The Larger Perspective*, pp. 39–58.
28. Said, "Yeats and Decolonization," in Eagleton, Jameson, and Said, *Nationalism, Colonialism, and Literature*, p. 70.
29. Feroza Jussawalla and Reed Way Dasenbrock, eds., *Interviews with Writers of the Post-Colonial World*, p. 15.
30. Fanon says of colonialism: "It is violence in its natural state, and it will yield only when confronted with greater violence." *The Wretched of the Earth*, p. 55. He also argues that the notion of transcending nationalism belies colonial liberation movements and that national movements cannot be divided. See pp. 247, 158–62.
31. Chatterjee, *The Nation and Its Fragments*, p. 13.
32. Freud, *Group Psychology and the Analysis of the Ego*, pp. 52, 22, 68.
33. Ibid., p. 39.
34. Adorno, "Freudian Theory," pp. 118–37.
35. Harold Laski, reply to Walter Lippmann, *New Republic*, May 31, 1919, p. 149; quoted in Zylstra, *From Pluralism to Collectivism*, p. 46.
36. Jones, *Social Darwinism and English Thought*, p. 132.
37. The lines of influence between psychologists and politicians went both ways. As Hearnshaw says, social psychology did not develop in England until the hold of individualism over British political thinking broke in the 1870's. *A Short History of British Psychology*, p. 105.
38. Woolf, *A Room of One's Own*, pp. 51, 101, 102.
39. Joyce, *Ulysses*, 8.718.
40. Prince, *Psychotherapy and Multiple Personality*, pp. 213, 198.
41. Ibid., p. 193–95.
42. Woolf, *Three Guineas*, pp. 133, 137.

CHAPTER 2

1. Aneurin Bevan, *In Place of Fear* (London: Heinemann, 1953); quoted in Beer, *Modern British Politics*, p. 85.
2. Virginia Woolf, "A Sketch of the Past," in *Moments of Being*, pp. 79–80.
3. Collini, *Public Moralists*, pp. 355–56.
4. Ibid., pp. 190–91.
5. Eliot, introduction to Barnes, *Nightwood*, p. xv.

6. Albert Guerard, introduction to Joseph Conrad, *Heart of Darkness and The Secret Sharer* (New York: New American Library, 1983), p. 14.

7. In-text citations refer to Woolf, *To the Lighthouse*, and to the Gabler edition of Joyce, *Ulysses*.

8. Zwerdling, *Virginia Woolf and the Real World*, p. 193.

9. Kenner, *Joyce's Voices*, p. 49.

10. To construct "Oxen," Joyce used *The History of English Prose Rhythms* by George Saintsbury and *English Prose: Mandeville to Ruskin* by W. Peacock. For a discussion of these and other books Joyce used as his sources for "Oxen," see J. S. Atherton, "The Oxen of the Sun," in Hart and Hayman, eds., *James Joyce's 'Ulysses.'*

11. Gilbert and Gubar, *No Man's Land*, 1: 260. Leo Bersani also argues that *Ulysses* as a whole "actually works to increase literature's authority." *The Culture of Redemption*, p. 169.

12. Bonnie Kime Scott, "'The Look in the Throat of a Stricken Animal,'" p. 160.

13. Karen Lawrence, "Joyce and Feminism," in Attridge, *The Cambridge Companion to James Joyce*, p. 251.

14. Virginia Woolf, "Mr. Bennett and Mrs. Brown," in *The Captain's Death Bed*, pp. 118–19, 96. Zwerdling quotes the end of the passage on change, after the scene with the cook, to indicate Woolf's interest in changes in family structures. *Virginia Woolf and the Real World*, p. 145.

15. Woolf, introduction to Margaret Lleweln Davies, *Life as We Have Known It*.

16. Kate Flint pointed out this fact in "Virginia Woolf and the General Strike," in *Essays in Criticism: A Quarterly Journal of Literary Criticism* 36, no. 4 (October 1986): 319–34.

17. James M. Haule, "*To the Lighthouse* and the Great War: The Evidence of Virginia Woolf's Revisions of 'Time Passes,'" in Hussey, ed., *Virginia Woolf and War*, p. 166.

18. Jane Marcus notes this fact about the manuscript in her introduction to *Virginia Woolf and the Languages of Patriarchy*, p. 12.

19. See, for example, Elgar, *Picasso*, p. 56.

20. Janson and Janson, *History of Art*, p. 522.

21. Ashcroft, Griffins, and Tiffin, *The Empire Writes Back*, p. 158.

22. Janson and Janson, *History of Art*, pp. 27–28.

23. For a discussion of the use of the primitive in modern art, see Torgovnick, *Gone Primitive*.

24. Ibid., pp. 85–104.

25. Fry, *Vision and Design*, pp. 19, 96, 90.

26. Ibid., p. 94.

27. Maier, *Recasting Bourgeois Europe*, pp. 10–11.

28. Beer, *Modern British Politics*, p. 78.

29. Maier, *Recasting Bourgeois Europe*, pp. 353, 9.

30. Joyce, *Stephen Hero*, p. 202.   31. Joyce, *Portrait*, p. 188.

32. Joyce, *Finnegans Wake*, p. 215.   33. Joyce, *Portrait*, p. 101.

34. Stephen even seems to have a woman's foot, both as part of his anatomy and as a unit of rhythm in his poetry. Stephen is wearing Buck Mulligan's cast-off shoe, which seems to carry with it a rhythm Stephen hates. Stephen thinks

that he would be happier in a woman's shoe: "His gaze brooded on his broadtoed boots, a buck's castoffs. . . . He counted the creases of rucked leather wherein another's foot had nested warm. The foot that beat the ground in tripudium, foot I dislove. But you were delighted when Esther Osvalt's shoe went on you: girl I knew in Paris." *Ulysses*, 3.448–50.

35. Joyce, *Portrait*, p. 187.

36. Torgovnick, *Gone Primitive*, p. 85.

37. Haule, "*To the Lighthouse* and the Great War," in Hussey, ed., *Virginia Woolf and War*, p. 167.

38. Yeats, "Easter, 1916" in *Poems*, p. 180.

39. Dangerfield, *The Strange Death of Liberal England*, p. 371.

40. Harold Laski, *Authority in the Modern State* (New Haven: Yale University Press, 1919), pp. 313–14; quoted in Zylstra, *From Pluralism to Collectivism*, p. 46.

41. William James, *Essays in Radical Empiricism and A Pluralistic Universe* (New York: Longmans, Green, 1943), pp. 320–21; quoted in Laski, *Foundations of Sovereignty*, p. 169.

42. Donzelot says that the government becomes a third party to all family disputes, policing the family in the name of helping family members to "liberate" themselves. The government interfering inside families may be a form of policing, something Woolf opposed, but in this novel Woolf shows another kind of interference of one social structure on another that may even promise to loosen, not increase, the policing of society. *The Policing of Families*, chapter 3, particularly pp. 90–95.

43. Woolf, introduction to Davies, *Life as We Have Known It*, p. xxiii.

44. Jane Marcus, *Virginia Woolf and the Languages of Patriarchy*, p. xv.

CHAPTER 3

1. Dicey, *Lectures*, p. 217.

2. Cited in the *Oxford English Dictionary* (1989) s.v. *individualism*.

3. Mill, *Utilitarianism*, p. 78.

4. Maier, *Recasting Bourgeois Europe*, p. 23.

5. Arblaster, *The Rise and Decline of Western Liberalism*.

6. Dangerfield, *The Strange Death of Liberal England*, p. 215.

7. Dicey, *Lectures*, p. liv.   8. Ibid.

9. Ibid., p. lv.   10. Webb, *Our Partnership*, p. 442.

11. Auden, introduction to *Victorian and Edwardian Poets*, p. xxii.

12. Mill, *Utilitarianism*, p. 213.

13. Dangerfield, *The Strange Death of Liberal England*, p. 385.

14. Brantlinger, "Imperial Gothic," p. 243.

15. Masterman, *From the Abyss*, p. 2.

16. Levenson, *Modernism and the Fate of Individuality*, p. 77.

17. D. H. Lawrence, *Women in Love*, in *The Penguin Great Novels of D. H. Lawrence*, p. 979.

18. Levenson, in chapter 2 of *Modernism and the Fate of Individuality*, similarly sees Forster as preserving liberalism. See pp. 78–101.

19. Harvena Richter, *Virginia Woolf: The Inward Voyage*, p. 14.

20. Pitt, "The Exploration of Self," p. 146.

21. DuPlessis, *Writing Beyond the Ending*, p. 52.

22. DeKoven, *Rich and Strange*, p. 85.

23. Torgovnick has shown the complex ways that the category of the primitive becomes "engendered" feminine. See *Gone Primitive*, pp. 141–76.

24. The problem can be neatly epitomized in the contrast between the name of Woolf's most famous feminist text, *A Room of One's Own*, and the name of the journal of the suffrage movement in England: *Time and Tide*. Woolf sought to break out of the bourgeois home that submerges women inside male space by providing separate rooms for each person (or each gender). But as the suffrage journal suggests, the alternative to the world of men may not be a world of separate spaces for male and female individuals, but rather a world of tides.

25. Naremore, *The World Without a Self*, p. 49.

26. Sir James Barr, "Some Reasons Why the Public Should Oppose the Insurance Act," *British Medical Journal*, December 30, 1911; quoted in Evans, *Social Policy 1830–1914*, p. 280.

27. Quoted in Lambert, " 'And Darwin says they are nearer the cow,' " p. 1.

28. DeSalvo, introduction to Woolf, *Melymbrosia*, p. xxiii.

29. Gillian Beer, "Virginia Woolf and Pre-History," in Warner, ed., *Virginia Woolf: A Centenary Perspective*, p. 111.

30. Atkinson, "Africa," p. 28.

31. C. F. G. Masterman, *The Condition of England* (London: Methuen, 1911); quoted in Gill Davies, "Foreign Bodies," p. 64.

32. Booth, *Darkest England*, pp. 11–12, 44.

33. Mill, *Utilitarianism*, pp. 213–14.

34. DeKoven interprets Pepper's monsters as "fetal images and a repressed desire for autonomy; the ocean at once the womb and the unconscious." Bringing them up is "the de-repression of the maternal." *Rich and Strange*, p. 105. I agree that they represent the results of seeking autonomy, but not simply because the maternal is given no place in bourgeois society, but also because the search for a realm of female autonomy simply leads out into the "masses" outside the bourgeois world.

35. Woolf, *A Room of One's Own*, pp. 88–89.

36. DeSalvo, *Virginia Woolf*, pp. 159, 177. On pp. 162–68, DeSalvo discusses Rachel Vinrace as a victim of sexual abuse.

37. Masterman, *From the Abyss*, pp. 2, 26, 37.

CHAPTER 4

1. Eliot, *Notes Towards the Definition of Culture*, p. 45.

2. For summaries of critiques of plutocracy and fears of loss of cultural cohesion in the United States at the turn of the century, see Lears, *No Place of Grace*.

3. Eliot, *After Strange Gods*, p. 16.

4. For an account of the nativist movement, see Higham, *Strangers in the Land*.

5. Henry Cabot Lodge, "Lynch Law and Unrestricted Immigration," p. 606.

6. Sigg, *The American T. S. Eliot*, pp. 147–48.

7. Eliot, *After Strange Gods*, pp. 19–20, 30.

8. Lears discusses in separate chapters the attractions of medievalism, Catholicism, and aestheticism. *No Place of Grace*, pp. 141–67, 183–203, 77–78.

9. Eliot is quoted in Sigg, *The American T. S. Eliot*, p. 110.

10. E. L. C. Morse, *The Nation*, June 15, 1903, p. 515.

11. Eliot, "The Humanism of Irving Babbitt," in *Essays*, p. 81.

12. Ibid., pp. 81–82.

13. Freud, *Group Psychology*, p. 22.

14. Freud, *Civilization and Its Discontents*, p. 88.

15. Lears, *No Place of Grace*, p. 102.

16. Frances Parkman, "The Failure of Universal Suffrage," *North American Review* 127 (July–August 1878), p. 2.

17. Ibid., pp. 18–20.

18. Babbitt, "Julian Benda," in *On Being Creative*, p. 191.

19. Eliot, *Letters*, p. 96.

20. Ackroyd, *T. S. Eliot*, p. 20; Howarth makes the same comment in *Notes on Some Figures*, p. 24.

21. Howarth, *Notes on Some Figures*, p. 24.

22. Eliot, *Notes Towards the Definition of Culture*, p. 26.

23. See Pinkney, *Women in the Poetry of T. S. Eliot*; Carol Christ, "Gender, Voice and Figuration in Eliot's Early Poetry," in Bush, ed., *T. S. Eliot: The Modernist in History*, pp. 23–40; Gelpi, *A Coherent Splendor*, pp. 91–168.

24. Christ, "Gender, Voice and Figuration," in Bush, ed., *T. S. Eliot: The Modernist in History*, p. 25.

25. Gelpi, *A Coherent Splendor*, p. 98.

26. The manuscript notebook and folder are among the Quinn papers in the Berg Collection of the New York Public Library. I examined the manuscripts, but Valerie Eliot will not permit direct quotation from unpublished poems before there is a published edition.

27. Pound, *Personae*, p. 85.

28. Yeats, "The Second Coming," in *Poems*, p. 187.

29. Yeats, "To-morrow's Revolution," in *Explorations*, p. 425.

30. Joyce, *Portrait*, p. 23.

31. Kershner, "Genius, Degeneration, and the Panopticon," p. 385.

32. Yeats, "Crazy Jane Talks with the Bishop," in *Poems*, p. 259.

33. Page numbers in parentheses in this chapter refer to Eliot, *Complete Poems and Plays*.

34. Eliot, *After Strange Gods*, pp. 19–20.

35. Doris L. Eder first pointed out that Louis was modeled on Eliot. "Louis Unmasked," p. 13.

36. Miller, *T. S. Eliot's Personal Waste Land*, p. 11.

37. Ward, "The Restriction of Immigration," p. 236.

38. Depew is quoted in Higham, *Strangers in the Land*, p. 111.

39. Parkman, "The Failure of Universal Suffrage," pp. 2, 10.

40. Walker, "Restriction of Immigration, pp. 828–29. Others also used the image of drains: Ward quotes James Bryce as speaking of "the more and more thorough 'drainage' of the inland regions of Europe which is illustrated for us in the new immigration." "The Restriction of Immigration," p. 228.

41. Eliot, *The Waste Land: A Facsimile*, pp. 58–59.

CHAPTER 5

1. Joyce, "The Day of the Rabblement," in *Critical Writings*, pp. 69, 71.

2. Manganiello, *Joyce's Politics*.

3. Trevor L. Williams similarly views Stephen as struggling to resist the dominant ideologies of Ireland. "Dominant Ideologies: The Production of Stephen Dedalus," in Benstock, ed., *James Joyce: The Augmented Ninth*, p. 312.

4. Eco, The *Aesthetics of Chaosmos: The Middle Ages of James Joyce*; Reynolds, "Joyce's Villanelle and D'Annunzio's Sonnet Sequence"; Zingrone, "Joyce and D'Annunzio"; Lucente, "D'Annunzio's *Il Fuoco* and Joyce's *Portrait*"; Lobner, *James Joyce's Italian Connection*, chapter 3.

5. Lobner, *James Joyce's Italian Connection*, pp. 68, 73.

6. D'Annunzio, *The Flame of Life*. All in-text citations refer to this translation.

7. D'Annunzio is quoted in Klopp, *Gabriele D'Annunzio*, p. 84.

8. D'Annunzio is quoted in Rhodes, *The Poet as Superman*, p. 58.

9. Joyce, *Stephen Hero*, pp. 49, 80–81.

10. Joyce, *Letters*, 2: 187.

11. Sorel, *Reflections on Violence*, p. 53.

12. Joyce, *Stephen Hero*, p. 147.

13. For a summary of the arguments about Stephen's future, see Beja, *Joyce, the Artist Manqué*.

14. Gregory L. Lucente, "D'Annunzio's *Il Fuoco* and Joyce's *Portrait*," p. 25.

15. James Naremore calls Stephen's aesthetic a "defense mechanism" against what seems dirty inside him. "Consciousness and Society in *A Portrait of the Artist*," in Staley and Benstock, eds., *Approaches to Joyce's 'Portrait,'* p. 121.

16. Gabriele D'Annunzio, *The Child of Pleasure*, quoted in Reynolds, "Joyce's Villanelle and D'Annunzio's Sonnet Sequence," p. 26.

17. Theweleit, *Male Fantasies*, 2: 3, 4.

18. D'Annunzio, *The Flame*, p. 118.

19. Gabriele D'Annunzio, *Laus vitae*, 18.463–70, quoted in Klopp, *Gabriele D'Annunzio*, p. 69.

20. Theweleit, *Male Fantasies*, 2: 159.

21. Ibid., 1: 249, 300.

22. Woolf, *A Room of One's Own*, p. 104.

23. Ibid., p. 106.

24. James Joyce, conversation of February 21, 1908, quoted in Ellman, *James Joyce*, p. 265.

25. Joyce, *Stephen Hero*, pp. 35, 54.

26. D'Annunzio is quoted in Antongini, *D'Annunzio*, p. 378.

27. Joyce, *Stephen Hero*, p. 40.   28. Ellman, *James Joyce*, p. 279.

29. Joyce, *Exiles*, p. 88.   30. Joyce, *Ulysses*, 15.4599.

CHAPTER 6

1. For a range of opinions about Yeats's politics, see Cullingford, *Yeats, Ireland, and Fascism*; Connor Cruse O'Brien, "Passion and Cunning: An Essay on the Politics of W. B. Yeats," in Jeffares and Cross, eds., *In Excited Reverie*; Deane, *Celtic Revivals*; Said, "Yeats and Decolonization," in Eagleton, Jameson, and

Said, *Nationalism, Colonialism, and Literature*; and John S. Kelly, "The Fifth Bell: Race and Class in Yeats's Political Thought," in Komesu and Sekine, eds., *Irish Writers and Politics.*

2. Georges Sorel, letter to Benedetto Croce, May 6, 1907; quoted in Roth, *The Cult of Violence*, p. 39.

3. Critics who have emphasized Yeats's desire to combine opposites include Engelberg, *The Vast Design*, and Hazard Adams, *The Book of Yeats's Poems.*

4. Sorel, *Reflections on Violence*, p. 55.

5. Ibid., pp. 163–64, 164–65, 167, 271.

6. Yeats, *Autobiography*, p. 90.

7. For an account of Yeats's conflicts with the Young Ireland movement, see Phillip L. Marcus, *Yeats and the Beginning of the Irish Renaissance*, pp. 9–19.

8. Yeats, *Autobiography*, p. 117.

9. Yeats, *Memoir*, p. 176.

10. Phillip L. Marcus, *Yeats and the Beginning of the Irish Renaissance*, pp. 28, xix.

11. Ibid., p. 29.

12. All in-text citations of Yeats's poetry in this chapter are from Yeats, *Poems.*

13. Norman Jeffares's comments are cited in Byrd, *The Early Poetry of W. B. Yeats*, p. 6.

14. Yeats, "The Happiest of Poets," in *Essays and Introductions*, pp. 54–56.

15. Roth, *The Cult of Violence*, p. 133.

16. Yeats, "The Happiest of Poets," in *Essays and Introductions*, p. 61.

17. Sorel, *Reflections on Violence*, p. 36.

18. Yeats, *Autobiography*, p. 176.

19. Yeats is quoted in the introduction to Yeats, *'Where There is Nothing' and 'The Unicorn from the Stars,'* pp. 12, 86.

20. Ibid., p. 86.

21. Sorel, *Reflections on Violence*, p. 264.

22. Yeats, *'Where There is Nothing' and 'The Unicorn from the Stars,'* pp. 114, 102.

23. Yeats, *Autobiography*, p. 218.

24. Yeats, *Memoirs*, p. 60.

25. Bornstein says that Yeats's "study of Shelley impelled him toward an Intellectual vision of life in which he rejected the flawed, quotidian world for an ideal vision of Intellectual Beauty. Later he renounced that position. . . . His well-known movement downward upon life rather then upward out of it marks his change from the Shelleyan work of his youth." *Yeats and Shelley*, p. xi.

26. Yeats, "The Galway Plain," in *Ideas of Good and Evil*, p. 336.

27. Lloyd, *Anomalous States*, p. 69.

28. Roth, *The Cult of Violence*, p. 37.

29. Sorel, *Reflections on Violence*, p. 39.

30. Yeats, *Autobiography*, p. 165.

31. Yeats, *A Vision* (1938), p. 263.

32. Yeats, "Michael Robartes: Two Occult Manuscripts," in G. M. Harper,

Yeats and the Occult (London: 1976), p. 221; quoted in Cullingford, *Yeats, Ireland, and Fascism*, p. 122.

33. Yeats, *Autobiography*, p. 118.

34. James Lovic Allen interprets the beast as "a new secular Messiah who will espouse a mass-oriented and anti-individualistic political materialism—a levelling socialism." I agree with Allen that the Beast represents a mass-oriented, anti-individualistic politics, but not a levelling socialism at all—the beast is an emblem of hierarchy in its division into head and thigh. "What Rough Beast?" p. 263.

35. Yeats, "Fighting the Waves," in *Explorations*, p. 373.

36. Yeats, *Autobiography*, p. 117.

37. Ibid., p. 212.

38. Yeats, *A Vision* (1925), pp. 213–14.

39. Dangerfield, *The Strange Death of Liberal England*, p. 145.

40. Sorel, *Reflections on Violence*, pp. 47, 247.

41. Yeats, *Pages from a Diary Written in Nineteen Hundred and Thirty* (Dublin: Cuala Press, 1944), p. 33; quoted in Krimm, *W. B. Yeats and the Emergence of the Irish Free State*, p. 151.

42. Blackmur, *Language as Gesture*, p. 122.

43. For accounts of Yeats's involvement with the Blueshirts, see Cullingford, *Yeats, Ireland, and Fascism*, chapter 11, and Stansfield, *Yeats and Politics in the 1930s*, chapter 2.

CHAPTER 7

1. Eliot, *Notes Towards the Definition of Culture*, p. 26.

2. Several critics have located *The Waste Land* as part of the debates about the breakdown of gender and class hierarchies. See Tate, "The Master-Narrative of Modernism"; West, *Crisis and Criticism*; Cooper, *T. S. Eliot and the Politics of Voice*, esp. chapter 5.

3. Dangerfield, *The Strange Death of Liberal England*, pp. 368, 395.

4. Butler and Sloman, eds., *British Political Facts*, pp. 182–83; the quote about two-thirds of the constituencies is from Kinnear, *The British Voter*, pp. 122–24.

5. Eliot, "Tradition and the Individual Talent," in *Selected Prose*, pp. 39–40.

6. Eliot, "A Commentary," *Criterion* 12, no. 49 (July 1933), p. 644.

7. Sorel, *Reflections on Violence*, pp. 167, 140.

8. Eliot, "The Three Voices of Poetry," in *On Poetry and Poets*, p. 98.

9. Eliot, "Tradition and the Individual Talent," in *Selected Prose*, p. 39.

10. Eliot, "*Ulysses*, Order and Myth" in *Selected Prose*, p. 177.

11. Robert Langbaum says that Eliot "introduces a new method of characterization deriving from the reaction against the nineteenth-century belief in the individual as the one reality you could be sure of." "New Characterization in *The Waste Land*," in Litz, ed., *Eliot in His Time*, p. 11.

12. All in-text citations of line numbers in *The Waste Land* are from Eliot, *Complete Poems and Plays*, pp. 37–55. Other poems and plays from that collection are cited in the text by page number.

13. Le Bon, *The Crowd*, p. 20.

14. Anthony Ludovici, *The False Assumptions of Democracy* (London: Heath Cranton, 1921), p. 212; quoted in Webber, *The Ideology of the British Right*, p. 61.

15. Woolf, *A Room of One's Own*, p. 15.

16. Koestenbaum, "*The Waste Land*," p. 119.

17. Sigmund Freud and Joseph Breuer, *Studies on Hysteria*, p. 96.

18. Koestenbaum, "*The Waste Land*," p. 136.

19. Eliot, *The Waste Land: A Facsimile*, p. 93.

20. Ibid., p. 37.

21. Eliot, "A Commentary," *Criterion* 12, no. 40 (April 1931), p. 485.

22. Bedient, *He Do the Police in Different Voices*, p. 198.

23. Bedient similarly sees Coriolanus as a figure who has to overcome "his natural egotism." Ibid., p. 199.

24. Harold Macmillan, interview in the *London Star*, June 26, 1926; quoted in Beer, *Modern British Politics*, p. 271.

25. Ardolino, *Thomas Kyd's Mystery Play*, pp. 96, 148.

26. Kyd, *The Spanish Tragedy*, 4.4.75, p. 116.

27. Eliot, "The Humanism of Irving Babbitt," in *Essays*, pp. 78–79.

28. Eliot, *Complete Poems and Plays*, pp. 217, 221.

CHAPTER 8

1. Gregor, *Italian Fascism*, p. 71.

2. Ibid., p. 51.

3. For a more detailed history of Italian syndicalism, see ibid., pp. 50–58, 64–96.

4. Arturo Labriola, *Ríforme é Rivoluzione Sociale*, quoted in Tridon, *The New Unionism*, p. 156.

5. Joyce, *Letters*, 2: 188.

6. Ibid., 2: 174.

7. Cole, *Guild Socialism Re-Stated*, p. 95 n.

8. Ibid., p. 33.

9. Laski, *The Foundations of Sovereignty*, p. 27.

10. Manganiello, *Joyce's Politics*, p. 108.

11. Laski, *Authority in the Modern State*; quoted in Zylstra, *From Pluralism to Collectivism*, p. 46.

12. Herr, *Joyce's Anatomy of Culture*, pp. 3–6, 8–9.

13. Karen Lawrence, *The Odyssey of Style in 'Ulysses'*; Riquelme, *Teller and Tale*; Meisel, *The Myth of The Modern*.

14. Foucault, "What Is an Author?" in *The Foucault Reader*, pp. 101–19.

15. Critics who have written on Joyce and popular culture include Kershner, *Joyce, Bakhtin, and Popular Literature*; Wicke, *Advertising Fictions*; and Richards, *The Commodity Culture of Victorian England*. For discussions of Joyce's presentation of gender, see Henke and Unkeles, *Women in Joyce*; Bonnie Kime Scott, *Joyce and Feminism*; MacCabe, *James Joyce and the Revolution of the Word*; and Gilbert and Gubar, *No Man's Land: The Place of the Woman Writer in the Twentieth Century*.

16. Herr, *Joyce's Anatomy of Culture*, p. 153.

17. Chapter and line numbers in parentheses refer to the Gabler edition of Joyce, *Ulysses*.

18. Karen Lawrence, *The Odyssey of Style in 'Ulysses,'* p. 64.

19. See Richards, *The Commodity Culture of Victorian England*, pp. 205–49; Leonard, "Women on the Market"; and Suzette Henke, "Gerty MacDowell: Joyce's Sentimental Heroine," in Henke and Unkeles, eds., *Women in Joyce*, pp. 123–49.

20. Leonard, "Women on the Market," p. 31.

21. Foucault, *History of Sexuality*, 1: 156–57.

22. Sanderson summarizes the change effected by the introduction of research into universities at the end of the nineteenth century: "with research whole new subject areas would arise—history, economics, English literature—which in the end would surpass classics as the tools of general higher education." Sanderson talks about the "pressure on libraries" exerted by the need to keep up with constantly changing texts. He also provides excerpts from central documents in the debate about research, which engaged such eminent Victorians as John Stuart Mill, Cardinal Newman, Matthew Arnold, and T. H. Huxley. *The Universities in the Nineteenth Century*, pp. 7, 5, 115–40.

23. Ralph Rader, "The Logic of *Ulysses*; or, Why Molly Had to Live in Gibraltar," p. 570.

24. Theweleit, *Male Fantasies*, 1: 3.

25. Ibid., 1: 90–99.

26. Ibid., 1: 229–34.

27. Rader, "The Logic of *Ulysses*," p. 571.

CHAPTER 9

1. M. H. Abrams et al., eds., *Norton Anthology of English Literature* (1993), 2: 1687.

2. Woolf, *Three Guineas*, pp. 70, 74.

3. The most detailed account of Woolf's political concerns, Zwerdling, *Virginia Woolf and the Real World*, leaves out *The Waves* except in passing comments; so does the early feminist treatment of Woolf, Marder's *Feminism and Art: A Study of Virginia Woolf*. Jane Marcus, after editing three collections of essays on Woolf and feminism, admitted in 1987 that she had "avoided the subject of Woolf's mysticism, and of *The Waves*," preferring Woolf's "most anti-capitalist, anti-imperialist novels." *Virginia Woolf and the Languages of Patriarchy*, p. 132. In contrast, critics who focus on form usually highlight *The Waves* as the peak of Woolf's aesthetic development: for example, Love, *Worlds in Consciousness*; McCluskey, *Reverberations*; and Naremore, *The World Without a Self*. A few critics such as Proudfit, *The Fact and The Vision*, and Kelley, *The Novels of Virginia Woolf*, have tried to bridge the two camps by calling the conflict between politics and aesthetics, or "fact" and "vision," the central principle on which Woolf built her works. Recent feminist critics have in a sense adopted the aestheticians' view of the novel as "visionary," but have examined how visionary aesthetics become a female way of relating to the world as opposed to the male concern with "facts." See, for example, Transue, *Vir-*

ginia Woolf and the Politics of Style, p. 128; Pearce, *The Politics of Narration*, p. 156–71; and Minow-Pinkney, *Virginia Woolf and the Problem of the Subject*, pp. 152–87.

4. Jane Marcus, "Brittania Rules *The Waves*," in Karen Lawrence, ed., *Decolonizing Tradition*, p. 139.

5. Booker, "Tradition, Authority, and Subjectivity," p. 36.

6. Visualizing the novel as diagrammed in this illustration is especially useful for teaching it.

7. Laski, *The Foundations of Sovereignty*, pp. 157, 156.

8. Both ellipses in this passage are Woolf's.

9. Woolf, *Three Guineas*, pp. 69–72.

10. Leslie Stephen, *The Life of Sir James Fitzjames Stephen* (London, 1856); quoted in Collini, *Public Moralities*, pp. 195–96. Stephen's credo of manliness is discussed in detail in chapter 5.

11. Booker, "Tradition, Authority, and Subjectivity," p. 38.

12. Althusser, "Ideology and Ideological State Apparatuses," in *Lenin and Philosophy*, pp. 174, 178.

13. Ibid., p. 182.

14. Woolf, *Between the Acts*, pp. 161–62.

15. Miller, *The Novel and the Police*, p. 25.

16. Woolf, *Between the Acts*, p. 172.

17. Jane Marcus, "Brittania Rules *The Waves*," in Karen Lawrence, ed., *Decolonizing Tradition*, p. 155.

18. Eagleton summarizes and critiques theories of ideology as the "naturalizing of power." *Ideology: An Introduction*, pp. 58–61, 199–200.

19. Leonard Woolf, *Imperialism and Civilization*, pp. 115–16.

20. Ibid.

21. Tawney, *The Acquisitive Society*, pp. 48–49.

22. Althusser, "Ideology and Ideological State Apparatuses," in *Lenin and Philosophy*, p. 172.

23. Philip Snowden, *An Autobiography*, vol. 1 (London: I. Nicholson and Watson, 1934); quoted in Beer, *Modern British Politics*, p. 153.

24. Beer, *Modern British Politics*, p. 154.

25. The consequence of the unifying effect of school is described by Bernard at the end of the novel: "We exist not only separately but in undifferentiated blobs of matter. With one scoop a whole brakeful of boys up and goes cricketing, footballing. An army marches across Europe. We assemble in parks and halls and sedulously oppose any renegade (Neville, Louis, Rhoda) who sets up a separate existence" (p. 347). The games of school create the unified groups that go to war and oppose domestic rebellion.

EPILOGUE

1. Woolf, *Between the Acts*, p. 188.

2. Yeats, *Poems*, p. 236.

3. See, for example, Wicke, *Advertising Fictions*; Moretti, *Signs Taken for Wonders*; and Kershner, *Joyce, Bakhtin, and Popular Literature*.

Selected Bibliography

Abrams, M. H., et al., eds. *The Norton Anthology of English Literature*. 1st ed. 2 vols. New York: W. W. Norton, 1962.
———. *The Norton Anthology of English Literature*. 6th ed. 2 vols. New York: W. W. Norton, 1993.

Abrams, Philip. *The Origins of British Sociology: 1834–1914: An Essay with Selected Papers*. Chicago: University of Chicago Press, 1968.

Ackroyd, Peter. *T. S. Eliot: A Life*. New York: Simon and Schuster, 1984.

Adams, Hazard. *The Book of Yeats's Poems*. Tallahassee: Florida State Press, 1990.

Adams, Robert Martin. *Surface and Symbol: The Consistency of James Joyce's Ulysses*. New York: Oxford University Press, 1962.

Adorno, Theodor. "Freudian Theory and the Pattern of Fascist Propaganda." In Andreio Arato and Eike Gebhardt, eds., *The Essential Frankfurt Reader*. New York: Continuum, 1985, pp. 118–137.

Alexander, Jean. *The Venture of Form in the Novels of Virginia Woolf*. Port Washington, N.Y.: Kennikat Press, 1974.

Allen, James Lovic. "What Rough Beast: Yeats's 'The Second Coming' and *A Vision*." *REAL: The Yearbook of Research in English and American Literature* 3 (1985): 223–63.

Althusser, Louis. *Lenin and Philosophy and Other Essays*. Trans. Ben Brewster. New York: Monthly Review Press, 1971.

Annan, Noel Gilroy. *Leslie Stephen: The Godless Victorian*. London: Weidenfeld & Nicolson, 1984.

Antongini, Tommaso. *D'Annunzio*. Boston: Little Brown, 1938.

Arblaster, Anthony. *The Rise and Decline of Western Liberalism*. Oxford: Basil Blackwell, 1984.

Ardolino, Frank R. *Thomas Kyd's Mystery Play: Myth and Ritual in 'The Spanish Tragedy.'* New York: Peter Lang, 1985.

Ashcroft, Bill, Gareth Griff, and Helen Tiffin. *The Empire Writes Back: Theory and Practice in Post-Colonial Literatures.* New York: Routledge, 1989.

Atkinson, William. "Africa: A Common Topos in Lawrence and Eliot." *Twentieth Century Literature* 37, no. 1 (Spring 1991): 22–37.

Attridge, Derek, ed. *The Cambridge Companion to James Joyce.* Cambridge: Cambridge University Press, 1990.

Auden, W. H. Introduction to *Victorian and Edwardian Poets, Tennyson to Yeats.* Vol. 5 of *Poets of the English Language.* Ed. W. H. Auden and Norman Holmes Pearson. London: Eyre and Spottiswoode, 1952.

Babbitt, Irving. *On Being Creative and Other Essays.* Boston: Houghton Mifflin, 1932.

Ball, Alan R. *British Political Parties.* 2nd ed. London: Macmillan, 1987.

Barnes, Djuna. *Nightwood.* New York: New Directions, 1961.

Bazin, Nancy Topping. *Virginia Woolf and the Androgynous Vision.* New Brunswick, N.J.: Rutgers University Press, 1973.

Bedient, Calvin. *He Do the Police in Different Voices: 'The Waste Land' and Its Protagonist.* Chicago: University of Chicago Press, 1986.

Beer, Samuel H. *Modern British Politics: Parties and Pressure Groups in the Collectivist Age.* New York: W. W. Norton, 1982.

Beja, Morris. *Joyce, the Artist Manqué, and Indeterminacy: A Lecture and an Essay.* Gerrards Cross, Eng.: Colin Smythe, 1989.

Bell, Quentin. *Virginia Woolf: A Biography.* New York: Harcourt Brace Jovanovich, 1972.

Benstock, Bernard. *Joyce-Again's Wake: An Analysis of 'Finnegans Wake.'* Seattle: University of Washington Press, 1965.

———, ed. *Critical Essays on Joyce's 'Ulysses.'* Boston: G. K. Hall, 1985.

———, ed. *James Joyce: The Augmented Ninth.* Proceedings of the Ninth International James Joyce Symposium. Syracuse, N.Y.: Syracuse University Press, 1988.

Bentley, Arthur F. *The Process of Government: A Study of Social Pressures.* 1908. Reprint, Evanston: The Principia Press of Illinois, 1935.

Berman, Russell. *Modern Culture and Critical Theory: Art, Politics, and the Legacy of the Frankfurt School.* Madison: University of Wisconsin Press, 1989.

Bernstein, Michael André. *The Tale of the Tribe: Ezra Pound and the Modern Verse Epic.* Princeton, N.J.: Princeton University Press, 1980.

Bersani, Leo. *The Culture of Redemption.* Cambridge, Mass.: Harvard University Press, 1990.

Blackmur, R. P. *Language as Gesture: Essays in Poetry.* London: George Allen and Unwin, 1954.

Bloom, Harold. *Yeats.* New York: Oxford University Press, 1970.

Bollettieri, Rosa Maria Bosinelli. "The Importance of Trieste in Joyce's Work, with Reference to His Knowledge of Pscyhoanalysis." *James Joyce Quarterly* 7, no. 3 (Spring 1970): 177–85.

Booker, M. Keith. "Tradition, Authority, and Subjectivity: Narrative Constitution of the Self in *The Waves.*" *Literature Interpretation Theory* 3, no. 1 (1991): 33–55.

Boone, Joseph Allen. "A New Approach to Bloom as 'Womanly Man': The Mixed Middling's Progress in *Ulysses.*" *James Joyce Quarterly* 20, no. 1 (Fall 1982): 67–86.

Booth, William. *In Darkest England and the Way Out.* London: International Headquarters of the Salvation Army, 1890.

Bornstein, George. *Yeats and Shelley.* Chicago: University of Chicago Press, 1970.

Bowra, C. M. *Poetry and Politics, 1900–1960.* Cambridge; Cambridge University Press, 1966.

Bradley, Francis Herbert. *Ethical Studies.* Glasgow: Oxford University Press, 1876.

Bramsback, Birgit, and Martin Croghan, eds. *Anglo-Irish and Irish Literature: Aspects of Language and Culture.* Proceedings of the Ninth International Congress of the International Association for the Study of Anglo-Irish Literature, vol. 1. Uppsala: S. Academiae Upsaliensis, 1988.

Brantlinger, Patrick. "Imperial Gothic: Atavism and the Occult in the British Adventure Novel, 1880–1914." *English Literature in Transition, 1880–1920* 28, no. 3 (1985): 243–52.

Briggs, Asa. *Victorian People.* Chicago: University of Chicago Press, 1955.

Brown, Dennis. *The Modernist Self in Twentieth-Century English Literature: A Study in Self-Fragmentation.* London: Macmillan, 1989.

Bruce, Maurice. *The Coming of the Welfare State.* London: William Clowes & Sons, 1961.

Budgen, Frank. *James Joyce and the Making of Ulysses.* Bloomington: Indiana University Press, 1960.

Bush, Ronald, ed. *T. S. Eliot: The Modernist in History.* Cambridge: Cambridge University Press, 1991.

Butler, David, and Anne Sloman, eds. *British Political Facts, 1900–1975.* London: Macmillan, 1975.

Byrd, Thomas L. *The Early Poetry of W. B. Yeats: The Poetic Quest.* Port Washington, N.Y.: Kennikat Press, 1978.

Calverton, V. F. "T. S. Eliot: Inverted Marxism." *Modern Monthly,* July 1934, pp. 371–72.

Canary, Robert H. *T. S. Eliot: The Poet and His Critics.* Chicago: American Library Association, 1982.

Chace, William M. *The Political Identities of Ezra Pound and T. S. Eliot.* Stanford, Calif.: Stanford University Press, 1973.

Chadwick, Joseph. "Violence in Yeats's Later Politics and Poetry." *ELH* 55, no. 4 (Winter 1988): 869–93.

Chatterjee, Partha, *The Nation and Its Fragments.* Princeton, N.J.: Princeton University Press, 1993.

Cixous, Hélène. *The Exile of James Joyce.* Trans. Sally A. J. Purcell. New York: David Lewis, 1972.

Clarke, Graham, ed. *T. S. Eliot: Critical Assessments.* Vol. 2. London: Christopher Helm, 1990.

Colby, Robert A. *Fiction with a Purpose: Major and Minor Nineteenth-Century Novels.* Bloomington: Indiana University Press, 1968.

Cole, G. D. H. *Guild Socialism Re-Stated.* London: Leonard Parsons, 1920.

Collini, Stefan. *Liberalism and Sociology: L. T. Hobhouse and Political Argument in England, 1880–1914.* Cambridge: Cambridge University Press, 1979.

———. *Public Moralists: Political Thought and Intellectual Life in Britain, 1850–1930.* Oxford: Clarendon Press, 1991.

Connolly, Thomas E. *The Personal Library of James Joyce: A Descriptive Bibliography.* Buffalo, N.Y.: University of Buffalo Press, 1955.

Cooper, John Xiros. *T. S. Eliot and the Politics of Voice: The Argument of 'The Waste Land.'* Ann Arbor, Mich.: UMI Research Press, 1987.

Costanzo, William V. "Joyce and Eisenstein: Literary Reflections of the Reel World." *The Journal of Modern Literature* 11, no. 1 (March 1984): 175–80.

Craig, Cairns. *Yeats, Eliot, Pound, and the Politics of Poetry.* Pittsburgh: University of Pittsburgh Press, 1982.

Cullingford, Elizabeth. "Venus or Mrs. Pankhurst: Yeats's Love Poetry and the Culture of Suffrage." *Yeats: An Annual of Critical and Textual Studies* 9 (1991): 11–29.

———. *Yeats, Ireland, and Fascism.* New York: New York University Press, 1981.

Dangerfield, George. *The Strange Death of Liberal England, 1910–1914.* Reprint, New York: Capricorn, 1961.

D'Annunzio, Gabriele. *The Flame of Life.* Trans. Kassandra Vivaria. New York: Howard Fertig, 1990.

Davies, Gill. "Foreign Bodies: Images of the London Working Class at the End of the Nineteenth Century." *Literature and History* 14, no. 1 (Spring 1988): 64–80.

Davies, Margaret Lleweln. *Life as We Have Known It: By Co-operative Working Women.* London: Virago, 1977. Introduction by Virginia Woolf.

Deane, Seamus. *Celtic Revivals: Essays in Modern Irish Literature, 1880–1980.* London: Faber and Faber, 1985.

DeKoven, Marianne. *Rich and Strange.* Princeton, N.J.: Princeton University Press, 1992.

DeSalvo, Louise. Introduction to *Melymbrosia,* by Virginia Woolf. New York: The New York Public Library, 1982.

———. *Virginia Woolf: The Impact of Childhood Sexual Abuse on Her Life and Work.* New York: Ballantine, 1989.

Dicey, A. V. *Lectures on the Relation Between Law and Public Opinion in England During the Nineteenth Century.* London: Macmillan, 1914.

Dinnerstein, Leonard, Roger L. Nichols, and David M. Reimers. *Natives and Strangers: Blacks, Indians, and Immigrants in America.* 2nd. ed. New York: Oxford University Press, 1990.

Donoghue, Denis. *William Butler Yeats.* London: Faber and Faber, 1971.

Donzelot, Jacques. *The Policing of Families.* New York: Pantheon, 1979.

DuPlessis, Rachel Blau. *Writing Beyond the Ending: Narrative Strategies of Twentieth-Century Women Writers.* Bloomington: Indiana University Press, 1985.

Eagleton, Terry. *Exiles and Emigrés: Studies in Modern Literature*. New York: Schocken, 1970.

——. *Ideology: An Introduction*. London: Verso, 1991.

Eagleton, Terry, Fredric Jameson, and Edward Said. *Nationalism, Colonialism, and Literature*. Minneapolis: University of Minneapolis Press, 1990.

Easthope, Anthony. "Why Most Contemporary Poetry Is So Bad and How Post-Structuralism May be Able to Help." *PN Review 48*, 12, no. 4 (November–December 1985): 36–38.

Eco, Umberto. *The Aesthetics of Chaosmos: The Middle Ages of James Joyce*. Trans. Ellen Esrock. Tulsa, Okla.: University of Tulsa Press, 1982.

Eder, Doris L. "Louis Unmasked: T. S. Eliot in *The Waves*." *Virginia Woolf Quarterly* 2, nos. 1–2 (Winter, Spring 1975): 13–27.

Eliot, T. S. *After Strange Gods: A Primer of Modern Heresy*. London: Faber and Faber, 1934.

——. *The Complete Poems and Plays, 1909–1950*. New York: Harcourt, Brace and World, 1971.

——. *Essays Ancient and Modern*. New York: Harcourt Brace, 1936.

——. *The Idea of A Christian Society*. New York: Harcourt Brace, 1940.

——. *The Letters of T. S. Eliot*. Ed. Valerie Eliot. New York: Harcourt Brace Jovanovich, 1988.

——. *Notes Towards the Definition of Culture*. London: Faber and Faber, 1948.

——. *On Poetry and Poets*. London: Faber and Faber, 1957.

——. *The Sacred Wood: Essays on Poetry and Criticism*. New York: Barnes & Noble, 1928.

——. *Selected Prose*. Ed. Frank Kermode. Harcourt Brace Jovanovich, 1975.

——. *The Waste Land: A Facsimile and Transcript of the Original Drafts*. Ed. Valerie Eliot. New York: Harcourt Brace Jovanovich, 1971.

Elgar, Frank, and Robert Maillard. *Picasso*. Trans. Frank Scarfe. New York: Praeger, 1960.

Ellman, Richard. *The Consciousness of Joyce*. New York: Oxford University Press, 1977.

——. *James Joyce*. New York: Oxford University Press, 1982.

Engelberg, Edward. *The Vast Design: Patterns in W. B. Yeats's Aesthetic*. 2nd ed. Washington, D.C.: Catholic University of America Press, 1988.

Estey, William. *Revolutionary Syndicalism*. London: Leonard Parsons, 1910.

Evans, Eric J. *Social Policy 1830–1914: Individualism, Collectivism and the Origins of the Welfare State*. London: Routledge & Kegan Paul, 1978.

Fanon, Frantz. *The Wretched of the Earth*. Trans. Constance Farrington. New York: Grove Press, 1965.

Fleishman, Avrom. *Virginia Woolf: A Critical Reading*. Baltimore: Johns Hopkins University Press, 1975.

Flint, Kate. "Virginia Woolf and the General Strike." *Essays in Criticism: A Quarterly Journal of Literary Criticism* 36, no. 4 (October 1986): 319–34.

Foucault, Michel. *The Foucault Reader*. Ed. Paul Rabinow. New York: Pantheon, 1984.

——. *The History of Sexuality*. Vol. 1. *An Introduction*. Trans. Robert Hurley. New York: Vintage, 1980.

Freedman, Ralph, ed. *Virginia Woolf: Revaluation and Continuity.* Berkeley: University of California Press, 1980.

Freud, Sigmund. *Civilization and Its Discontents.* Trans. James Strachey. New York: W. W. Norton, 1961.

———. *Group Psychology and the Analysis of the Ego.* Trans. James Strachey. New York: Bantam, 1960.

———. *The Psychopathology of Everyday Life.* Trans. Alan Tyson. Ed. James Strachey. New York: W. W. Norton, 1965.

———. *Three Essays on the Theory of Sexuality.* Trans. James Strachey. New York: Avon, 1961.

Freud, Sigmund, and Joseph Breuer. *Studies on Hysteria.* Trans. James Strachey. New York: Basic Books, 1957.

Freyer, Grattan. *W. B. Yeats and the Anti-Democratic Tradition.* Dublin: Gill and Macmillan, 1981.

Friedman, Ellen G., and Miriam Fuchs, eds. *Breaking the Sequence: Women's Experimental Fiction.* Princeton, N.J.: Princeton University Press, 1989.

Fry, Roger. *Vision and Design.* Harmondsworth: Penguin, 1940.

Gallagher, Catherine. *The Industrial Reformation of English Fiction: Social Discourse and Narrative Form, 1832–1867.* Chicago: University of Chicago Press, 1985.

Gelpi, Albert. *A Coherent Splendor: The American Poetic Renaissance, 1910–1950.* Cambridge: Cambridge University Press, 1987.

Gifford, Don. *Joyce Annotated.* Berkeley: University of California Press, 1982.

———. *Notes For Joyce: An Annotation of James Joyce's 'Ulysses.'* New York: E. P. Dutton, 1974.

Gilbert, Bentley B. *The Evolution of National Insurance in Great Britain: The Origins of the Welfare State.* London: Michael Joseph, 1966.

Gilbert, Sandra M., and Susan Gubar. *No Man's Land: The Place of the Woman Writer in the Twentieth Century.* 3 vols. New Haven: Yale University Press, 1988–94.

Gilbert, Stuart. *James Joyce's 'Ulysses': A Study.* London: Faber and Faber, 1952.

Gordon, Lyndall. *Eliot's Early Years.* Oxford: Oxford University Press, 1977.

———. *Eliot's New Life.* New York: Farrar, Straus & Giroux, 1988.

Greenberg, Elaine K., and Laura Moss Gottlieb, eds. *Virginia Woolf: Centennial Essays.* Troy, N.Y.: Whitson, 1983.

Gregor, A. James. *Italian Fascism and Developmental Dictatorship.* Princeton, N.J.: Princeton University Press, 1979.

Guerard, Albert. Introduction to *Heart of Darkness and The Secret Sharer,* by Joseph Conrad. New York: New American Library, 1983.

Hamilton, Alastair. *The Appeal of Fascism: A Study of Intellectuals and Fascism, 1919–1945.* New York: Macmillan, 1971.

Hannah, Leslie. *The Rise of the Corporate Economy.* London: Methuen, 1976.

Harrison, John. *The Reactionaries: A Study of the Anti-Democratic Intelligentsia.* New York: Schocken, 1967.

Hart, Clive, and David Hayman, eds. *James Joyce's 'Ulysses': Critical Essays.* Berkeley: University of California Press, 1974.

Hassett, Joseph M. *Yeats and the Poetics of Hate.* New York: St. Martin's Press, 1986.

Hayes, Carlton J. H. *The Historical Evolution of Modern Nationalism*. New York: Russell and Russell, 1968.

Hearnshaw, L. S. *A Short History of British Psychology*. New York: Barnes & Noble, 1964.

Henke, Suzette. *James Joyce and the Politics of Desire*. New York: Routledge, 1990.

Henke, Suzette, and Elaine Unkeles, eds. *Women in Joyce*. Chicago: University of Illinois Press, 1982.

Herr, Cheryl. *Joyce's Anatomy of Culture*. Urbana: University of Illinois Press, 1986.

Higham, John. *Strangers in the Land: Patterns of American Nativism, 1860–1925*. New Brunswick, N.J.: Rutgers University Press, 1955.

Hobson, J. A. *The Crisis of Liberalism: New Issues of Democracy*. Ed. P. F. Clarke. Hassocks: Harvester, 1979.

Howarth, Herbert. *Notes on Some Figures Behind T. S. Eliot*. Boston: Houghton Mifflin, 1964.

Hughes, H. Stuart. *Consciousness and Society: The Reorientation of European Social Thought 1890–1930*. New York: Vintage, 1977.

Humphreys, Susan L. "Ferrero, Etc.: James Joyce's Debt to Guglielmo Ferrero." *James Joyce Quarterly* 16, no. 3 (Spring 1979): 239–52.

Hussey, Mark, ed. *Virginia Woolf and War: Fiction, Reality, and Myth*. Syracuse, N.Y.: Syracuse University Press, 1991.

Huyssen, Andreas. *After the Great Divide: Modernism, Mass Culture, Postmodernism*. Bloomington: Indiana University Press, 1987.

James, William. *The Principles of Psychology*, vol. 2. New York: Henry Holt, 1890.

Jameson, Fredric. *Fables of Aggression: Wyndham Lewis, the Modernist as Fascist*. Berkeley: University of California Press, 1979.

Janson, H. W., with Dora Jane Janson. *History of Art*. Englewood Cliffs, N.J.: Prentice-Hall, 1968.

Jardine, Alice. *Gynesis: Configurations of Woman and Modernity*. Ithaca, N.Y.: Cornell University Press, 1985.

Jeffares, A. Norman. *W. B. Yeats*. New York: Farrar, Straus, Giroux, 1989.

Jeffares, A. Norman, and K. G. W. Cross, eds. *In Excited Reverie: A Centenary Tribute to William Butler Yeats, 1865–1939*. New York: Macmillan, 1965.

Jones, Greta. *Social Darwinism and English Thought: The Interaction Between Biological and Social Theory*. Atlantic Highlands, N.J.: Humanities Press, 1980.

Joyce, James. *The Critical Writings of James Joyce*. Ed. Ellsworth Mason and Richard Ellman. New York: Viking Press, 1964.

———. *Dubliners*. Harmondsworth, Middlesex: Penguin, 1976.

———. *Exiles*. Norfolk, Conn.: New Classics Series, 1918.

———. *Finnegans Wake*. Harmondsworth: Penguin, 1976.

———. *Letters of James Joyce*. 3 vols. Ed. Stuart Gilbert. New York: Viking, 1957.

———. *A Portrait of the Artist as a Young Man*. New York: Viking, 1970.

———. *Stephen Hero*. Ed. John J. Slocum and Herbert Cahoon. New York: New Directions, 1963.

————. *Ulysses.* Ed. Hans Walter Gabler. New York: Random House, 1986.

Joyce, Stanislaus, and Richard Ellman. *My Brother's Keeper.* London: Faber and Faber, 1982.

Jussawalla, Feroza, and Reed Way Dasenbrock. *Interviews with Writers of the Post-Colonial World.* Jackson: University of Mississippi Press, 1992.

Kearns, Cleo McNelly. *T. S. Eliot and the Indic Traditions: A Study in Poetry of Belief.* Cambridge: Cambridge University Press, 1987.

Keating, Peter. *Into Unknown England: Selections from the Social Explorers, 1866–1913.* Manchester, Eng.: Manchester University Press, 1971.

Kelley, Alice Van Buren. *The Novels of Virginia Woolf: Fact and Vision.* Chicago: University of Chicago Press, 1973.

Kenner, Hugh. *Joyce's Voices.* Berkeley: University of California Press, 1978.

————. *The Pound Era.* London: Faber and Faber, 1972.

————. *Ulysses.* Boston: George Allen & Unwin, 1980.

Kermode, Frank. *The Sense of Ending: Studies in the Theory of Fiction.* New York: Oxford University Press, 1967.

Kershner, R. Brandon. "Genius, Degeneration, and the Panopticon." In James Joyce, *A Portrait of the Artist as a Young Man.* Ed. R. Brandon Kershner. Boston: St. Martin's Press, 1993.

————. *Joyce, Bakhtin, and Popular Literature: Chronicles of Disorder.* Chapel Hill: University of North Carolina Press, 1989.

Kiely, Robert. *Beyond Egotism: The Fiction of James Joyce, Virginia Woolf and D. H. Lawrence.* Cambridge, Mass.: Harvard University Press, 1980.

Kinnear, Michael. *The British Voter, An Atlas and Survey Since 1885.* Ithaca, N.Y.: Cornell University Press, 1968.

Klopp, Charles. *Gabriele D'Annunzio.* Boston: Twayne, 1988.

Knapp, James F. *Literary Modernism and the Transformation of Work.* Evanston, Ill.: Northwestern University Press, 1988.

Koestenbaum, Wayne. "*The Waste Land*: T. S. Eliot's and Ezra Pound's Collaboration on Hysteria." *Twentieth Century Literature* 34, no. 1 (Summer 1988): 113–19.

Kojecky, Roger. *T. S. Eliot's Social Criticism.* London: Faber and Faber, 1971.

Komesu, Okifumi, and Masaru Sekine, eds. *Irish Writers and Politics.* Gerrards Cross, Eng.: Colin Smythe, 1990.

Kraditor, Aileen S. *Ideas of the Woman Suffrage Movement, 1890–1920.* New York: Columbia University Press, 1965.

Krafft-Ebbing, Richard Von. *Psychopathia Sexualis.* New York: Pioneer Publications, 1946.

Krimm, Bernard G. *W. B. Yeats and the Emergence of the Irish Free State, 1918–1939: Living in the Explosion.* Troy, N.Y.: Whitson, 1981.

Kyd, Thomas. *The Spanish Tragedy.* Ed. J. R. Mulroyne. New York: W. W. Norton, 1989.

Lambert, Elizabeth G. " 'And Darwin says they are nearer the cow': Evolutionary Discourse in *Melymbrosia* and *The Voyage Out.*" *Twentieth Century Literature* 37, no. 1 (Spring 1991): 1–21.

Langbaum, Robert Woodrow. *The Mysteries of Identity: A Theme in Modern Literature.* New York: Oxford University Press, 1977.

Laski, Harold J. *Authority in the Modern State*. New Haven: Yale University Press, 1919.

———. *The Foundations of Sovereignty and Other Essays*. New York: Harcourt, Brace, 1921.

———. *A Grammar of Politics*. London: George Allen & Unwin, 1925.

Lawrence, D. H. *Women in Love*. *The Penguin Great Novels of D. H. Lawrence*. Harmondsworth: Penguin, 1984, pp. 705–1076.

Lawrence, Karen. *The Odyssey of Style in 'Ulysses.'* Princeton, N.J.: Princeton University Press, 1981.

———, ed. *Decolonizing Tradition: New Views of Twentieth-Century "British" Literary Canons*. Urbana: University of Illinois Press, 1992.

Lears, T. Jackson. *No Place of Grace: Antimodernism and the Transformation of American Culture, 1880–1920*. New York: Pantheon, 1981.

Le Bon, Gustave. *The Crowd: A Study of the Popular Mind*. 2nd ed. New York: Macmillan, 1897.

Leonard, Garry. "Women on the Market: Commodity Culture, 'Femininity,' and 'Those Lovely Seaside Girls' in Joyce's *Ulysses*." *Joyce Studies Annual* 2 (1991): 27–68.

Levenson, Michael. *Modernism and the Fate of Individuality: Character and Novel Form from Conrad to Woolf*. Cambridge: Cambridge University Press, 1991.

Lewis, Wyndham. *Time and Western Man*. London: Chatto & Windus, 1927.

Litz, A. Walton, ed. *Eliot in His Time: Essays on the Occasion of the Fiftieth Anniversary of 'The Waste Land.'* Princeton, N.J.: Princeton University Press, 1973.

Lloyd, David. *Anomalous States: Irish Writing and the Post-Colonial Moment*. Durham, N.C.: Duke University Press, 1993.

Lobner, Corinna del Greco. *James Joyce's Italian Connection: The Poetics of the Word*. Iowa City: University of Iowa Press, 1989.

Lodge, Henry Cabot. "Lynch Law and Unrestricted Immigration." *North American Review* 152, no. 1 (May 1891), p. 605.

Love, Jean O. *Virginia Woolf: Sources of Madness and Art*. Berkeley: University of California Press, 1977.

———. *Worlds in Consciousness: Mythopoetic Thought in The Novels of Virginia Woolf*. Berkeley: University of California Press, 1970.

Lowi, Theodore J. *The End of Liberalism: The Second Republic of the United States*. New York: W. W. Norton, 1979.

Lucente, Gregory L. "D'Annunzio's *Il Fuoco* and Joyce's *Portrait of the Artist*: From Allegory to Irony." *Italica* 57, no. 1 (Spring, 1980): 19–33.

Lukács, Georg. *The Meaning of Contemporary Realism*. Atlantic Highlands, N.J.: Humanities Press, 1980.

Lukes, Steven. *Individualism*. Basil Blackwell, 1973.

MacCabe, Colin. *James Joyce and the Revolution of the Word*. London: Macmillan, 1978.

Magid, Henry Meye. *English Political Pluralism: The Problem of Freedom and Organization*. New York: Columbia University Press, 1941.

Maier, Charles. *Recasting Bourgeois Europe: Stabilization in France, Germany, and Italy in the Decade After World War I.* Princeton, N.J.: Princeton University Press, 1975.

Manganiello, Dominic. *Joyce's Politics.* London: Routledge & Kegan Paul, 1980.

Marcus, Jane. "No More Horses: Woolf on Art and Propaganda." *Women's Studies* 4, nos. 2–3 (1977): 265–90.

——. *Virginia Woolf and the Languages of Patriarchy.* Bloomington: Indiana University Press, 1987.

——, ed. *Virginia Woolf: A Feminist Slant.* Lincoln: University of Nebraska Press, 1985.

Marcus, Phillip L. *Yeats and Artistic Power.* New York: Macmillan, 1992.

——. *Yeats and the Beginning of the Irish Renaissance.* Syracuse, N.Y.: Syracuse University Press, 1987.

Marder, Herbert. *Feminism and Art: A Study of Virginia Woolf.* Chicago: University of Chicago Press, 1968.

Margolis, John D. *T. S. Eliot's Intellectual Development: 1922– 1939.* Chicago: University of Chicago Press, 1972.

Marks, Elaine, and Isabelle de Courtivron, eds. *New French Feminisms.* Amherst: University of Massachusetts Press, 1980.

Marx, Karl, and Friedrich Engels. *On Britain.* Moscow: Foreign Languages Publishing House, 1962.

Masterman, C. F. G. *From the Abyss: Of Its Inhabitants by One of Them.* London: R. Brimley Johnson, 1902.

Mayo, Elton. *The Social Problems of an Industrial Civilization.* London: Routledge & Kegan Paul, 1949.

McCluskey, Kathleen. *Reverberations: Sound and Structure in the Novels of Virginia Woolf.* Ann Arbor: University of Michigan Press, 1983.

McCormack, W. J., and Alistair Stead, eds. *James Joyce and Modern Literature.* London: Routledge & Kegan Paul, 1982.

McDougall, William. *The Group Mind: A Sketch of the Principles of Collective Psychology, with Some Attempt to Apply Them to the Interpretation of National Life and Character.* London: G. P. Putnam's Sons, 1920.

——. *An Introduction to Social Psychology.* Boston: John W. Luce, 1918.

McHugh, Roland. *Annotations to Finnegans Wake.* Baltimore: Johns Hopkins University Press, 1980.

Meisel, Perry. *The Myth of The Modern.* New Haven: Yale University Press, 1989.

Mill, John Stuart. *Mill on Bentham and Coleridge.* Ed. F. R. Leavis. London: Chatto & Windus, 1950.

——. *Utilitarianism, On Liberty, and Considerations on Representative Government.* Ed. H. B. Acton. London: J. M. Dent & Sons, 1971.

Miller, D. A. *The Novel and the Police.* Berkeley: University of California Press, 1988.

Miller, James E., Jr. *T. S. Eliot's Personal Waste Land: Exorcism of the Demons.* University Park: Pennsylvania State University Press, 1978.

Milne, A. J. M. *The Social Philosophy of English Idealism.* London: George Allen & Unwin, 1962.

Minow-Pinkney, Makiko. *Virginia Woolf and the Problem of the Subject: Femi-*

nine Writing in the Major Novels. New Brunswick, N.J.: Rutgers University Press, 1987.

Moore, Benjamin. *The Dawn of the Health Age*. Edinburgh: Ballantyne Press, 1911.

Moretti, Franco. *Signs Taken for Wonders: Essays in the Sociology of Literary Forms*. Trans. Susan Fischer, David Forgacs, and David Miller. London: Verso, 1988.

——. *The Way of the World: The Bildungsroman in European Culture*. London: Verso, 1987.

Morris, William. *News From Nowhere*. London: Routledge & Kegan Paul, 1970.

Murphy, Frank Hughes. *Yeats's Early Poetry: The Quest for Reconciliation*. Baton Rouge: Louisiana State University Press, 1975.

Naremore, James. *The World Without a Self: Virginia Woolf and the Novel*. New Haven: Yale University Press, 1973.

Nelson, Cary, and Lawrence Grossberg, eds. *Marxism and the Interpretation of Culture*. Urbana: University of Illinois Press, 1988.

Newman, Robert P., and Weldon Thornton, eds. *Joyce's 'Ulysses': The Larger Perspective*. Newark: University of Delaware Press, 1987.

North, Michael. *The Political Aesthetic of Yeats, Eliot and Pound*. Cambridge: Cambridge University Press, 1991.

O'Connor, Emmet. *Syndicalism in Ireland, 1917–1923*. Cork: Cork University Press, 1989.

Parkman, Frances. "The Failure of Universal Suffrage." *North American Review* 127 (July–August 1878): 1–20.

Pearce, Richard. *The Politics of Narration*. New Brunswick, N.J.: Rutgers University Press, 1991.

Pecora, Vincent P. *Self and Form in Modern Narrative*. Baltimore: Johns Hopkins University Press, 1989.

Perkin, Harold. *The Rise of Professional Society: England Since 1880*. New York: Routledge & Kegan Paul, 1989.

Perloff, Marjorie. *The Futurist Moment: Avant-Garde, Avant Guerre, and the Language of Rupture*. Chicago: University of Chicago Press, 1986.

Pierson, Stanley. *Marxism and the Origins of British Socialism: The Struggle for a New Consciousness*. Ithaca, N.Y.: Cornell University Press, 1973.

Pinkney, Tony. *Women in the Poetry of T. S. Eliot*. London: Macmillan, 1984.

Pitt, Rosemary. "The Exploration of Self in Conrad's *Heart of Darkness* and Woolf's *The Voyage Out*." *Conradiana* 10, no. 2 (1978): 141–59.

Poirier, Richard. "The Difficulties of Modernism and the Modernism of Difficulty." *Humanities in Society* 1, no. 4 (Fall 1978): 270–82.

Polhemus, Robert M. *Erotic Faith: Being in Love From Jane Austen to D. H. Lawrence*. Chicago: University of Chicago Press, 1990.

Poliakov, Leon. *The Aryan Myth: A History of Racist and Nationalist Ideas in Europe*. Trans. Edmund Howard. Sussex, Eng.: Sussex University Press, 1974.

Poole, Roger. *The Unknown Virginia Woolf*. Cambridge: Cambridge University Press, 1978.

Pound, Ezra. *Personae: The Shorter Poems of Ezra Pound*. Revised by Lea Baechler and A. Walton Litz. New York: New Directions, 1990.

Prince, Morton. *The Dissociation of a Personality: A Biographical Study in Abnormal Psychology.* New York: Meridian, 1957.

——. *Psychotherapy and Multiple Personality: Selected Essays.* Ed. Nathan G. Hale, Jr. Cambridge, Mass.: Harvard University Press, 1975.

Proudfit, Sharon Louise Wood. *The Fact and The Vision: Virginia Woolf's and Roger Fry's Post-Impressionist Aesthetic.* Ann Arbor, Mich.: Xerox University Microfilms, 1975.

Rader, Ralph W. "The Logic of *Ulysses*; or Why Molly Had to Live in Gibraltar." *Critical Inquiry* 10, no. 4 (June 1984): 567–78.

Reynolds, Mary T. "Joyce's Villanelle and D'Annunzio's Sonnet Sequence." *The Journal of Modern Literature* 5, no. 1 (February 1976): 19–45.

Rhodes, Anthony. *D'Annunzio: The Poet as Superman.* New York: McDowell Obolensky, 1960.

Richards, Thomas. *The Commodity Culture of Victorian England: Advertising and Spectacle, 1851–1914.* Stanford, Calif.: Stanford University Press, 1990.

Richter, Harvena. *Virginia Woolf: The Inward Voyage.* Princeton, N.J.: Princeton University Press, 1970.

Richter, Melvin. *The Politics of Conscience: T. H. Green and His Age.* Cambridge, Mass.: Harvard University Press, 1964.

Riquelme, John Paul. *Teller and Tale in Joyce's Fiction.* Baltimore: Johns Hopkins University Press, 1983.

Rose, Phyllis. *Woman of Letters: A Life of Virginia Woolf.* New York: Oxford University Press, 1978.

Ross, Andrew. *The Failure of Modernism: Symptoms of American Poetry.* New York: Columbia University Press, 1986.

Roth, Jack. *The Cult of Violence: Sorel and the Sorelians.* Berkeley: University of California Press, 1980.

Rover, Constance. *Women's Suffrage and Party Politics in Britain, 1866–1914.* London: Routledge & Kegan Paul, 1967.

Ruotolo, Lucio. *The Interrupted Moment: A View of Virginia Woolf's Novels.* Stanford, Calif.: Stanford University Press, 1986.

Said, Edward. *Orientalism.* New York: Vintage, 1979.

Sanderson, Michael, ed. *The Universities in the Nineteenth Century.* London: Routledge & Kegan Paul, 1975.

Scott, Anne F., and Andrew M. Scott. *One-Half the People: The Fight for Woman's Suffrage.* Philadelphia: Lippincott, 1975.

Scott, Bonnie Kime. *Joyce and Feminism.* Bloomington: Indiana University Press, 1984.

——. " 'The Look in the Throat of a Stricken Animal': Joyce as Met by Djuna Barnes." *Joyce Studies Annual* 2 (1991): 153–76.

Semmel, Bernard. *Imperialism and Social Reform: English Social-Imperial Thought, 1895–1914.* Cambridge, Mass.: Harvard University Press, 1960.

Sigg, Eric. *The American T. S. Eliot.* Cambridge: Cambridge University Press, 1989.

Smith, Stan. *Inviolable Voice: History and Twentieth-Century Poetry.* Dublin: Gill and Macmillan, 1982.

Soffer, Reba. *Ethics and Society in England: The Revolution in the Social Sciences, 1870–1914.* Berkeley: University of California Press, 1978.

Sorel, Georges. *Reflections on Violence.* Trans. T. E. Hulme and J. Roth. Glencoe, Ill.: The Free Press, 1950.

Spencer, Herbert. *The Evolution of Society: Selections from Herbert Spencer's 'Principles of Sociology.'* Ed. Robert L. Carneiro. Chicago: The University of Chicago Press, 1967.

Squier, Susan. *Virginia Woolf and London: The Sexual Politics of the City.* Chapel Hill: University of North Carolina Press, 1985.

Staley, Thomas F., ed. *'Ulysses': Fifty Years.* Bloomington: Indiana University Press, 1974.

Staley, Thomas F., and Bernard Benstock, eds. *Approaches to Joyce's 'Portrait': Ten Essays.* Pittsburgh: University of Pittsburgh Press, 1976.

Stansfield, Paul Scott. *Yeats and Politics in the 1930s.* London: Macmillan, 1988.

Stead, C. K. *Pound, Yeats, Eliot and the Modernist Movement.* Hampshire: Macmillan, 1986.

Sternhell, Zeev. *Neither Right Nor Left: Fascist Ideology in France.* Trans. David Maisel. Berkeley: University of California Press, 1986.

Sutherland, Gillian, ed. *Studies in the Growth of Nineteenth-Century Government.* Totowa, N.J.: Rowman and Littlefield, 1972.

Sypher, Wylie. *Loss of Self in Modern Literature.* New York: Random House, 1962.

Tate, Alison. "The Master-Narrative of Modernism: Discourses of Gender and Class in *The Waste Land.*" *Literature and History* 14, no 2. (Autumn 1988): 160–71.

Tawney, R. H. *The Acquisitive Society.* New York: Harcourt, Brace & World, 1920.

———. *The British Labor Movement.* New Haven: Yale University Press, 1925.

Theweleit, Klaus. *Male Fantasies.* Vol. 1, *Women, Floods, Bodies, History.* Trans. Stephen Conway, with Erica Carter and Chris Turner. Minneapolis: University of Minnesota Press, 1987.

———. *Male Fantasies.* Vol. 2, *Male Bodies: Psychoanalyzing the White Terror.* Trans. Erica Carter, Chris Turner, and Stephen Conway. Minneapolis: University of Minnesota Press, 1989.

Thomas, R. Hinton. "Culture and T. S. Eliot," *Modern Quarterly* 2, no. 4 (Spring 1951): 147–62.

Thurlow, Richard. *Fascism in Britain: A History, 1918–1985.* London: Basil Blackwell, 1987.

Timms, Edward, and Peter Collier, eds. *Visions and Blueprints: Avant-Garde Culture and Radical Politics in Early Twentieth-Century Europe.* Manchester: Manchester University Press, 1988.

Torgovnick, Marianna. *Gone Primitive: Savage Intellects, Modern Lives.* Chicago: University of Chicago Press, 1990.

Transue, Pamela J. *Virginia Woolf and the Politics of Style.* Albany: State University of New York Press, 1986.

Tridon, André. *The New Unionism.* New York: B. W. Huebsch, 1913.

Trilling, Lionel. *Beyond Culture: Essays on Literature and Learning.* New York: Viking, 1965.

Trotter, Wilfred. *Instincts of the Herd in Peace and War.* London: T. Fisher Unwin, 1922.

Walker, Frances. "Restriction of Immigration." *Atlantic Monthly* 77, no. 464 (June 1896), 822–29.

Wallas, Graham. *Human Nature in Politics.* London: Constable, 1948.

Ward, Robert de Courcy. "The Restriction of Immigration." *North American Review* 179, no. 2 (August 1904): 226–37.

Warner, Eric, ed. *Virginia Woolf: A Centenary Perspective.* New York: St. Martin's Press, 1984.

Waters, Chris. *British Socialists and the Politics of Popular Culture: 1884–1914.* Stanford, Calif.: Stanford University Press, 1990.

Watt, Ian. *The Rise of the Novel.* Berkeley: University of California Press, 1965.

Webb, Beatrice. *My Apprenticeship.* New York: Longmans, Green, 1926.

———. *Our Partnership.* Ed. Barbara Drake and Margaret I. Cole. New York: Longmans, Green, 1948.

Webber, G. C. *The Ideology of the British Right, 1918–1939.* London: Croom Helm, 1986.

West, Alick. *Crisis and Criticism and Other Essays.* London: Lawrence and Wishart, 1937.

Wicke, Jennifer. *Advertising Fictions: Literature and Advertisement and Social Reading.* New York: Columbia University Press, 1988.

Wiener, Martin J. *Between Two Worlds: The Political Thought of Graham Wallas.* Oxford: Clarendon Press, 1971.

Williams, Raymond. *Culture and Society.* New York: Columbia University Press, 1960.

———. *The Politics of Modernism.* London: Verso, 1989.

Wilson, Edmund. *Axel's Castle: A Study in the Imaginative Literature of 1870–1930.* New York: Charles Scribner's Sons, 1931.

Woolf, Leonard. *After the Deluge: A Study of Communal Psychology.* London: The Hogarth Press, 1953.

———. *Imperialism and Civilization.* New York: Harcourt Brace, 1928.

Woolf, S. J. *Fascism in Europe.* New York: Methuen, 1981.

Woolf, Virginia. *Between the Acts.* New York: Harcourt Brace Jovanovich, 1969.

———. *The Captain's Death Bed and Other Essays.* New York: Harcourt Brace Jovanovich, 1978.

———. *Flush.* New York: Harcourt Brace Jovanovich, 1933.

———. *Moments of Being.* 2nd ed. Ed. Jeanne Schulkind. New York: Harcourt Brace Jovanovich, 1985.

———. *Mrs. Dalloway.* New York: Harcourt Brace Jovanovich, 1953.

———. *Mrs. Dalloway's Party: A Short Story Sequence.* Ed. Stella McNichol. New York: Harcourt Brace Jovanovich, 1973.

———. *Night and Day.* New York: Harcourt Brace Jovanovich, 1948.

———. *Orlando.* New York: Harcourt Brace Jovanovich, 1956.

———. *The Pargiters: The Novel-Essay Portion of 'The Years.'* Ed. Mitchell A. Leaska. New York: Harcourt Brace Jovanovich, 1977.

———. *A Room of One's Own.* New York: Harcourt Brace Jovanovich, 1957.

———. *Selections from Her Essays.* Ed. Walter James. London: Chatto & Windus, 1966.

————. *Three Guineas*. New York: Harcourt, Brace & World, 1966.

————. *To the Lighthouse*. New York: Harcourt Brace Jovanovich, 1955.

————. *The Voyage Out*. New York: Harcourt Brace Jovanovich, 1948.

————. *The Waves*. New York: Harcourt Brace Jovanovich, 1959.

————. *The Years*. New York: Harcourt Brace Jovanovich, 1965.

Yeats, William Butler. *The Autobiography of William Butler Yeats*. New York: Macmillan, 1953.

————. *Essays and Introductions*. London: Macmillan, 1961.

————. *Explorations*. London: Macmillan, 1962.

————. *Ideas of Good and Evil*. London: A. H. Bullen, 1907.

————. *Memoirs, Autobiography, and First Draft of Journal*. Transcribed and edited by Denis Donoghue. London: Macmillan, 1972.

————. *The Poems of W. B. Yeats*. Ed. Richard Finneran. New York: Macmillan, 1983.

————. *A Vision*. London: T. W. Laurie, 1925.

————. *A Vision*. New York: Macmillan, 1938.

Yeats, William Butler, with Lady Gregory. *'Where There is Nothing' and 'The Unicorn from the Stars.'* Ed. Katharine Worth. Washington, D.C.: Catholic University of America Press, 1987.

Zingrone, Frank. "Joyce and D'Annunzio: The Marriage of Fire and Water." *James Joyce Quarterly* 16, no. 3 (Spring 1979): 253–66.

Zwerdling, Alex. *Virginia Woolf and the Real World*. Berkeley: University of Caliifornia Press, 1986.

Zylstra, Bernard. *From Pluralism to Collectivism: The Development of Harold Laski's Political Thought*. Lassen, The Netherlands: Van Gorcun, 1968.

Index

In this index "f" after a number indicates a separate reference on the next page, and "ff" indicates separate references on the next two pages. A continuous discussion over two or more pages is indicated by a span of numbers. *Passim* is used for a cluster of references in close but not consecutive sequence.

Original printing 1995

Last figure below indicates year of this printing

05 04 03 02 01 00 99 98 97 96

Library of Congress Cataloging-in-Publication Data

Tratner, Michael.

    Modernism and mass politics : Joyce, Woolf, Eliot, Yeats / Michael Tratner.

        p.   cm.

    Includes bibliographical references and index.

    ISBN 0-8047-2516-0 (alk. paper)

      1. English literature—20th century—History and criticism.
2. Politics and literature—Great Britain—History—20th century.
3. Literature and society—Great Britain—History—20th century.
4. Popular culture—Great Britain—History—20th century.   5. Joyce,
James, 1882–1941—Political and social views.   6. Woolf, Virginia,
1882–1941—Political and social views.   7. Eliot, T. S. (Thomas
Stearns), 1888–1965—Political and social views.   8. Yeats, W. B.
(William Butler), 1865–1939—Political and social views.
9. Modernism (Literature)—Great Britain.   10. Crowds in literature.
I. Title.

PR478.P64T73   1995

820.9′1—dc20

95-10586
CIP